Piloting the Next Generation
www.stpaulswels.org/school

Karen,

Here is a copy of Luther's small catechism. If you'd like to purchase this one it costs $22.00

Piloting the Next Generation
www.stpaulswels.org/school

Or, if you just want to borrow it for a bit that is fine too :).

—Pastor Knox

St. Paul's Evangelical
LUTHERAN SCHOOL

LUTHER'S CATECHISM

THE SMALL CATECHISM
of Dr. Martin Luther

EVANGELICAL HERITAGE VERSION

NORTHWESTERN PUBLISHING HOUSE
Milwaukee, Wisconsin

Interior Stained Glass Photographs: Robert Koester
Art Director: Karen Knutson
Design Team: Diane Cook, Pamela Dunn

The text of the enchiridion used in this catechism is the version adopted by WELS at the 1995 synod convention.

Northwestern Publishing House
N16W23379 Stone Ridge Dr., Waukesha, WI 53188-1108
www.nph.net

Published 2019
Printed in the United States of America
ISBN 978-0-8100-3066-4
ISBN 978-0-8100-3067-1 (e-book)

7701511
ISBN 978-0-8100-3066-4
9780810030664

20 21 22 23 24 25 26 27 28 10 9 8 7 6 5 4 3 2

CONTENTS

PREFACE

Luther's Small Catechism is a treasure that has graced the church ever since it was first published in 1529. Throughout the centuries since, the catechism, along with its exposition, has been the textbook used by hundreds of thousands of students to learn the truths of Scripture.

But Luther understood that the value of this treasure was not limited to young people. He used the catechism throughout his life, and he urged others to follow his example.

Those two factors have influenced the design and development of this Reformation Anniversary Edition of the Small Catechism.

Because of the catechism's enduring role as an instructional tool, this book contains a clear and orderly presentation of Bible doctrine. The Bible verses that follow the questions let Scripture speak for itself and encourage students to search the Scriptures to discover God's answers. Often, additional explanations are included to summarize Bible truths.

Because of the catechism's potential to serve as an ongoing source of encouragement and guidance, its contents have been designed to flow for a more natural read. The text and its indices will always permit Christians to search out a particular topic and the Bible verses that apply. However, introductions as well as transitional thoughts also promote the reading of the material as a unit. And transitional units promote the reading of the catechism as a book.

Two other features are noteworthy:

- As saint and sinner, each Christian faces an ongoing struggle with sin. The transitional units highlight the role of law and gospel in this new-self-versus-old-self struggle.
- To highlight even more the catechism's potential as an ongoing spiritual tool, each of the 51 units ends with a Connections section that could be the basis of an individual or joint family devotion. The participants are guided through a Bible history narrative and corresponding thought questions, which apply

the truths learned in that unit. Those are followed by a related quote from Luther or the Lutheran Confessions and a closing hymn. We hope that this section will also help the students grow in appreciation of their Lutheran heritage.

The Lutheran church is a catechetical church. We consider it a remarkable, though undeserved, privilege that we have been able to participate in the development of this book. We pray that you will use your catechism regularly, throughout your entire life, and that God will bless you through it.

Professor Stephen Geiger, Wisconsin Lutheran Seminary
Professor Joel Otto, Wisconsin Lutheran Seminary
Pastor John Braun, Northwestern Publishing House
Pastor Ray Schumacher, Northwestern Publishing House

LUTHER'S SMALL CATECHISM

THE TEN COMMANDMENTS

As the head of the family should teach them in the simplest way to those in his household.

The First Commandment

You shall have no other gods.

What does this mean?

We should fear, love, and trust in God above all things.

The Second Commandment

You shall not misuse the name of the Lord your God.

What does this mean?

We should fear and love God that we do not use his name to curse, swear, lie, or deceive, or use witchcraft, but call upon God's name in every trouble, pray, praise, and give thanks.

The Third Commandment

Remember the Sabbath day by keeping it holy.

What does this mean?

We should fear and love God that we do not despise preaching and his Word, but regard it as holy and gladly hear and learn it.

The Fourth Commandment

Honor your father and mother, that it may go well with you and that you may enjoy long life on the earth.

What does this mean?

We should fear and love God that we do not dishonor or anger our parents and others in authority, but honor, serve, and obey them, and give them love and respect.

The Fifth Commandment

You shall not murder.

What does this mean?

We should fear and love God that we do not hurt or harm our neighbor in his body, but help and befriend him in every bodily need.

The Sixth Commandment

You shall not commit adultery.

What does this mean?

We should fear and love God that we lead a pure and decent life in words and actions, and that husband and wife love and honor each other.

The Seventh Commandment

You shall not steal.

What does this mean?

We should fear and love God that we do not take our neighbor's money or property, or get it by dishonest dealing, but help him to improve and protect his property and means of income.

The Eighth Commandment

You shall not give false testimony against your neighbor.

What does this mean?

We should fear and love God that we do not tell lies about our neighbor, betray him, or give him a bad name, but defend him, speak well of him, and take his words and actions in the kindest possible way.

The Ninth Commandment

You shall not covet your neighbor's house.

What does this mean?

We should fear and love God that we do not scheme to get our neighbor's inheritance or house, or obtain it by a show of right, but do all we can to help him keep it.

The Tenth Commandment

You shall not covet your neighbor's wife, workers, animals, or anything that belongs to your neighbor.

What does this mean?

We should fear and love God that we do not force or entice away our neighbor's spouse, workers, or animals, but urge them to stay and do their duty.

The Conclusion

What does God say about all these commandments?

He says, "I, the Lord your God, am a jealous God, punishing the children for the sin of the fathers to the third and fourth generation of those who hate me, but showing love to a thousand generations of those who love me and keep my commandments."

What does this mean?

God threatens to punish all who transgress these commandments. Therefore we should fear his anger and not disobey what he commands.

But he promises grace and every blessing to all who keep these commandments. Therefore we should love and trust in him and gladly obey what he commands.

THE CREED

As the head of the family should teach it in the simplest way to those in his household.

The First Article (Creation)

I believe in God the Father almighty, maker of heaven and earth.

What does this mean?

I believe that God created me and all that exists, and that he gave me my body and soul, eyes, ears, and all my members, my mind and all my abilities.

And I believe that God still preserves me by richly and daily providing clothing and shoes, food and drink, property and home, spouse and children, land, cattle, and all I own, and all I need to keep my body and life. God also preserves me by defending me against all danger, guarding and protecting me from all evil. All this God does only because he is my good and merciful Father in heaven, and not because I have earned or deserved it. For all this I ought to thank and praise, to serve and obey him.

This is most certainly true.

The Second Article (Redemption)

I believe in Jesus Christ, his only Son, our Lord, who was conceived by the Holy Spirit, born of the virgin Mary, suffered under Pontius Pilate, was crucified, died, and was buried. He descended into hell. The third day he rose again from the dead. He ascended into heaven and is seated at the right hand of God the Father almighty. From there he will come to judge the living and the dead.

What does this mean?

I believe that Jesus Christ, true God, begotten of the Father from eternity, and also true man, born of the virgin Mary, is my Lord.

He has redeemed me, a lost and condemned creature, purchased and won me from all sins, from death, and from the power of the devil, not with gold or silver but with his holy, precious blood and with his innocent suffering and death.

All this he did that I should be his own, and live under him in his kingdom, and serve him in everlasting righteousness, innocence, and blessedness, just as he has risen from death and lives and rules eternally.

This is most certainly true.

The Third Article
(Sanctification)

I believe in the Holy Spirit; the holy Christian church, the communion of saints; the forgiveness of sins; the resurrection of the body; and the life everlasting. Amen.

What does this mean?

I believe that I cannot by my own thinking or choosing believe in Jesus Christ, my Lord, or come to him.

But the Holy Spirit has called me by the gospel, enlightened me with his gifts, sanctified and kept me in the true faith. In the same way he calls, gathers, enlightens, and sanctifies the whole Christian church on earth, and keeps it with Jesus Christ in the one true faith.

In this Christian church he daily and fully forgives all sins to me and all believers.

On the Last Day he will raise me and all the dead and give eternal life to me and all believers in Christ.

This is most certainly true.

THE LORD'S PRAYER

As the head of the family should teach it in the simplest way to those in his household.

The Address

Our Father in heaven.

What does this mean?

With these words God tenderly invites us to believe that he is our true Father and that we are his true children, so that we may pray to him as boldly and confidently as dear children ask their dear father.

The First Petition

Hallowed be your name.

What does this mean?

God's name is certainly holy by itself, but we pray in this petition that we too may keep it holy.

How is God's name kept holy?

God's name is kept holy when his Word is taught in its truth and purity and we as children of God lead holy lives according to it. Help us to do this, dear Father in heaven! But whoever teaches and lives contrary to God's Word dishonors God's name among us. Keep us from doing this, dear Father in heaven!

The Second Petition

Your kingdom come.

What does this mean?

God's kingdom certainly comes by itself even without our prayer, but we pray in this petition that it may also come to us.

How does God's kingdom come?

God's kingdom comes when our heavenly Father gives his Holy Spirit, so that by his grace we believe his holy

Word and lead a godly life now on earth and forever in heaven.

The Third Petition

Your will be done on earth as in heaven.

What does this mean?

God's good and gracious will certainly is done without our prayer, but we pray in this petition that it may be done among us also.

How is God's will done?

God's will is done when he breaks and defeats every evil plan and purpose of the devil, the world, and our sinful flesh, which try to prevent us from keeping God's name holy and letting his kingdom come. And God's will is done when he strengthens and keeps us firm in his Word and in the faith as long as we live. This is his good and gracious will.

The Fourth Petition

Give us today our daily bread.

What does this mean?

God surely gives daily bread without our asking, even to all the wicked, but we pray in this petition that he would lead us to realize this and to receive our daily bread with thanksgiving.

What, then, is meant by daily bread?

Daily bread includes everything that we need for our bodily welfare, such as food and drink, clothing and shoes, house and home, land and cattle, money and goods, a godly spouse, godly children, godly workers, godly and faithful leaders, good government, good weather, peace and order, health, a good name, good friends, faithful neighbors, and the like.

The Fifth Petition

Forgive us our sins, as we forgive those who sin against us.

What does this mean?

We pray in this petition that our Father in heaven would not look upon our sins or because of them deny our prayers; for we are worthy of none of the things for which we ask, neither have we deserved them, but we ask that he would give them all to us by grace; for we daily sin much and surely deserve nothing but punishment.

So we too will forgive from the heart and gladly do good to those who sin against us.

The Sixth Petition

Lead us not into temptation.

What does this mean?

God surely tempts no one to sin, but we pray in this petition that God would guard and keep us, so that the devil, the world, and our flesh may not deceive us or lead us into false belief, despair, and other great and shameful sins; and though we are tempted by them, we pray that we may overcome and win the victory.

The Seventh Petition

But deliver us from evil.

What does this mean?

In conclusion, we pray in this petition that our Father in heaven would deliver us from every evil that threatens body and soul, property and reputation, and finally when our last hour comes, grant us a blessed end and graciously take us from this world of sorrow to himself in heaven.

The Doxology

For the kingdom, the power, and the glory are yours now and forever. Amen.

What does this mean?

We can be sure that these petitions are acceptable to our Father in heaven and are heard by him, for he himself has commanded us to pray in this way and has promised to hear us. Therefore we say, "Amen. Yes, it shall be so."

THE SACRAMENT OF HOLY BAPTISM

As the head of the family should teach it in the simplest way to those in his household.

The Institution of Baptism

First: *What is Baptism?*

Baptism is not just plain water, but it is water used by God's command and connected with God's Word.

Which is that word of God?

Christ our Lord says in the last chapter of Matthew, "Go and make disciples of all nations, baptizing them in the name of the Father and of the Son and of the Holy Spirit."

The Blessings of Baptism

Second: *What does Baptism do for us?*

Baptism works forgiveness of sin, delivers from death and the devil, and gives eternal salvation to all who believe this, as the words and promises of God declare.

What are these words and promises of God?

Christ our Lord says in the last chapter of Mark, "Whoever believes and is baptized will be saved, but whoever does not believe will be condemned."

The Power of Baptism

Third: *How can water do such great things?*

It is certainly not the water that does such things, but God's Word which is in and with the water and faith which trusts this Word used with the water.

For without God's Word the water is just plain water and not Baptism. But with this Word it is Baptism, that is, a gracious water of life and a washing of rebirth by the Holy Spirit.

Where is this written?

Saint Paul says in Titus, chapter 3, "[God] saved us through the washing of rebirth and renewal by the Holy Spirit, whom he poured out on us generously through Jesus Christ our Savior, so that, having been justified by his grace, we might become heirs having the hope of eternal life. This is a trustworthy saying."

The Meaning of Baptism for Our Daily Life

Fourth: *What does baptizing with water mean?*

Baptism means that the old Adam in us should be drowned by daily contrition and repentance, and that all its evil deeds and desires be put to death. It also means that a new person should daily arise to live before God in righteousness and purity forever.

Where is this written?

Saint Paul says in Romans, chapter 6, "We were . . . buried with [Christ] through baptism into death in order that, just as Christ was raised from the dead through the glory of the Father, we too may live a new life."

THE USE OF THE KEYS AND CONFESSION

As the head of the family should teach them in the simplest way to those in his household.

The Keys

First: *What is the use of the keys?*

The use of the keys is that special power and right which Christ gave to his church on earth: to forgive the sins of penitent sinners but refuse forgiveness to the impenitent as long as they do not repent.

Where is this written?

The holy evangelist John writes in chapter 20, "[Jesus] breathed on [his disciples] and said, 'Receive the Holy Spirit. If you forgive anyone his sins, they are forgiven; if you do not forgive them, they are not forgiven.' "

The Public Use of the Keys

Second: *How does a Christian congregation use the keys?*

A Christian congregation with its called servant of Christ uses the keys in accordance with Christ's command by forgiving those who repent of their sin and are willing to amend, and by excluding from the congregation those who are plainly impenitent that they may repent. I believe that when this is done, it is as valid and certain in heaven also, as if Christ, our dear Lord, dealt with us himself.

Where is this written?

Jesus says in Matthew, chapter 18, "Whatever you bind on earth will be bound in heaven, and whatever you loose on earth will be loosed in heaven."

Confession

First: *What is confession?*

Confession has two parts. The one is that we confess our sins; the other, that we receive absolution or forgiveness from the pastor as from God himself, not doubting but firmly believing that our sins are thus forgiven before God in heaven.

Second: *What sins should we confess?*

Before God we should plead guilty of all sins, even those we are not aware of, as we do in the Lord's Prayer.

But before the pastor we should confess only those sins which we know and feel in our hearts.

Third: *How can we recognize these sins?*

Consider your place in life according to the Ten Commandments. Are you a father, mother, son, daughter, employer, or employee? Have you been disobedient, unfaithful, or lazy? Have you hurt anyone by word or deed? Have you been dishonest, careless, wasteful, or done other wrong?

Fourth: *How will the pastor assure a penitent sinner of forgiveness?*

He will say, "By the authority of Christ, I forgive you your sins in the name of the Father and of the Son and of the Holy Spirit. Amen."

THE SACRAMENT OF HOLY COMMUNION

As the head of the family should teach it in the simplest way to those in his household.

The Institution of Holy Communion

First: *What is the Sacrament of Holy Communion?*

It is the true body and blood of our Lord Jesus Christ under the bread and wine, instituted by Christ for us Christians to eat and to drink.

Where is this written?

The holy evangelists Matthew, Mark, Luke, and the apostle Paul tell us: Our Lord Jesus Christ, on the night he was betrayed, took bread; and when he had given thanks, he broke it and gave it to his disciples, saying, "Take and eat; this is my body, which is given for you. Do this in remembrance of me."

Then he took the cup, gave thanks, and gave it to them, saying, "Drink from it, all of you; this is my blood of the new covenant, which is poured out for you for the forgiveness of sins. Do this, whenever you drink it, in remembrance of me."

The Blessings of Holy Communion

Second: *What blessing do we receive through this eating and drinking?*

That is shown us by these words: "Given" and "poured out for you for the forgiveness of sins."

Through these words we receive forgiveness of sins, life, and salvation in this sacrament.

For where there is forgiveness of sins, there is also life and salvation.

The Power of Holy Communion

Third: *How can eating and drinking do such great things?*

It is certainly not the eating and drinking that does such things, but the words "Given" and "poured out for you for the forgiveness of sins."

These words are the main thing in this sacrament, along with the eating and drinking.

And whoever believes these words has what they plainly say, the forgiveness of sins.

The Reception of Holy Communion

Fourth: *Who, then, is properly prepared to receive this sacrament?*

Fasting and other outward preparations may serve a good purpose, but he is properly prepared who believes these words: "Given" and "poured out for you for the forgiveness of sins."

But whoever does not believe these words or doubts them is not prepared, because the words "for you" require nothing but hearts that believe.

THE NICENE CREED

We believe in one God, the Father, the Almighty, maker of heaven and earth, of all that is, seen and unseen.

We believe in one Lord, Jesus Christ, the only Son of God, eternally begotten of the Father, God from God, Light from Light, true God from true God, begotten, not made, of one being with the Father. Through him all things were made. For us and for our salvation, he came down from heaven, was incarnate of the Holy Spirit and the virgin Mary, and became fully human. For our sake he was crucified under Pontius Pilate. He suffered death and was buried. On the third day he rose again in accordance with the Scriptures. He ascended into heaven and is seated at the right hand of the Father. He will come again in glory to judge the living and the dead, and his kingdom will have no end.

We believe in the Holy Spirit, the Lord, the giver of life, who proceeds from the Father and the Son, who in unity with the Father and the Son is worshiped and glorified, who has spoken through the prophets. We believe in one holy Christian and apostolic Church. We acknowledge one baptism for the forgiveness of sins. We look for the resurrection of the dead and the life of the world to come. Amen.

DAILY PRAYERS

How the head of the family should teach those in his household to pray morning and evening, to ask a blessing, and to say grace at meals.

Morning Prayer

In the name of God the Father, Son, and Holy Spirit. Amen.

I thank you, my heavenly Father, through Jesus Christ, your dear Son, that you have kept me this night from all harm and danger. Keep me this day also from sin and every evil, that all my doings and life may please you. Into your hands I commend my body and soul and all things. Let your holy angel be with me, that the wicked foe may have no power over me. Amen.

Evening Prayer

In the name of God the Father, Son, and Holy Spirit. Amen.

I thank you, my heavenly Father, through Jesus Christ, your dear Son, that you have graciously kept me this day. Forgive me all my sins, and graciously keep me this night. Into your hands I commend my body and soul and all things. Let your holy angel be with me, that the wicked foe may have no power over me. Amen.

To Ask a Blessing

The eyes of all look to you, O Lord, and you give them their food at the proper time. You open your hand and satisfy the desires of every living thing. Amen.

Lord God, heavenly Father, bless us through these gifts which we receive from your bountiful goodness, through Jesus Christ, our Lord. Amen.

Come, Lord Jesus, be our guest, and let these gifts to us be blest. Amen.

To Say Grace

Give thanks to the Lord, for he is good; his love endures forever. Amen.

Lord God, heavenly Father, we thank you for all your gifts, through Jesus Christ, our Lord. Amen.

TABLE OF DUTIES

Pastors

A pastor must be above reproach, the husband of but one wife, temperate, self-controlled, respectable, hospitable, able to teach, not given to much wine, not violent but gentle, not quarrelsome, not a lover of money. He must manage his own family well and see that his children obey him with proper respect. He must not be a recent convert. He must hold firmly to the trustworthy message as it has been taught, so that he can encourage others by sound doctrine and refute those who oppose it. (See 1 Timothy 3:2,3,4,6; Titus 1:9.)

What We Owe to Our Pastors and Teachers

Anyone who receives instruction in the Word must share all good things with his instructor. (See Galatians 6:6.)

In the same way, the Lord has commanded that those who preach the gospel should receive their living from the gospel. (See 1 Corinthians 9:14.)

The elders who direct the affairs of the church well are worthy of double honor, especially those whose work is preaching and teaching. For the Scripture says, "The worker deserves his wages." (See 1 Timothy 5:17,18.)

Obey your leaders and submit to their authority. They keep watch over you as men who must give an account. Obey them so that their work will be a joy, not a burden, for that would be of no advantage to you. (See Hebrews 13:17.)

Government

Everyone must submit himself to the governing authorities, for there is no authority except that which God has established. The authorities that exist have been established by God. Consequently, he who rebels against the authority is rebelling against what God has instituted, and those who do so will bring judgment on themselves. For he is God's servant to do you good. But if you do wrong, be afraid, for he does not bear the sword for nothing. He is God's servant, an agent of wrath to bring punishment on the wrongdoer. (See Romans 13:1,2,4.)

Husbands

Husbands, be considerate as you live with your wives, and treat them with respect as the weaker partner and as heirs with you of the gracious gift of life, so that nothing will hinder your prayers. Husbands, love your wives and do not be harsh with them. (See 1 Peter 3:7; Colossians 3:19.)

Wives

Wives, submit to your husbands as to the Lord, like Sarah, who obeyed Abraham and called him her master. You are her daughters if you do what is right and do not give way to fear. (See Ephesians 5:22; 1 Peter 3:6.)

Parents

Fathers, do not exasperate your children; instead, bring them up in the training and instruction of the Lord. Fathers, do not embitter your children, or they will become discouraged. (See Ephesians 6:4; Colossians 3:21.)

Children

Children, obey your parents in the Lord, for this is right. "Honor your father and mother"—which is the first commandment with a promise—"that it may go well with you and that you may enjoy long life on the earth." (See Ephesians 6:1-3.)

Employees

Obey your earthly masters with respect and fear, and with sincerity of heart, just as you would obey Christ. Obey them not only to win their favor when their eye is on you, but like slaves of Christ, doing the will of God from your heart. Serve wholeheartedly, as if you were serving the Lord, not men, because you know that the Lord will reward everyone for whatever good he does. (See Ephesians 6:5-8.)

Employers

Treat your employees in the same way. Do not threaten them, since you know that he who is both their Master and yours is in heaven, and there is no favoritism with him. (See Ephesians 6:9.)

Young People

Young men, be submissive to those who are older. Clothe yourselves with humility toward one another, because "God opposes the proud but gives grace to the humble." Humble yourselves, therefore, under God's mighty hand, that he may lift you up in due time. (See 1 Peter 5:5,6.)

Widows

The widow who is really in need and left all alone puts her hope in God and continues night and day to pray and to ask God for help. But the widow who lives for pleasure is dead even while she lives. (See 1 Timothy 5:5,6.)

A Word for All

Love your neighbor as yourself. This is the sum of all the commandments. (See Romans 13:8-10; Galatians 5:14.) And continue praying for everyone. (See 1 Timothy 2:1.)

Let each the lesson learn with care,
And all the household well shall fare.

MARTIN LUTHER
The Author of the Small Catechism

Luther's Early Life

Eisleben sits in the beautiful, green, hilly region of western Germany. Over five hundred years ago, Hans and Margarethe Luther moved to this small mining town because it offered excellent opportunities to make a good living.

While they were there, the Luthers welcomed a son into their family. He was born on November 10, 1483, in a two-story house, not far from the center of town. The day after his birth, according to the custom of the day, Hans and Margarethe brought their newborn son to St. Peter's Church to be baptized. And since the baptism took place on the Festival of St. Martin, Hans named his son Martin.

A few months later, the Luthers moved again, this time to Mansfeld, in the heart of the copper-mining region. It appears that the move provided just the chance for advancement that Martin's father, Hans, desired. By the time Martin started school, his father was a respected citizen in Mansfeld.

Martin was a diligent student. He demonstrated a keen mind and the ability to excel in his studies. Hans was proud of his ambitious and intelligent son and had great expectations for him. When it came time for the university, Hans paid for Martin to attend the university in Erfurt in order to become a lawyer. In fact, he purchased a set of law books for his son as an encouragement and a proof of his approval.

Luther Becomes a Monk

But something troubled Martin. He was sensitive and wondered if he was good enough for God. After a visit home, Martin made his way back to the university. Whether he noticed the sky or not along the way, the weather began to change. He quickened his step as he heard the thunder rumble in the distance. The storm was moving quickly in his direction. Then suddenly it broke, and he found himself in the middle of a fierce storm. A flash of lightning and the crack of thunder were so near he thought he would die with the next flash and crack. In desperation and panic, he prayed, "St. Anne, help me. I'll become a monk."

The storm with its flashes of lightning and cracks of thunder changed his life. In the days that followed, Luther wondered if his vow, "I'll become a monk," came only from a spur of the moment panic. But finally, it didn't matter. He decided to fulfill his vow.

He became a monk and believed that if he was diligent in his fasting, vigils, prayers, confession, and study, he could make himself good enough for God. He believed that God welcomed only people who made themselves good and that God was angry with everyone else. So Luther sought to offer God what the church demanded. He worked hard to become the perfect monk so he could change God's anger to love.

Luther Discovers the Gospel

In spite of all his efforts, Luther was still troubled. He found no peace. As he punished himself with fasting and work, hope slipped away instead of growing. All he did was not enough, no matter how hard he tried. His troubles led him to his superior, John Staupitz; he advised Luther to turn only to Jesus Christ for peace and comfort.

That advice helped, but in those early days, Luther was still confused. In order to help Luther, Staupitz sent him to Wittenberg to teach at the new university established by Elector Frederick the Wise. There Luther read, he taught, and he thought. He lectured on the Psalms and eventually on Romans.

His study of Romans was a turning point, much like the storm that had led him to become a monk. His study turned his thinking away from the angry God of the thunderbolt. As Luther studied Romans, he learned that what God requires does not come from what he did or any sinner does. It is something entirely different. God freely gives the sinner what is required for the sake of Christ. Luther had realized all his efforts were not good enough. Now he found that the Bible says that God gives sinners the perfect and complete good that

Christ achieved. God simply declares humans good, perfect, and holy because Jesus suffered and died for them. They possess the goodness of Christ by trust—by faith—in God's promises and not by what they do.

Luther Bases Everything on God's Word

Then came another turning point. While Luther's studies were deepening his understanding of God's grace, John Tetzel appeared. Tetzel received authority from the Roman Catholic Church to sell indulgences to raise money. Indulgences were official documents of the Roman Catholic Church that promised to release those who bought them from the obligations required by the church. As Tetzel traveled in the Holy Roman Empire, he boasted, "As soon as the money clinks in the chest, the soul flits into heavenly rest." Selling indulgences challenged Luther's new thinking. Could Christians offer a gift in order to remove the church's requirement of satisfaction for sin? Could they buy peace, hope, and forgiveness, even heaven, when they paid for an indulgence? Luther objected. His Ninety-five Theses challenged the abuse he saw. Through his theses he wanted to discuss and debate whether the church could sell indulgences and whether or not indulgences could help someone get into heaven.

The resistance from the Roman Catholic Church came quickly. Luther was summoned before Cardinal Cajetan in Augsburg to withdraw his objections. Cajetan, one of the leading theologians of his day, pointed out that the decrees and pronouncements of the popes supported the teaching on indulgences. Luther was wrong, he said, for objecting to the teachings of the church. But Luther realized that the revered cardinal had no scriptural proof for the practice. Luther wrote, "Nothing is mentioned in the Holy Scriptures about indulgences. . . . The Scriptures commend faith and are as devoid of references to indulgences as they are full of teaching concerning faith" (LW 31:276).

Luther based his thinking on God's Word, not on human decrees, so he moved on unconvinced and undaunted. In addition, Luther's understanding of the gift of God through faith in Christ provided him the courage to write and object even more. He was sure that the Bible was more important than what any human said. A little later the emperor, Charles V, summoned Luther to Worms to retract his teachings. Luther stood before the emperor, the princes, and many leaders of the Roman Catholic Church and confessed, "Unless I am convinced by the testimony of Sacred Scripture or by evident reason—since I do not accept the authority of popes and councils, for it is evident that they have contradicted each other—my conscience is captive to the Word of God. I cannot and I will not recant anything, for to go against my conscience is neither right nor safe. Here I stand, I can do no other. God help me. Amen."

That important truth—teaching must be based on the Bible—motivated Luther and guided his thoughts for the rest of his life. But he left Worms as an outlaw. The emperor signed the Edict of Worms, which was a warrant for Luther's arrest and capture. The Edict also threatened anyone "favoring Luther and his works in any way."

Luther Continues to Write and Teach

On the way back home, Luther was suddenly abducted by a band of horsemen. But they were not agents of the emperor. Instead, Frederick the Wise had ordered his men to take Luther into protective custody. They led him off that night to the Wartburg Castle.

For the next few months, Luther grew a beard and learned the ways of a knight. To all at the castle he became Knight George. For Luther, this became a time to write. He sent his writings back to Wittenberg where they were published.

The most important task Luther began while at the Wartburg was the translation of the New Testament into German. He wanted to put the Bible into the hands of the common people so that they could read it for themselves. "When you open the book containing the gospels," he wrote, "and read or hear how Christ comes here or there, or how someone is brought to him, you should therein perceive the sermon or the gospel through which he is coming to you, or you are being brought to him" (LW 35:121).

After about a year at the Wartburg Castle, Luther returned to Wittenberg. The Edict of Worms still condemned Luther as a heretic and guilty of high treason. But the truths of the Bible were more important than even life itself. Luther did not look over his shoulder. His faith drove him forward.

Luther's ideas spread quickly throughout Germany, and throughout Europe. He continued to write. So the presses all over Germany and Europe printed more, and people read more. But his ideas were not new. He tested his ideas and compared them to the Bible. He wrote what agreed with the Bible. Many theologians of the church throughout the ages also believed the same things Luther confessed. Luther and many who agreed with him felt it was time to bring the Christian church back to what the Bible said—time to reform the church.

Luther became a magnet, drawing people to Wittenberg to study and learn. The university grew in spite of the threat of the Edict. Together with his coworkers in Wittenberg, Luther finished translating the Old Testament into German so that people could read the entire Bible. His writings were eagerly read not only in Germany but all over Europe. Luther's collected works were packed in the goods that were traded and shipped even to England and Italy. He had two central thoughts: the Bible is the only authority for what we believe and God declares the sinner good and righteous by grace through faith in Christ. Humans cannot earn that status by their good works. His thoughts are summarized by three short phrases: *by grace alone, by faith alone,* and *by Scripture alone.*

Luther wanted to make sure that everyone understood God's promises and truth. When he saw how many did not understand the Bible, he also wrote the Small Catechism. It is a simple outline of what the Bible teaches. The Small Catechism wasn't anything new—only what God's people believed and taught for centuries. It includes the Ten Commandments, the Apostles' Creed, the Lord's Prayer, Baptism, Confession and Absolution, and the Lord's Supper.

Luther's Small Catechism also includes a Table of Duties as a guideline from the Bible for Christian people—husbands, wives, parents, children, employees, employers, and others. The Bible teaches that God gives every man, woman, and child a role to play in their lives. Pastors, teachers, clerks, shoemakers, farmers, butchers, barbers, and students all serve God. "Here faith is truly active through love [Gal 5:6], that is, it finds expression in works of the freest service, cheerfully and lovingly done, with which a Christian willingly serves another without hope of reward; and for themselves they are satisfied with the fullness and wealth of their faith [in Christ]" (LW 31:365).

When people came to listen to Luther and the other reformers, they were encouraged to let their lights of faith shine in their daily lives, in other words, to love others just as Jesus and the apostles had taught. Throughout his later years, Luther taught and wrote a great deal—volumes and volumes. He never tired of helping people understand what the Bible taught.

Luther himself lived like anyone else. He married a former nun, Katherine von Bora. They had six children and lived in Wittenberg the rest of Luther's life. Late in January 1546, Luther traveled to Eisleben, the town of his birth, to help settle a dispute there. But while he was in Eisleben, he became sick. He died on February 18, 1546. On his deathbed, his friends asked him if he was willing to die still confessing the doctrine he spent his life teaching. He answered clearly, "Yes." His body was taken back to Wittenberg and laid to rest under the floor of the Castle Church just in front of the pulpit.

Luther may have stood alone at Worms, but he did not remain alone. Many joined him. Many still join him in protesting teachings that violate the Scriptures. We are among them. We believe that we are saved by God's grace alone, through faith alone, on account of Christ alone. Those are the teachings of the Bible, and we are captive to the Word of God, the Scripture alone. Here we stand; God help us. Amen.

THE BIBLE

The Truth About God and Us

Like most Christians of his day, Luther had grown up with a serious misunderstanding regarding the answer to a very important question: How can we be confident that anyone is good enough to go to heaven after death? For a long time that question tormented him as he tried to find peace for his soul. The answer to that question eventually changed the direction of his life.

That question is the most important question we will ever ask. Because there is still so much confusion about the answer, it is important that we learn the truth. In order to do that, we must start from the beginning to learn what God tells us about himself and about ourselves.

God and His Word

1. By now you know that many people deny there is a god. They don't want to admit that there is a being who has power over them or to whom they owe obedience. In reality, it should be obvious to everyone that there is a God. **Why should it be clear to everyone that there is a God?**

> **Hebrews 3:4** Every house is built by someone, and God is the one who built everything.
>
> **Psalm 19:1,2** *The heavens tell about the glory of God. The expanse of the sky proclaims the work of his hands.* Day after day they pour out speech. Night after night they display knowledge.

2. The magnificent creation gives us hints about the God who created all things. **What can we learn about God from the things he created?**

> **Romans 1:20** His invisible characteristics—*his eternal power and divine nature—have been clearly seen* since the creation of the world, because they are understood from the things he made. As a result, people are without excuse.
>
> **Psalm 104** (The psalmist speaks of the way God has arranged the creation and of the power God has over the creation. Verse 24 summarizes what these truths tell us about God.) How many are your works, O LORD! *In wisdom* you made them all. The earth is full of your creatures.

3. The voice of our conscience also proves that God exists. **How does the conscience within each of us testify to the truth that there is a God?**

Romans 2:14,15 Whenever Gentiles, who do not have the law, do by nature what the law requires—even though they do not have the law—they are a law for themselves. They demonstrate the work of the law that is written in their hearts, since *their conscience also bears witness* as their thoughts go back and forth, at times accusing or at times even defending them.

Romans 1:32 *They know God's righteous decree* that those who do these things are worthy of death, such people not only continue to do them, but also approve of others who continue to commit such sins.

A CLOSER LOOK

The word *Gentiles,* found in Romans 2, refers to non-Jews. To understand better how these two groups of people, Jews and Gentiles, came to be, consider the following history:

Because of God's great love for all people, he initiated a plan to save them from the deadly consequences of their sins. The human race was extremely wicked. The people easily and quickly wandered away from God's promises and rebelled against him. But God planned to send a Savior for all people and set aside the descendants of Abraham to carry out his plan. Everyone aside from these descendants of Abraham was considered a Gentile. Because the Savior of the world—which included the Gentiles—would come from the Jewish nation, God set the Jewish nation apart from all other nations. God gave the people of Israel laws to remind them of their special status. For example, they weren't to eat certain foods. They weren't to work on the Sabbath, a day set aside for worship. As they followed these laws, they were reminded that they were the recipients of a very special promise from God—they were the nation from which the Savior would come.

We can better understand what the inspired writer is saying in Romans 2:14,15 if we understand this history of God's people.

Paul reminds us in these verses that although the Gentiles (non-Jews) hadn't received the Word of God and the laws of God, they showed that God's law was written in their hearts. Their consciences bore witness to the fact that there is a standard of right and wrong—a law for judging their lives and actions. Our consciences tell us the same.

---

4. God's creation and the conscience within each of us testify clearly that there is a God. **Why do we still need the Bible?**

Isaiah 40:13 Who has directed the Spirit of the LORD? Who can teach him anything or serve as his advisor?

1 Corinthians 2:9,10 What no eye has seen and no ear has heard and no human mind has conceived—that is what God has prepared for those who love him. *But God revealed it to us through his Spirit.*

2 Peter 1:19 We also have the completely reliable prophetic word. You do well to pay attention to it, as to a lamp shining in a dark place.

Romans 10:14 So then, how can they call on the one they have not believed in? And how can they believe in the one about whom they have not heard? And how can they hear without a preacher?

5. According to the Bible, what has spoiled my relationship with God?

Genesis 6:5 The LORD saw that the wickedness of mankind was great on the earth, and that *all the thoughts and plans they formed in their hearts were only evil* every day.

Romans 3:23 All have sinned and fall short of the glory of God.

Romans 7:18 I know that *good does not live in me,* that is, in my sinful flesh. The desire to do good is present with me, but I am not able to carry it out.

Psalm 51:5 Certainly, *I was guilty when I was born.* I was sinful when my mother conceived me.

6. What is the result of this sin in my life?

Mark 7:21-23 *From within, out of people's hearts, come evil thoughts,* sexual sins, theft, murder, adultery, greed, wickedness, deceit, unrestrained immorality, envy, slander, arrogance, and foolishness. All these evil things proceed from within and make a person unclean.

Isaiah 59:2 *It is your guilt that has separated you from your God, and* your sins have hidden God's face from you, so that he does not hear.

Romans 6:23 The wages of sin is death.

Ephesians 2:3 Formerly, we all lived among them in the passions of our sinful flesh, as we carried out the desires of the sinful flesh and its thoughts. Like all the others, *we were by nature objects of God's wrath.*

A CLOSER LOOK

Sin has totally destroyed our relationship with God. Our sinful nature produces evil thoughts, words, and actions that *defile* us. To *defile* means "to make unclean or to contaminate." God is holy and perfect; he can't stand sin. Our sin is repulsive to God. He tells us that we deserve *death* because of our sins (Romans 6:23). If you have stood beside the casket of someone you love, you know how horrible death is. You know how death hurts. Death is one of the consequences of sin. But sin brings more than just physical death, it brings eternal, spiritual death—separation from God in the punishment of hell.

Because of sin, we deserve *wrath*—God's anger and lasting punishment.

7. My sin has separated me from God. It has earned God's wrath. It has earned death. **What does God tell me in his Word that brings peace to my relationship with him?**

1 Timothy 2:4 [God] wants all people to be saved and to come to the knowledge of the truth.

John 3:16 For God so loved the world that he gave his only-begotten Son, that *whoever believes in him shall not perish, but have eternal life.*

Romans 6:23 The wages of sin is death, *but the undeserved gift of God is eternal life in Christ Jesus our Lord.*

Isaiah 43:25 I, yes *I, am he. I blot out your rebellious deeds* for my own sake, and I will not remember your sins.

8. Can I trust what the Bible tells me?

2 Peter 1:16 We were not following cunningly devised fables when we made known to you the powerful appearance of our Lord Jesus Christ, but *we were eyewitnesses of his majesty.*

1 Corinthians 2:12,13 What we received is not the spirit of the world, but the Spirit who is from God, so that we might know the blessings freely given to us by God. *We also speak about these things, not in words taught by human wisdom, but in words taught by the Spirit,* combining spiritual truths with spiritual words.

Matthew 24:35 Heaven and earth will pass away, but my words will never pass away.

John 17:17 Sanctify them by the truth. *Your word is truth.* (words of Jesus)

9. How can the words of the Bible be God's Word if human writers wrote them?

John 14:26 The Counselor, the Holy Spirit, whom the Father will send in my name, *will teach you all things and remind you of everything I told you.*

2 Timothy 3:16 *All Scripture is God breathed* and is useful for teaching, for rebuking, for correcting, and for training in righteousness.

2 Peter 1:21 No prophecy ever came by the will of man, but men *spoke from God as they were being carried along by the Holy Spirit.*

10. Why is the Bible so important?

2 Timothy 3:15 From infancy you have known the Holy Scriptures, which are able to *make you wise for salvation* through faith in Christ Jesus.

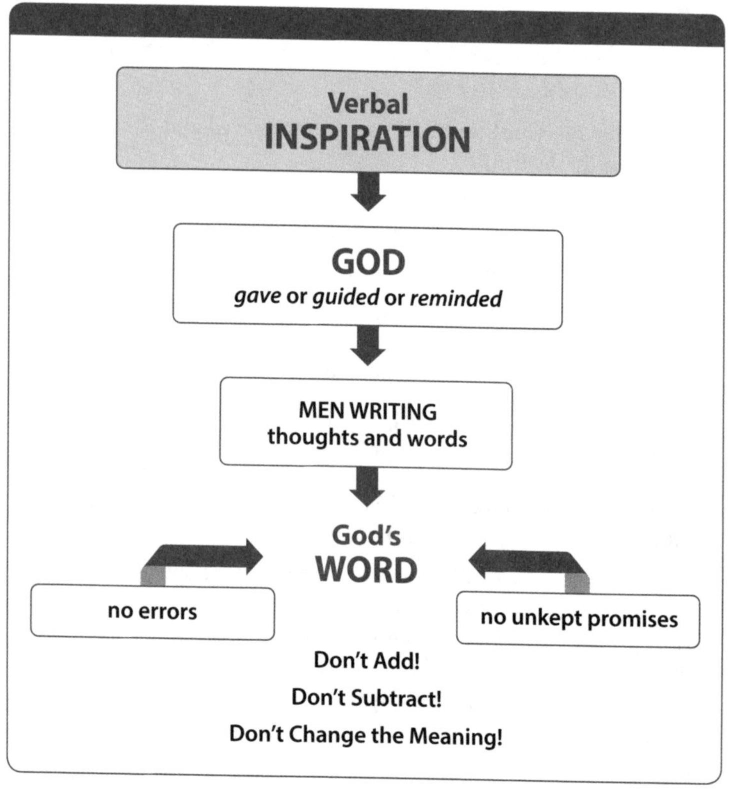

John 20:31 These are *written that you may believe that Jesus is the Christ,* the Son of God, and that by believing you may have life in his name.

Ephesians 2:19,20 You are no longer foreigners and strangers, but you are fellow citizens with the saints and members of God's household. You have been *built on the foundation of the apostles and prophets,* with Christ Jesus himself as the Cornerstone.

11. The Bible is God's Word that tells us about our salvation. God wants all people of all time to know the salvation he has provided. **What does God forbid anyone to do with the Bible?**

Deuteronomy 4:2 *Do not add* to the word that I am commanding you, and *do not subtract from it,* so that you keep the commandments of the LORD your God that I am commanding you.

Revelation 22:18,19 I give this warning to everyone who hears the words of the prophecy of this book: *If anyone adds to them,* God will add to him the plagues that are written in this book. And *if anyone takes away* from the words of the book of this prophecy, God will take away his share in the Tree of Life and in the Holy City, which are written in this book.

Jeremiah 14:14 Then the LORD said this to me: Those prophets are prophesying lies in my name, but I did not send them. I did not command them, and I did not speak to them. They are prophesying a false vision to you and providing worthless omens—*something from their own imagination.*

Matthew 15:9 They worship me in vain, *teaching human rules* as if they are doctrines.

A CLOSER LOOK

The Books of the Bible The Bible contains a total of 66 separate books and is divided into two parts—the Old Testament and the New Testament.

- God revealed the Old Testament to the world before the coming of Jesus, and it was written by Moses and the prophets.
- God revealed the New Testament to the world after Jesus came, and it was written by the apostles and evangelists.
- All the writers of the Bible were inspired by the Holy Spirit, so their messages are God's words—true and reliable.
- Both the Old Testament and the New Testament teach two main principles, or doctrines. The first is the *law,* which tells us what we must do and not do. The second is the *gospel,* which tells us what God has done for us in giving us a Savior.

Old Testament
Genesis
Exodus
Leviticus
Numbers
Deuteronomy
Joshua
Judges
Ruth
1 Samuel
2 Samuel
1 Kings
2 Kings
1 Chronicles
2 Chronicles
Ezra
Nehemiah
Esther
Job
Psalms
Proverbs
Ecclesiastes
Song of Solomon
Isaiah
Jeremiah
Lamentations
Ezekiel
Daniel
Hosea
Joel
Amos
Obadiah
Jonah
Micah
Nahum
Habakkuk
Zephaniah
Haggai
Zechariah
Malachi

New Testament
Matthew
Mark
Luke
John
Acts
Romans
1 Corinthians
2 Corinthians
Galatians
Ephesians
Philippians
Colossians
1 Thessalonians
2 Thessalonians
1 Timothy
2 Timothy
Titus
Philemon
Hebrews
James
1 Peter
2 Peter
1 John
2 John
3 John
Jude
Revelation

When Luther discovered the answer to the question about how we can have a good relationship with God and be confident that we will be in heaven when we die, it changed his life. It also helped him understand the message of the entire Bible. Because there was so much confusion and misunderstanding, he knew it was vitally important to teach these truths to the world. That was the reason he wrote the Small Catechism. He wanted a book that could be used to teach these important truths to future generations. He knew these truths would change our lives as well.

Luther saw how important it was and still is to listen to God's Word. Read about a group of people who eagerly used the Scriptures:

Acts 17:10-12

The Bereans were looking to see if the message of Jesus was true. They checked the words of the apostle Paul and compared them with the Bible. Why was it important to know if Paul spoke the truth? Why is it important for you to know the truth of the Bible? Explain what can make it hard for you to be like the Bereans. What is one thing you could do that would follow the example of the Bereans?

Luther

Let us learn the art of letting the world boast of great wealth, honor, power, etc. After all, these are light, unstable, perishable commodities, which God throws away. . . . But to his children, He gives the true treasure. Therefore, as dear children and heirs of God, we should not boast of our wisdom, strength, or wealth; we should boast of the fact that we have the precious pearl, the dear Word, through which we know God, our dear Father, and Jesus Christ, whom He has sent. This is our treasure and heritage; it is certain and eternal and better than the goods of all the world. (*What Luther Says,* Ewald M. Plass, p. 1465, par. 4732)

One Thing's Needful (Stanza 1)

One thing's needful; Lord, this treasure
Teach me highly to regard.
All else, though it first give pleasure,
Is a yoke that presses hard.
Beneath it the heart is still fretting and striving,
No true, lasting happiness ever deriving.
This one thing is needful; all others are vain—
I count all but loss that I Christ may obtain.

GOD'S LAW

In Need of a Savior

The message that God loved the world so that he gave his Son to die for us is good news—extremely good news. Unfortunately, many people refuse to believe that they need a savior. They compare their lives to those of murderers, terrorists, drug dealers, and others and feel that they are good people by comparison. Actually, the sinful nature within each of us believes that way. It wants to believe that we are able to have a good relationship with God on our own, but that is a serious mistake with deadly consequences.

As we learn about God's law, we will see that it keeps us from making such serious spiritual mistakes.

God's Law: A Great Blessing

12. What do we mean when we speak of God's law?

Luke 10:27 Love the Lord your God with all your heart, with all your soul, with all your strength, and with all your mind; and, love your neighbor as yourself.

Matthew 4:10 Worship the Lord your God, and serve him only.

Matthew 19:17-19 If you want to enter life, keep *the commandments.* . . . "You shall not murder. You shall not commit adultery. You shall not steal. You shall not give false testimony. Honor your father and mother." And, "You shall love your neighbor as yourself."

A CLOSER LOOK

Laws tell us what is right and wrong—what we should do and what we shouldn't do. God's laws do the same.

When we speak of God's laws, though, it is important to understand that there are different categories of law. Some of God's laws were meant for the Jews for a specific time period. For example, some of God's laws were meant to govern the Jewish nation of Israel. Some very explicitly dictated how the nation of Israel was to worship God. Other laws of God apply to all people of all time.

We refer to God's commands that governed the nation of Israel as *civil laws.* An example of some of the civil laws would be those laws that spelled out the punishment for those caught stealing or those who hurt others.

God's laws that commanded how his people should worship were called *ceremonial laws.* Those laws included regulations for the priesthood, the Sabbath Day, and the sacrifices. The ceremonial laws pointed ahead to Christ, reminding the people that God would send a Savior and how important the work of the Savior would be.

The laws of God that are meant for all people of all times are called the *moral law.* The moral law expresses people's duty toward God and toward one another and remains in effect forever.

---

13. How does God give his law (moral law) to everyone?

Romans 2:14,15 Whenever Gentiles, who do not have the law, do by nature what the law requires—even though they do not have the law—they are a law for themselves. They demonstrate the work of the law that is *written in their hearts,* since their conscience also bears witness as their thoughts go back and forth, at times accusing or at times even defending them.

When God made us, he wrote his law on our hearts (natural law). When we sin, our consciences bother us. That tells us of the law God wrote on our hearts. Because of sin, however, our consciences can be mistaken. We may become so accustomed to certain sins that our consciences no longer tell us they are wrong. We may also be ignorant and believe that something is a sin when it isn't or isn't sin when it is. In order that we would know what sin is without a doubt, God also gave us his law in a second way (written law).

14. How did God give his law in a second way?

John 1:17 The law was given through Moses.

Exodus 20 (God gave his law to the nation of Israel at Mount Sinai.)

Deuteronomy 4:13 He declared to you his covenant that he commanded you to carry out, namely, the Ten Commandments. Then he *wrote them on two tablets of stone.*

A CLOSER LOOK

God's law is very important because it serves three different functions in our lives. It serves outwardly, in the lives of all people, as a *curb* by threatening punishment to those who disobey the law and promising rewards to those who obey. It also works inwardly, in the hearts of all people, as a *mirror* by showing us our sin. Finally, it has a function that serves only believers in Jesus—it serves as a *guide* for Christian living.

---

15. How does the law serve as a curb in the lives of all people, even unbelievers?

1 Timothy 1:9,10 The law is not laid down for a righteous person, but for lawless and rebellious people, for godless people and sinners, for unholy and worldly people, for those who kill their fathers and those who kill their mothers, for murderers, for sexually immoral people, for homosexuals, for kidnappers, for liars, for perjurers, and for whatever else is opposed to sound teaching.

Psalm 119:120 My flesh trembles because I am afraid of you, because I fear your judgments.

Deuteronomy 4:24 The LORD your God is a consuming fire, a jealous God.

Romans 13:2,3 The one who rebels against the authority is opposing God's institution, and *those who oppose will bring judgment on themselves.* For rulers are not a terror to good conduct, but to evil.

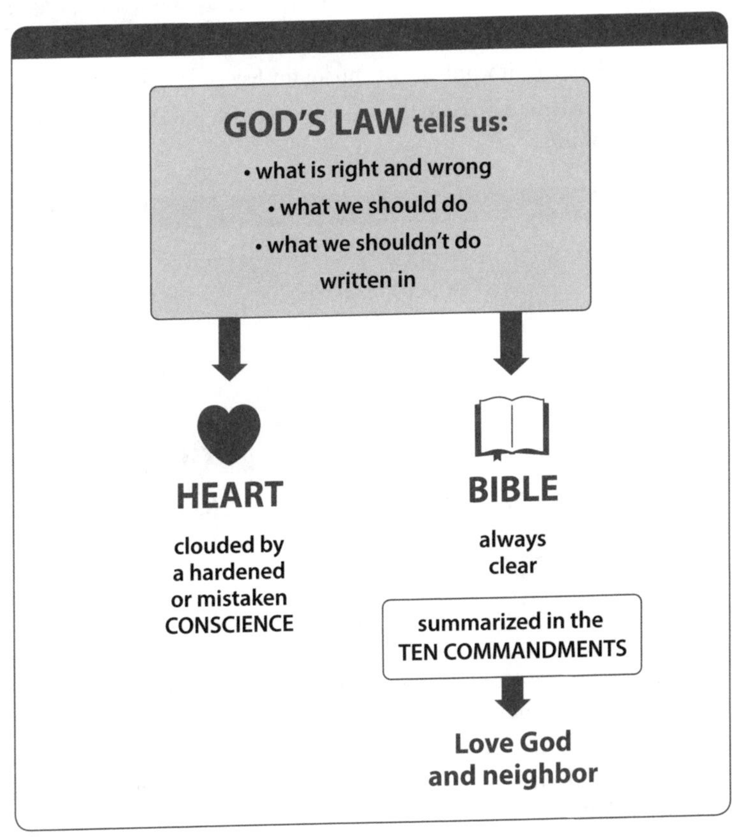

16. What do we mean when we say that God's law acts as a mirror in the hearts of all people?

Romans 3:20 No one will be declared righteous in his sight by works of the law, *for through the law we become aware of sin.*

Romans 7:7 *I would not have recognized sin except through the law.* For example, I would not have known about coveting if the law had not said, "You shall not covet."

17. Why is it so important that we look into the mirror of God's law?

Luke 18:13 The tax collector stood at a distance and would not even lift his eyes up to heaven, but was beating his chest and saying, "God, be merciful to me, a sinner!"

Acts 4:12 *There is salvation in no one else,* for there is no other name under heaven given to people by which we must be saved.

18. What do we mean when we say that God's law serves as a guide for Christians?

Psalm 119:105 Your words are a lamp for my feet and a light for my path.

Psalm 119:9 How can a young man keep his path pure? *By guarding it with your words.*

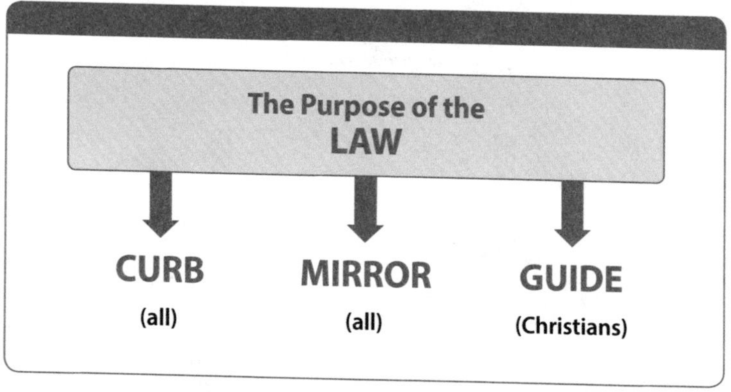

19. Why do we want to follow God's law?

Romans 12:1 I urge you, brothers, *by the mercies of God,* to offer your bodies as a living sacrifice—holy and pleasing to God—which is your appropriate worship.

2 Corinthians 5:15 He died for all, so that those who live would *no longer live for themselves but for him, who died in their place and was raised again.*

God's Word teaches the amazing truth that Jesus offered his life as a sacrifice for our sins. Because he did, our sins are forgiven and we are confident that we will go to heaven when we die. When, by faith, we grasp this truth, God changes us and we want to live for Christ. We want to obey his will so that our entire lives honor him.

CONNECTIONS

We measure the value of things people give to us in different ways. We may measure the value of something according to how much it costs. We may measure another thing according to its practical value—what we can do with the gift or how much time it will save us. We may consider other gifts to be important because of their beauty.

God's written law is a valuable and important gift for us all. God emphasized that by the striking and unusual way he first gave his law to the people of Israel. Read the following section of the Bible and learn how God gave his law to the Israelites:

Exodus 19:10–20:21

In what special and striking ways did God show the people how important the law was? Sometimes we don't think God's law is important. Can you remember a time when you thought God's commands were unimportant? How did you learn it was more important to obey than to disobey?

Luther

Since we are still clothed in flesh and blood, the preaching of the letter [law] is also necessary in order first to put people to death by the Law and destroy all their self-confidence, so that they may know themselves, become hungry for the Spirit, thirsty for grace, and so be a people prepared for the preaching of the Spirit. (*What Luther Says,* Ewald M. Plass, p. 736, par. 2284)

We therefore unanimously believe, teach, and confess that in its strict sense the law is a divine teaching in which the righteous, unchanging will of God revealed how human beings were created in their nature, thoughts, words, and deeds to be pleasing and acceptable to God. This law also threatens those who transgress it with God's wrath and temporal and eternal punishments. (FC SD V:17)

The Law of God Is Good and Wise (Stanzas 1,3,4)
The law of God is good and wise;
It sets his will before our eyes,
Shows us the way of righteousness,
But dooms to death when we transgress.

Its light of holiness imparts
The knowledge of our sinful hearts
That we may see our lost estate
And seek relief before too late.

To Jesus we for refuge flee,
Who from the curse has set us free,
And humbly worship at his throne,
Saved by his grace through faith alone.

TEN COMMANDMENTS

God gave Moses the Ten Commandments on two stone tablets at Mount Sinai.

COMMANDMENTS

The Ten Commandments*

The Ten Commandments are a summary of God's will for us in our lives. Many people think of the commandments as out-of-date rules that take away our freedom to do the things we want and should have the right to do. But the more we study the commandments, the more clearly we see that they are given to us to bless us. They remain important. We have every reason to want to learn what they mean, and we have every reason to obey them.

*Note: When God gave the Ten Commandments to Moses on Mount Sinai, he did not assign numbers to individual commandments. Luther chose to keep the numbering used by the ancient church and the church of his day. Others have numbered the commandments in a different way, keeping the number at ten but changing the way they are numbered.

God's Will for Our Lives

20. To understand why the Ten Commandments are blessings for us, we first have to grasp the condition of our relationship with God. **At birth what is wrong in our natural relationship with God?**

> **Genesis 2:16,17; 3:6** (When Adam and Eve disobeyed God's command and ate of the tree of the knowledge of good and evil, they brought sin and death into the world.)
>
> **John 3:6** Whatever is born of the flesh is flesh. Whatever is born of the Spirit is spirit.
>
> **Romans 5:12** Just as sin entered the world through one man and death through sin, so also death spread to all people because all sinned.
>
> **Psalm 51:5** Certainly, I was guilty when I was born. I was sinful when my mother conceived me.

Adam and Eve sinned when they chose to disobey God. Their sin brought them guilt along with many other consequences, including death. Because "whatever is born of flesh is flesh" (John 3:6), their descendants have been born with that sin and, therefore, are guilty and subject to death. Psalm 51 makes it very clear that at the moment of conception in our mother's womb, we each became guilty of sin. The consequences of sin were devastating for Adam and Eve. The consequences we inherit from them by birth are devastating to us also.

21. What are the results of our inborn sin?

Ephesians 2:1,3 *You were dead in your trespasses and sins. . . .* Like all the others, *we were by nature objects of God's wrath.*

Romans 8:7 *The mind-set of the sinful flesh is hostile to God,* since it does not submit to God's law, and in fact, it cannot.

Matthew 15:19 *Out of the heart come evil thoughts,* murders, adulteries, sexual sins, thefts, false testimonies, and blasphemies.

Isaiah 59:2 *It is your guilt that has separated you from your God, and* your sins have hidden God's face from you, so that he does not hear.

Because this guilt comes to us from our forefather Adam and so thoroughly corrupts our nature, we often refer to our natural sinful condition as our old Adam, sinful nature, inherited sin, or original sin. This sinful nature puts us under God's judgment, makes us enemies of God, and leads us to sins of thought, word, and deed, which separate us from our holy God.

22. How do we know that this description applies to us?

Romans 3:23 All have sinned and fall short of the glory of God.

Romans 5:12 Sin entered the world through one man and death through sin, *so also death spread to all people because all sinned.*

1 John 1:8 If we say we have no sin, we deceive ourselves, and the truth is not in us.

23. How do we come to the realization of our sin?

Romans 7:7 I would not have known about coveting if the law had not said, "You shall not covet."

Romans 3:20 No one will be declared righteous in his sight by works of the law, for *through the law we become aware of sin.*

Some people try to avoid medical tests because they fear the results, but medical tests can uncover diseases that, without treatment, could kill us.

God's commandments uncover the truth about the evil thoughts and deeds that spring from our old Adam and earn death for us.

24. Why is the work of the law a blessing as it uncovers our sins?

1 John 1:9 If we confess our sins, he is faithful and just to forgive us our sins and to cleanse us from all unrighteousness.

Luke 13:3 Unless you repent, you will all perish too.

God's law shows us that by ourselves we are lost because of our sins. It shows us that we are unable to save ourselves and that we need a Savior. It prepares our hearts so that we are ready to hear God's wonderful promise.

25. Who alone kept God's law?

Romans 3:12 They all turned away; together they became useless. There is *no one who does what is good;* there is not even one.

Hebrews 4:14,15 Since we have a great high priest, who has gone through the heavens, namely, Jesus the Son of God, let us continue to hold on to our confession. For we do not have a high priest who is unable to sympathize with our weaknesses, *but one who has been tempted in every way, just as we are, yet was without sin.*

Hebrews 7:26 This is certainly the kind of high priest we needed: one who is holy, innocent, pure, separated from sinners, and exalted above the heavens.

26. Why is it important to us that Jesus kept the law for us?

Galatians 4:4,5 When the set time had fully come, God sent his Son to be born of a woman, so that he would be *born under the law, in order to redeem those under the law,* so that we would be adopted as sons.

2 Corinthians 5:21 God made him, who did not know sin, to become sin for us, *so that we might become the righteousness of God in him.*

A CLOSER LOOK

Redeem: to pay a ransom; to buy back; to pay the price required to free someone from slavery or captivity

Vicarious: taking the place of another; substitutionary

Atonement: establishing peace between God and us by removing the guilt of sin through Christ's perfect life and death

Jesus kept God's law perfectly in our place—as our substitute. He also died as our substitute, paying for the guilt of our sins. We refer to this as *vicarious atonement.*

27. The result of Adam's sin is devastating for us. **How has the result of Jesus' life and death turned our lives around?**

Romans 5:17 If by the trespass of the one man, death reigned through the one man, it is even more certain that those who receive the overflowing grace of the gift of righteousness will reign in life through the one man Jesus Christ!

Ephesians 1:7 *In him we also have redemption through his blood,* the forgiveness of sins, in keeping with the riches of his grace.

Ephesians 2:1,3-5 You were dead in your trespasses and sins. . . . Like all the others, we were by nature objects of God's wrath. But *God, because he is rich in mercy,* because of the great love with which he loved us, *made us alive with Christ* even when we were dead in trespasses. It is by grace you have been saved!

1 John 1:7 The blood of Jesus Christ, his Son, cleanses us from all sin.

2 Corinthians 5:17,18 *If anyone is in Christ, he is a new creation.* The old has passed away. The new has come! And all these things are from God, who reconciled us to himself through Christ and gave us the ministry of reconciliation.

Ephesians 4:22-24 As far as your former way of life is concerned, you were taught *to take off the old self,* which is corrupted by its deceitful desires, and *to be renewed* continually in the spirit of your mind, and to put on the new self, which has been created to be like God in righteousness and true holiness.

Once we were controlled by the old Adam and were dead in sin and enemies of God. When we came to faith, a new person came to life within each of us, with a new attitude toward sin and righteousness. We often refer to this as the new person, the new self, the spiritual person (being).

28. Though the new self has come to life within us, the old Adam is still alive within us too. **What is the result of having both the old Adam and the new self within us?**

Galatians 5:17 The sinful flesh desires what is contrary to the spirit, and the spirit what is contrary to the sinful flesh. In fact, *these two continually oppose one another,* so that you do not continue to do these things you want to do.

Romans 7:18-23 I know that good does not live in me, that is, in my sinful flesh. *The desire to do good is present with me, but I am not able to carry it out.* So I fail to do the good I want to do. Instead, the evil I do not want to do, that is what I keep doing. Now if I do what I do not want to do, it is no longer I who am doing it, but it is sin living in me. So I find this law at work: *When I want to do good, evil is present with me.* I certainly delight in God's law according to my inner self, but I see a different law at work in my members, waging war against the law of my mind and taking me captive to the law of sin, which is present in my members.

29. We so often give in to the old Adam and fall into sin. But God's promise of forgiveness in Jesus strengthens the new self within us. **How does the new self within us respond to the gift of forgiveness and eternal life that Jesus has earned for us?**

Romans 12:1 I urge you, brothers, by the mercies of God, to *offer your bodies as a living sacrifice*—holy and pleasing to God—which is your appropriate worship.

2 Corinthians 5:14,15 The love of Christ compels us, because we came to this conclusion: One died for all; therefore, all died. And *he died for* *all, so that those who live would no longer live for themselves* but for him, who died in their place and was raised again.

30. Some people think of the commandments as rules that take all the fun out of life. In Genesis 3:1-6, we see how Satan deceived Eve into thinking that disobeying God would bring happiness. The results of Adam and Eve's disobedience, however, were misery, slavery to sin, and ultimately death. These things are always the results of sin. Obedience to God's commands, on the other hand, does bring blessings. **What blessings are ours as we obey his laws?**

Psalm 19:7,8,11 The law of the LORD is perfect. *It revives the soul.* The testimony of the LORD is trustworthy. It gives wisdom to the inexperienced. The precepts of the LORD are right. *They give joy to the heart.* The commandment of the LORD is bright. *It gives light to the eyes.* Yes, by them your servant is warned. In keeping them there is great reward.

Psalm 119:14,35,45 I rejoice in the way that is taught by your testimonies as much as I delight in all riches. Make me walk on the path of your commandments, *for I take pleasure in it.* Then I will walk around freely, because I have sought your precepts.

Matthew 5:3-10 (In this section of blessings, Jesus teaches that obedience to God's will is the way of true happiness.)

31. Why is God's law (the Ten Commandments) a blessing for us as we wish to show our gratitude to God for saving us?

Psalm 119:105 Your words are a lamp for my feet and a light for my path.

CONNECTIONS

Sometimes unpleasant experiences are actually blessings. Even pain can be a good thing. Pain can be the signal that tells us something serious is happening inside of us so that we get help from the doctor. Pain can also cause us to pull away from something that is hot and could burn us and do permanent damage. God might also use pain to lead us to his Word for hope and comfort. The result is a stronger faith.

The experience of looking into God's law is not always pleasant. Sometimes it is downright painful. God's law shows us that we fall short of what he wants us to be. It reveals the painful truth that we are sinners who deserve God's everlasting punishment. As unpleasant and painful as those truths are, they are blessings because they show us that we need a Savior. God shows us our sins and what we deserve because of them, but then he graciously points us to the forgiveness we have in our Savior. Read the account of Jonah; see how God's law accomplished its purpose of bringing an entire city of people to realize their sins.

Jonah 1–3

Notice how God brought the city of Nineveh to repentance. He used the words of his prophet. How has God shown you your sin? How has he assured you of his love and forgiveness? What Bible truths or passages have been most comforting to you when you have felt the guilt of your sin?

Luther

If the Law accuses me of not having done this or that or being unjust and a sinner in God's record, I must confess that all these charges are true. . . . To be sure, according to the Law, which computes my guilt, I am a poor, damned sinner. However, I appeal from the Law to the Gospel; for, in addition to the Law, God has given us another message called the Gospel. This bestows on us His grace, the forgiveness of sins, eternal righteousness and life. (*What Luther Says,* Ewald M. Plass, p. 743, par. 2300)

Salvation Unto Us Has Come (Stanzas 2-4)

What God does in his law demand And none to him can render
Brings wrath and woe on ev'ry hand
For man, the vile offender.
Our flesh has not those pure desires
The spirit of the law requires,
And lost is our condition.

It is a false, misleading dream That God his law has given
That sinners can themselves redeem
And by their works gain heaven.
The law is but a mirror bright
To bring the inbred sin to light
That lurks within our nature.

Yet as the law must be fulfilled Or we must die despairing,
Christ came and has God's anger stilled,
Our human nature sharing.
He has for us the law obeyed
And thus the Father's vengeance stayed
Which over us impended.

THE FIRST COMMANDMENT
You shall have no other gods.

What does this mean?
We should fear, love, and trust in God above all things.

NO OTHER GODS

Honor God Above All Else

With the First Commandment, God plainly teaches us that we should have no gods other than him, the only true God. As Christians, we may think that it will be easy to keep this commandment. After all, we believe in the true God who tells us about himself in the Bible. But as we study this commandment, we will see that we often break this commandment by honoring other gods. We often place more importance on something or someone other than God, making that something or someone our god. We need God's strong reminder to fear, love, and trust the true God above all things.

32. The greatest blessing we have, our most prized treasure, is to know the true God. **Why is it so important for us to know the true God?**

John 17:3 *This is eternal life: that they may know you, the only true God,* and Jesus Christ, whom you sent.

Acts 4:12 *There is salvation in no one else,* for there is no other name under heaven given to people by which we must be saved.

1 Peter 3:12 The eyes of the Lord are on the righteous, and his ears are open to their requests. But the face of the Lord is against those who do evil.

John 16:23 Amen, Amen, I tell you: *Whatever you ask the Father in my name, he will give you.*

Psalm 46:1 God is our refuge and strength, a helper who can always be found in times of trouble.

Psalm 67:1 May God be gracious to us and bless us. May his face shine on us.

Psalm 145:15,16 The eyes of all look eagerly to you, and you give them their food at the proper time. He opens his hand, and he *satisfies the desire of every living thing.*

33. Who is the true God?

1 Corinthians 8:4 There is no God but *one.*

Isaiah 45:21 *There is no god except me,* a righteous God and Savior. There is no one except me.

Matthew 28:19 Go and gather disciples from all nations by baptizing them *in the name of the Father and of the Son and of the Holy Spirit.*

2 Corinthians 13:14 The grace of the *Lord Jesus Christ,* and the love of *God,* and the fellowship of the *Holy Spirit* be with you all.

34. People break this commandment in many ways. **What are some ways people dishonor the true God?**

Psalm 14:1 The fool says in his heart, "There is no God."

Psalm 115:4 Their idols are silver and gold, the work of human hands.

Isaiah 44:12-19 (The prophet speaks of the foolishness of people who bow down to idols. He talks about the blacksmith who creates an image of metal that can't satisfy his hunger. He describes a craftsman who takes a block of wood, using half of it for fuel to cook his food and the other half to create an image that can do nothing.)

A CLOSER LOOK

Some people believe that there is no God. They are called atheists. They want to believe that they are masters of their own destinies and that they aren't responsible to anyone else. Other people acknowledge that there may be a god, but they say we can't know for sure. They are called agnostics. Neither atheists nor agnostics believe what the Bible tells us. They don't believe in the true God. It is worth noting the demons described in James 2:19. Though these demons believed there is one God, they had reason to shudder in fear.

---

35. We understand what the words *love* and *trust* mean. However, when we speak of loving and trusting God, those words take on special significance. To love God means to treasure him and his Word above everything else. To trust him is to be confident that his Word is true and that he always provides everything we need, keeps us safe, and gives us everything he has promised. Unfortunately, our actions often reveal that the sinful nature lives within us and leads us to love and trust in other gods instead of in the true God. **What are some of the ways that we may be guilty of sinning against God by breaking this commandment?**

Matthew 6:24 No one can serve two masters. Either he will hate the one and love the other, or he will be devoted to the one and despise the other. You cannot *serve both God and mammon.*

Psalm 62:10 If your wealth grows, *do not set your heart on it.*

Proverbs 11:28 *Whoever trusts his wealth will fall,* but righteous people will flourish like green plants.

1 John 2:15 *Do not love the world or the things in the world.* If anyone loves the world, the love of the Father is not in him.

Matthew 10:37 *Whoever loves father or mother more than me is not worthy of me,* and whoever loves son or daughter more than me is not worthy of me.

Our material possessions, our families, and our friends are all blessings from God. We thank him for them. But when they become too important to us, they begin to take God's place in our hearts; they become our idols. We love them more than we love God.

Proverbs 3:5 Trust in the LORD with all your heart, and *do not rely on your own understanding.*

Jeremiah 17:5 This is what the LORD says. *Cursed is anyone who trusts in mankind,* who seeks his strength from human flesh, and who turns his heart away from the LORD.

God has blessed us so we can learn many things. We know more about this complex world than previous generations did. We develop medicines and invent technology that can do amazing things. But if we trust our human knowledge so much that we believe we do not need God's care, love, and forgiveness, we make gods of our understanding, knowledge, and technology.

John 5:23 Whoever does not honor the Son does not honor the Father who sent him.

1 John 2:22,23 Who is a liar but the one who denies that Jesus is the Christ? This is an antichrist: the one who denies the Father and the Son. *Everyone who denies the Son does not have the Father.* But the one who confesses the Son has the Father as well.

Many people claim to believe in the God of the Bible but don't believe that Jesus is true God. They really believe in a god created by human imagination. In reality, they are following an idol.

36. In his explanation of the First Commandment, Luther says that we are to love and trust God above all things. If we love and trust other things more than God, we are making them into false gods. **In the**

explanation, he also tells us to fear God above all things. What does that mean?

Matthew 10:28 Do not fear those who kill the body but cannot kill the soul. Rather, *fear the one who is able to destroy both soul and body in hell.*

Ephesians 3:20,21 Now to him, who is able, according to the power that is at work within us, to do infinitely more than we can ask or imagine, to him be the glory in the church and in Christ Jesus throughout all generations, forever and ever! Amen.

1 Samuel 12:24 Above all, *fear the Lord, and serve him in truth,* with all your heart, considering the great things he has done for you.

Daniel 6:1-23 (Daniel feared God more than the king's decree. He was willing to die rather than bow down to the king.)

To fear God doesn't mean simply to be afraid of him. To fear God means to recognize his power and authority and be filled with great awe and respect. When our sinful flesh leads us to sin, God wants us to fear the punishment that we deserve because of our sin. But we do not receive punishment; we receive forgiveness. As we rejoice in the forgiveness of our sins, our fear of God includes appreciation that his power and authority gave us a Savior.

37. All of us struggle with this commandment. We don't always fear, love, and trust in God more than anything or anyone else. **How can we then hope that God will love us as his children, that he will listen to our prayers, and that he will someday take us to heaven?**

Matthew 4:1-10 (Jesus was tempted to put himself first, but he didn't. He put God first.)

Romans 5:19 Just as through the disobedience of one man the many became sinners, so also *through the obedience of one man the many will become righteous.*

We are sinners who have heard the wonderful message that Jesus kept God's commandments in our place. Out of thanks to Jesus for saving us, we turn away from our sins and want to obey God.

38. How does God's Word serve as a guide for those of us who want to keep the First Commandment?

Matthew 22:37 Jesus said to him, "Love the Lord your God with all your heart, with all your soul, and with all your mind."

Psalm 73:25,26 Who else is there for me in heaven? And besides you, I desire no one else on earth. My flesh and my heart fail, but God is the rock of my heart and my portion forever.

Genesis 22:1-19 (Abraham so feared, loved, and trusted God that he was willing to offer his son.)

1 Samuel 17 (David trusted that God would give him victory against Goliath.)

1 Peter 5:6,7 Humble yourselves under God's powerful hand so that he may lift you up at the appointed time. Cast all your anxiety on him, because he cares for you.

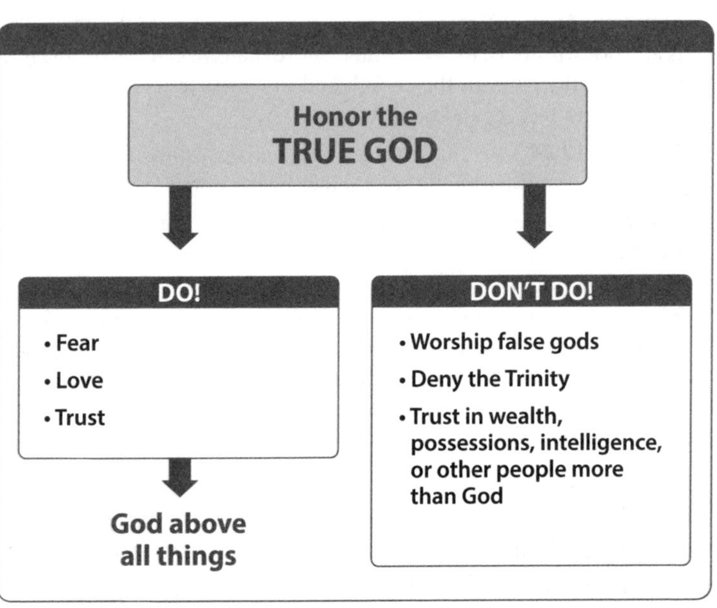

CONNECTIONS

Fear. Love. Trust. Those three words summarize Luther's explanation of the First Commandment. We fear God above all things when we are afraid of his punishment because of our sins and when we are filled with such awe and respect that we don't want to sin. We love him above all things when his promise of salvation through Jesus is our most valuable treasure and the focus of our hearts. We trust him above all things when we bring all of our challenges and needs to him in prayer, believing he can help us. We demonstrate that trust especially when we look to him to help us with our greatest problem—our sin—and believe his promise that he has forgiven us through Jesus. In the Bible we can find many examples of people for whom the promises of God were more valuable than even life itself. In the book of Daniel, read about how three men feared, loved, and trusted God to the point that they were ready to die rather than worship a false god.

Daniel 3:1-18

God miraculously rescued these three men from the fire. But before the men were thrown into the flames, they did not know what God would do. They were willing to risk their lives because they believed God was more important than life. Describe a time when putting God first means you might lose something. What Bible truths can help you when you are in such a situation?

Luther

You shall have me alone as your God. What is the meaning of this? . . . Answer: A god means that from which we are to expect all good and in which we are to take refuge in all distress. So, to have a god is nothing other than trusting and believing him with the heart. I have often said that the confidence and faith of the heart alone make both God and an idol. If your faith and trust is right, then your God is also true. On the other hand, if your trust is false and wrong, then you do not have the true God. For these two belong together, faith and God [Hebrews 11:6]. Now, I say that whatever you set your heart on and put your trust in is truly your god. (Large Catechism, I, par. 1,2)

The Ten Commandments Are the Law (Stanzas 2,11,12)

"I am your Lord and God alone!
No other god but me enthrone!
Put your whole confidence in me;
Give me your heart totally."
Have mercy, Lord!

God gave these laws to show therein,
O child of man, your life of sin,
And help you rightly to perceive
How unto God you should live.
Have mercy, Lord!

Our works cannot salvation gain;
They merit only endless pain.
Forgive us, Lord! To Christ we fly,
Our mediator on high.
Have mercy, Lord!

I Am Trusting You, Lord Jesus (Stanzas 1,4,6)

I am trusting you, Lord Jesus,
Trusting only you,
Trusting you for full salvation,
Free and true.

I am trusting you to guide me;
You alone shall lead,
Ev'ry day and hour supplying
All my need.

I am trusting you, Lord Jesus;
Never let me fall.
I am trusting you forever
And for all.

THE SECOND COMMANDMENT

You shall not misuse the name of the Lord your God.

What does this mean?

We should fear and love God that we do not use his name to curse, swear, lie, or deceive, or use witchcraft, but call upon God's name in every trouble, pray, praise, and give thanks.

GOD'S NAME

Use God's Name Properly

The names that God uses for himself in the Bible tell us much of what we know about God. Names like *God Almighty, the Lord, Jesus, Savior, Holy Spirit,* and *the First and the Last,* and many more, express important truths about God. It is vital that we know and believe in the true God. Therefore, it is easy to understand why God gave us a commandment that forbids us to misuse his name in any way. Because God is holy and is our Creator and Savior, he deserves our respect. The Second Commandment reminds us that we very often show a lack of respect for his name and so dishonor it. The commandment shows us how to treat his name with the utmost honor and respect.

A CLOSER LOOK

When we hear someone's name, we naturally think about the things we know about that person—what the person looks like, the things he or she likes to do, and so on. A name is like a signpost, pointing our minds to everything we associate with the person. In a similar way, when we speak of God's name, we aren't just talking about the sounds of the letters *G-o-d.* God's name brings to mind everything that is true about him. God's name recalls everything God has told us about himself in the Bible.

39. We are very blessed that God has revealed his name to us. His name is so important that God gave a commandment to warn us against misusing it. **Why did God reveal his name to us?**

Romans 10:13 *Everyone who calls on the name of the Lord will be saved.*

Proverbs 18:10 The name of the LORD is a strong tower. *A righteous person runs inside and is protected.*

Psalm 9:10 Those who know your name will *trust in you,* for you, O LORD, have not forsaken those who seek you.

Psalm 54:6 *I will praise your name,* O LORD, because it is good.

Psalm 50:15 Call on me in the day of distress. I will deliver you, and you will honor me.

Psalm 20:1 May the LORD answer you in the day of distress. *May the name* of the God of Jacob *lift you up.*

Psalm 22:22 *I will declare your name* to my brothers.

God's name is very important to us. Through it, God calls us to be saved. He protects those who believe in his name. He reveals his name to us so that we might trust in his power and pray to him in every need. He teaches us his name so that we might praise him and tell others of the great things he has done.

With all of these blessings coming to us through his name, one might think that we would always honor his name and treat it with the highest respect. However, our sinful nature opposes God and leads us to misuse God's name—the very thing God forbids in the Second Commandment.

40. God's law serves as a mirror for us, revealing that we are guilty of breaking the Second Commandment. **How do we misuse God's name?**

James 3:10 Blessing and *cursing* come out of the same mouth. My brothers, these things should not be this way.

Romans 12:14 Bless those who persecute you; bless, and *do not curse.*

To **curse** here means to use God's name to wish evil on someone. We find an example in Numbers 22:1-6. There we read how Balak tried to hire Balaam to curse God's people so that Balak could conquer them.

Leviticus 19:12 You shall not swear falsely by my name so that you do not profane the name of your God. I am the LORD.

Matthew 26:69-75 (Peter swore to support his lie that he didn't know Jesus.)

James 5:12 Above all, my brothers, *do not swear*—not by heaven or by earth or by anything else. Just let your "yes" be "yes" and your "no" be "no," so that you do not fall under judgment.

Swearing here means to use God's name to pledge that you are telling the truth. We sin if we use God's name to defend a lie. We also sin if we swear unnecessarily.

Matthew 15:9 They worship me in vain, *teaching human rules* as if they are doctrines.

Matthew 7:15 Watch out for *false prophets.* They come to you in sheep's clothing, but inwardly they are ravenous wolves.

Jeremiah 23:31 Indeed, *I am against the prophets,* declares the LORD, *who use their own tongues to say, "This is what the LORD declares!"*

We use God's name to **lie** if we teach false doctrine (claim that our own false beliefs come from God).

Matthew 15:7,8 Hypocrites! Isaiah was right when he prophesied about you: These people honor me with their lips, but *their heart is far from me.*

Acts 5:1-11 (Ananias and Sapphira tried to deceive the other disciples into believing that they were giving all their proceeds from the sale of property to the church as a gift.)

Matthew 23:23-33 (Jesus condemned the teachers of the law and the Pharisees for being hypocrites. The Pharisees were members of a Jewish group that focused on keeping laws [they even added laws to those given in the Bible]. Although they claimed to follow God and tried to show off their "goodness" and "godliness," their zeal didn't flow from love for God. Often they tried to use their "godliness" as a cover for their greed and the evil things they were doing.)

We use God's name to **deceive** if we try to pretend that we are faithful followers of God in order to cover our sins.

Deuteronomy 18:10-12 Let no one be found among you who *makes his son or his daughter pass through fire, or who uses divination, or who engages in fortune telling, or who observes omens, or who practices witchcraft, or who casts a magic spell, or who consults a ghost or a familiar spirit, or who inquires of the dead.* Anyone doing these things is detestable to the LORD, and because of these abominations, the LORD your God is driving them out before you.

If we practice **witchcraft,** are involved with the **occult,** or are **superstitious** (believing in good luck charms, etc.), we are sinning against God's name because we are trusting in power that ultimately comes from Satan and is opposed to the power and will of God.

41. We often sin by the things we do, but we also sin when we don't do the things we should. When we do what God forbids (commit sinful acts), we call those sins of commission. When we fail to do what God commands, we call those sins of omission. **How do we sometimes dishonor God's name by our failure to use it?**

1 Thessalonians 5:17 Pray without ceasing.

James 4:2 You want something but do not get it, so you murder. You desire something but cannot obtain it, so you quarrel and fight. You do not have *because you do not ask.*

Isaiah 43:21 This people that I formed for myself *will declare my praise.*

Psalm 105:1 Give thanks to the LORD. *Proclaim his name.* Make his deeds known among the peoples.

Psalm 118:1 *Give thanks to the LORD,* for he is good, for his mercy endures forever.

Ephesians 5:4 *Obscenity, foolish talk, and coarse joking are also out of place.* Instead, give thanks.

42. Jesus spoke through his apostle James, telling us, "Whoever keeps the whole law but stumbles in one point has become guilty of breaking all of it" (James 2:10). We are all guilty of breaking the Second Commandment. Perhaps we can think of specific times we have cursed, used God's name to swear needlessly, or placed our trust in good luck charms. At other times we may have failed to use his name to pray, to praise, or to give thanks. **How do we know that our sins against the Second Commandment are forgiven?**

2 Corinthians 5:21 God made him, who did not know sin, to become sin for us, so that we might become the righteousness of God in him.

43. We are sinners who have heard the wonderful message that Jesus' perfect obedience to God's law is credited to us. Because of Jesus, we are counted righteous (sinless) in the sight of God; therefore, we want to obey his commandments and honor God's name. **How does God's Word serve as a guide for those of us who want to keep the Second Commandment?**

Acts 4:12 *There is salvation in no one else,* for there is no other name under heaven given to people by which we must be saved.

Psalm 50:15 Call on me in the day of distress. *I will deliver you,* and you will honor me.

John 16:23 In that day you will not ask me anything. Amen, Amen, I tell you: *Whatever you ask the Father in my name, he will give you.*

1 Thessalonians 5:17 Pray without ceasing.

Psalm 52:9 *I will thank you forever because you have done this.* I will hope in your name in the presence of your favored ones because it is good.

Ephesians 5:18-20 Be filled with the Spirit by speaking to one another with psalms, hymns, and spiritual songs (singing and making music with your hearts to the Lord), by *always giving thanks for everything to God the Father, in the name of our Lord Jesus Christ.*

Acts 4:20 We cannot stop speaking about what we have seen and heard.

Matthew 28:19,20 Therefore go and gather disciples from all nations by *baptizing them in the name of the Father and of the Son and of the Holy Spirit, and by teaching them to keep all the instructions I have given you.* And surely I am with you always until the end of the age.

God's name is precious to us. In his name we find salvation. We are invited to pray to him in every need. We offer thanks and praise to his name. We tell others the great things he has done.

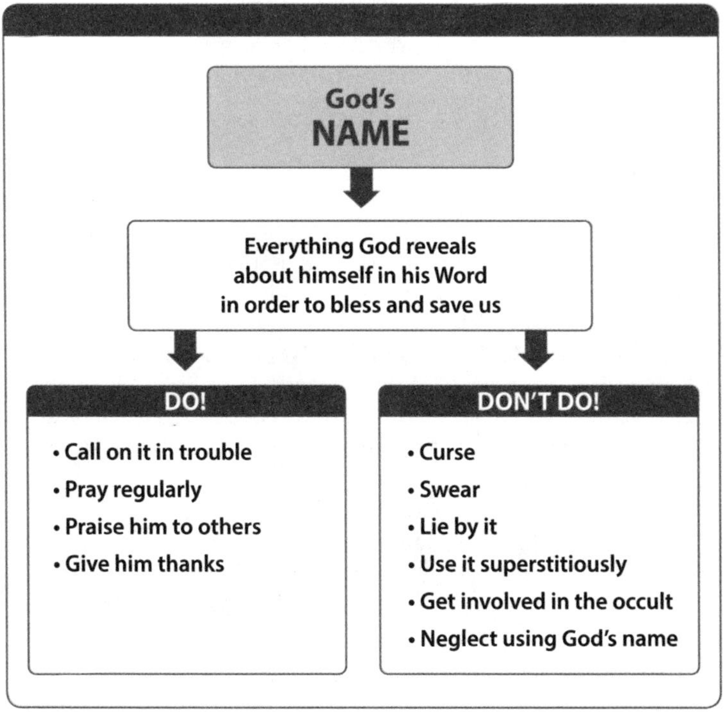

God's NAME

↓

Everything God reveals about himself in his Word in order to bless and save us

DO!	DON'T DO!
• Call on it in trouble	• Curse
• Pray regularly	• Swear
• Praise him to others	• Lie by it
• Give him thanks	• Use it superstitiously
	• Get involved in the occult
	• Neglect using God's name

CONNECTIONS

The names of God tell us many important truths about him.

One day when Moses was taking care of his father-in-law's sheep, he saw something unusual. A bush was on fire, but it didn't burn up. From there God revealed one of his names to Moses—a simple name, yet one that taught Moses a lot about God.

Exodus 3:1-17

When God revealed himself to Moses at the burning bush, he said, "I AM WHO I AM." This name "I AM" teaches us a number of important things about God. First, God simply "is," and he doesn't depend on anything else to exist. Second, God doesn't change. He is the same yesterday, today, and forever. When Jesus applied the name "I am" to himself (John 8:58), the people knew he was claiming to be God, who had revealed himself to Moses, with that name. Describe a situation in life when you can find comfort in knowing that God doesn't depend on anything else to exist. Then, think of a circumstance when knowing that God never changes would be helpful.

Luther

God's name cannot be misused worse than for the support of falsehood and deceit. . . . All misuse of the divine name happens first in worldly business and in matters that concern money, possessions, and honor. This applies publicly in court, in the market or wherever else people make false oaths in God's name or pledge their souls in any matter. This is especially common in marriage affairs. . . . But the greatest abuse occurs in spiritual matters. These have to do with the conscience, when false preachers rise up and offer their lying vanities as God's Word. (Large Catechism, I, par. 52,53)

Oh, Bless the Lord, My Soul (Stanzas 1,2,5)

Oh, bless the Lord, my soul! Let all within me join
And aid my tongue to bless his name Whose favors are divine.

Oh, bless the Lord, my soul, Nor let his mercies lie
Forgotten in unthankfulness And without praises die.

His wondrous works and ways He made by Moses known,
But sent the world his truth and grace By his beloved Son.

THE THIRD COMMANDMENT
Remember the Sabbath day by keeping it holy.

What does this mean?
We should fear and love God that we do not despise preaching and his Word, but regard it as holy and gladly hear and learn it.

WORSHIP
Hear and Learn God's Word

Are you tired? The body can get worn out after a long day of school, a busy day of work, or a full day of fun and play. Our souls can get worn out too, burdened by doubts and guilt and fear. We long for peace and rest. *Sabbath* is the Hebrew word for "rest." When God invites us to remember the Sabbath, he wants us to enjoy the true rest he offers for weary souls. He gives us this rest when we worship him and especially when he assures us that our sins are forgiven through Jesus.

44. For the Old Testament people, the Sabbath Day began at sundown on Friday and ended at sundown on Saturday. God emphasized the importance of the day by forbidding that the people do any work during that time. **How were the people blessed as they observed the Sabbath Day?**

> **Exodus 20:9-11** Six days you are to serve and do all your regular work, but the seventh day shall be a sabbath rest to the LORD your God. Do not do any regular work, neither you, nor your sons or daughters, nor your male or female servants, nor your cattle, nor the alien who is residing inside your gates, for in six days the LORD made the heavens and the earth, the sea, and everything that is in them, but he *rested on the seventh day.* In this way the LORD blessed the seventh day and made it holy.

> **Ezekiel 20:12** I also gave them my Sabbaths *to be a sign* between me and them, so that they could know that I, the LORD, am the one who sanctifies them.

Psalm 122:1 I rejoiced with those who said to me, "Let us go to the house of the LORD."

Isaiah 40:31 Those who wait for the LORD will receive new strength.

Hebrews 4:1-3 *Since the promise of entering his rest still stands,* let us be fearful that any one of you may be judged to have failed to reach it. In fact, we have had the gospel preached to us, just as they did. But the message they heard did not benefit them, because they were not united in faith with those who did listen. Indeed, we who believe are going to enter his rest.

God commanded the people of Israel to rest from their weekly work and worship him (Leviticus 23:3). They were to rest on the seventh day, the Sabbath. The Sabbath as a day of rest reminded them that God worked six days to create the world and then he rested on the seventh day, or the Sabbath. The rest God commanded for them made them different from other nations and also reminded them that they were a special people he had set apart from all the nations to fulfill his promise of a Savior. Lastly, the Sabbath reminded them of the great spiritual rest the Savior would bring—rest for their souls, the forgiveness of sins.

45. Why aren't we required to observe the Sabbath Day in the way the Old Testament people were?

Colossians 2:13,14,16,17 Even when you were dead in your trespasses and the uncircumcision of your flesh, God made you alive with Christ by forgiving us all our trespasses. God erased the record of our debt brought against us by his legal demands. This record stood against us, but he took it away by nailing it to the cross. Therefore, do not let anyone judge you in regard to food or drink, or in regard to a festival or a New Moon or a Sabbath day. *These are a shadow of the things that were coming, but the body belongs to Christ.*

Matthew 11:28,29 *Come to me* all you who are weary and burdened, and I will give you rest. Take my yoke upon you and learn from me, because I am gentle and humble in heart, and *you will find rest for your souls.*

Jesus fulfilled the Sabbath. The Old Testament day of rest was a shadow of the perfect rest for our souls given to us through the Savior.

46. What does the Third Commandment then mean for us in the New Testament?

Romans 10:17 *Faith comes from hearing* the message, and the message comes through the word of Christ.

Luke 10:16 *Whoever listens to you listens to me.* Whoever rejects you rejects me. And whoever rejects me rejects the one who sent me.

John 8:47 *Whoever belongs to God listens to what God says.* The reason you do not listen is that you do not belong to God.

Colossians 3:16 *Let the word of Christ dwell in you richly,* as you teach and admonish one another with all wisdom, singing psalms, hymns, and spiritual songs, with gratitude in your hearts to God.

Acts 17:10-12 (The Bereans were eager to hear God's Word, and they studied it diligently.)

God's Word brings rest to our troubled hearts and lives through its comforting message of forgiveness. In the Third Commandment, God warns us not to despise his Word but, rather, to consider it sacred and hear it and study it gladly.

47. How does God's Word serve as a mirror, showing us how we sin by despising his Word?

John 8:47 Whoever belongs to God listens to what God says.

Hebrews 10:24,25 Let us also consider carefully how to spur each other on to love and good works. *Let us not neglect meeting together,* as some have the habit of doing. Rather, let us encourage each other, and all the more as you see the Day approaching.

1 Samuel 15:1-23 (Saul rejected the Word of God. God had commanded him to destroy the king of the Amalekites and his people and everything that belonged to them. However, Saul and his men spared the king and kept the best sheep and cattle for themselves.)

Luke 8:14 The seeds that fell into the thorns are the ones who hear the word, but as they go on their way they are choked by the worries, riches, and pleasures of life, so they do not mature.

1 John 2:15 Do not love the world or the things in the world. *If anyone loves the world, the love of the Father is not in him.*

James 1:22-24 *Be people who do what the word says, not people who only hear it.* Such people are deceiving themselves. In fact, if anyone hears the word and does not do what it says, he is like a man who carefully looks at his own natural face in a mirror. Indeed, he carefully looks at himself; then, he goes away and immediately forgets what he looked like.

We can despise God's Word in many ways. If we don't hear his Word, we are acting as if it is not important to us. This can happen as we stay away from worship services or fail to study God's Word on our own because we consider other concerns or pleasures more important. We can also despise God's Word when we hear it but refuse to take it to heart.

48. How did Jesus keep this commandment perfectly as our substitute?

1 John 3:5 You know that he appeared in order to take away our sins and *in him there is no sin.*

Luke 4:16 He went to Nazareth, where he had been brought up. *As was his custom, he went into the synagogue on the Sabbath day* and stood up to read.

Matthew 4:1-10 (When Jesus was tempted by the devil, he always used God's Word to resist temptation. See verses 4,7,10.) *"It is written:* Man shall not live by bread alone, but by every word that comes out of the mouth of God. . . . *Again, it is written:* You shall not test the Lord your God." Then Jesus said to him, "Go away, Satan! *For it is written:* Worship the Lord your God, and serve him only."

49. Recognizing that Jesus kept the Third Commandment perfectly and has forgiven our sins, we want to honor him by keeping his Word. **How does God's Word guide us to keep the Third Commandment?**

Psalm 122:1 I rejoiced with those who said to me, "Let us go to the house of the LORD."

Isaiah 66:2 *This is the person I will watch over:* the one who is afflicted and whose spirit is crushed, the one who *trembles at my word.*

Joshua 1:8 *This Book of the Law must never depart from your mouth, and you are to meditate on it day and night, so that you will act faithfully according to everything written in it,* because then you will prosper in everything you do, and you will succeed.

John 20:31 These are written *that you may believe* that Jesus is the Christ, the Son of God, and that by believing you may have life in his name.

Luke 11:28 He said, "Even more blessed are *those who hear* the word of God *and keep it.*"

Acts 17:11 Now the Bereans were more noble-minded than the Thessalonians. They received the word very eagerly and examined the Scriptures *every day* to see if these things were so.

1 Thessalonians 2:13 There is also another reason we give thanks to God unceasingly, namely, when you received God's word, which you heard from us, you did not receive it as the word of men *but as the word of God (as it really is),* which is now at work in you who believe.

Mark 16:15 *He said to them, "Go into all the world and preach the gospel to all creation."*

1 Peter 1:25; 2:2 The word of the Lord endures forever. And this is the word that was preached to you. Like newborn babies, *crave the pure milk of the word* so that by it you may grow up with the result being salvation.

50. Why is God's Word especially important to us?

Romans 10:17 Faith comes from hearing the message, and the message comes through the word of Christ.

Deuteronomy 32:47 *It is not empty talk for you, because it is your life.* By this word you will live long on the land that you are crossing the Jordan to possess.

Because God's Word is so important to us—it is the source of life—the Christian church provides regular opportunities for God's people to come together to worship God and hear his Word. Shortly after the time of Jesus, Christians began to meet regularly on Sundays in memory of several important events that took place on Sundays: the first day of creation, Jesus' resurrection, and the sending of the Holy Spirit on Pentecost. Eventually, in much of the world, Sunday was set aside as a day of rest and worship. Yet, today, many people are expected to work on Sundays and their opportunities for worship become limited. In New Testament freedom, many congregations offer opportunities for people to worship together and hear God's Word on other days of the week.

Sunday is still the primary day of worship for the majority of Christians. But what matters most is not the specific day but, rather, that we are gathering together with fellow Christians to hear God's Word, to benefit from the sacraments, and to encourage one another in the faith.

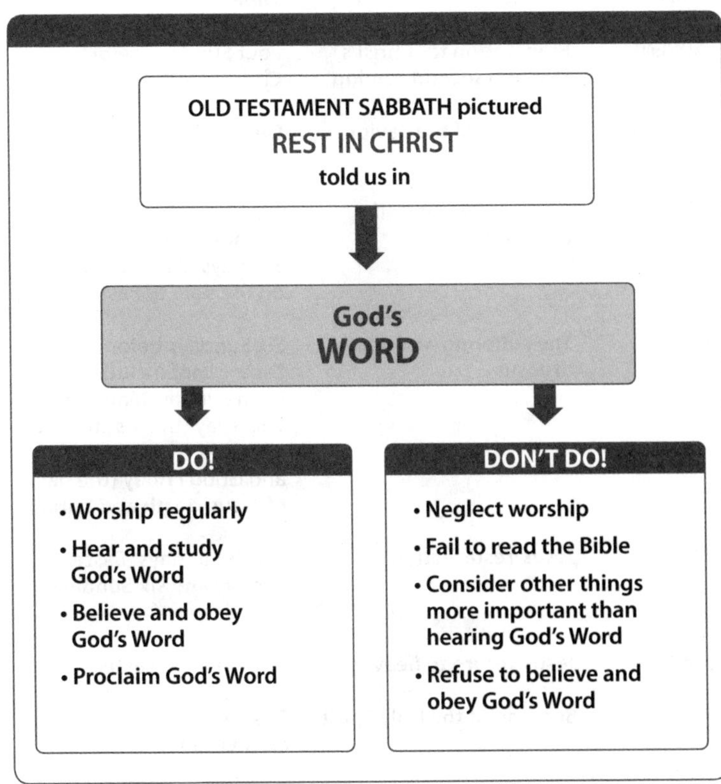

Sundays of the Church Year

The early Christian church developed a system to provide an annual review of the chief teachings of the Bible. The Sundays of the year are divided into units, or seasons, that focus on major events in the life of Jesus as well as the important lessons God teaches us in the Bible. The church year begins with Advent, four Sundays before Christmas. Because the system doesn't follow the calendar year exactly, we call it the church year.

The first half of the church year is called the festival half. On the Sundays in the festival half of the church year, we review the life of Christ, especially his birth (Advent and Christmas) and then his suffering, death, and resurrection (Lent and Easter).

The second half of the church year is the non-festival half. During this portion of the church year, we focus on how the life of a Christian can reflect the love that Christ has shown to us.

The Festival Half of the Church Year

THE LIFE OF CHRIST		
Season	**Theme**	**Time**
ADVENT	Preparation for Christ's first and second coming	Four Sundays before Christmas
CHRISTMAS	The birth of the Savior	December 25 to January 6
EPIPHANY	Jesus shows himself as Savior	January 6 through the next four to nine Sundays, depending on the date of Easter
LENT	The suffering and death of Jesus	Six Sundays before Easter; Lent includes Palm Sunday, Maundy Thursday (the institution of the Lord's Supper), and Good Friday (the day of Jesus' death and burial)
EASTER	Jesus' resurrection	Seven Sundays (Easter Sunday and six Sundays after Easter)
ASCENSION	Jesus' return to heaven	40 days after Easter
PENTECOST	Sending of the Holy Spirit	The Sunday 50 days after Easter

The Non-Festival Half of the Church Year

The non-festival half of the church year begins with Trinity Sunday at the end of May or beginning of June and extends through November. Trinity Sunday is the first Sunday after the celebration of Pentecost. The Sundays that follow Pentecost are referred to as Sundays after Pentecost. They offer Christians the opportunity to review what a Christian life looks like. The last Sundays of the non-festival half of the church year focus on the Reformation and the end times as we prepare for Christ's return.

During the non-festival half of the church year, we celebrate several special days. In addition to the Reformation, we observe Thanksgiving Day (the fourth Thursday of November in the United States and the second Monday of October in Canada). Many congregations also celebrate a special mission festival during this half of the church year.

Although God's Word doesn't bind us to this plan or any other, many churches follow it because they recognize the value of studying the life and teachings of Christ every year.

Over the centuries, the leaders of the church designated a set of readings from the Bible for each Sunday of the church year. The list of readings is called the lectionary, and each Sunday's set consists of an Old Testament reading, a reading from one of the gospels, and a reading from one of the letters, or epistles, of the New Testament. These readings highlight the unique emphasis for that particular Sunday.

The church year guides worship over the course of a year. Many churches have also adopted a pattern that provides structure for worship every Sunday. We call that pattern the liturgy. The liturgy has two key parts.

First, there is a part that regularly changes. Every Sunday, the lessons (the pericope), hymns, and some of the prayers focus on the particular theme of the day. They change according to the part of Jesus' life we are considering or the aspect of Christian living that we are studying.

Second, there is a part that doesn't change as much. For example, in most services we confess our sins and receive the assurance that we are forgiven. In most services we have a special song of praise that rises from our hearts as we are reminded that our sin is taken away. There are different variations of this "unchanging" portion of the liturgy. Historically, this unchanging portion had five special songs:

FIVE SONGS OF THE LITURGY	
Lord, Have Mercy *(Kyrie)*	**Psalm 123 Whenever we pray to the Lord, we remember that we depend completely on his mercy.**
Glory Be to God *(Gloria in Excelsis)*	**Luke 2:13,14 Using words of the angels, we praise our great and glorious God.**
Creed *(Credo)*	**We acknowledge who God is and what he has done.**
Holy, Holy, Holy *(Sanctus)*	**Isaiah 6:3 We join the angels around the throne of God, acknowledging that he is the God of grace and power.**
O Christ, Lamb of God *(Agnus Dei)*	**John 1:29 We point to Jesus as the Savior and pray that he will direct his saving work to each of us.**

The church year and the liturgy highlight the works and words of Christ. Because many Christians before us have worshiped in a similar way, these patterns in our worship remind us of the connection we have with the Christians who have lived before us. These patterns also remind us of the connection we have with other churches and Christians of our denomination. When we visit these churches, we often find that they use the same liturgy. At the same time, we rejoice in the freedom we have in worship—the freedom to use different patterns of worship with joy and with responsibility.

CONNECTIONS

People can be very busy. We work or go to school, and the rest of our days are jam-packed with activities. We want to participate. All of the opportunities that keep us busy demonstrate the truth that God has richly blessed us. We probably have more opportunities to do more different things than previous generations ever imagined. But because we are so busy, it is easy for us to neglect the most important activity of all: turning our attention to the Word of God. Through his Word, the Holy Spirit nourishes our faith and keeps us alive spiritually.

When we draw near to the end of our lives, we may find satisfaction looking back at all the things we have done. But at that time, what will give us peace and hope are the promises that God has given, which we receive through his Word. In order to stay alive spiritually, we need a steady diet of God's Word. One of

Jesus' followers understood that very clearly. Read about how Mary wouldn't let herself be distracted by busyness and was commended by Jesus because she knew the one thing that was most important.

Luke 10:38-42

Mary wanted what was most needed. What was it? List distractions and temptations that can keep you from coming to church to worship Jesus or from reading your Bible. For each distraction and temptation, suggest a way to follow Mary's example and to seek the one thing needful.

Luther

We come together to hear and use God's Word, and then to praise God, to sing and to pray [Colossians 3:16]. However, this keeping of the Sabbath, I point out, is not restricted to a certain time, as with the Jewish people. It does not have to be just on this or that day. For in itself no one day is better than another [Romans 14:5-6]. Instead, this should be done daily. However, since the masses of people cannot attend every day, there must be at least one day in the week set apart. (Large Catechism, I, par. 84,85)

Speak, O Savior; I Am Listening (Stanzas 1,3)

Speak, O Savior; I am list'ning,
As a servant to his lord.
Let me show respect and honor
To your holy, precious Word,
That each day, my whole life through,
I may serve and follow you.
Let your Word e'er be my pleasure
And my heart's most precious treasure.

Lord, your words are waters living
Where I quench my thirsty needs.
Lord, your words are bread life-giving;
On your words my spirit feeds.
Lord, your words will be my light
Through death's cold and dreary night;
Yes, they are my sword prevailing
And my cup of joy unfailing.

THE FOURTH COMMANDMENT
Honor your father and mother, that it may go well with you and that you may enjoy long life on the earth.

What does this mean?
We should fear and love God that we do not dishonor or anger our parents and others in authority, but honor, serve, and obey them, and give them love and respect.

HONOR AND OBEY

God's Representatives

The first three commandments speak of our personal relationship with God. The Fourth Commandment begins a new focus: our relationships with one another. Each of the remaining commandments addresses a specific aspect of our relationships with others. In the Fourth Commandment, God directs our attitudes and actions toward those in authority. The authorities we are most familiar with are our parents, but, for our own good, God also has placed representatives over us in the government and the church.

51. The Fourth Commandment speaks specifically about our fathers and mothers. They are the primary representatives God has placed over us. But this commandment really addresses our relationships with *all* of those God has placed over us. **Who are the representatives God has placed over us?**

Ephesians 6:1,2 Children, *obey your parents* in the Lord, for this is right. *"Honor your father and mother,"* which is the first commandment with a promise.

Hebrews 13:7,17 Remember your *leaders, who spoke the word of God to you. . . .* Obey your leaders and submit to them.

Romans 13:1 Everyone must submit to the *governing authorities.* For no authority exists except by God, and the authorities that do exist have been established by God.

Colossians 3:22,23 Slaves, obey your human masters in everything, not just when they are watching you, like people-pleasers, but with a sincere heart, out of respect for the Lord. Whatever you do, keep working at it with all your heart, as for the Lord and not for people.

52. How does God bless us through those he has placed over us?

Representatives in the home

1 Timothy 5:8 If anyone does not *provide for his own family,* and especially for his own household, he has denied the faith and is worse than an unbeliever.

Proverbs 1:1,3,8 The proverbs of Solomon, son of David, . . . to acquire discipline to act sensibly. . . . Listen, my son, to *your father's discipline,* and do not forsake *your mother's teaching.*

Deuteronomy 11:18,19 *Put these words of mine in your hearts* and in your soul, and tie them on your wrists as signs and as symbols on your forehead. *Teach them to your children by* talking about them when you sit in your house and when you travel on the road, when you lie down and when you get up.

Representatives in the church

Hebrews 13:7,17 Remember your leaders, who spoke the word of God to you. . . . They are *keeping watch over your souls* as men who will give an account.

1 Timothy 4:16 Pay close attention to yourself and to the doctrine. Persevere in them, because by doing this *you will save both yourself and those who listen to you.*

Representatives in the government

Romans 13:1,3,6 Everyone must submit to the governing authorities. . . . For rulers are not a *terror* to good conduct, but *to evil.* . . . For this reason you also pay taxes, because the authorities are God's ministers, who are employed to do this very thing.

1 Peter 2:13,14 Submit to every human authority because of the Lord, whether to the king as the supreme authority or to governors as those who have been sent by him to *punish those who do what is wrong* and to *praise those who do what is right.*

53. How does God emphasize his desire to bless us through the people he has placed in positions of authority over us?

Ephesians 6:2,3 "Honor your father and mother," which is *the first commandment with a promise:* "that it may go well with you and that you may live a long life on the earth."

54. Though God gives us a multitude of blessings through his representatives, our sinful nature doesn't want to be under the authority of others. **In what different ways do we dishonor those God has placed over us?**

Deuteronomy 21:18-21 (This Old Testament law demonstrates how serious God was about children who were stubborn and rebellious and *refused to obey* their parents or listen to them.)

Romans 13:2 The one who *rebels against* the authority is opposing God's institution, and those who oppose will bring judgment on themselves.

Proverbs 30:11,17 There is a type of person who curses his father and does not bless his mother. An eye that *mocks its father and despises the obedience due its mother—ravens of the valley* will peck it out, and young vultures will eat it.

2 Timothy 3:1,2 But know this: In the last days there will be terrible times. For people will be lovers of themselves, lovers of money, boastful, arrogant, blasphemous, *disobedient to their parents,* ungrateful, unholy.

2 Samuel 15:1-12; 18:14-17 (Absalom rebelled against his father, David. Because David was king, Absalom's rebellion also undermined the stability of the government.)

55. What responsibility do God's representatives have toward those who break this commandment?

Proverbs 13:24 A person who withholds his rod hates his son, but one who loves him *administers discipline* promptly.

2 Timothy 4:2 Preach the word. Be ready whether it is convenient or not. *Correct, rebuke, and encourage,* with all patience and teaching.

Romans 13:2-4 The one who rebels against the authority is opposing God's institution, and those who oppose will bring judgment on themselves. For rulers are not a terror to good conduct, but to evil. Would you like to have no fear of the one in authority? . . . But if you do wrong, be afraid, because he does not *carry the sword* without reason. He is God's servant, *a punisher to bring wrath on the wrongdoer.*

56. God's representatives are charged with disciplining us when we do wrong. **Why can we consider such discipline to be a blessing for us?**

Proverbs 19:18 Discipline your son *while there is hope.* Do not make yourself responsible for his death.

1 Samuel 3:11-14; 4:10,11 (Eli didn't discipline his sons. As a result, they died young, having fallen away from God.)

Matthew 18:15 If your brother sins against you, go and show him his sin just between the two of you. *If he listens to you, you have regained your brother.*

We often think of discipline as something that hurts us or takes away something good. Perhaps we remember the discipline of our parents. God has given parents the duty to discipline their children, but parents are not to abuse their children. Christian discipline in the home is ideally done in love to correct and train. Though discipline is generally unpleasant at the time, it is important training for life.

Discipline is not limited to the home and children. The government must also oppose bad behavior. This means police and judges correct or punish crime and disobedience to the law. At work, we have supervisors who also must discipline and train. In the church, leaders must oppose and discipline those who teach and act contrary to God's Word.

Christians are directed to obey all those the Lord has placed over them in all areas of life.

---

57. It is possible that someone in authority over us could ask us to do something against God's will. **What should we do if someone in authority asks us to do something that is wrong?**

Daniel 6 (Daniel was ordered to do evil but disobeyed and remained faithful to God.)

Matthew 10:37 Whoever loves father or mother more than me is not worthy of me, and whoever loves son or daughter more than me is not worthy of me.

Acts 5:29 We must *obey God rather than men.*

58. How can we be confident that our sins against the Fourth Commandment are forgiven?

1 Peter 2:22 [Christ] did not commit a sin, and no deceit was found in his mouth.

Matthew 22:19-22 (Jesus obeyed and honored the government.)

Luke 2:51 (Jesus was obedient to his parents.)

Ephesians 1:7 In him *we also have redemption through his blood, the forgiveness of sins,* in keeping with the riches of his grace.

59. Jesus obeyed the law perfectly as our substitute. He redeemed us from the guilt of our sin by shedding his blood on the cross. Out of thanks to him, we want to obey his commandments. **How does the Fourth Commandment serve as a guide to show us how to express our gratitude to God?**

Colossians 3:20 Children, *obey your parents* in everything, for this is pleasing in the Lord.

1 Timothy 5:4 If any widow has children or grandchildren, let them first learn *to be devoted to their own household* and repay their parents, for this is pleasing in the sight of God.

Ephesians 6:7 *Serve with eagerness,* as for the Lord and not for people.

1 Thessalonians 5:12,13 Brothers, we ask you to take note of those who work hard among you, who exercise leadership over you in the Lord, and who admonish you. *Hold them in the highest regard in love,* on account of their work. *Live at peace* with each other.

Hebrews 13:7,17 *Remember your leaders,* who spoke the word of God to you. Carefully consider the outcome of their way of life and imitate their faith. *Obey* your leaders and submit to them, for they are keeping watch over your souls as men who will give an account.

Romans 13:7 Pay what you owe to all of them: taxes to whom taxes are owed, revenue to whom revenue is owed, respect to whom respect is owed, and honor to whom honor is owed.

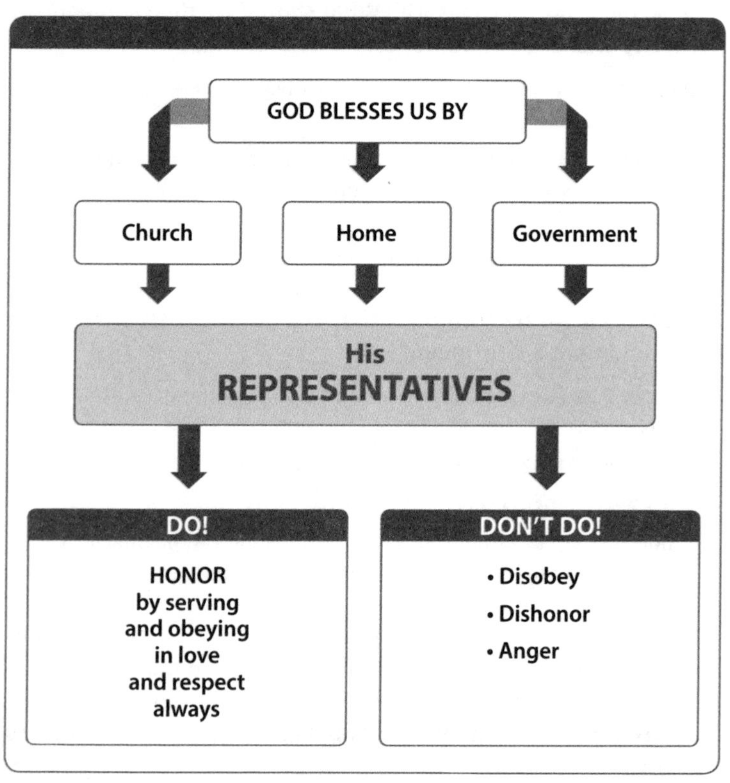

Titus 3:1 Remind them to *be subject to rulers and authorities, to obey,* to be ready to do any good work.

Leviticus 19:32 You must rise in the presence of gray hair and *show respect in the presence of an elder, so that you fear your God.* I am the LORD.

Genesis 39:1-6 (Joseph was a slave in Potiphar's house, yet he served Potiphar diligently and honestly.)

CONNECTIONS

Those God has placed over us as his representatives are also sinners. We may not always agree with their wishes, and we may be tempted to show disrespect when we do not agree. David gives us a wonderful example of how we can continue to honor those in authority even when we disagree with what they are doing. Read about how David honored the Lord's anointed king even when the king was trying to kill him.

---

1 Samuel 26:1-21

Saul hunted David to arrest him and perhaps kill him. Yet David resisted the temptation to harm King Saul. Explain why it is so hard to avoid sin when someone in authority seems to treat you unfairly. List ways you can overcome evil with good (Romans 12:21).

Luther

God knows very well this perverseness of the world; therefore, He admonishes and urges by commandments that everyone consider what his parents have done for him. Each child will discover that he has from them a body and life. He has been fed and reared when otherwise he would have perished a hundred times in his own filth. Therefore, this is a true and good saying of old and wise people: "To God, to parents, and to teachers we can never offer enough thanks and compensation." The person who thinks about and considers this will give all honor to his parents without force and bear them up on his hands as those through whom God has done him all good [Psalm 91:12]. Over and above all this, another great reason that should move us more to obey this commandment is that God attaches to it a temporal promise: "That your days may be long in the land that the LORD your God is giving you" [Exodus 20:12]. (Large Catechism, I, par. 129-131)

For Christian Homes, O Lord, We Pray (Stanzas 1-3)

For Christian homes, O Lord, we pray,
That you might dwell with us each day.
Make ours a place where you are Lord,
Where all is governed by your Word.

We are the children of your grace;
Our homes are now your dwelling place.
In you we trust and daily live;
Teach us to serve and to forgive.

United in a bond of love,
We lift our eyes to you above.
From you we gain the strength to live,
The wish to share, the joy to give.

THE FIFTH COMMANDMENT
You shall not murder.

What does this mean?
We should fear and love God that we do not hurt or harm our neighbor in his body, but help and befriend him in every bodily need.

LIFE

Protect God's Gift of Life

Life certainly is important to each of us. Our own lives are valuable and important to us and to our families and friends. The lives of others are just as important to their families and friends. God protects this precious gift with the Fifth Commandment. He warns us against harming the life of another and invites us to consider how we can protect and honor life.

60. Why is human life so precious?

Genesis 2:7 The *LORD God formed the man* from the dust of the ground and breathed into his nostrils the breath of life, and the man became a living being.

Acts 17:25,28 Neither is he served by human hands, as if he needed anything, since *he* himself *gives all people life* and breath and everything they have. "For in him we live and move and have our being." As some of your own poets have said, "Indeed, *we are also his offspring.*"

Genesis 9:6 Whoever sheds man's blood, by man his blood shall be shed, for God made man in his own image.

Human life is a unique and wonderful gift from God, who created our first parents in his own image.

A CLOSER LOOK

Image of God The Bible clearly teaches that Adam and Eve were created in the image of God. "In his own image" doesn't mean they looked like God in the way children often look like their parents. God is a spirit. Adam and Eve were created holy, like God, with a will that wanted exactly the same things that God wanted. See the First Article (question 127) for an in-depth study of the image of God.

Isaiah 55:6 Seek the Lord *while he may be found!* Call on him while he is near!

2 Corinthians 6:2 Look, now is the favorable time! See, *now is the day of salvation!*

Matthew 25:1-13 (The five foolish virgins missed their opportunity to participate in the wedding celebration. Those who die without faith in Jesus don't have another opportunity to be saved.)

When Adam and Eve fell into sin, the image of God was lost. Our life on earth is precious because it is our *time of grace*—the time when we have the opportunity to learn about God's love for us and about all the blessings he has promised to those who believe.

61. Who alone has the right to end a person's life?

Psalm 31:15 My times are in *[God's]* hand. Deliver me from the hand of my enemies and from those who pursue me.

Deuteronomy 32:39 Now see that I, only I, am he, and there is not a god comparable to me. *I put to death and I make alive.*

Romans 13:4 *He is God's servant* for your benefit. But if you do wrong, be afraid, because *he does not carry the sword without reason.* He is God's servant, a punisher to bring wrath on the wrongdoer.

God alone has the right to end a person's life, but he delegates that right also to his representatives in government. A person serving under the authority of the government as God's representative—a government official, a soldier, or a police officer—may carry out capital punishment, take life in a war, or take life in order to protect the lives of others.

62. The explanation to this commandment shows that God means to protect our bodies as well as our lives. The explanation helps us see that there are many ways people sin by breaking this commandment. **In order to protect our bodies and lives, what does God forbid with the Fifth Commandment?**

Genesis 9:5,6 I will hold each animal and each person responsible for your lifeblood. . . . Whoever *sheds man's blood,* by man his blood shall be shed, for God made man in his own image.

2 Samuel 11:2-17 (David arranged things so that Uriah would be killed in battle. David was responsible for Uriah's death.)

God forbids that we take another person's life (unless we are serving as God's representative in the government).

Psalm 139:13 You created my inner organs. *You wove me together in my mother's womb.*

Exodus 21:22-24 If men are fighting and they injure a pregnant woman . . . if any harm follows, then you are to take life for life, eye for eye, tooth for tooth, hand for hand, foot for foot.

God forbids taking the life of the unborn. Abortion is murder. Because our lives are in God's hands, deliberately causing the death of someone who is in misery because of illness or injury is also murder.

Leviticus 19:16 *You shall not go around spreading slander* among your people. *You shall not testify falsely against your neighbor* in a capital case. I am the LORD.

Exodus 21:29 (If a farmer knew his bull was dangerous but did nothing to protect others, he would be responsible if the bull killed someone.)

God forbids that we cause the death of another person by deliberate carelessness.

Romans 12:19 *Do not take revenge,* dear friends, but leave room for God's wrath. For it is written, "Vengeance is mine; I will repay," says the Lord.

God forbids us to seek revenge when we have been wronged.

Proverbs 23:20,31-33 *Do not be among those who drink too much wine, or those who eat too much* meat. Do not look at wine when it is red, when it sparkles in the cup, when it goes down smoothly. Later it bites like a snake, and it strikes like a venomous viper. Your eyes will see strange things, and your mind will say senseless things.

God forbids that we harm our bodies by eating or drinking too much or by abusing alcohol or drugs.

Psalm 31:15 My times are in your hand. Deliver me from the hand of my enemies and from those who pursue me.

1 Samuel 31:4; Matthew 27:5 (Saul and Judas committed suicide.)

God forbids that we take our own lives (suicide).

1 John 3:15 *Everyone who hates his brother* is a murderer, and you know that no murderer has eternal life remaining in him.

Matthew 5:21,22 You have heard that it was said to people long ago, "You shall not murder, and whoever murders will be subject to judgment." But I tell you that *everyone who is angry* with his brother without a cause *will be subject to judgment,* and whoever says to his brother, "*Raca,*" will have to answer to the Sanhedrin. But *whoever says, "You fool!" will be in danger of hell fire.*

God forbids hatred and other cruel thoughts and words against others.

63. How does God's Word serve as a mirror, showing us that we are also guilty of breaking this commandment?

Galatians 5:19-21 The works of the sinful flesh are obvious: sexual immorality, impurity, complete lack of restraint, idolatry, sorcery, *hatred, discord, jealousy, outbursts of anger,* selfish ambition, *dissensions,* heresies, envy, murders, drunkenness, orgies, and things similar to these. I warn you, just as I also warned you before, that those who continue to do such things will not inherit the kingdom of God.

64. When God leads us to recognize our sin, feel sorry for it, and long for forgiveness, he assures us of forgiveness. Then his forgiveness strengthens us to turn away from our sin. **How do we know that our sins against the Fifth Commandment are forgiven?**

1 Peter 2:22-24 He did not commit a sin, and no deceit was found in his mouth. When he was insulted, he did not insult in return. When he suffered, he made no threats. Instead, he entrusted himself to him who judges justly. He himself carried our sins in his body on the tree so that we would be dead to sins and alive to righteousness. By his wounds you were healed.

65. Jesus took our sins on his body and suffered for them on the cross. Out of gratitude for his healing our souls, we want to obey his commandments. **How does the Fifth Commandment serve as a guide to show us how to express our gratitude to God?**

Proverbs 31:8 *Speak up* for those who cannot speak. Speak for the rights of all those who are defenseless.

1 John 4:7,20 Dear friends, let us love one another, because love comes from God. Everyone who loves has been born of God and knows God. *If anyone says, "I love God," but hates his brother, he is a liar.* For how can anyone who does not love his brother, whom he has seen, love God, whom he has not seen?

Ephesians 4:31,32 *Get rid of every kind of bitterness, rage, anger, quarreling, and slander, along with every kind of malice.* Instead, be kind and compassionate to one another, forgiving one another, just as God in Christ has forgiven us.

1 Thessalonians 5:14,15 We also encourage you, brothers, to admonish those who are idle. *Encourage* those who are discouraged, *help* those who are weak, and *be patient with everyone.* See to it that no one repays evil with evil, but instead, always *strive to do good to each other* and to everyone else.

Luke 10:33-35 (The good Samaritan helped the Jewish man who had been robbed and beaten, even though Jews and Samaritans were generally hostile toward each other.)

Colossians 3:12,13 As God's elect, holy and loved, clothe yourselves with *heartfelt compassion, kindness, humility, gentleness, and patience.* Bear with one another and *forgive each other* if anyone has a complaint against anyone else. Forgive, just as Christ forgave you.

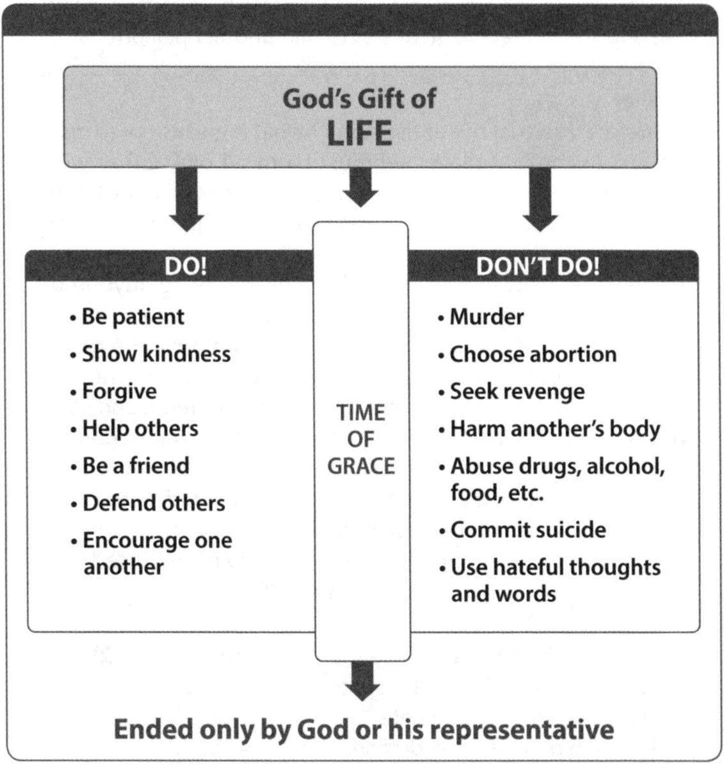

God's Gift of LIFE

DO!		DON'T DO!
• Be patient • Show kindness • Forgive • Help others • Be a friend • Defend others • Encourage one another	TIME OF GRACE	• Murder • Choose abortion • Seek revenge • Harm another's body • Abuse drugs, alcohol, food, etc. • Commit suicide • Use hateful thoughts and words

Ended only by God or his representative

CONNECTIONS

Most people would acknowledge that the Fifth Commandment is correct. It is wrong to murder. However, our sinful nature bristles at the suggestion that our thoughts and words can make us guilty of breaking this commandment. But if we hate someone, we wish harm for that person. We may be pleased if the person were dead. Thoughts of hatred are murderous thoughts. Read the story of Cain and Abel, and see how sinful thoughts lead to sinful actions.

Genesis 4:1-16

Genesis 4 tells the account of how Cain killed his brother Abel. Cain obviously was guilty of murder. But hatred was there even before he committed the murder. Explain the image of "sin is crouching at the door" (Genesis 4:7). First John 3:15 shows us that Cain was guilty of murder even before his brother was dead. What passage or example from the Bible can help you when you are tempted to hate someone or to hurt another person?

Luther

Therefore, [here is] the entire sum of what it means *not to murder*. . . . In the first place, we must harm no one, either with our hand or by deed. We must not use our tongue to instigate or counsel harm. We must neither use nor agree to use any means or methods by which another person may be injured. Finally, the heart must not be ill disposed toward anyone or wish another person ill in anger and hatred. . . . Second, a person who does evil to his neighbor is not the only one guilty under this commandment. It also applies to anyone who can do his neighbor good, prevent or resist evil, defend, and save his neighbor so that no bodily harm or hurt happened to him—yet does not do this [James 2:15-16]. If, therefore, you send away someone who is naked when you could clothe him, you have caused him to freeze to death. If you see someone suffer hunger and do not give him food, you have caused him to starve. (Large Catechism, I, par. 188,189)

The Ten Commandments Are the Law (Stanzas 6,11,12)

"You shall not murder, hurt, nor hate;
Your anger dare not dominate.
Be kind and patient; help, defend,
And treat your foe as your friend."
Have mercy, Lord!

God gave these laws to show therein,
O child of man, your life of sin,
And help you rightly to perceive
How unto God you should live.
Have mercy, Lord!

Our works cannot salvation gain;
They merit only endless pain.
Forgive us, Lord! To Christ we fly,
Our mediator on high.
Have mercy, Lord!

THE SIXTH COMMANDMENT
You shall not commit adultery.

What does this mean?
We should fear and love God that we lead a pure and decent life in words and actions, and that husband and wife love and honor each other.

MARRIAGE

Honor God's Gift of Marriage

God designed marriage to be a lifelong commitment of one man and one woman to live together as husband and wife. It is at the heart of God's design for human relationships. In the intimate relationship of marriage, God brings companionship and great joy. Through husband and wife, children enter this world and God establishes families. Then God uses the family to nourish and train children and to pass along the truths of salvation to another generation.

It is no surprise that Satan, the world, and our own sinful nature seek to undermine God's gift of marriage. Often people enjoy the pleasures of marriage without the commitment. Husbands and wives are tempted to break the promises they made to each other. So many forces around us seek to ruin this beautiful gift. In the Sixth Commandment, we discover how God helps us treasure and defend the blessing of marriage.

66. With the Sixth Commandment, God protects marriage. **What is marriage?**

> **Genesis 2:22,24** The LORD God built a woman from the rib that he had taken from the man and brought her to the man. For this reason a man *will leave his father and his mother and will remain united with his wife,* and they will become one flesh.
>
> **Proverbs 18:22** The man who finds a wife finds a good thing, and he obtains favor from the LORD.

Romans 7:2 A married woman is bound to her husband by law *as long as he is alive,* but if he dies, she is released from this law regarding her husband.

Marriage is a one-of-a-kind relationship God established when he first created Adam and Eve. In marriage, a man and woman leave their fathers and mothers to form a new family unit. Under a solemn promise, they join their lives together for as long as they live.

A CLOSER LOOK

Marriage Is a Public Declaration In our society, a man and a woman enter into marriage by declaring their commitment to each other in a public ceremony. They publicly speak their promises in front of a pastor or an official who is authorized by the government to perform weddings. Witnesses are present as well. For Christians, this public ceremony is a clear statement that the man and woman are making a commitment to each other for life.

This lifelong commitment is at the heart of God's plan for marriage. Until this lifelong commitment is openly declared—which in our society happens though an official ceremony—Christians honor God by refraining from the sexual relationship.

Engagement Before the actual marriage takes place, a man and a woman have already made a promise to each other—the promise to get married. We often refer to that as the engagement. Christian couples will give serious prayerful consideration to their relationship before making that promise. Breaking any promise involves sin. Breaking the promise to get married inflicts deep emotional pain on another person and affects his or her future in a significant way. Christians don't wish to harm another person or cause such pain. The agreement to marry another is made only after a person is thoroughly convinced of his or her own desire to marry.

---

67. Marriage is a special relationship because of the many unique blessings God gives through it. **What blessings does God intend to give through marriage?**

Genesis 2:18 The LORD God said, "It is not good for the man to be *alone.* I will make a helper who is a suitable partner for him."

Genesis 2:24 For this reason a man will leave his father and his mother and will remain united with his wife, and they will become *one flesh.*

1 Corinthians 7:2-4,9 Because of sexual sins, *each man is to have his own wife,* and *each woman is to have her own husband.* The husband is to fulfill his obligation to his wife, and likewise the wife to her husband. The wife does not have authority over her own body—her husband does. Likewise, the husband does not have authority over his own body—his wife does. But if they do not have self-control, they should marry, because *it is better to marry than to burn with desire.*

Song of Songs 1:15,16; 4:1-7; 5:10-16 (Describes the physical attraction between a husband and wife. It is natural, beautiful, and pleasing.)

Genesis 1:28 God blessed them and said to them, "*Be fruitful, multiply,* fill the earth, and subdue it."

Psalm 127:3 *Children are a heritage* from the LORD. The fruit of the womb is a reward from him.

1 Samuel 1:1-20 (For years, Hannah wanted a child and had endured the sadness of having no children. Then God blessed her with a son.)

Through marriage, God blesses a husband and wife with companionship, the opportunity to express love in a very special and intimate way in their sexual relationship, and the possibility of children.

A CLOSER LOOK

Marriage—The Foundation for the Family As we contemplate the blessings God gives through marriage, we clearly see the importance of protecting and strengthening the marriage relationship. Marriage provides the foundation for the family unit. This family structure is designed to play a huge role in the spiritual, social, and financial stability of every member of the family. In Christian homes, husbands and wives encourage each other with the Word of God. In Deuteronomy 6, God instructs parents to teach God's Word to their children. The teamwork of a committed husband and wife makes it easier to support and raise children.

68. Marriage is not simply a custom or a tradition. Rather, it is a solemn and binding agreement between two people. God's Word underscores the fact that in marriage a man and woman are making a commitment. **What promises are included in the marriage commitment?**

Romans 7:2 A married woman is bound to her husband by law *as long as he is alive,* but if he dies, she is released from this law regarding her husband.

Hebrews 13:4 Marriage is to be held in honor by all, and *the marriage bed is to be kept undefiled,* for God will judge sexually immoral people and adulterers.

Ephesians 5:21-25,28 *[Submit] to one another* in reverence for Christ. *Wives, submit to your own husbands* as to the Lord. For the husband is the head of the wife, just as Christ is the head of the church, his body, of which he himself is the Savior. Moreover, as the church submits to Christ, so also wives are to submit to their husbands in everything.

Husbands, love your wives, in the same way as Christ loved the church and gave himself up for her. In the same way, husbands have an obligation to love their own wives as their own bodies. He who loves his wife loves himself.

A CLOSER LOOK

Christ Is Our Model By comparing the marriage relationship to the model of Jesus and his church, God teaches important truths about marriage.

Husbands and wives are equal in value in the sight of God. Yet God has revealed that in marriage, as in most other relationships, there is benefit in having someone take the leadership role. God asks the husband to serve in this role with an attitude of sacrifice. A husband's goals are not to be selfish. He uses his position of responsibility to do all he can to serve, just as Christ used his authority to be a blessing to others. A husband seeks to love his wife as Christ loved the church, ready to give up everything—including his own life—for her.

And as the Christian church submits to Christ, so a wife submits to her husband. Christians submit to Christ not with resentment but with joy. A Christian wife honors her husband and respects him as the head, holding a deep appreciation for the responsibility God has given him. She seeks to support, encourage, and assist him. Husband and wife work together to build their marriage and family.

Christian husbands and wives can and do sin in their marriage relationships. Christ's perfect model is not always lived perfectly. A Christian husband can fail to love unselfishly; he can fail to lead. A Christian wife can fall short of honoring her husband as her head. When husbands and wives see their faults, how blessed they are to know Jesus. Though they are imperfect, he loves them perfectly. He gave his life for their sins. In him, husbands and wives have forgiveness. Jesus' divine love gives them reason and power to grow and to model their marriage after the relationship between Christ and the church.

69. The Sixth Commandment speaks to all: young and old, male and female, married and unmarried. **As we study how God established marriage, what do we learn about the blessing of the sexual relationship?**

Genesis 2:24 *For this reason a man will leave his father and his mother and will remain united with his wife, and they will become one flesh.*

God connects the sexual blessings of marriage to the leaving of a person's father and mother and uniting with a spouse—a permanent marriage relationship. If a couple has not publicly declared the promise to establish a permanent marriage, the blessing of the sexual relationship is not to be enjoyed.

70. God designed the sexual relationship to be a blessing of marriage. **In what way, then, do some who are not yet married sin against the Sixth Commandment?**

1 Thessalonians 4:3-5 This is God's will: that you be sanctified, namely, that you keep yourselves away from *sexual immorality*. He wants each of you to learn to obtain a wife for yourself in a way that is holy and honorable, not in *lustful passion* like the heathen, who do not know God.

Genesis 39:6-12 (Potiphar's wife tried to entice Joseph into a sexual relationship with her, but he refused. He acknowledged that it would be wicked—a sin against God.)

The unmarried sin when they enjoy blessings designed only for marriage. Living arrangements that involve enjoyment of the blessings of marriage without the commitment of marriage are contrary to God's will.

71. The Sixth Commandment also has much to say to those who are married. **When do some who are married sin against the Sixth Commandment?**

Colossians 3:19 Husbands, love your wives and *do not treat them harshly.*

Proverbs 21:19 Better to live in an arid region than with a *nagging, ill-tempered wife.*

Husbands and wives sin if their words or actions destroy the loving companionship that is to be a part of marriage. (Domestic violence violates the example of love and consideration God intends in marriage.)

Hebrews 13:4 Marriage is to be held in honor by all, and *the marriage bed is to be kept undefiled,* for God will judge sexually immoral people and adulterers.

2 Samuel 11:1-4 (David lusted for Bathsheba, the wife of one of his most courageous soldiers, and brought her to his house so that he could have sexual intercourse with her.)

Psalm 32:3,4 (David expressed how the guilt of his sin with Bathsheba weighed so heavily on him.)

1 Corinthians 6:9,10 Do you not know that the unrighteous will not inherit the kingdom of God? Do not be deceived. *Neither the sexually immoral, nor idolaters, nor adulterers* . . . will inherit the kingdom of God.

People sin if they are involved in any sexual activity outside of marriage.

Matthew 19:9 I tell you that whoever divorces his wife, except on the grounds of her sexual immorality, and marries another woman is committing adultery.

1 Corinthians 7:15 If the unbeliever leaves, let him leave. The brother or the sister is not bound in such cases, and God has called us to live in peace.

People sin if they divorce their spouses for any reason other than marital unfaithfulness or desertion.

72. Sins against the Sixth Commandment are so common and so accepted by the majority of people. **In what ways can both married and unmarried sin against the Sixth Commandment?**

Matthew 5:27,28 You have heard that it was said, "You shall not commit adultery," but I tell you that *everyone who looks at a woman with lust has already committed adultery with her in his heart.*

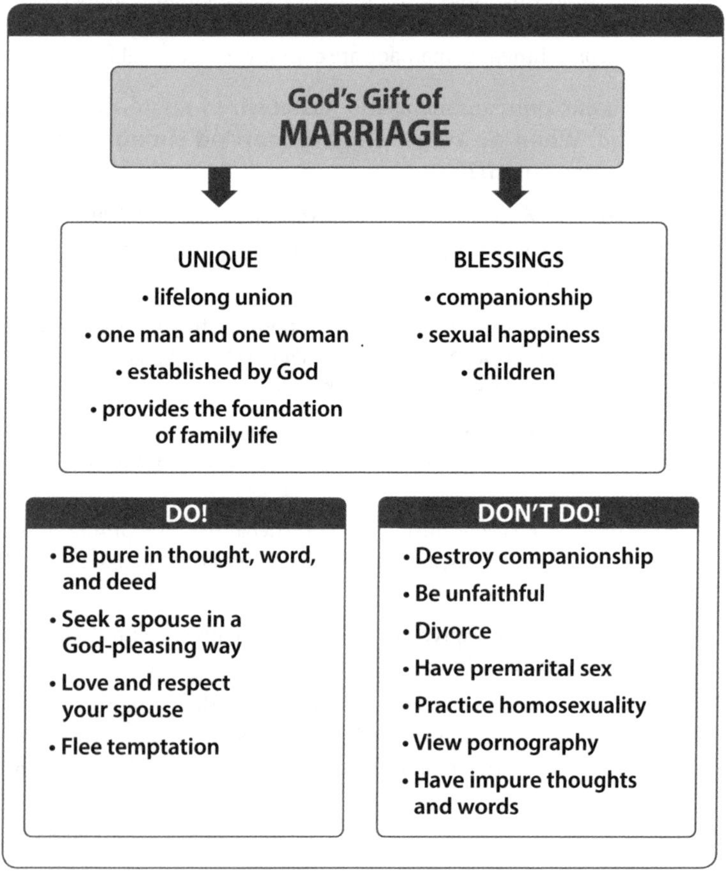

God's Gift of MARRIAGE

UNIQUE	BLESSINGS
• lifelong union	• companionship
• one man and one woman	• sexual happiness
• established by God	• children
• provides the foundation of family life	

DO!

- Be pure in thought, word, and deed
- Seek a spouse in a God-pleasing way
- Love and respect your spouse
- Flee temptation

DON'T DO!

- Destroy companionship
- Be unfaithful
- Divorce
- Have premarital sex
- Practice homosexuality
- View pornography
- Have impure thoughts and words

Ephesians 5:3-5 *Do not let sexual immorality, any kind of impurity, or greed even be mentioned among you,* as is proper for saints. *Obscenity,* *foolish talk, and coarse joking* are also out of place. Instead, give thanks. Certainly you are aware of this: No immoral, impure, or greedy person—such a person is an idolater—has an inheritance in the kingdom of Christ, who is God.

Ephesians 5:12 It is shameful even to mention the things that are done by people in secret.

The Sixth Commandment forbids sexual immorality. That includes sexual intercourse outside of marriage, incest, rape, sexual abuse, obscene jokes, and the use of pornography.

Serving as a mirror, the Sixth Commandment shows that we are sinning by having lust in our hearts; by speaking coarse, demeaning, and suggestive words; and by taking delight when these immoralities are the focus of our entertainment or the gossip we hear.

73. What does God say about homosexuality?

Romans 1:26,27 For this reason God handed them over to disgraceful passions. Even their females exchanged natural sexual relations for unnatural ones. And, in the same way, their males, after abandoning natural sexual relations with females, *were consumed by their lust for one another.* Males perform indecent acts with males and receive in themselves the penalty that is fitting for their perversion.

1 Corinthians 6:9,10 Do you not know that the unrighteous will not inherit the kingdom of God? Do not be deceived. *Neither the sexually immoral, nor idolaters, nor adulterers, nor males who have sex with males,* nor thieves, nor the greedy, nor drunkards, nor the verbally abusive, nor swindlers will inherit the kingdom of God.

1 Timothy 1:9,10 The law is not laid down for a righteous person, but for lawless and rebellious people, for godless people and sinners, for unholy and worldly people, for those who kill their fathers and those who kill their mothers, for murderers, for sexually immoral people, *for homosexuals,* for kidnappers, for liars, for perjurers, and for whatever else is opposed to sound teaching.

God clearly states that homosexuality is sin.

74. In his Word, God tells us that there is something unique about the sins against the Sixth Commandment. **In what way does God help us appreciate the seriousness of sexual sins?**

1 Corinthians 6:18-20 Flee from sexual immorality! Every sin that a person commits is outside the body, but he who commits sexual immorality *sins against his own body.* Or do you not know that *your body is a temple of the Holy Spirit,* who is within you, whom you have from God? You are not your own, for you were bought at a price. Therefore glorify God with your body.

75. What should we do when the Sixth Commandment shows us our sins?

Mark 1:15 "The time is fulfilled," he said. "The kingdom of God has come near! *Repent,* and believe in the gospel."

Matthew 3:8 *Produce fruit in keeping with repentance!*

76. What good news gives us the confidence that our sins against the Sixth Commandment are forgiven and helps us do as God commands?

Hebrews 4:15 We do not have a high priest who is unable to sympathize with our weaknesses, but one who has been tempted in every way, just as we are, *yet was without sin.*

Hebrews 7:26 This is certainly the kind of high priest we needed: one who is holy, innocent, pure, separated from sinners, and exalted above the heavens.

2 Corinthians 5:21 *God made him, who did not know sin, to become sin for us,* so that we might become the righteousness of God in him.

77. It is an amazing truth that God counted all of our sins against Jesus and that he counts Jesus' righteousness for us. As we consider this great truth, we want to obey God's commandments. **How does God's Word serve as a guide as we want to honor God by keeping the Sixth Commandment?**

Colossians 3:5 *Put to death whatever is worldly in you:* sexual immorality, uncleanness, lust, evil desire, and greed, which is idolatry.

Ephesians 5:3,4 *Do not let sexual immorality, any kind of impurity, or greed even be mentioned among you,* as is proper for saints. Obscenity, foolish talk, and coarse joking are also out of place. Instead, give thanks.

Ephesians 5:22-25 Wives, submit to your own husbands as to the Lord. For the husband is the head of the wife, just as Christ is the head of the church, his body, of which he himself is the Savior. Moreover, *as the church submits to Christ, so also wives are to submit to their husbands in everything. Husbands, love your wives, in the same way as Christ loved the church and gave himself up for her.*

Ephesians 5:33 Each one of you also is to love his wife as himself, and each wife is to respect her husband.

Romans 13:13,14 Let us walk decently as in the daytime, not in carousing and drunkenness, not in sexual sin and wild living, not in strife and jealousy. Instead, *clothe yourselves with the Lord Jesus*

Christ, and do not give any thought to satisfying the desires of your sinful flesh.

Philippians 4:8 Finally, brothers, whatever is true, whatever is honorable, whatever is right, whatever is pure, whatever is lovely, whatever is commendable, if anything is excellent, and if anything is praiseworthy, think about these things.

1 Peter 3:1,3,4,7 Wives, in the same way, be submissive to your own husbands, so that even if some do not obey the word, they might be won over without a word by the behavior of their wives. Do not let your beauty be something outward, such as braided hair or wearing gold jewelry or fine clothes. Rather let your beauty be the hidden person of your heart—the lasting beauty of a gentle and quiet spirit, which is precious in God's sight. Husbands, in the same way, continue to live with your wives with the knowledge that, as the wife, she is the weaker vessel. Also continue to accord them honor as fellow heirs with you of the gracious gift of life, so that your prayers will not be hindered.

CONNECTIONS

In his Word, God provides examples of husbands and wives who cherish the marriage relationship as a gift of God. In their marriages, they demonstrate a partnership focused on the goal of serving the Lord. Aquila and Priscilla provide us with an example of such a marriage. Their marriage partnership is a wonderful example of how God's design for marriage can bring great blessing to other people.

Acts 18:2,3,18,19,24-26; Romans 16:3,4
In what different ways was the marriage of Aquila and Priscilla a blessing to other people?

- For those not married, create a list of blessings you may expect from the marriage partnership you may have one day.
- Make a list of the blessings God can bring to you and others through a Christian marriage today.

Luther
But this commandment is aimed directly at the state of marriage and gives us an opportunity to speak about it. First, understand and mark well how gloriously God honors and praises this estate. For by his commandment he both approves and guards it. He has proved it above in the Fourth Commandment, "Honor your father and your mother." But here he has (as we said) hedged it

about and protected it. Therefore, he also wishes us to honor it [Hebrews 13:4] and to maintain and govern it as a divine and blessed estate because, in the first place, he has instituted it before all others. He created man and woman separately, as is clear [Genesis 1:27]. This was not for lewdness, but so that they might live together in marriage, be fruitful, bear children, and nourish and train them to honor God [Genesis 1:28; Psalm 128; Proverbs 22:6; Ephesians 6:4]. (Large Catechism, I, par. 206,207)

Oh, Blest the House, Whate'er Befall (Stanzas 1,2)

Oh, blest the house, whate'er befall,
Where Jesus Christ is all in all!
A home that is not wholly his—
How sad and poor and dark it is!

Oh, blest that house where faith you find
And all within have set their mind
To trust their God and serve him still
And do in all his holy will.

THE SEVENTH COMMANDMENT
You shall not steal.

What does this mean?
We should fear and love God that we do not take our neighbor's money or property, or get it by dishonest dealing, but help him to improve and protect his property and means of income.

PROPERTY

Use Possessions as God's Gifts

God warns us against attaching too much importance to our possessions. Many people mistakenly believe that they will be happy and secure if they have a lot of money and many possessions. But trusting that happiness and security will come from having lots of money and possessions is dangerous. Wealth can become our god. To get that wealth, we can be tempted to do things that are wrong.

God actually wants us to have possessions. He gives us what we need for our lives, and he even invites us to enjoy the things that money can buy. Though God obviously doesn't want us to worship our possessions or take what belongs to others, the Seventh Commandment teaches us to appreciate the possessions God gives to us.

78. How does God give us our money and property?

Genesis 3:19 By the sweat of your face you will eat bread.

2 Thessalonians 3:10-12 If anyone does not want to work, he should not eat. Indeed, we hear that some among you are idle. . . . In the Lord Jesus Christ, we command and urge these people to work quietly and eat their own bread.

Deuteronomy 8:17,18 You might say in your heart, "My ability and the power of my hand have earned this wealth for me." But then you are to remember that the LORD your God is the one who gives you the ability to produce wealth, to confirm his covenant that he promised to your fathers with an oath, as he does to this day.

Genesis 24:35,36 (When Abraham's servant went to find a wife for Isaac, God directed him to the family of Bethuel. The servant described how God had blessed his master.) *The LORD has blessed my master greatly.* He has become great. The LORD has given him flocks and herds, silver and gold, male servants and female servants, camels and donkeys. Sarah, my master's wife, bore a son for my master when she was old. My master has given him everything that he owns.

Genesis 23:1-18 (Abraham used some of the wealth God had given him to purchase a field and a cave as a burial place for his wife.)

Luke 15:11-20 (The prodigal son asked for his *inheritance.*)

1 Kings 21:1-15 (Naboth had *inherited* his vineyard.)

Matthew 7:11 If you know how to give good gifts to your children, even though you are evil, how much more will your Father in heaven give good gifts to those who ask him!

79. Because God is the source of all of our blessings, what will our attitude be toward the things we have?

James 1:17 Every good act of giving and every perfect gift is from above, coming down from the Father of the lights, who does not change or shift like a shadow.

Psalm 107:8,9 Let them *give thanks* to the LORD for his mercy and his wonderful deeds for all people, because he satisfies the desire of the thirsty, and he fills the desire of the hungry with good things.

Psalm 24:1 *The earth is the LORD's* and everything that fills it, the world and all who live in it.

1 Corinthians 4:2 Moreover, it is required of stewards that they be *found faithful.*

Matthew 25:14-30 (God teaches us that we are to manage the gifts he has given us to the best of our abilities. *We are stewards of his blessings.)*

80. Our money and possessions are blessings that we can use in many ways. **For what purposes does God give these blessings?**

1 Timothy 5:8 If anyone does not *provide for his own family,* and *especially for his own household,* he has denied the faith and is worse than an unbeliever.

1 John 3:17 Whoever has worldly wealth and sees his brother in need but closes his heart against him—how can God's love remain in him?

Romans 13:6,7 For this reason you also *pay taxes,* because the authorities are God's ministers, who are employed to do this very thing. Pay what you owe to all of them: taxes to whom taxes are owed, revenue to whom revenue is owed, respect to whom respect is owed, and honor to whom honor is owed.

1 Corinthians 16:2 On the first day of every week, each of you is to set something aside in keeping with whatever he gains, saving it up at home, so that when I come, no collections will need to be carried out.

2 Corinthians 9:7 Each one should *give as he has determined in his heart,* not reluctantly or under pressure, for God loves a cheerful giver.

Mark 12:41-44 (A widow gave all she had.)

81. Because of our sinful nature, we aren't content with the abundant blessings God gives to us. Our lack of contentment leads us to sin against this commandment. **What are some ways people sin against God in the way they use the gifts that he gives?**

Luke 15:11-20 (The lost son *wasted* his possessions by sinful selfish living.)

Luke 10:30-37 (Several men beat and robbed a traveler.)

Leviticus 19:35 *You shall not use dishonest measurements of weight or volume.*

Proverbs 11:1 *Dishonest* scales are disgusting to the LORD, but an accurate weight wins his approval.

Proverbs 22:16,22 Whoever oppresses the poor to become great, and whoever gives gifts to the rich—both are sure to suffer loss. Do not *rob a poor person because he is* poor, and do not crush an oppressed person in court.

Psalm 37:21 The wicked *borrow and do not repay,* but the righteous are gracious and give.

1 Corinthians 6:8 You yourselves *do the wronging* and defrauding, and you do it to your brothers!

1 Timothy 6:9,10 Those who want to get rich fall into temptation and a trap and many foolish and harmful desires, which plunge them into complete destruction and utter ruin. For the love of money is a root of all sorts of evils. By striving for money, some have wandered away from the faith and have pierced themselves with many pains.

James 5:4 Listen, the wages that you *failed to pay* the workers who reaped your fields are crying out! And the cries of the harvesters have entered the ears of the Lord of Armies.

Malachi 3:8 Will a man rob God? *You are robbing me!* You say, "How have we robbed you?" In regard to the tithe and the special offering.

2 Thessalonians 3:10 When we were with you, this was our command to you: If anyone *does not want to work,* he should not eat.

James 2:15,16 If a brother or sister needs clothes and lacks daily food and one of you tells them, "Go in peace, keep warm, and eat well," but *does not give them what their body needs,* what good is it?

82. An Old Testament prophet stated a sobering truth that applies to all of us: "All of us have become like something unclean, and all our righteous acts are like a filthy cloth" (Isaiah 64:6). Our sinful nature is alive within us and taints our use of God's gifts with sins such as selfishness and greed. **How can we be sure that our sins against the Seventh Commandment are forgiven?**

2 Corinthians 8:9 You know the grace of our Lord Jesus Christ, that although he was rich, yet *for your sakes he became poor, so that through his poverty you might become rich.*

Romans 5:19 Just as through the disobedience of one man the many became sinners, so also *through the obedience of one man the many will become righteous.*

Galatians 3:13 *Christ redeemed us from the curse of the law by becoming a curse for us.* As it is written, "Cursed is everyone who hangs on a tree."

83. Because of sin we were under a curse. Yet, in his amazing mercy, Jesus took our curse upon himself. He freed us from our curse and forgave us. Freed and forgiven, we want to honor him with our lives and with our possessions. **How does the Seventh Commandment serve as a guide, showing us how to serve God with our possessions?**

Hebrews 13:5 *Keep your life free from the love of money, and be content* with what you have. For God has said: I will never leave you, and I will never forsake you.

1 Timothy 6:6-8 Godliness with contentment is great gain. For we brought nothing into the world, and we certainly cannot take anything out. But if we have food and clothing, with these *we will be satisfied.*

Luke 12:15 He said to them, "Watch out and *be on guard against all greed,* because a man's life is not measured by how many possessions he has."

Ephesians 4:28 Let the one who has been stealing *steal no longer.* Instead, let him work hard doing what is good with his own hands, so that he has something to share with a person who is in need.

1 Corinthians 16:2 On the first day of every week, each of you is to *set something aside in keeping with whatever he gains, saving it up at home.*

Colossians 3:22,23 Slaves, obey your human masters in everything, not just when they are watching you, like people-pleasers, but with a sincere heart, out of respect for the Lord. Whatever you do, keep working at it with all your heart, as for the Lord and not for people.

1 Corinthians 10:24 Let no one *seek* his own good, but *that of others.*

Genesis 13:5-12 (Abraham helped Lot prosper by allowing him to choose the best land for himself.)

Proverbs 28:25 A greedy person stirs up strife, but *a person who trusts in the* L*ORD* will prosper.

Romans 8:31,32 What then will we say about these things? If God is for us, who can be against us? Indeed, he who did not spare his own Son, but gave him up for us all—how will he not also graciously give us all things along with him?

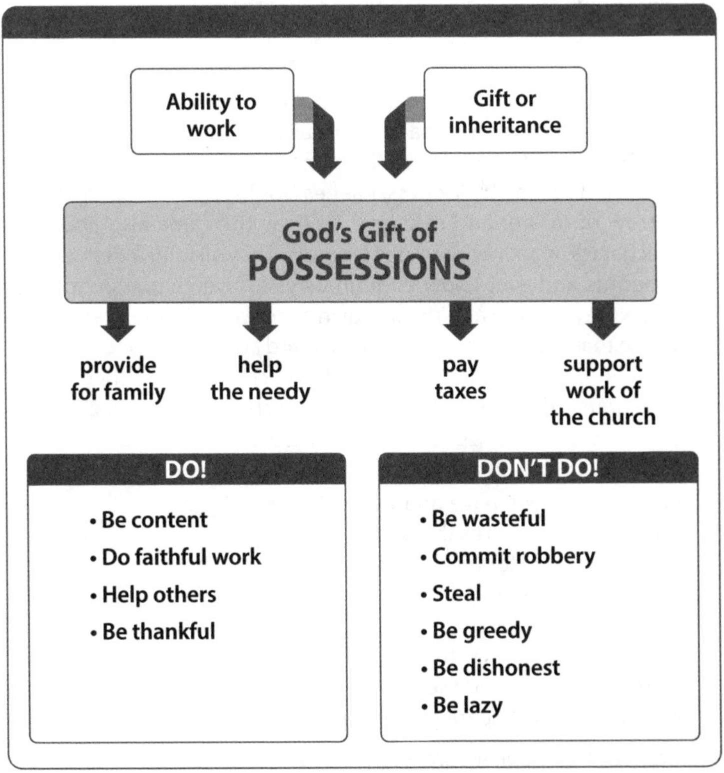

Ability to work → **God's Gift of POSSESSIONS** ← **Gift or inheritance**

God's Gift of POSSESSIONS → **provide for family** | **help the needy** | **pay taxes** | **support work of the church**

DO!	DON'T DO!
• Be content	• Be wasteful
• Do faithful work	• Commit robbery
• Help others	• Steal
• Be thankful	• Be greedy
	• Be dishonest
	• Be lazy

CONNECTIONS

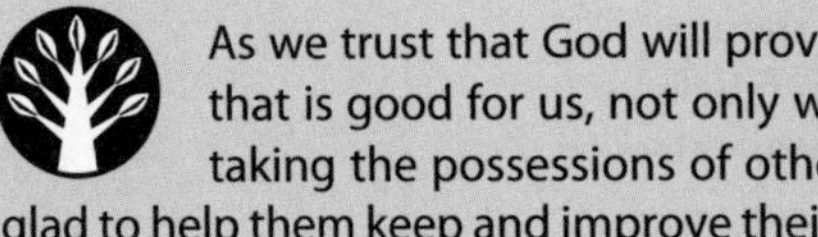

As we trust that God will provide all we need and all that is good for us, not only will we be able to resist taking the possessions of others but we will also be glad to help them keep and improve their property. Once, Abraham risked his life to rescue Lot and the wealthy leader of some neighboring lands. When he was offered a reward, Abraham declined. He wasn't greedy and eager to take whatever he could get. Instead, he expressed his trust that his blessings would come from God and was confident God would provide him with whatever he needed.

Genesis 14:1-24

Abraham trusted God to provide all he needed and chose to do what would benefit Lot and his neighbors. Make a list of ways you could use your possessions to help others.

Luther

Consider a manservant or maidservant who does not serve faithfully in the house, does damage, or allows damage to be done when it could be prevented. He ruins and neglects the goods entrusted to him, by laziness, idleness, or hate, to the spite and sorrow of master and mistress. . . . I say the same also about mechanics, workmen, and day laborers. They all follow their evil thoughts and ever know enough ways to overcharge people, while they are lazy and unfaithful in their work. All these are far worse than burglars, whom we can guard against with locks and bolts and, if caught, can be treated in such a way that they will not commit the crime again. (Large Catechism, I, par. 225,226)

Lord of Glory, You Have Bought Us (Stanzas 1,2)

Lord of glory, you have bought us
With your lifeblood as the price,
Never grudging for the lost ones
That tremendous sacrifice,
And with that have freely given
Blessings countless as the sand
To th' unthankful and the evil
With your own unsparing hand.

Grant us hearts, dear Lord, to give you
Gladly, freely, of your own.
With the sunshine of your goodness
Melt our thankless hearts of stone
Till our cold and selfish natures,
Warmed by you, at length believe
That more happy and more blessed
'Tis to give than to receive.

THE EIGHTH COMMANDMENT
You shall not give false testimony against your neighbor.

What does this mean?
We should fear and love God that we do not tell lies about our neighbor, betray him, or give him a bad name, but defend him, speak well of him, and take his words and actions in the kindest possible way.

REPUTATION

Defend and Protect the Reputation of Others

What is your most valuable possession?

God answers that question for us: "A good name is worth more than great wealth. Respect is worth more than silver and gold" (Proverbs 22:1). What makes a good name worth so much? The reputation we have affects almost everything we do with other people.

God doesn't want us to lose our good name, and God doesn't want us to hurt the good name of others. The Eighth Commandment protects reputations—our own and those of others.

84. Why is a good name an important blessing?

Genesis 39:16-20 (Joseph was thrown into prison because of a lie Potiphar's wife told.)

1 Samuel 19:1-6 (Jonathan defended David's life by speaking well of him.)

1 Samuel 20:18-42 (Jonathan defended David again.)

A good name is important because it determines whether people will respect us, trust us, or believe the truth about us.

85. When God forbids false testimony, he reminds us that anything that hurts a person's good name is sin. **How does the Eighth Commandment serve as a mirror, showing us that we also sin against God when we fail to respect our neighbor's good name?**

Leviticus 19:16 You shall not go around *spreading slander* among your people. You shall not testify falsely against your neighbor in a capital case. I am the Lord.

Proverbs 19:5 A *false witness* will not go unpunished. He breathes lies and will not escape.

Colossians 3:9 Do not *lie* to each other since you have put off the old self with its practices.

We sin by lying to or about someone. This includes everything from lying in our daily conversations to lying as a witness in court (perjury).

Proverbs 11:9 *With his mouth the godless person destroys* his neighbor, but righteous people are rescued by knowledge.

Proverbs 16:28 A perverse man *spreads conflict,* and *a gossip separates intimate friends.*

Proverbs 17:19 A person who loves sin loves conflict.

2 Samuel 15:1-6 (Absalom said bad things about his father in order to give David a bad name and turn people against him.)

1 Timothy 5:13 They also learn to be lazy as they go about from house to house. They not only learn to be lazy, but also to be gossips and *busybodies, saying things that they should not say.*

We sin by spreading gossip or by saying anything that will give a person a bad name.

Proverbs 11:13 A gossip *goes around betraying secrets, but a trustworthy spirit keeps a matter confidential.*

Proverbs 25:9 Argue your case with your neighbor, but do not *reveal someone else's secret.*

We sin when we betray a person's confidence (reveal private information that could hurt the person).

Proverbs 6:16-19 These are six things the Lord hates, seven things that really disgust him: arrogant eyes, *a lying tongue,* hands that shed innocent blood, *a heart that devises wicked plans,* feet that run quickly to do evil, *a false witness who breathes lies,* and *a person who spreads conflict between brothers.*

We sin against the Eighth Commandment when we use our words to cause pain or trouble for others.

86. Sins against the Eighth Commandment are so common that we may not even realize we are sinning with our words. **How does God emphasize that our speech can make us guilty of sin?**

Romans 1:29-32 They are filled with every kind of *unrighteousness,* evil, greed, and *wickedness.* They are full of envy, murder, quarreling, *deceit, and malice.* They are *gossipers, slanderers. . . .* Even though they know God's righteous decree that *those who do these things are worthy of death,* such people not only continue to do them, but also approve of others who continue to commit such sins.

James 3:2,6 We all stumble in many ways. If anyone does not stumble in what he says, he is a fully mature man, able to bridle his whole body as well. And the tongue is a fire. It is set among the parts of our body as a world of unrighteousness that stains the whole body, sets the whole course of life on fire, and is *set on fire by hell.*

God's Word emphasizes the damage we do with our tongues and what we deserve because of our damaging words.

87. How can we be sure that our sins against the Eighth Commandment are forgiven?

Isaiah 53:9 They would have assigned him a grave with the wicked, but he was given a grave with the rich in his death, because he had done no violence, *and no deceit was in his mouth.*

1 Peter 2:22,23 He did not commit a sin, and no deceit was found in his mouth. When he was insulted, he did not insult in return. When he suffered, he made no threats. Instead, he entrusted himself to him who judges justly.

Romans 5:8,10 God shows his own love for us in this: While we were still sinners, *Christ died for us.* For if, while we were enemies, *we were reconciled to God* by the death of his Son, it is even more certain that, since we have been reconciled, we will be saved by his life.

88. Though our sinful nature is hostile toward God, Jesus kept this commandment and all others perfectly in our place. Because of his love for us, we want our words to others and about others to honor God. **How does the Eighth Commandment guide us in the way we speak about others?**

Ephesians 4:15 *Speaking the truth in love,* we would in all things grow up into Christ, who is the head.

Ephesians 4:25 Therefore, after you *put away lying,* let each of you *speak truthfully* with your neighbor, because we are all members of one body.

1 Peter 3:8-10 Finally, all of you, live in harmony with one another. Show *sympathy, brotherly love, compassion,* and humility. *Do not repay evil with evil or insult with insult.* Instead, speak a blessing, because you were called for the purpose of inheriting a blessing. Indeed: Let the one who wants to love life and to see good days *keep his tongue from evil and his lips from saying anything deceitful.*

Proverbs 31:8,9 *Speak up for those who cannot speak.* Speak for the rights of all those who are defenseless. Speak up, judge fairly, and *defend the oppressed* and needy.

1 Corinthians 13:5-7 [Love] does not behave indecently. It is not selfish. *It is not irritable. It does not keep a record of wrongs. It does not rejoice over unrighteousness but rejoices with the truth. It bears all things, believes all things, hopes all things,* endures all things.

Matthew 26:6-13 (Jesus defended Mary and modeled what it means to take someone's words and actions in the kindest possible way.)

89. How does God want us to show love to those whom we have sinned against?

Matthew 5:23,24 So if you are about to offer your gift at the altar, and there you remember that your brother has something against you, leave your gift there in front of the altar and go. First *be reconciled to your brother.* Then come and offer your gift.

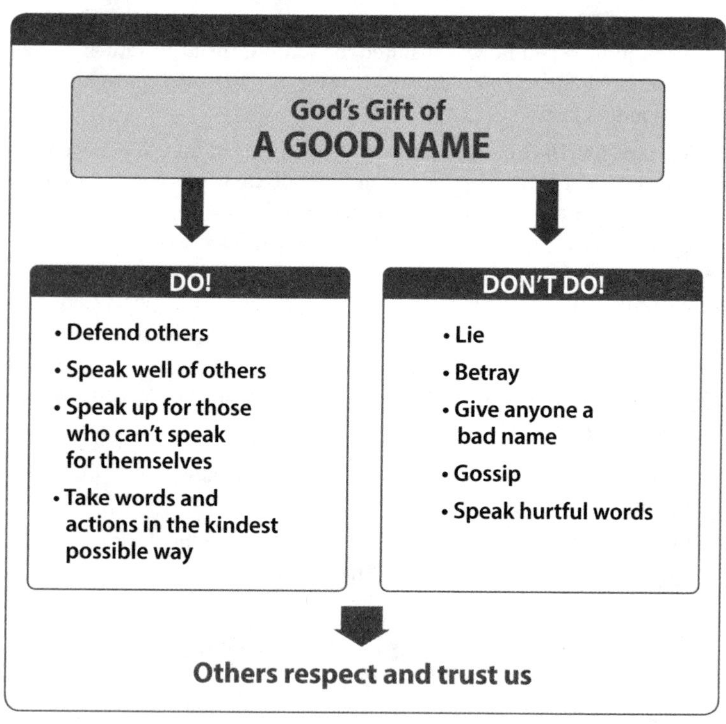

90. How does God want us to show love to those who have sinned against us?

Matthew 18:15 If your brother sins against you, *go and show him his sin just between the two of you.* If he listens to you, you have regained your brother.

Luke 17:3 *If your brother sins, rebuke him. If he repents, forgive him.*

CONNECTIONS

We are guilty of sin like all others, but God has brought us to repentance, forgiven our sin, and helped us to resist sin. We have the responsibility to warn others who continue in their sins without repentance. We can warn them and urge them to repent rather than continue and then suffer the consequences of their disobedience. As we do this, we pray that God would lead them to repentance. Speaking to another about sin is not easy, but it is a true act of love.

Nathan, a prophet, once had to confront David, a king of Israel, with David's sin. Read about how Nathan boldly confronted David's sin and about how God blessed the results.

---

2 Samuel 12:1-14

Nathan's bold rebuke was followed by a joyful sharing of God's forgiveness. Nathan's goal was to bring David to see his sin, to repent, and to trust God's forgiveness again. Before Nathan's rebuke, David showed no repentance. Consider how you can warn someone and help him or her repent and trust God's forgiveness. Explain how speaking a humble rebuke is similar to being a doctor.

Luther

This commandment forbids all sins of the tongue [James 3], by which we may injure or confront our neighbor. To bear false witness is nothing else than a work of the tongue. Now, God prohibits whatever is done with the tongue against a fellow man.... Here belongs particularly the detestable, shameful vice of speaking behind a person's back and slandering, to which the devil spurs us on, and of which much could be said. For it is a common evil plague that everyone prefers hearing evil more than hearing good about his neighbor. We ourselves are so bad that we cannot allow anyone to say anything bad about us. Everyone would much prefer that all the world should speak of him in glowing terms. Yet we cannot bear that the best is spoken about others. (Large Catechism, I, par. 263,264)

Take My Life and Let It Be (Stanzas 1-3)
Take my life and let it be
Consecrated, Lord, to thee.
Take my moments and my days;
Let them flow in ceaseless praise.

Take my hands and let them move
At the impulse of thy love.
Take my feet and let them be
Swift and beautiful for thee.

Take my voice and let me sing
Always, only for my King.
Take my lips and let them be
Filled with messages from thee.

THE NINTH COMMANDMENT

You shall not covet your neighbor's house.

What does this mean?

We should fear and love God that we do not scheme to get our neighbor's inheritance or house, or obtain it by a show of right, but do all we can to help him keep it.

THE TENTH COMMANDMENT

You shall not covet your neighbor's wife, workers, animals, or anything that belongs to your neighbor.

What does this mean?

We should fear and love God that we do not force or entice away our neighbor's spouse, workers, or animals, but urge them to stay and do their duty.

COVETING

Keep the Desires of the Heart Pure

Many sins we commit can be seen or heard by others: a child hits his brother or we speak an angry word. But sin is not always so obvious. We can offend our perfect God simply with our thoughts.

Consider God's warnings in the Ninth and Tenth Commandments. Both commandments warn us that sin starts with the thoughts and desires in our hearts. God knows what we think, but he also forgives us fully so that we can turn away from sin and live as his children.

91. To **covet** means to have a sinful desire or craving in our hearts for something God hasn't given us. The Ninth Commandment points to our neighbor's house and property. The Tenth Commandment points especially to those people who bring blessings to our neighbor's life and occupation. **What does God forbid in these two commandments?**

> **Micah 2:1,2** Woe to those who plan wickedness. . . . They *covet fields* and seize them. They covet houses and take them away. *They deprive a person of his house, and a man of his inheritance.*

Luke 20:46,47 Beware of the experts in the law, who like to walk around in long robes and love greetings in the marketplaces. . . . *They devour widows' houses* and offer long prayers to look good.

Isaiah 5:8 Woe to you who *join house to house,* who connect field to field, until there is no room left, except room for you alone to live in the middle of the land!

Joshua 7:1-21 (Achan had a sinful desire to take the spoils of war that were supposed to be dedicated and given to God.)

Matthew 14:3,4 (Herod had taken his brother's wife for himself.)

2 Samuel 15:2-6 (Absalom coveted his father's kingdom and tried to take it away from David by turning the people against him.)

1 Kings 21:1-16 (Jezebel devised a devious plan to get Naboth's vineyard by a show of right.)

A CLOSER LOOK

The explanation to the Ninth Commandment says that we should not obtain our neighbor's property by a "show of right." What does that mean? *Show of right* means that someone tries to get someone else's property in a way that may appear legal but is really not ethical or the right thing to do.

92. By giving *two* commands that address coveting, God impresses upon us that even if we haven't actually stolen something, a sinful desire to have something that is not ours is wrong. **How do the Ninth and Tenth Commandments serve as a mirror, unmasking the sin of coveting within our hearts?**

Romans 7:7,8 I would not have recognized sin except through the law. For example, *I would not have known about coveting if the law had not said, "You shall not covet."* But sin, seizing the opportunity provided by this commandment, produced every kind of sinful desire in me. For apart from the law, sin is dead.

James 4:1,2 Where do conflicts and quarrels among you come from? Don't they come from your *cravings* for pleasure, *which are at war in the parts of your body?* You want something but do not get it, so you murder. You desire something but cannot obtain it, so you quarrel and fight. You do not have because you do not ask.

1 Timothy 6:9,10 Those who *want to get rich* fall into temptation and a trap and many foolish and harmful desires, which plunge them into complete destruction and utter ruin. For the love of money is a root of all sorts of evils. *By striving for money,* some have wandered away from the faith and have pierced themselves with many pains.

Mark 7:21,22 In fact, *from within, out of people's hearts,* come evil thoughts, sexual sins, theft, murder, adultery, greed, wickedness, deceit, unrestrained immorality, envy, slander, arrogance, and foolishness.

These commandments convict us, exposing our sinful desires to have things God has not given to us.

93. Coveting is a sin. We want something that is not his will to give us. Coveting also leads to many other sins. **How might coveting lead to other sins?**

James 1:14,15 Each person is tempted when he is *dragged away and enticed by his own desire.* Then when desire has conceived, it *gives birth to sin.* And sin, when it is full grown, gives birth to death.

Genesis 3:6 When the woman *saw that the tree was good for food, and that it was appealing to the eyes, and that the tree was desirable to make one wise, she took some of its fruit and ate.* She gave some also to her husband, who was with her, and he ate it.

1 Timothy 6:10 The love of money is a root of all sorts of evils. *By striving for money, some have wandered away from the faith and have pierced themselves with many pains.*

Deuteronomy 27:17 Cursed is anyone who moves the boundary marker of his neighbor. All the people will say, "Amen!"

James 5:5,6 You have lived for pleasure on the earth and led a life of luxury. You have fattened your hearts on the day of slaughter. You condemned and murdered the Righteous One. Does he not oppose you?

2 Samuel 11:1-17 (David's sin of coveting Uriah's wife led to sins of adultery and murder.)

94. How do we know that our sins against the Ninth and Tenth Commandments are also forgiven?

Hebrews 4:15 We do not have a high priest who is unable to sympathize with our weaknesses, but one who has been tempted in every way, just as we are, *yet was without sin.*

1 John 3:5 You know that *he appeared in order to take away our sins* and *in him there is no sin.*

1 Corinthians 15:3 I delivered to you as of first importance what I also received: that *Christ died for our sins* in accordance with the Scriptures.

Hebrews 9:26 He has appeared once and for all, at the climax of the ages, in order to *take away sin* by the sacrifice of himself.

95. Contentment is the opposite of coveting. **Why can we say that contentment is a gift from God?**

Psalm 145:15,16 The eyes of all look eagerly to you, and *you give them their food at the proper time.* He opens his hand, and he satisfies the desire of every living thing.

Ecclesiastes 2:24 There is nothing better for a man than to eat and to drink and to find joy in his work. This too, I saw, is *from God's hand.*

1 Timothy 6:6,7 *Godliness with contentment is great gain.* For we brought nothing into the world, and we certainly cannot take anything out.

Proverbs 3:5,6 *Trust in the LORD* with all your heart, and do not rely on your own understanding. In all your ways acknowledge him, and he will make your paths straight.

Psalm 37:25 I was a young man. Now I am old. But I have never seen a righteous person forsaken or his children begging for bread.

Contentment comes with the realization that we can trust God to give us the things we need.

96. Jesus came to do away with our sin. Because of his sacrifice, we want our hearts to be pure so that all we do honors him. **How do the Ninth and Tenth Commandments serve as a guide for our daily lives?**

Luke 12:15 Then he said to them, "*Watch out and be on guard against all greed,* because a man's life is not measured by how many possessions he has."

1 Timothy 6:8 If we have food and clothing, *with these we will be satisfied.*

1 Peter 1:14-16 As obedient children, *do not conform to the evil desires you had when you lived in ignorance.* Rather, just as the one who called you is holy, so also be holy in everything you do. For it is written, "Be holy, because I am holy."

Genesis 13:1-12 (Abram unselfishly allowed Lot to choose the best land for himself.)

Genesis 14:1-24 (Abram refused to take even what was offered as a reward for saving the kings. He was content with what God gave him, and he wanted everyone to know that he trusted God to provide for him.)

Genesis 39:6-8 (Joseph remembered God's will and resisted coveting his master's wife.)

Hebrews 13:5 *Keep your life free from the love of money, and be content with what you have.* For God has said: I will never leave you, and I will never forsake you.

Colossians 3:5 *Put to death* whatever is worldly in you: sexual immorality, uncleanness, lust, *evil desire, and greed,* which is idolatry.

Philippians 2:4 Let each of you *look carefully not only to your own interests, but also to the interests of others.*

COVETING
(Sinful Desires)

DO!	DON'T DO!
Have holy desires • Contentment • Generosity • Gratitude • Concern for others • Trust in God	**Desire something we should not want** **Neighbor's** • House • Property • Wealth • Spouse • Workers **Anything that belongs to our neighbor**
God-pleasing words and actions	**Sinful words and deeds**

CONNECTIONS

Coveting what belongs to someone else can quickly lead to other sins. King Ahab was interested in a vineyard that was owned by a man named Naboth. Discover how dangerous coveting is as you read what happens next.

1 Kings 21:1-16
Make a list of the sins that were committed as a consequence of Ahab's coveting. Imagine that you were Ahab. What could you

have done to stop the sins that led to Naboth's death? Imagine you were Jezebel. What could you have done to stop the sins that led to Naboth's death?

What different things can you do to fight against the sins of your own heart?

Luther

We must know that God does not want you to deprive your neighbor of anything that belongs to him, so that he suffer the loss and you gratify your greed with it. . . . So these commandments are especially directed against envy and miserable greed. God wants to remove all causes and sources from which arises everything by which we harm our neighbor. Therefore, He expresses it in plain words, "You shall not covet," and so on. For He especially wants us to have a pure heart [Matthew 5:8], although we will never attain to that as long as we live here. So this commandment will remain, like all the rest, one that will constantly accuse us and show how godly we are in God's sight! (Large Catechism, I, par. 307,310)

God's Own Child, I Gladly Say It (Stanzas 1,5)

God's own child, I gladly say it: I am baptized into Christ!
He, because I could not pay it, Gave my full redemption price.
Do I need earth's treasures many?
I have one worth more than any
That brought me salvation free, Lasting to eternity!

There is nothing worth comparing To this lifelong comfort sure!
Open-eyed my grave is staring: Even there I'll sleep secure.
Though my flesh awaits its raising,
Still my soul continues praising:
I am baptized into Christ; I'm a child of paradise!

THE CONCLUSION

What does God say about all these commandments?

He says, "I, the LORD your God, am a jealous God, punishing the children for the sin of the fathers to the third and fourth generation of those who hate me, but showing love to a thousand generations of those who love me and keep my commandments."

What does this mean?

God threatens to punish all who transgress these commandments. Therefore we should fear his anger and not disobey what he commands.

But he promises grace and every blessing to all who keep these commandments. Therefore we should love and trust in him and gladly obey what he commands.

CONCLUSION

God Threatens and Promises

Though there are only ten, the commandments cover all areas of our lives. They speak to our relationship with God and to our relationships with fellow humans. In addition to our actions, the commandments govern our words and even our thoughts. God clearly cares about every aspect of our lives, and he wants us to follow his perfect design for human behavior.

To help us know how seriously he wants us to view his commands and any sins against them, God adds both threats and promises.

97. The first three commandments speak about our thoughts, words, and actions toward God. The last seven commandments speak about our thoughts, words, and actions toward one another. **What one word summarizes all of God's law?**

Matthew 22:37-40 Jesus said to him, "'*Love the Lord your God* with all your heart, with all your soul, and with all your mind.' This is the first and greatest commandment. The second is like it: '*Love your* *neighbor* as yourself.' All the Law and the Prophets depend on these two commandments."

Romans 13:9,10 The commandments—do not commit adultery, do not murder, do not steal, do not covet (and if there is any other commandment)—are summed up in this statement: "Love your neighbor as yourself." Love does no harm to a neighbor, so *love is the fulfillment of the law.*

98. How diligently should we keep the commandments?

Leviticus 19:2 You shall be holy, because I, the LORD your God, am holy.

Matthew 5:48 So then, be perfect, as your heavenly Father is perfect.

James 2:10 Whoever keeps the whole law but stumbles in one point has become guilty of breaking all of it.

99. The Conclusion to the commandments quotes the Lord's words in Exodus 20:5,6. **What does God mean when he calls himself a jealous God?**

Isaiah 42:8 I am the LORD; that is my name. *I will not give my glory to another, nor my praise to idols.*

Ezekiel 6:9 I was heartbroken by their lustful hearts, which turned away from me, and by their eyes, which lusted for their filthy idols.

Psalm 5:4,5 You are not a God who takes pleasure in evil. With you the wicked cannot dwell. The arrogant cannot stand before your eyes. You hate all evildoers.

Leviticus 11:45 I am the LORD, who brought you up from the land of Egypt to be your God. You therefore shall be holy, for I am holy.

Exodus 3:1-5 (The Angel of the Lord [God himself] appeared to Moses in a burning bush. God taught Moses that God is holy by having Moses take off his sandals as he neared the unusual sight.)

God is holy. He cannot tolerate sin. He will not share the love and honor we owe him with idols.

100. The Bible uses several different terms to describe disobedience to the commandments. The terms are descriptive and help us clearly understand what our disobedience means. **What does God call disobedience to his commandments?**

1 John 3:4 Everyone who *commits sin* also commits lawlessness. Sin is lawlessness.

Isaiah 53:5 It was because of *our rebellion* that he was pierced. He was crushed for *the guilt our sins deserved.* The punishment that brought us peace was upon him, and by his wounds we are healed.

Psalm 25:11 For the sake of your name, O Lord, you forgive my *guilt,* although it is great.

To *sin* is to miss the mark—to miss the target of perfection our holy God demands. To *transgress* is to cross the line or to rebel against God's law. *Iniquity* is crooked or perverse behavior. (These are some of the words God uses to describe disobedience.)

101. In what two ways do we disobey God's commandments?

James 4:17 For the one who *knows the right thing to do and doesn't do it,* this is a sin.

Leviticus 5:17 If, however, a person sins by *doing anything against the Lord's commands by doing something that should not be done,* even though he is not aware of it, he is liable and shall bear the punishment for his guilt.

We disobey God when we don't do what God wants us to do (sins of omission) and when we do things God doesn't want us to do (sins of commission).

102. What are the results of our disobedience to God?

Isaiah 59:2 It is your guilt that has *separated you from your God, and* your sins have hidden God's face from you, so that he does not hear.

103. What does God threaten will happen to all who break his commandments?

Genesis 3:16-19 (God told Adam and Eve that the consequences of sin which they brought upon themselves and all humankind would be felt in their work, their relationships, and all of life—even in giving birth to children.)

Romans 1:18 *God's wrath* is being revealed from heaven against all the ungodliness and unrighteousness of people who try to suppress the truth by unrighteousness.

Isaiah 57:21 There is *no peace,* says my God, for the wicked.

John 16:33 In this world you are going to have trouble.

1 Kings 17:1; 18:16-18 (God subjected the people of Israel to a severe famine because they followed Ahab in worshipping Baal.)

God threatens all who disobey his commandments with his wrath (anger) and with trouble.

Romans 6:23 The wages of sin is *death.*

Matthew 25:41,46 Then he will say to those on his left, "Depart from me, you who are cursed, into the eternal fire, which is prepared for the Devil and his angels." And they will go away to *eternal punishment,* but the righteous to eternal life.

Matthew 10:28 Do not fear those who kill the body but cannot kill the soul. Rather, fear the one who is able to destroy both soul and body in *hell.*

God threatens all who disobey his commandments with death and eternal punishment.

104. Why does God threaten punishment for those who break his commandments, even to the third and fourth generation?

Ecclesiastes 12:13,14 This is the conclusion of the matter. Everything has been heard. *Fear God and keep his commandments.* For mankind, this is everything. Yes, God will bring everything that is done into judgment, including everything that is hidden, whether good or evil.

Deuteronomy 6:13,15 *Fear the LORD your God, serve him,* and swear by his name. . . . The LORD your God will be a jealous God in your midst, and the anger of the LORD your God will burn against you, and he will destroy you from the face of the earth.

Deuteronomy 5:9 Do not bow down to them or be subservient to them, for I the LORD your God am a jealous God. I follow up on the guilt of the fathers with their children, their grandchildren, and their great-grandchildren if they also hate me.

2 Kings 9:7,8; 10:11 (The family of wicked Ahab and Jezebel followed in the footsteps of their parents and were destroyed.)

The consequences that God threatens make his anger toward sin very clear. His threat to punish to the third and fourth generation reminds us that God is serious about sins against his commandments. It also reminds us how patterns of sin and unbelief are naturally passed down from parents to their children. The effect of the sins of parents can be felt for generations to come.

105. Why do Christians need God's threat of punishment?

Romans 8:7,8 The *mind-set of the sinful flesh is hostile to God,* since it does not submit to God's law, and in fact, it cannot. Those who are in the sinful flesh cannot please God.

Genesis 8:21 *The thoughts [man] forms in his heart are evil from his youth.*

Our sinful nature rebels against God and does not want to obey him. God's threats are a curb. They keep the wicked actions of all people in check and help people to consider the consequences of their disobedience.

106. What does God promise for those who love him and obey his commandments?

Psalm 103:11 As high as the heavens are above the earth, *so powerful is his mercy toward those who fear him.*

Psalm 147:11 The LORD is pleased with those who fear him, those who wait for his mercy.

Genesis 22:1-18 (Abraham obeyed God's difficult command. God promised that he would *richly bless Abraham,* and through Abraham, he would also bless us.)

Luke 1:50 *His mercy is for those who fear him from generation to generation.*

1 Timothy 4:8 Bodily training is beneficial to an extent, but godliness is beneficial in all things, because it holds promise both for life now and for the life to come.

Deuteronomy 7:9 Know that the LORD your God, yes, he is God, the faithful God who *maintains both his covenant and his mercy* for those who love him and keep his commandments, *to a thousand generations.*

A CLOSER LOOK

A covenant is a solemn agreement, especially one in which God promises to bless and save. God makes his promise to bless and save us only because of his grace and mercy. He does not require anything from us. In addition, he makes another gracious covenant, or promise, to continue to bless the faithful obedience of those who believe.

107. What is God emphasizing by promising to bless those who fear him and obey his commandments?

Deuteronomy 5:9,10 I the LORD your God am a jealous God. . . . But I show mercy to thousands who love me and keep my commandments.

Deuteronomy 5:29 If only this would be in their hearts—to fear me and to keep all my commandments always, so that it might go well for them and for their children continually.

God's pledge to keep the covenant of love to a thousand generations of those who love him and keep his commandments shows us how seriously he takes obedience.

108. In what way is God's grace evident in his promise to bless obedience?

Romans 11:35 Who has first given to God that he will be repaid?

Luke 17:10 So also you, when you have done all that you were commanded, say, "We are unworthy servants. We have only done what we were supposed to do."

When God graciously works obedience in us, that doesn't mean God owes us something in return. We are simply doing what we are supposed to do. The fact that he does bless our obedience is purely a result of his grace.

109. What does the combination of God's threat and his promise urge us to do?

Deuteronomy 11:26-28,32 You see, I am placing before you today a blessing and a curse: the blessing, *if you listen to the commandments of the LORD* your God that I am giving you today, or the curse, if you do not listen to the commandments of the LORD your God and you turn away from the path that I am commanding you today by walking after other gods whom you did not know. But *be careful to carry out all the statutes and the ordinances that* I am giving you today.

Deuteronomy 10:12 So now, Israel, what is the LORD your God asking of you but to *fear the LORD your God,* to *walk in all his ways, and* to *love him and* to *serve the LORD your God with all your heart and with all your soul.*

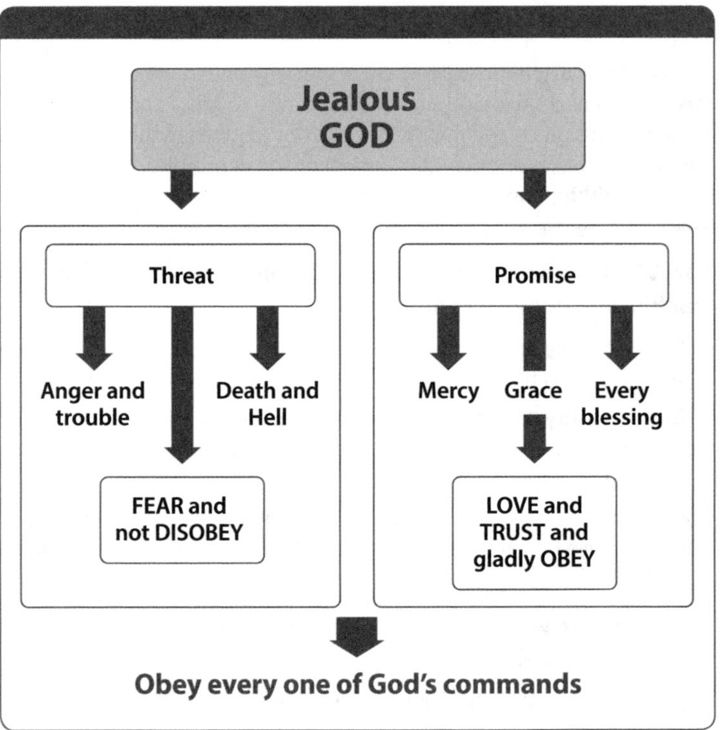

110. Though we fail in our attempts to keep God's commandments perfectly, why can we be confident that we are saved?

John 3:16 God so loved the world that he gave his only-begotten Son, that *whoever believes in him shall not perish, but have eternal life.*

Romans 3:28 We conclude that *a person is justified by faith without the works of the law.*

Colossians 1:13,14 The Father rescued us from the domain of darkness and transferred us into the kingdom of the Son he loves, *in whom we have redemption, the forgiveness of sins.*

1 Timothy 2:6 [He] gave himself as a ransom for all.

CONNECTIONS

If people want us to do something that is very important, they may emphasize the importance in a variety of ways. They might explain very seriously how important it is. They may warn us that if we don't do what they ask, we will face discipline or some serious consequences. They may promise that if we do what they are asking, they will reward us in some way. God emphasized the importance of our keeping his commandments by threatening punishment for those who would disobey and promising blessing for those who would obey. In these verses God promises wonderful blessings for people who obey his commandments.

Exodus 19:3-6

In Exodus 19:4 God reminds his people that he brought them out of Egypt and cared for them. Why does God mention this event before asking them to obey? Then God gives them additional promises that will benefit them as they obey his commandments. How did his added promises encourage the people to obey? Make a list of things God has done for you that encourage you to obey his commandments.

Luther

Let this be considered and laid to heart that these things are not human games, but are the commandments of the Divine Majesty. He insists on them with great seriousness. He is angry with and punishes those who despise them. On the other hand, He abundantly rewards those who keep them. In this way there will be a spontaneous drive and a desire gladly to do God's will. (Large Catechism, I, par. 330)

Dear Christians, One and All, Rejoice (Stanzas 2-4)

Fast bound in Satan's chains I lay;
Death brooded darkly o'er me.

Sin was my torment night and day;
In sin my mother bore me.
Yet deep and deeper still I fell;
Life had become a living hell,
So firmly sin possessed me.

My own good works availed me naught,
No merit they attaining;
My will against God's judgment fought,
No hope for me remaining.
My fears increased till sheer despair
Left naught but death to be my share
And hell to be my sentence.

But God beheld my wretched state
Before the world's foundation,
And, mindful of his mercies great,
He planned my soul's salvation.
A Father's heart he turned to me,
Sought my redemption fervently;
He gave his dearest treasure.

LAW AND GOSPEL

The Difference Between the Law and the Gospel

When we hear or read God's law, we learn that God is serious about sin. Martin Luther understood the message of the law. It accused him of sin and convinced him that he should be punished. In order to try to appease God's anger against sin, Luther became a monk. (See Luther's biography pp. 20-25.) He also punished himself in the hope that he could impress God with his zeal and his self-denial. He sometimes slept on the cold floor in a cold room. He went without food. He wanted to make himself good enough—righteous enough—for God. But all he did was not enough. He still sinned and could not make himself good enough for God. At that time, Luther was looking for the solution to his sin in God's law. But there had to be more. Praise God that he led Luther to discover something more in the Bible. Luther found good news, extremely good news: God has declared sinners good and righteous because of Jesus, not because they work to be good and righteous. God himself gives sinners perfect righteousness through faith in Jesus. This good news is called the gospel. Luther realized that the gospel—not the law—provided the solution to his sin.

Both the law and gospel are at the heart of God's message to humans. While both are important, they are different in several ways. First, they are different in the way they were given to us.

In What Way Is the Gospel Different From the Law?

111. How does God give his law to us?

> **Romans 2:14,15** In fact, whenever Gentiles, who do not have the law, do by nature what the law requires—even though they do not have the law—they are a law for themselves. They demonstrate the work of the law that is written in their hearts, since their conscience also bears witness as their thoughts go back and forth, at times accusing or at times even defending them.

The Old Testament Gentiles didn't have the written law of God, because they did not have the Scriptures to read. Yet, by nature they did things God's law required. They knew right from wrong because God has written his law in the hearts of all humans, and our consciences are often guided by that law within. However, because of sin, our consciences aren't completely dependable. For that reason, God gave his law another way.

> **Exodus 20:1-17; 31:18** (On Mount Sinai, God presented to the people of Israel the Ten Commandments inscribed on tablets of stone.)

> **Deuteronomy 31:9** *Moses wrote down this law,* and he gave it to the priests, the sons of Levi.

In addition to the law written in human hearts, God also gave his law written in physical form.

112. How does God give the gospel to us?

> **1 Corinthians 2:9,10** As it is written: What no eye has seen and no ear has heard and no human mind has conceived—that is what God has prepared for those who love him. But *God revealed it to us through his Spirit.* For the Spirit searches all things, even the depths of God.

> **2 Timothy 3:15** From infancy you have known the *Holy Scriptures, which are able to make you wise for salvation* through faith in Christ Jesus.

We do not know about Jesus and salvation on our own. The gospel is revealed to us only through the Bible.

Through the law and gospel, God reveals different truths to us.

113. What does God teach us through the law?

> **Matthew 19:17** Jesus said to him, "Why do you ask me about what is good? Only one is good. But if you want to enter life, *keep the commandments.*"

> **James 2:8** If you really fulfill the royal law according to the Scripture: "You shall *love your neighbor as yourself,*" you are doing well.

> **Romans 3:20** No one will be declared righteous in his sight by works of the law, for *through the law we become aware of sin.*

> **Romans 7:7** What will we say then? Is the law sin? Absolutely not! On the contrary, *I would not have recognized sin except through the law.* For example, I would not have known about coveting if the law had not said, "You shall not covet."

> **Galatians 3:10** *Those who rely on the works of the law are under a curse.* For it is written, "Cursed is everyone who does not continue to do everything written in the book of the law."

Through the law, God teaches us what to do and what not to do. The law shows us our sins, reveals God's anger against sin, and shows us that we deserve to be punished because of our sins.

114. What does God teach us through the gospel?

Genesis 3:15 I will put hostility between you and the woman, and between your seed and her seed. *He will crush your head,* and you will crush his heel. [The first gospel promise]

Luke 2:10,11 The angel said to them, "Do not be afraid. For behold, I bring you good news of great joy, which will be for all people: *Today in the town of David, a Savior was born for you.* He is Christ the Lord."

John 3:16 God so loved the world that he gave his only-begotten Son, that *whoever believes in him shall not perish, but have eternal life.*

Romans 1:17 In the gospel a *righteousness from God is revealed by faith, for faith,* just as it is written, "The righteous will live by faith."

Through the gospel, God teaches us the good news of all he has done and all he still does to save us from our sins. The gospel shows us our Savior and reveals God's grace toward us.

115. The law and the gospel are also different in the work that they do. **What is the work of the law? What is the work of the gospel?**

Romans 3:20 No one will be declared righteous in his sight by works of the law, for *through the law we become aware of sin.*

2 Corinthians 7:10 *Godly sorrow produces repentance,* which leads to salvation, leaving no regret. On the other hand, worldly sorrow produces death.

Luke 3:8 *Produce fruits* in keeping with repentance!

The law shows us our sin and leads us to repentance. It also shows us how God would have us live and serves as our guide as we turn away from sin and obey God.

Romans 1:16 I am not ashamed of the gospel, because *it is the power of God for salvation* to everyone who believes—to the Jew first, and also to the Greek.

Romans 10:17 Faith comes from hearing the message, and the message comes through the word of Christ.

1 John 2:1,2 My children, I write these things to you so that you will not sin. If anyone does sin, we have an Advocate before the Father: Jesus Christ, the Righteous One. *He is the atoning sacrifice for our sins,* and not only for ours but *also for the whole world.*

The gospel brings us to faith in Jesus as our Savior and comforts us daily with the assurance that our sins are forgiven because of Jesus' sacrifice.

116. Our sinful nature rebels against God's law. It doesn't want to keep the law. **How does the gospel change our attitude about obeying God's law?**

Romans 12:1 I urge you, brothers, *by the mercies of God, to offer your bodies as a living sacrifice*—holy and pleasing to God—which is your appropriate worship.

2 Corinthians 5:14,15 *The love of Christ compels us,* because we came to this conclusion: One died for all; therefore, all died. And he died for all, so that those who live would no longer live for themselves but for him, who died in their place and was raised again.

Colossians 3:17 *Everything you do,* whether in word or deed, *do it all in the name of the Lord Jesus,* giving thanks to God the Father through him.

117. The law and the gospel are the two key teachings of the Bible. **What is God's ultimate purpose in giving us these teachings?**

John 5:39 You search the Scriptures because you think you have eternal life in them. *They testify about me!*

John 20:31 *These are written that you may believe that Jesus is the Christ, the Son of God, and that by believing you may have life in his name.*

2 Timothy 3:15 From infancy you have known the Holy Scriptures, which are able to *make you wise for salvation* through faith in Christ Jesus.

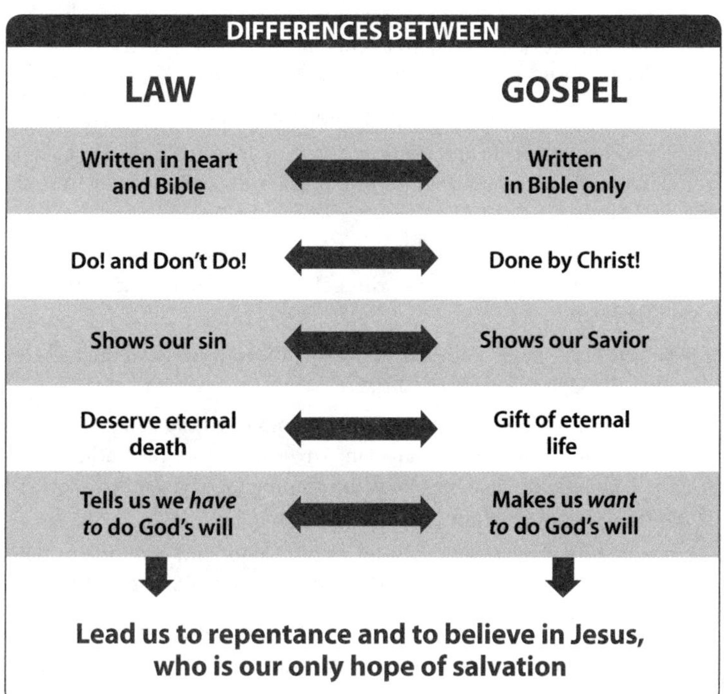

It is very important that we understand the difference between the law and the gospel and the purpose of the law and the gospel. Many who have not understood these two major teachings of the Bible have lost their faith. A man named Saul, who was alive at the time Jesus was crucified, misunderstood the purpose of the law. Though he was extremely zealous for God's law, he mistakenly believed that people would be saved by following the law. Saul was so zealous for God's law that he vowed to track down those who believed in Jesus—to imprison or even to kill them. Read about how Jesus stopped Saul as he was on his way to track down Christians in a distant city and about how, by God's grace, Saul became a believer in Jesus and a messenger of the gospel.

Acts 9:1-22

We have been brought to faith too. God has not come to us in a blinding light, yet he uses the same means to make us believers. In what ways did Jesus show Saul that he had disobeyed? Think of your own life; how does God point out your sins? How did Jesus show Saul the good news of forgiveness? In your own life, how has God assured you that he loves you and forgives you?

Luther

Throughout the gospel, Christ does no more than draw us out of ourselves and into himself; he spreads his wings and invites us to take shelter under him. (*What Luther Says,* Ewald M. Plass, p. 561, par. 1703)

The Law Commands and Makes Us Know

The law commands and makes us know
What duties to our God we owe,
But 'tis the gospel must reveal
Where lies our strength to do his will.

The law uncovers guilt and sin
And shows how vile our hearts have been;
The gospel only can express
Forgiving love and cleansing grace.

What curses does the law pronounce
Against the one who fails but once!

But in the gospel Christ appears,
Pard'ning the guilt of num'rous years.

My soul, no more attempt to draw
Your life and comfort from the law.
Flee to the hope the gospel gives;
The one who trusts the promise lives.

APOSTLES' CREED

The Father, Son, and Holy Spirit are three distinct persons of the Godhead. Yet God is one.

I BELIEVE

The Apostles' Creed

The Ten Commandments summarize God's law—his commands for all people. The Apostles' Creed summarizes the gospel, the good news of what the triune God has done and continues to do for us.

In the Apostles' Creed, we confess the gospel truths in three sections, each section highlighting the work of one of the three persons of the Trinity: Father, Son, and Holy Spirit. Each section of the creed is called an article. Each article tells us what one of the divine persons has done and is continuing to do for us.

A CLOSER LOOK

A creed is a statement that expresses what people believe and teach. The Apostles' Creed wasn't written by the apostles, but it is a statement that expresses the truths taught by the apostles. It can be traced back to the third century.

Two other Christian creeds have played an important part in the history of the Christian church. When false teachings arose within the Christian church, God's people needed to confess the truth and avoid the errors. The Nicene Creed (adopted in A.D. 325, see p. 15) and the Athanasian Creed (written about A.D. 500) were written to defend the truth of what the Bible teaches about God.

Most of our worship services include the confession of one of these creeds as an expression of our faith.

The Triune God

118. Christians worship the triune God. **What do we mean when we say that God is triune?**

Deuteronomy 6:4 Hear, O Israel! The LORD is our God. *The LORD is one!*

1 Corinthians 8:4 Concerning the eating of food from idol sacrifices, we know that an idol is not anything real in the world and that *there is no God but one.*

John 10:30 I and the Father are *one.*

Genesis 1:26 God said, "Let us make man *in our image, according to our likeness.*"

Matthew 3:16,17 After Jesus was baptized, he immediately went up out of the water. Suddenly, the heavens were opened for him! He saw the *Spirit of God,* descending like a dove and landing on him, and *a voice out of the heavens said, "This is my Son, whom I love.* I am well pleased with him."

Matthew 28:19 Go and gather disciples from all nations by baptizing them *in the name of the Father and of the Son and of the Holy Spirit.*

John 15:26 When the *Counselor* comes, *whom I will send to you from the Father—the Spirit of truth,* who proceeds from the Father—*he will testify about me.*

2 Corinthians 13:14 *The grace of the Lord Jesus Christ, and the love of God, and the fellowship of the Holy Spirit be with you all.*

A CLOSER LOOK

The word *triune* comes from two Latin words: *tria,* meaning "three," and *unus,* meaning "one." When we say that God is triune, we mean that he is three persons yet one God (Trinity). The word *trinity* is not found in the Bible, but it helps us describe what God tells us about himself.

119. Because of our limited understanding, the truth of the Trinity—three persons in one God—is impossible for us to grasp or explain. **Though we can't comprehend this great truth, why do we believe that God is triune?**

John 17:17 Sanctify them by the truth. *Your word is truth.*

Isaiah 55:9 As the heavens are higher than the earth, so my ways are higher than your ways, and *my plans are higher than your plans.*

Jeremiah 10:7 Is there anyone who should not fear you, King of the Nations? That is what you deserve. Among all the wise men of the nations and in all their kingdoms, *there is no one like you.*

1 Corinthians 2:13 *We also speak about these things, not in words taught by human wisdom, but in words taught by the Spirit,* combining spiritual truths with spiritual words.

1 John 5:20 *We know that the Son of God has come and has given us understanding so that we may know him who is true.* And we are in him who is true, in his Son, Jesus Christ. He is the true God and eternal life.

God is so much greater than our ability to understand, but the Holy Spirit reveals the truth to us. Because God's Word tells us that there are three persons yet one God, we believe that it is true.

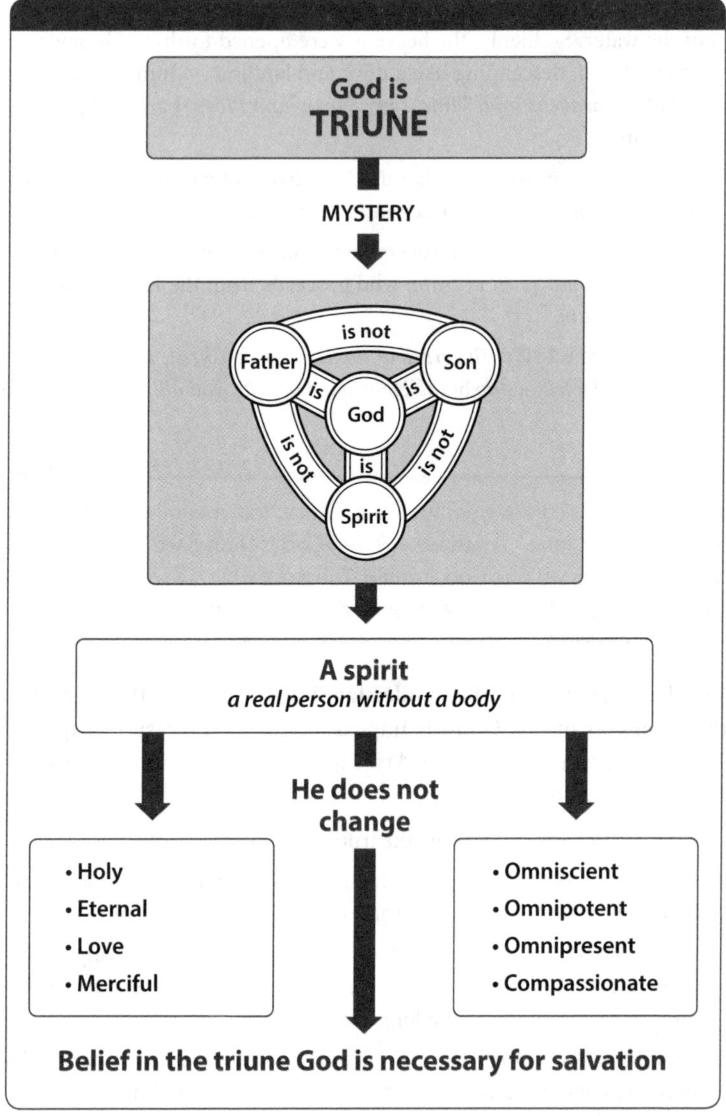

120. What does the Bible reveal about the characteristics of God?

John 4:24 *God is spirit,* and those who worship him must worship in spirit and in truth.

Psalm 42:2 My soul thirsts for God, for *the living God.* When can I go and appear before God?

Isaiah 6:3 One called to another and said, *Holy, holy, holy* is the LORD of Armies! The whole earth is full of his glory!

Malachi 3:6 *I, the LORD, do not change.* That is why you, sons of Jacob, have not come to an end.

Psalm 90:2 Before the mountains were born, before you gave birth to the earth and the world, *from eternity to eternity you are God.*

Genesis 17:1-8 (When Abram was 99 years old and his wife 89, God came to him to confirm the promise that they would yet have a son and that their descendants would be a great nation. To assure Abram that this could happen, God said about himself, *"I am God Almighty"* [v. 1].)

Matthew 19:26 Jesus looked at them and said, "With people this is impossible, but *with God all things are possible.*"

John 21:17 He asked him the third time, "Simon, son of John, do you care about me?" Peter was grieved because Jesus asked him the third time, "Do you care about me?" He answered, "*Lord, you know all things.* You know that I care about you." "Feed my sheep," Jesus said.

Psalm 139:1-4 LORD, you have investigated me, and you know. You know when I sit down and when I get up. You understand my thoughts from far off. You keep track of when I travel and when I stay, and you are familiar with all my ways. Before there is a word on my tongue, *you, LORD, already know it completely.*

Jeremiah 23:24 Can anyone hide in secret places so that I cannot see him? declares the LORD. Do I not fill heaven and earth? declares the LORD.

Psalm 139:7,8 Where can I go from your Spirit? Where can I flee from your Presence? *If I go up to heaven, you are there. If I make my bed in hell—there you are!*

1 John 4:8 The one who does not love has not known God, because *God is love.*

Psalm 103:8 *The LORD is compassionate and gracious,* slow to anger, abounding in mercy.

God is a spirit, and he is love. (His actions flow from compassion and grace—undeserved love.) He is holy (without sin and hates sin), and he does not change.

He is eternal. There never was a time when he didn't exist. He is all-powerful (omnipotent). He knows all things (omniscient). He is everywhere (omnipresent).

A CLOSER LOOK

Throughout history, people have attempted to understand or explain the nature of God. Yet sometimes they have reached conclusions that disagree with what God tells us about himself. Some have denied that God is triune. By doing so, they have denied any possibility or hope of eternal life. The Athanasian Creed, written approximately five hundred years after the time of Christ, very carefully and clearly states the truths that the Bible teaches about the triune God. It emphasizes that the Son of God did not come into existence when he was born in Bethlehem. Rather, "the Father is eternal, the Son eternal, the Holy Spirit eternal." Jesus and the Holy Spirit are not creations of the Father. Rather, "the Son is neither made nor created, but is begotten of the Father alone. The Holy Spirit is neither made nor created nor begotten, but proceeds from the Father and the Son."

---

121. Why is it so important that we teach the doctrine of the Trinity?

John 3:16 God so loved the world that he gave his only-begotten Son, that *whoever believes in him shall not perish, but have eternal life.*

Acts 4:12 *There is salvation in no one else,* for there is no other name under heaven given to people by which we must be saved.

2 Corinthians 5:21 God made him, who did not know sin, to become sin for us, so that we might become the righteousness of God in him.

Psalm 49:7,8 *No one can by any means redeem himself. He cannot give God a ransom for himself*[.] (Yes, the ransom for their souls is costly. Any payment would fall short.)

John 5:23 All should honor the Son just as they honor the Father. *Whoever does not honor the Son does not honor the Father who sent him.*

John 14:6 Jesus said to him, "I am the Way and the Truth and the Life. *No one comes to the Father, except through me.*"

Salvation is found in only one place. Whoever wishes to be saved must confess the triune God—Father, Son, and Holy Spirit—as the only true God.

CONNECTIONS

Some groups today claim to believe in the God of the Bible, but they deny that God is triune. They deny that Jesus is true God. The Church of Jesus Christ of Latter-day Saints (Mormons) and the Jehovah's Witnesses are examples of such groups. Many of the religious leaders in Jesus' day refused to accept that he was true God. As you read the account of John the Baptist, you will see examples of those who did not accept what God said about Jesus. At Jesus' baptism, you will also see clear evidence that God gave to prove he is triune.

Matthew 3:1-17

Reminders that we believe in and worship the triune God are found throughout our worship services. List some of the places in our worship services that remind us that God is triune. What artwork in the church or worship material shows that God is triune?

Luther

How can we, miserable, poor mortals comprehend this mystery? We do not know the how of our own speaking, laughing, or sleeping, although we daily perform and experience these natural functions. And yet we want to speak of God and the conditions existing within his divine Being. We want to do so without the Word of God, solely according to our own mind. Is it not blindness above all blindness for a man who cannot explain the most insignificant functions he daily observes in his own body to presume to know what is beyond and above all reason and of which no one except God alone can speak, and to have the audacity to state so rashly and bluntly that Christ is not God? (*What Luther Says,* Ewald M. Plass, p. 1388, par. 4466)

Holy, Holy, Holy! Lord God Almighty (Stanza 1)

Holy, holy, holy! Lord God Almighty!
Early in the morning our song shall rise to thee;
Holy, holy, holy, merciful and mighty,
God in three persons, blessed Trinity!

THE FIRST ARTICLE

Creation

I believe in God the Father almighty, maker of heaven and earth.

What does this mean?

I believe that God created me and all that exists, and that he gave me my body and soul, eyes, ears, and all my members, my mind and all my abilities.

And I believe that God still preserves me by richly and daily providing clothing and shoes, food and drink, property and home, spouse and children, land, cattle, and all I own, and all I need to keep my body and life. God also preserves me by defending me against all danger, guarding and protecting me from all evil. All this God does only because he is my good and merciful Father in heaven, and not because I have earned or deserved it. For all this I ought to thank and praise, to serve and obey him.

This is most certainly true.

CREATION

God the Father Almighty: The Creator

The First Article of the Apostles' Creed begins with the words "I believe." Both of those words are noteworthy. The "I" reminds you that when you speak these words, you are confessing what you personally believe. This is *your* confession. And when you confess that you "believe" in God, you are saying more than that you believe God exists: You are confessing that you trust in God. You trust all that the Bible says about God is true. You trust that all of God's promises will be fulfilled.

Many people, probably the majority of people, believe there is a higher power, an intelligent designer—a god. But many fashion this god to suit their personal beliefs. Because salvation is found in no other God, we want to learn what the Bible tells us about the true God. In the First Article of the Apostles' Creed, we learn what the Bible says about the first person of the Trinity, God the Father.

122. Why do we believers label the first person of the triune God "the Father"?

Malachi 2:10 Don't we all have one *Father?* Hasn't one God created us? Why then do we violate our vows to each other, polluting the covenant of our fathers?

Matthew 3:17 A voice out of the heavens said, "*This is my Son, whom I love.* I am well pleased with him."

John 20:17 Jesus told her, "Do not continue to cling to me, for I have not yet ascended to my Father. But go to my brothers and tell them, 'I am ascending *to my Father and your Father*—to my God and your God.'"

Galatians 4:4,5 When the set time had fully come, God sent his Son to be born of a woman, so that he would be born under the law, in order to redeem those under the law, so that we would be adopted as sons.

Galatians 3:26 *You are all sons of God* through faith in Christ Jesus.

123. How did God show his almighty power in the creation of the world?

Genesis 1:1–2:3 (God created everything in heaven and on earth out of nothing.)

Psalm 33:6,9 By the word of the LORD the heavens were made. By the breath of his mouth he made the whole army of stars. *For he said, "Let it be," and it was!* He gave a command, and there it stood.

CREATION	
DAY 1	Heavens and earth; light
DAY 2	Sky
DAY 3	Dry ground and seas; plants and trees
DAY 4	Sun, moon, and stars
DAY 5	Birds and fish
DAY 6	Land animals and humans

Exodus 20:11 *In six days the LORD made the heavens and the earth, the sea, and everything that is in them,* but he rested on the seventh day. In this way the LORD blessed the seventh day and made it holy.

Hebrews 11:3 By faith we know that the universe was created by God's word, so that what is seen did not come from visible things.

A CLOSER LOOK

Evolution

Many people do not believe what the Bible says about the creation of the world. Some don't believe that supernatural things could happen because they don't believe God exists. They believe that all living things developed by chance over a very long period of time (billions of years). This theory about the origin of the universe is called evolution.

Evolution is a human theory. The basic assumption is that primitive cells were formed by chance events. Over time, those cells evolved into more complex forms of life, eventually resulting in all the life-forms that exist now. According to this theory, humans are just highly developed animals.

What we believe about the origin of the world and the origin of life will have far-reaching effects on the way we look at our lives. If we believe that we are simply highly developed animals, then we will believe that we are the masters of our own destinies and that we are not accountable to a divine being (God). The only real purpose in life would be simply to survive.

The evidence revealed in the Bible, however, shows that God is almighty and perfectly wise. The testimony of the Bible is that God used his almighty power and divine wisdom to create the world and all the creatures that inhabit the world. The Bible testifies that he gave humans a special place and purpose in that world.

---

124. Some people try to reconcile the creation account with the theory of evolution. They suggest that God created the basic components of the earth and then allowed the process of evolution to continue the development of the universe. This belief is called theistic evolution. **However, what does the Bible clearly teach about the origin of all things?**

John 1:3 *Through him everything was made,* and without him not one thing was made that has been made.

Exodus 20:11 *In six days the LORD made the heavens and the earth, the sea, and everything that is in them,* but he rested on the seventh day. In this way the LORD blessed the seventh day and made it holy.

125. Why don't we accept human theories about the origin of the world and the origin of people?

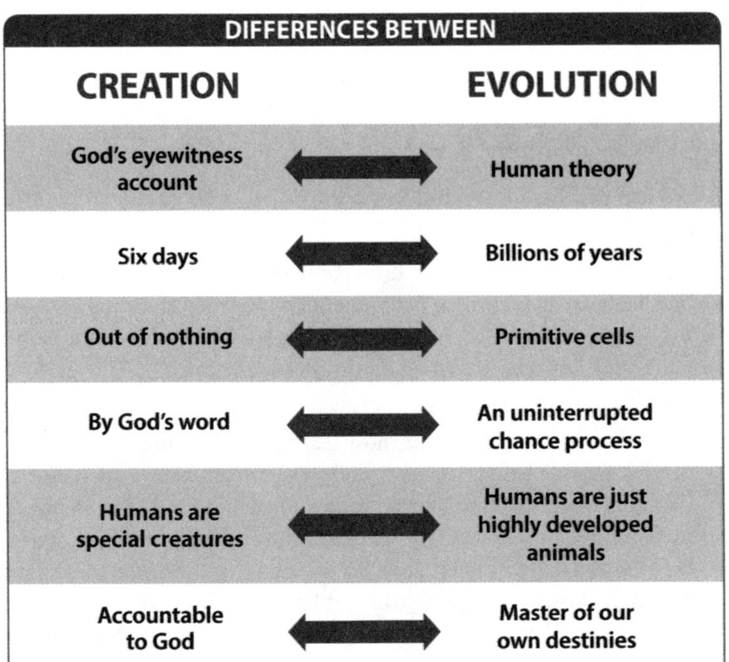

2 Peter 3:5 What they are intentionally forgetting is that the heavens *came into existence* long ago *by the word of God* and that the earth came together out of the water and between the waters.

1 Timothy 6:20,21 Guard what has been entrusted to you, turning away from godless, empty talk and the contradictions of what is falsely called "knowledge." By professing it, some have veered away from the faith.

Job 38 and 39 (God reminded Job that no humans witnessed the creation or can claim to be instrumental in preserving the creation.)

Hebrews 3:4 Every house is built by someone, and God is the one who built everything.

Hebrews 11:3 *By faith we know* that the universe was created by God's word, so that what is seen did not come from visible things.

Revelation 4:11 Worthy are you, our Lord and God, to receive the glory and the honor and the power, for *you have created all things,* and because of your will they existed and were created.

Matthew 19:4 (Jesus presented the biblical account of the creation as fact.)

Acts 4:24; 14:15-17; 17:22-31 (The apostles spoke of the creation of the world by God.)

The certainty that God created the entire world in six days and that humans occupy a special place and purpose in the creation is based on faith in God's message to us in the Bible. We don't accept human theories because they are human attempts to explain what no one has witnessed and what we can know only by faith.

126. How did God show that we humans were the focus of his creating activity?

Genesis 1:26 God said, "Let us *make man in our image,* according to our likeness, and let them *have dominion over* the fish of the sea, and over the birds of the sky, and over the livestock, and over all the earth, and over every creeping thing that crawls on the earth."

Genesis 2:7,20-22 The *Lord God formed the man* from the dust of the ground and breathed into his nostrils the breath of life, and the man became a living being. The *man gave names* to all the livestock, and to the birds of the sky, and to every wild animal, but for Adam no helper was found who was a suitable partner for him. The Lord God caused the man to fall into a deep sleep. As the man slept, the *Lord* God took a rib and closed up the flesh where it had been. *The Lord God built a woman from the rib that he had taken from the man* and brought her to the man.

Genesis 1:28 God blessed them and said to them, "Be fruitful, multiply, fill the earth, and subdue it. *Have dominion over* the fish of the sea, over the birds of the sky, and over every living thing that moves on the earth."

127. What does the Bible mean when it says that God created humans in his own image?

Colossians 3:10 Put on the new self, which is continually being renewed in knowledge, *according to the image of its Creator.*

Ephesians 4:24 Put on the new self, which has been created to be like God *in righteousness and true holiness.*

Because Adam and Eve were created in the image of God, their wills naturally conformed to the will of God. They were perfect and holy, only wanting to carry out God's will—and they were capable of doing so.

128. What was the consequence of the fall into sin on the image of God?

1 Corinthians 2:14 An *unspiritual person does not accept the truths taught by God's Spirit,* because they are foolishness to him, and he cannot understand them, because they are spiritually evaluated.

Romans 8:7 The mind-set of *the sinful flesh is hostile to God,* since it does not submit to God's law, and in fact, it cannot.

Genesis 5:3 Adam lived 130 years, and *he became the father of a son in his own likeness,* according to his own image, and he named him Seth.

Psalm 51:5 Certainly, I was guilty when I was born. I was sinful when my mother conceived me.

When Adam and Eve sinned, the image of God was lost. All of their descendants are born with a sinful nature that doesn't know God, and we are all enemies of God from birth.

129. Each of us has every reason to marvel at the way God made us. We can say with the psalmist, "I am fearfully and wonderfully made" (Psalm 139:14). **How has God shown his wisdom and goodness in the way he created you?**

Job 31:15 Didn't he who *made me in the womb also* make my servant? Didn't the same God fashion us both in the womb?

Job 10:11,12 You clothed me with skin and flesh. You wove me together with bones and tendons. *You provided me with life* and mercy, and your watchful care has guarded my spirit.

Genesis 2:7 The *Lord God formed the man* from the dust of the ground and breathed into his nostrils the breath of life, and *the man became a living being.*

Ecclesiastes 12:7 The dust goes back into the ground—just as it was before, and the spirit goes back to God who gave it.

1 Corinthians 12:14-26 (God gave each part of the body unique gifts that enable it to serve for the good of the body.)

James 1:5,17 If any one of you lacks wisdom, let him ask God, who gives it to all without reservation and without finding fault, and it will be given to him. *Every good act of giving and every perfect gift is from above, coming down from the Father of the lights,* who does not change or shift like a shadow.

God has shown his wisdom and goodness by giving you your body and soul, eyes, ears, and all your members, your mind, and all your abilities.

CONNECTIONS

In the depths of severe suffering, Job was tempted to question the wisdom and fairness of God in allowing such suffering. Part of God's answer to Job was to remind him of the magnificence and complexity of his splendid creation. The creation was evidence of God's power, wisdom, and love.

We often take for granted the world that God has given to us. As you read God's answer to Job, take a moment to marvel at the remarkable world God has created for you.

Job 38 and 39

God has created the world in which we live, but sometimes we take God's creation for granted because we don't stop to notice. Pause for a moment and consider God's marvelous creation. Write down at least three things that show God's power and wisdom in the world around us. Then pause again, look around, and add to your list.

Luther

The Ten Commandments have taught that we are to have not more than one God. So it might be asked, "What kind of a person is God? What does he do? How can we praise, or show and describe him, that he may be known?" . . . So the Creed is nothing other than the answer and confession of Christians arranged with respect to the First Commandment. It is as if you were to ask a little child, "My dear, what sort of a God do you have? What do you know about him?" The child could say, "This is my God: first, the Father, who has created heaven and earth. Besides this One only, I regard nothing else as God. For there is no one else who could create heaven and earth." (Large Catechism, II, par. 10,11)

Praise to the Lord, the Almighty (Stanzas 1,3)

Praise to the Lord, the Almighty, the King of creation!
O my soul, praise him, for he is your health and salvation!
Let all who hear Now to his temple draw near,
Joining in glad adoration!

Praise to the Lord, who has fearfully, wondrously, made you,
Health has bestowed and, when heedlessly falling, has stayed you.
What need or grief Ever has failed of relief?
Wings of his mercy did shade you.

PRESERVATION

God the Father Almighty: Our Provider and Protector

Often when we get something new that we really like, we pay a lot of attention to it. But after a while, we tire of it and may even forget about it. God doesn't feel that way about his creation. The universe exists because God created it. It continues to exist only because he continues to care for it and provide for it. The depth of God's love for his creation is demonstrated by the way he continues to care for it.

The explanation of the First Article speaks of how God preserves his creation in the way he provides for and protects his creatures.

God Provides for His Creation

130. What are all the things God does to provide for his creation?

Psalm 36:6,7 Your righteousness is as high as the mountains of God. Your justice is as deep as the ocean. *You save both man and animal, O Lord.* How precious is your mercy, O God! So all people find refuge in the shadow of your wings.

Psalm 147:8,9 He is the one who covers the sky with clouds. *He determines rain for the earth. He makes grass sprout* on the mountains. *He gives their food to the cattle* and to the young ravens when they call.

Psalm 147:4 He counts the number of the stars. *He calls them all by name.*

Hebrews 1:3 The Son is the radiance of God's glory and the exact imprint of the divine nature. *He sustains all things* by his powerful word.

Matthew 6:25-34 (Jesus assures us that we have no need to worry, because God provides our food and clothing.)

Psalm 37:25 I was a young man. Now I am old. But *I have never seen a righteous person forsaken or his children begging for bread.*

Psalm 50:15 Call on me in the day of distress. I will deliver you, and you will honor me.

Psalm 103:2,3 Bless the Lord, O my soul, and do not forget all his benefits—who pardons all your guilt, *who heals all your diseases.*

Psalm 121:3 He will not let your foot stumble. He who *watches over you* will not slumber.

Psalm 139:14 I praise you because *I am fearfully and wonderfully made.* Your works are wonderful, and my soul knows that very well.

131. What different methods does God use to provide for us?

2 Thessalonians 3:10 When we were with you, this was our command to you: If anyone does not want to work, he should not eat.

Leviticus 26:4 *I will give you rains in their season, so that the land will yield its produce and the trees in the farmland will yield their fruit.*

Psalm 104:14 He makes grass grow for the cattle, and plants that people use to *produce food from the earth.*

Psalm 67:6 *The earth will yield its harvest. God, our God, will bless us.*

3 John 2 *Dear friend, I pray that you are doing well in every way and have good health,* just as your soul is doing well.

1 Timothy 5:23 Stop drinking just water, but use a little wine because of your stomach and your frequent sicknesses.

Our heavenly Father preserves us using natural means. He blesses us with good health and gives us doctors and medicines to help us stay healthy. He provides work for us and gives us the abilities we need to do the work. He blesses our work and provides the rain and nutrients needed to produce our food.

1 Kings 17:1-16 (God provided for Elijah by means of miracles.)

John 6:3-13 (Jesus miraculously fed more than five thousand people.)

Mark 4:35-41 (Jesus calmed the storm.)

Matthew 19:26 With people this is impossible, but *with God all things are possible.*

Our heavenly Father can preserve us by means of miracles.

God Protects His Creation

132. Because of sin, the world is subjected to evil and suffering. We children of God find great comfort in knowing that our heavenly Father watches over us and protects us. **How does our heavenly Father protect us?**

Psalm 91:9,10 Yes, you LORD are *my refuge!* If you make the Most High your shelter, evil will not overtake you. Disaster will not come near your tent.

Psalm 50:15 Call on me in the day of distress. *I will deliver you,* and you will honor me.

Exodus 14 (God miraculously provided a way for Israel to escape through the Red Sea.)

Exodus 17:8-13 (God gave a visible demonstration of his protection. When Aaron and Hur held up Moses' hands, the army of Israel was defeating Amalek. When Moses let his arms drop, Amalek was defeating Israel.)

Daniel 6:16-23 (God protected Daniel in the lions' den.)

Our heavenly Father protects us by delivering us from evil and guarding us from harm.

Genesis 37:12-36; 39:1–46:4 (God used the many challenges in Joseph's life to save his people, with the ultimate purpose of carrying out his promise to send a Savior. Note especially Joseph's acknowledgment in Genesis 50:20.) You meant evil against me, but God meant it for good, to bring this to pass and to keep many people alive, as it is this day.

Romans 8:28 We know that all things work together for the good of those who love God, for those who are called according to his purpose.

Hebrews 12:5-10 (We receive blessings through our heavenly Father's discipline.)

Hebrews 12:10,11 They disciplined us for a little while, according to what seemed best to them, but *God disciplines us for our good,* so that we may have a share in his holiness. No discipline seems pleasant when it is happening, but painful, yet later it yields a peaceful harvest of righteousness for those who have been trained by it.

Our heavenly Father protects us by making all things in our lives serve for good.

133. What special creatures does God send for our protection?

Psalm 91:11 He will give a command to his angels concerning you, to guard you in all your ways.

2 Kings 6:8-17 (God sent an army of angels to protect Elisha.)

Daniel 6:16-23 (God protected Daniel in the lions' den by sending an angel.)

Matthew 2:13-21 (God used an angel to tell Joseph to take Mary and the baby Jesus and flee from impending slaughter.)

134. What does God tell us about angels?

Genesis 1:31 God saw everything that he had made, and indeed, *it was very good.*

Hebrews 1:14 Are not all angels *ministering spirits* sent out to serve for the benefit of those who are going to inherit salvation?

Psalm 103:20 Bless the LORD, *you his angels, you strong warriors who obey his word* by listening to what he says.

Daniel 7:10 A river of fire flowed out from his presence. Thousands upon thousands *served him, and* ten thousand times ten thousand stood before him.

Psalm 91:11,12 He will *give a command to his angels concerning you, to guard you* in all your ways. They will lift you up in their hands, so that you will not strike your foot against a stone.

Matthew 18:10 See to it that you do not look down on one of these little ones, because I tell you that *their angels in heaven always see the face of my Father* who is in heaven.

Angels are powerful spirit beings who were created sometime during the six days of creation. They are holy. There are many of them. They serve God and watch over us.

A CLOSER LOOK

Angel means "messenger." God often used angels to announce key events in his plan of salvation. Angels announced that John the Baptist and Jesus were about to be born. When Jesus was born, many angels announced the good news to the shepherds. When the baby Jesus' life was in danger because of Herod's evil decree, an angel instructed Joseph to flee with his family. When Jesus rose from the dead, angels at the tomb proclaimed the good news. When Jesus ascended, angels promised that he would come again. We are told that when Jesus returns on judgment day, angels will accompany him.

---

135. We can barely begin to comprehend all the ways God intervenes in our lives to preserve and protect us. We marvel at this comforting truth, especially as we realize that our sins make us unworthy of such care. **Why does our heavenly Father preserve and protect us?**

Romans 11:35 Who has first given to God that he will be repaid?

Lamentations 3:22,23 *By the mercies of the LORD we are not consumed, for his compassions do not fail.* They are new every morning. Great is your faithfulness.

Genesis 32:10 *I am not worthy* of even a bit of all the mercy and all the faithfulness that you have shown to your servant, for I crossed over this Jordan with just my staff, and now I have grown into two camps.

Romans 8:32 He who did not spare his own Son, but gave him up for us all—*how will he not also graciously give us all things along with him?*

God does all these great things only because he is our good and merciful Father in heaven, not because we have earned or deserved it.

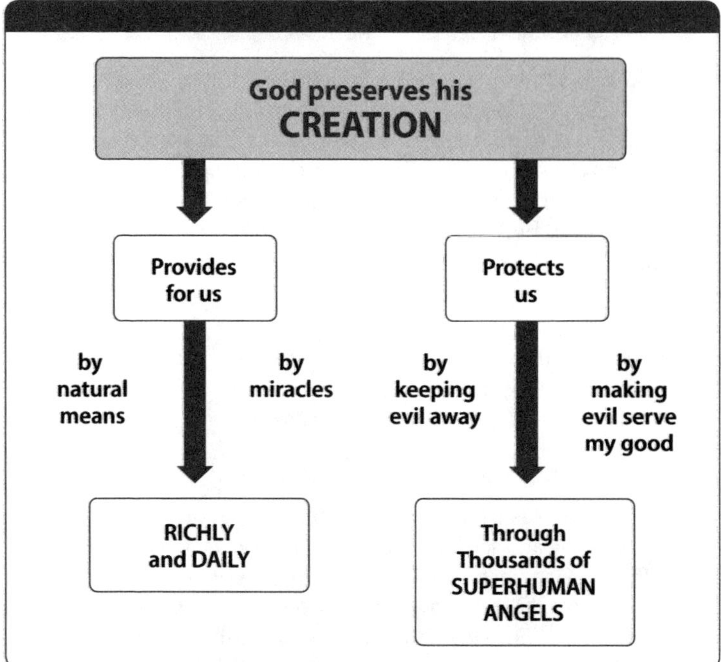

136. What does our heavenly Father's goodness and mercy move us to do?

Psalm 7:17 I will thank the LORD because of his righteousness, and I will make music to the name of the LORD Most High.

Psalm 150:1,2,6 Praise the LORD. Praise God in his sanctuary. Praise him in the expanse that shows his might. Praise him for his acts of power. Praise him according to his abundant greatness. Let everything that has breath praise the LORD. Praise the LORD.

1 Samuel 12:24 Above all, fear the LORD, and serve him in truth, with all your heart, considering the great things he has done for you.

Deuteronomy 10:12 So now, Israel, what is the LORD your God asking of you but to fear the LORD your God, to walk in all his ways, and to love him and to serve the LORD your God with all your heart and with all your soul.

Romans 12:1 I urge you, brothers, by the mercies of God, to offer your bodies as a living sacrifice—holy and pleasing to God—which is your appropriate worship.

1 Corinthians 10:31 Whether you eat or drink, or do anything else, do everything to the glory of God.

Sometimes when we think of the future, we are afraid. Certainly our world is marred by sin. But we can be confident that God loves us and that he has tremendous power to bless us. We see a great example of that in the account of the Israelites fleeing from Egypt. Read about how God showed both his love and his power by miraculously providing for and protecting his people.

Exodus 16:1–17:7

List some of the challenges in life that can lead you to worry and to doubt God. Explain how God's way of helping the Israelites in the wilderness is an encouragement to you.

Luther

We also confess that God the Father has not only given us all that we have and see before our eyes, but He daily preserves and defends us against all evil and misfortune. He directs all sorts of danger and disaster away from us. We confess that He does all this out of pure love and goodness, without our merit, as a kind Father. He cares for us so that no evil falls upon us. (Large Catechism, II, par. 17)

Now Thank We All Our God (Stanza 1)

Now thank we all our God With hearts and hands and voices,
Who wondrous things has done, In whom his world rejoices,
Who from our mother's arms Has blessed us on our way
With countless gifts of love And still is ours today.

THE FALL

The Ruin of God's Creation

When God created the world, he said that all he created was good. It's impossible for us to comprehend what life was like in God's perfect creation. What would life be like with no pain, no sickness, no arguments or hurt feelings, no death, no fear, no car accidents, no broken families, no wars, no murders—nothing to hurt us? Why does our world not look at all like God's perfect creation?

Sin and Its Effect on God's Creation

137. To get a better understanding of what happened to God's perfect creation, we go back to the time shortly after the creation. Remember that God had created the angels sometime during the six days of creation. Not long after the creation, some angels revolted against God and became evil. **What does the Bible tell us about the evil angels?**

> **Jude 6** The angels who did not keep their position of authority but *left their own dwelling place behind*—God has kept them in everlasting chains under darkness for the judgment of the great day.
>
> **2 Peter 2:4** God did not spare *angels when they sinned* but handed them over to chains of darkness by casting them into hell, to be kept under guard for judgment.
>
> **Matthew 25:41** Then he will say to those on his left, "Depart from me, you who are cursed, into the eternal fire, which is prepared for the Devil and his angels."

Some angels chose to disobey God and were condemned to eternal punishment in hell.

138. The devil is the chief of the evil angels. How did the devil ruin God's creation?

> **Genesis 3:1-6** (The devil succeeded in leading Adam and Eve to rebel against God.)

139. What was the result on God's creation of the fall into sin?

> **Genesis 3:6-19** (Adam and Eve's sin brought death upon them, alienated them from God, and brought many painful consequences to their lives.)
>
> **Romans 5:12** *Sin entered the world through one man* and death through sin, so also *death spread to all people* because all sinned.
>
> **Romans 8:22** We know that all of creation is groaning with birth pains right up to the present time.

A CLOSER LOOK

There are three kinds of death: spiritual death, temporal death, and eternal death. All involve separation. **Spiritual death** is the separation of the soul from God and separation from all the spiritual blessings God provides. By nature, all humans begin life spiritually dead. **Temporal death** is the separation of the soul from the body and separation from all the blessings of life here on earth. **Eternal death** is separation from the presence of God and separation from the joys of heaven forever in hell.

---

140. When Adam and Eve were created, they were created in the image of God—they were perfect, and they wanted what God wanted. **What was the impact of the fall into sin on the image of God?**

Genesis 8:21 The *thoughts [man] forms in his heart are evil* from his youth.

Romans 7:18 I know that *good does not live in me,* that is, in my sinful flesh. The desire to do good is present with me, but I am not able to carry it out.

Romans 8:7 The mind-set of the sinful flesh is *hostile to God,* since it does not submit to God's law, and in fact, it cannot.

1 Corinthians 2:14 An unspiritual person does not accept the truths taught by God's Spirit, because they are foolishness to him, and he cannot understand them, because they are spiritually evaluated.

Ephesians 2:1 *You were dead in your trespasses and sins.*

Genesis 5:3 Adam lived 130 years, and he became the father of a son in his own likeness, *according to his own image,* and he named him Seth.

The image of God was completely lost. Since the time that Adam and Eve sinned, all their descendants have been born spiritually dead and are by nature hostile to God.

141. What is the devil's goal as he continues to work in God's creation?

John 8:44 You belong to your father, the Devil, and you want to do your father's desires. *He was a murderer from the beginning and did not remain standing in the truth,* because there is no truth in him. Whenever he lies, he speaks from what is his, because he is a liar and the father of lying.

1 Peter 5:8 Have sound judgment. Be alert. Your adversary, *the Devil, prowls around like a roaring lion, looking for someone to devour.*

2 Timothy 2:25,26 . . . and gentle in correcting those who oppose him. God may grant them repentance, leading to the knowledge of the truth, and they may come to their senses and escape from *the Devil's trap, after they were captured by him to do his will.*

Revelation 12:12 Rejoice, you heavens and those who dwell in them. Woe to the earth and the sea, for *the Devil has gone down to you. He is full of rage,* because he knows that his time is short.

142. God certainly would have been justified in destroying Adam and Eve, along with the entire creation, when they turned against him. **Why didn't he destroy them?**

Lamentations 3:22 *By the mercies of the* L*ORD* we are not consumed, for his compassions do not fail.

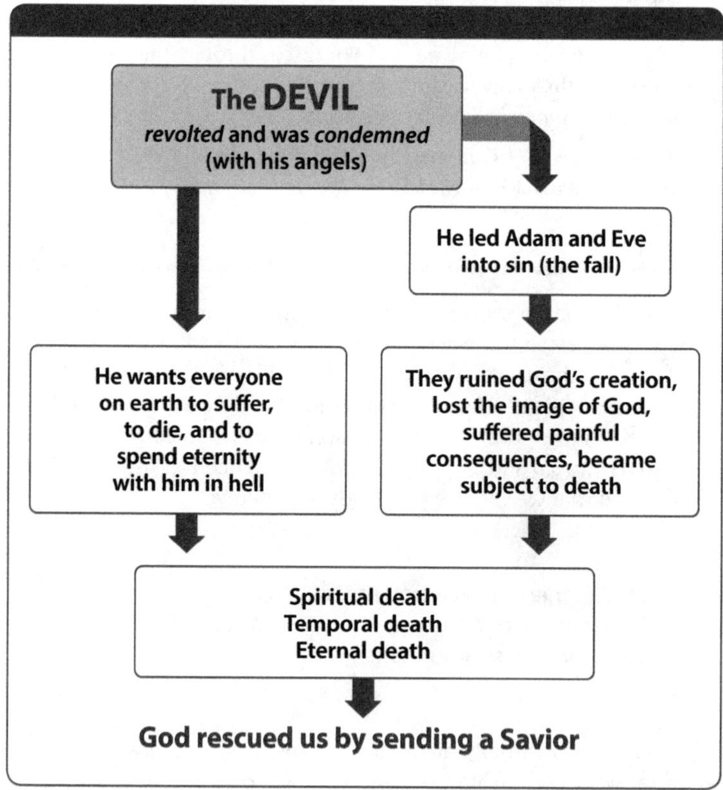

Ezekiel 33:11 Say to them, "As I live, declares the LORD *God, I take no pleasure in the death of the wicked,* but rather that the wicked turn from

their way and live. Turn back, turn back from your evil ways, for why should you die, O house of Israel?"

143. What has our heavenly Father done to rescue us from the devil's evil plan?

1 John 3:8 The one who continues to sin is of the Devil, because the Devil has been sinning from the beginning. This is why *the Son of God appeared: to destroy the works of the Devil.*

Genesis 3:15 I will put hostility between you and the woman, and between your seed and her seed. *He will crush your head,* and you will crush his heel.

John 3:16 God so loved the world that he gave his only-begotten Son, that whoever believes in him shall not perish, but have eternal life.

Romans 5:18,19 So then, just as one trespass led to a verdict of condemnation for all people, so also one righteous verdict led to life-giving justification for all people. For just as through the disobedience of one man the many became sinners, so also *through the obedience of one man the many will become righteous.*

2 Corinthians 5:21 God made him, who did not know sin, to become sin for us, so that *we might become the righteousness of God in him.*

CONNECTIONS

Satan spoiled God's creation by leading Adam and Eve into sin. If he had been able to lead Jesus into sin, the ruin of God's creation would have been complete. See how Jesus resisted Satan's temptations by using the truth of God's Word. That is a good lesson for us when Satan tries to lead us into sin and away from God. We too need to know God's Word so that we can use it to resist our enemy.

Matthew 4:1-11

What are some of the arguments Satan uses to try to get you to fall into temptation? What words of God do you find helpful for resisting those false arguments?

Luther

We have most briefly presented the meaning of this article . . . what we receive from God, and what we owe in return. This is a most excellent knowledge but a far greater treasure. For here we see how the Father has given himself to us, together with all creatures, and has most richly provided for us in this life. We see that He has overwhelmed us with unspeakable, eternal treasures by his Son and the Holy Spirit, as we shall hear [Colossians 2:2]. (Large Catechism, II, par. 24)

All Mankind Fell in Adam's Fall (Stanzas 1,2,4)

All mankind fell in Adam's fall;
One common sin infects us all.
From one to all the curse descends,
And over all God's wrath impends.

Through all our pow'rs corruption creeps
And us in dreadful bondage keeps;
In guilt we draw our infant breath
And reap its fruits of woe and death.

But Christ, the second Adam, came
To bear our sin and woe and shame,
To be our life, our light, our way,
Our only hope, our only stay.

THE SECOND ARTICLE

Redemption

I believe in Jesus Christ, his only Son, our Lord, who was conceived by the Holy Spirit, born of the virgin Mary, suffered under Pontius Pilate, was crucified, died, and was buried. He descended into hell. The third day he rose again from the dead. He ascended into heaven and is seated at the right hand of God the Father almighty. From there he will come to judge the living and the dead.

What does this mean?

I believe that Jesus Christ, true God, begotten of the Father from eternity, and also true man, born of the virgin Mary, is my Lord.

He has redeemed me, a lost and condemned creature, purchased and won me from all sins, from death, and from the power of the devil, not with gold or silver but with his holy, precious blood and with his innocent suffering and death.

All this he did that I should be his own, and live under him in his kingdom, and serve him in everlasting righteousness, innocence, and blessedness, just as he has risen from death and lives and rules eternally.

This is most certainly true.

GOD AND MAN

Christ's Person

Who is your master? Adam and Eve had a master, and then they met someone who wanted to be their new master. "I'm your friend," suggested the devil. But it was not the truth. The first humans obeyed him, only to discover that he was the very worst of enemies. He turned them away from God and all of God's love and blessings. As a result, all of us by nature are under the power of that master and are slaves to sin and death. But, in love, God did not abandon us. With the Second Article, we are reminded of how Jesus set us free from Satan so that we might serve a different and far superior Master.

144. Who is the second person of the Trinity?

1 John 5:20 We know that the *Son of God* has come and has given us understanding so that we may know him who is true. And we are in him who is true, in his Son, Jesus Christ. He is the *true God* and eternal life.

1 Timothy 2:5 There is one God and one mediator between God and mankind, *the man Christ Jesus.*

The second person of the Trinity is Jesus Christ, the Son of God, true God and true man.

145. How do we know Jesus Christ is true God?

Matthew 1:23 "Look, the virgin will be with child and will give birth to a son. And *they will name him Immanuel,*" which means, "God with us."

Luke 2:11 Today in the town of David, a Savior was born for you. *He is Christ the Lord.*

Romans 9:5 Theirs are the patriarchs, and from them, according to the flesh, came *the Christ, who is God over all,* eternally blessed. Amen.

John 20:26-28 After eight days, his disciples were inside again, and Thomas was with them. Though the doors were locked, Jesus came and stood among them. "Peace be with you," he said. Then he said to Thomas, "Put your finger here and look at my hands. Take your hand and put it into my side. Do not continue to doubt, but believe." Thomas answered him, *"My Lord and my God!"*

John 3:16 God so loved the world that *he gave his only-begotten Son,* that whoever believes in him shall not perish, but have eternal life.

The Bible clearly teaches that Jesus is God and often uses divine names for Jesus. These divine names aren't simply titles of honor. They tell us who Jesus is.

Matthew 28:18-20 Jesus approached and spoke to them saying, "*All authority in heaven and on earth has been given to me. . . . And surely I am with you always* until the end of the age." (Omnipotent, Omnipresent)

John 1:1,2 In the beginning was the Word, and the Word was with God, and the Word was God. He was with God in the beginning. (Eternal)

John 1:43-51 (Jesus knew all about Nathanael without being told.) (Omniscient)

John 21:17 He asked him the third time, "Simon, son of John, do you care about me?" Peter was grieved because Jesus asked him the third time, "Do you care about me?" He answered, "*Lord, you know* *all things.* You know that I care about you." "Feed my sheep," Jesus said. (Omniscient)

John 4:1-26 (Jesus knew all about the life of the Samaritan woman.) (Omniscient)

Hebrews 13:8 Jesus Christ is *the same yesterday and today and forever.* (Unchangeable)

Jesus has the characteristics of God.

John 2:1-11 (Jesus performed his first miracle, turning water into wine.)

Matthew 8:23-27 (Jesus calmed the storm.)

Mark 5:1-20 (Jesus freed a man who was possessed by demons.)

John 11:38-44 (Jesus raised Lazarus.)

Romans 1:4 [He] in the spirit of holiness was declared to be God's powerful Son by his resurrection from the dead—Jesus Christ, our Lord.

Matthew 9:6 "So that you may know that *the Son of Man has authority on earth to forgive sins,*" he then said to the paralyzed man, "Get up, take your stretcher, and go home."

Jesus does things only God can do.

John 5:22,23 The Father judges no one, but has entrusted all judgment to the Son, so that all should honor the Son just as they honor the Father. *Whoever does not honor the Son does not honor the Father who sent him.*

Hebrews 1:6 *When he brought his firstborn into the world, he said: Let all God's angels worship him.*

Philippians 2:10 *At the name of Jesus every knee will bow,* in heaven and on earth and under the earth.

Revelation 5:13 I also heard every creature that is in heaven and on earth and under the earth and on the sea, and all that is in them, saying: To him who sits on the throne and to the Lamb *be blessing and honor and glory and might forever and ever.*

Jesus is worshiped as God. We are commanded to honor and worship him as well.

146. How do we know that Jesus is true man?

Hebrews 2:14 Since the children share flesh and blood, *he also shared the same flesh and blood,* so that through death he could destroy the one who had the power of death (that is, the Devil).

Acts 17:31 He has set a day on which he is going to judge the world in righteousness *by the man he appointed.* He provided proof of this to everyone by raising him from the dead.

Romans 1:3 This gospel is about his Son—*who in the flesh was born a descendant of David.*

Romans 9:5 Theirs are the patriarchs, and from them, *according to the flesh, came the Christ,* who is God over all, eternally blessed. Amen.

Matthew 26:2 You know that after two days it will be the Passover, and the Son of Man will be handed over to be crucified.

The Bible reveals that Jesus is a man.

Galatians 4:4 When the set time had fully come, God sent his Son to be *born of a woman,* so that he would be born under the law.

Luke 2:12 This will be a sign for you: *You will find a baby* wrapped in swaddling cloths and lying in a manger.

Luke 24:39 Look at my hands and my feet. It is I myself. Touch me and see, because a ghost does not have flesh and bones as you see that I have.

Matthew 26:38 Then he said to them, "*My soul* is very sorrowful, even to the point of death. Stay here, and keep watch with me."

As true man, Jesus had a body and soul.

Matthew 4:2 After he had fasted forty days and forty nights, he was *hungry.*

Mark 4:38 Jesus himself was in the stern, *sleeping* on a cushion. They woke him and said, "Teacher, don't you care that we are about to drown?"

Luke 2:40 The child *grew and became strong.* He was filled with wisdom, and God's favor was on him.

John 11:35 Jesus *wept.*

John 19:28 After this, knowing that everything had now been finished, and to fulfill the Scripture, Jesus said, *"I thirst."*

Mark 15:37 Jesus cried out with a loud voice and *breathed his last.*

Jesus had normal, but sinless, human feelings. He died.

147. How did God's Son become man?

Luke 1:26-38 (Jesus' birth is announced.)

Matthew 1:20 As he was considering these things, an angel of the Lord suddenly appeared to him in a dream and said, "Joseph, son of David, do not be afraid to take Mary home as your wife, because the child conceived in her is from the Holy Spirit."

Matthew 1:22,23 All this happened to fulfill what was spoken by the Lord through the prophet: "Look, the virgin will be with child and will give birth to a son. And they will name him Immanuel," which means, "God with us."

Jesus became a man through the miracle of the virgin birth. Mary had no sexual relations before Jesus was born. Through the power of the Holy Spirit, she conceived and gave birth to a son, Jesus. We call the truth that the Son of God took a human nature upon himself the *incarnation.*

When Jesus ascended into heaven, he didn't cease being true man. He will remain true God and true man forever.

Jesus Christ is true God and true man in one person. God didn't reveal that truth simply to satisfy our curiosity. It is extremely important that we know this.

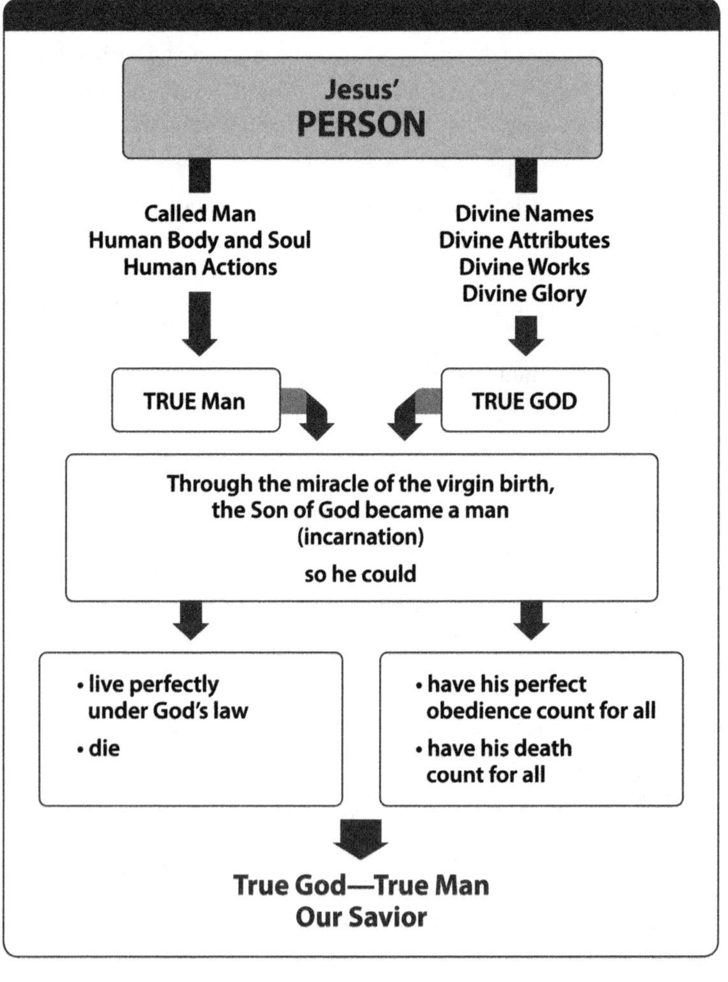

148. Why is it necessary for our salvation that Jesus is true God and true man?

Galatians 4:4,5 When the set time had fully come, God sent his Son to be born of a woman, so that he would be born under the law, in order to redeem those under the law, *so that we would be adopted as sons.*

Romans 5:19 Just as through the disobedience of one man the many became sinners, so also *through the obedience of one man the many will become righteous.*

It was necessary for Jesus to be both God and man so that he could be subject to God's law and keep all the commandments perfectly in the place of all humanity. This is called Christ's *active obedience.*

John 1:29 The next day, John saw Jesus coming toward him and said, "Look! The Lamb of God, *who takes away the sin of the world!*"

Hebrews 2:14 Since the children share flesh and blood, *he also shared the same flesh and blood, so that through death he could destroy the one who had the power of death* (that is, the Devil).

Psalm 49:7,8 No one can by any means redeem himself. He cannot give God a ransom for himself[.] (Yes, the ransom for their souls is costly. Any payment would fall short.)

Mark 10:45 The Son of Man did not come to be served, but to serve, and *to give his life as a ransom for many.*

Romans 3:23,24 *All* have sinned and fall short of the glory of God *and are justified freely by his grace through the redemption that is in Christ Jesus.*

Galatians 3:13 *Christ redeemed us from the curse of the law by becoming a curse for us.* As it is written, "Cursed is everyone who hangs on a tree."

2 Timothy 1:10 [Grace] has now been revealed through the appearance of our Savior *Christ Jesus, who abolished death and brought life and immortality to light* through the gospel.

It was necessary for Jesus to be both God and man so that he could die and so that his death could count for everyone, as a ransom for us from death. This is called Christ's *passive obedience.*

CONNECTIONS

During the three years of Jesus' ministry, he performed many miracles. Though his miracles always brought blessings to people, his purpose for performing them was greater than simply to help people who were in need. His miracles were meant to show everyone that he was the Son of

God, just as he claimed. The disciples witnessed many miracles. It was important for them to understand that Jesus is true man and true God.

John 21:1-14

Think of a person who is going through a serious challenge in his or her life. It could be that the person is very sick, is facing financial challenges, or is grieving the death of someone they love. In what different ways could the knowledge that Jesus is true God and true man be comforting to that person?

Luther

Here [the Second Article] we learn to know the Second Person of the Godhead. We see what we have from God over and above the temporal goods mentioned before [the First Article]. We see how he has completely poured forth himself and withheld nothing from us. Now this article is very rich and broad. But in order to explain it briefly . . . we shall take up one phrase and sum up the entire article. As we have said, we may learn from this article how we have been redeemed. We shall base this on these words, "In Jesus Christ, our Lord." (Large Catechism, II, par. 26)

Savior of the Nations, Come (Stanzas 1,2)

Savior of the nations, come;
Virgin's Son, make here your home.
Marvel now, O heav'n and earth,
That the Lord chose such a birth.

Not by human flesh and blood,
By the Spirit of our God
Was the Word of God made flesh,
Woman's offspring, pure and fresh.

Christ's Offices

In many parts of the world, Christians suffer persecution. Some are killed for their faith. Why are people willing to follow Jesus if in following him they endure suffering?

The answer is that they grasp the significance of what Jesus has done for them and they sincerely appreciate what he is still doing.

We refer to the special roles Jesus filled, or the services Jesus came to perform, as his *offices.*

The Second Article helps us understand the important offices the heavenly Father gave to his Son.

Our study of the offices of Christ will help us grow in our appreciation for what Christ has done and is doing for us.

A CLOSER LOOK

His Names Declare His Purpose

When the angel explained to Joseph that the child in Mary's womb was the Son of God, the angel said that they should name him Jesus "because he will save his people from their sins." (*Jesus* means "the Lord Saves" or "Savior.")

The Bible often uses the name *Christ* along with Jesus. To our ears, that sounds like a last name. But actually it is a title. *Christ* is the Greek word for "anointed." It is equivalent to the Hebrew word *Messiah.* The title *Christ* tells us that the heavenly Father anointed Jesus for special work.

Prophet, Priest, and King

149. To *anoint* means "to pour or sprinkle oil on a person's body." **What was the significance of anointing throughout the Old Testament?**

1 Kings 19:16 *You will also anoint Jehu* son of Nimshi *as king* over Israel *and Elisha* son of Shaphat from Abel Meholah *as prophet in your place.*

Exodus 30:30 *You shall anoint Aaron and his sons* and set them apart, so that they may minister to me *in the priest's office.*

1 Samuel 16:13 *So Samuel took the horn of oil and anointed him* in the presence of his brothers. The Spirit of the Lord rushed on David with power from that day forward.

Throughout the Old Testament, people were anointed with oil to show that they had been set apart for special positions or offices—as prophets, priests, or kings.

150. To what office was Christ anointed?

Deuteronomy 18:15 *The LORD your God will raise up for you a prophet* like me from among you, from your brother Israelites. Listen to him.

Hebrews 3:1 Holy brothers, who share in the heavenly calling, focus your attention on *Jesus, the apostle and high priest* whom we confess.

Isaiah 9:6,7 To us a child is born. To us a son is given. *The authority to rule will rest on his shoulders.* He will be named: Wonderful Counselor, Mighty God, Everlasting Father, *Prince of Peace.* There will be no limit to his authority and no end to the peace he brings. He will rule on David's throne and over his kingdom, to establish it and to uphold it with justice and righteousness from now on, into eternity. The zeal of the LORD of Armies will accomplish this.

Psalm 2 (The one enthroned in heaven terrifies the kings of the earth, saying, "I have installed my King on Zion, my holy mountain" [verse 6].)

John 18:37 "You are a king then?" Pilate asked. Jesus answered, "I am, as you say, a king. For this reason I was born, and for this reason I came into the world, to testify to the truth. Everyone who belongs to the truth listens to my voice."

151. What were the Old Testament prophets anointed to do?

Jeremiah 1:7 The LORD said to me, "Do not say, 'I am only a child.' You must go to everyone to whom I send you and *say whatever I command you.*"

Acts 3:18 In this way God fulfilled what he had foretold through the mouth of all the prophets: *that his Christ would suffer.*

Prophets were to speak God's Word to the people, especially the good news of the coming Savior.

152. How did Jesus serve as prophet while he was on earth?

Isaiah 61:1 The Spirit of the LORD God is upon me, because the LORD has anointed me *to preach good news* to the afflicted. He sent me to bind up the brokenhearted, *to proclaim freedom for the captives* and release for those who are bound.

Matthew 17:5 While he was still speaking, suddenly a bright cloud overshadowed them. Just then, a voice came out of the cloud, saying, "This is my Son, whom I love; with him I am well pleased. *Listen to him.*"

Luke 8:1 Soon afterward Jesus was traveling from one town and village to another, *preaching and proclaiming the good news of the kingdom of God.* The Twelve were with him.

Mark 1:38 [Jesus] told them, "Let's go somewhere else, to the neighboring villages, *so that I can preach* there too. In fact, that is why I have come."

John 6:68 Simon Peter answered him, "Lord, to whom will we go? *You have the words of eternal life.*"

153. How does Jesus continue to serve as prophet even now?

Ephesians 4:11,12 *[Christ] himself gave the apostles, as well as the prophets, as well as the evangelists, as well as the pastors and teachers,* for the purpose of training the saints for the work of serving, in order to build up the body of Christ.

Mark 16:15 *He said to them, "Go into all the world and preach the gospel to all creation."*

Luke 10:16 *Whoever listens to you listens to me.* Whoever rejects you rejects me. And whoever rejects me rejects the one who sent me.

2 Corinthians 5:20 *We are ambassadors for Christ,* inasmuch as God is making an appeal through us. We urge you, on Christ's behalf: Be reconciled to God.

154. What were the Old Testament priests anointed to do?

Exodus 30:30 *You shall anoint* Aaron and his sons and set them apart, *so that they may minister to me in the priest's office.*

Hebrews 5:1 Every high priest is chosen from the people and *is appointed to represent the people in the things pertaining to God, so that he may offer gifts, as well as sacrifices, for sins.*

Leviticus 16 (The high priest and the great Day of Atonement portrayed the atonement accomplished for us by Christ.)

A CLOSER LOOK

Before God established laws of worship on Mount Sinai, believers often worshiped God by offering sacrifices. God's design for their worship in the tabernacle, and later in the temple, included sacrifices that were to remind the Old Testament worshipers that they were sinners and that sin is serious. The sacrifices reminded them that they needed a substitute to make the payment that would do away with the guilt of their sin. The sacrifices taught them that it would be through the shedding of blood that their guilt would be removed.

The shedding of the blood of animals could never pay for sin by itself. The sacrifice of animals pointed to the coming Savior, the Christ, whose perfect sacrifice would take away the guilt of their sins.

When people wanted to make a sacrifice to God, they couldn't do it on their own. They needed someone to represent them, a priest. The need for a priest was yet another reminder that sin separated people from God.

One of the priests was set apart and anointed as high priest. He wore special vestments (clothing) that symbolized purity, set him apart from the others, and reminded him that he represented God's people. Also in other ways, he was removed from the life of the rest of the people.

Every human high priest was sinful. Jesus, however, was perfect and holy. He offered the perfect sacrifice that took away the sins of the world.

---

155. How did Christ serve as High Priest while he was on earth?

John 1:29 The next day, John saw Jesus coming toward him and said, "Look! The *Lamb of God, who takes away the sin of the world!*"

Ephesians 5:2 Walk in love, just as Christ loved us and *gave himself for us, as a fragrant offering and sacrifice to God.*

Hebrews 7:26,27 This is certainly the kind of high priest we needed: one who is holy, innocent, pure, separated from sinners, and exalted above the heavens. Unlike the other high priests, he does not need to offer sacrifices on a daily basis, first for his own sins and then for the sins of the people. In fact, *he sacrificed for sins once and for all when he offered himself.*

2 Corinthians 5:19 *God was in Christ reconciling the world to himself,* not counting their trespasses against them. And he has entrusted to us the message of reconciliation.

156. How does Jesus continue to serve as High Priest even now?

1 Timothy 2:5,6 There is one God and *one mediator between God and mankind, the man Christ Jesus,* who gave himself as a ransom for all, the testimony given at the proper time.

1 John 2:1,2 *If anyone does sin, we have an Advocate before the Father: Jesus Christ, the Righteous One.* He is the atoning sacrifice for our sins, and not only for ours but also for the whole world.

Hebrews 2:17,18 For this reason, he had to become like his brothers in every way, in order that he would be a merciful and faithful high priest in the things pertaining to God, so that he could pay for the sins of the people. Indeed, because he suffered when he was tempted, *he is able to help those who are being tempted.*

Jesus pleads for us by virtue of the sacrifice he made for us.

A CLOSER LOOK

Atonement refers to Christ's work of reconciling God and people. Christ did this by giving his life as a sacrifice to pay for the guilt of our sins. He did this vicariously, that is, as our substitute. He kept God's law in our place and died the death we deserved to die. His sacrifice was not for himself but for us and for the whole world **(vicarious atonement).**

---

157. What were the Old Testament kings anointed to do?

1 Samuel 8:20 *We also can be like all the nations, and* our king *can judge us and lead us out to fight our battles.*

1 Samuel 9:17 When Samuel saw Saul, the LORD told him, "There, that is the man I was talking about! *He will exercise authority over my people.*"

1 Samuel 16:12,13 (Samuel anointed David to be king.)

158. How did Christ serve as King while he was on earth?

Hebrews 2:14 Since the children share flesh and blood, he also shared the same flesh and blood, so that *through death he could destroy the one who had the power of death* (that is, the Devil).

1 Corinthians 15:56,57 The sting of death is sin, and the power of sin is the law. But thanks be to God, *who gives us the victory through our Lord Jesus Christ!*

1 Corinthians 6:20 *You were bought at a price.* Therefore glorify God with your body.

Jesus conquered sin, death, and the devil and gave us the victory.

159. How does Jesus continue to serve as King even now?

Matthew 28:18,19 Jesus approached and spoke to them saying, "*All authority in heaven and on earth has been given to me. Therefore go and gather disciples from all nations.*"

Luke 17:21 *The kingdom of God is within you.*

John 18:36,37 Jesus replied, "*My kingdom is not of this world.* If my kingdom were of this world, my servants would fight so that I would not be handed over to the Jews. But now my kingdom is not from here." "You are a king then?" Pilate asked. Jesus answered, "*I am, as you say, a king. For this reason I was born, and for this reason I came into the world, to testify to the truth. Everyone who belongs to the truth listens to my voice.*"

Acts 20:28 *Always keep watch over yourselves and over the whole flock in which the Holy Spirit has placed you as overseers, to shepherd the church of God, which he purchased with his own blood.*

Jesus brings new souls under his gracious rule and preserves them in faith through the proclamation of the Word (kingdom of grace).

Psalm 2 (The heavenly Father has established his Son as the King who rules over the world.)

Romans 14:9 For this reason [Christ] died, rose, and lived, to be *Lord of both the dead and the living.*

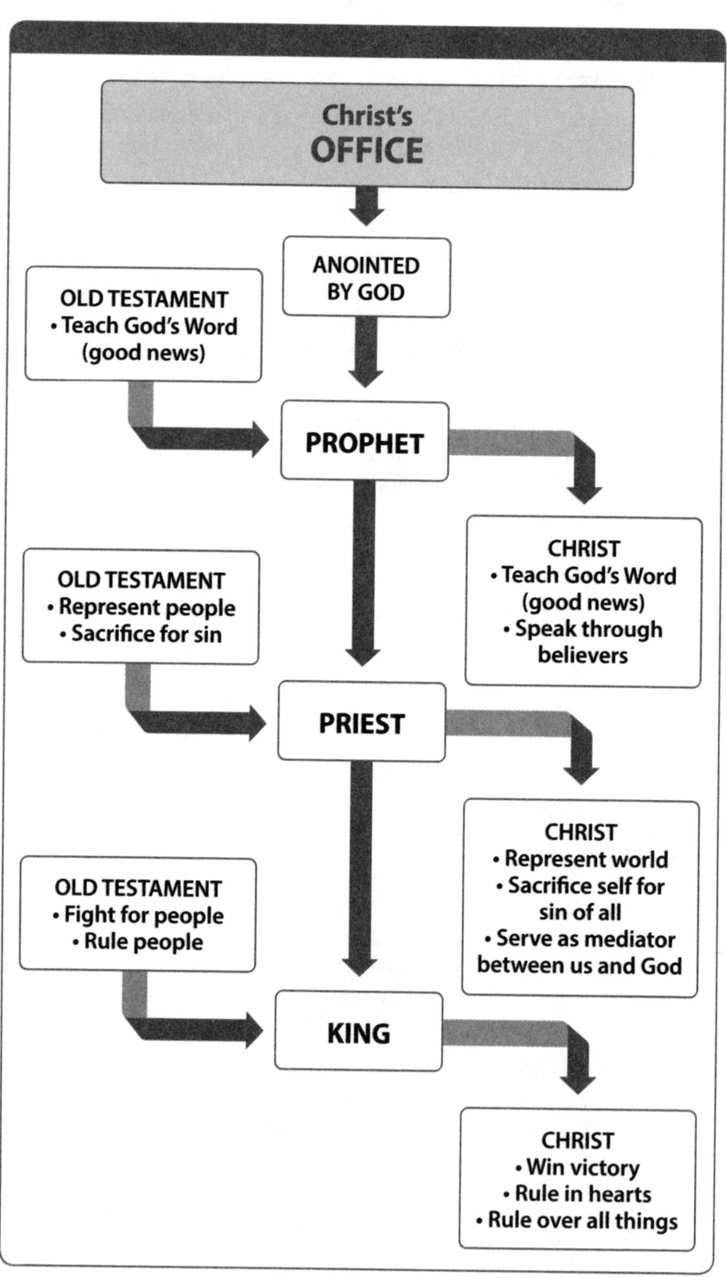

2 Timothy 4:18 The Lord will rescue me from every evil work and will bring me safely into his heavenly kingdom. To him be the glory forever and ever. Amen.

Romans 8:28 We know that *all things work together for the good of those who love God,* for those who are called according to his purpose.

Jesus rules over all things (kingdom of power) for the good of the church.

Revelation 7:14-17 (Jesus rules for the perfect blessing and enjoyment of those who are with him in heaven [kingdom of glory].)

CONNECTIONS

As Christians, we focus on the cross and the empty tomb. There we see Jesus as he paid a great price for our sins. There we receive the assurance of our forgiveness. There we find our hope. There we have reason for our joy.

In the shadow of the cross and in the light of the empty tomb, we see the focus of Jesus' work as Prophet, Priest, and King.

As you read the account of Jesus' suffering and death, take note that what happened to Jesus didn't happen because God lost control of the world. Just the opposite. What happened was in fulfillment of the very promises he had made through the prophets of long ago. It happened exactly as God had said it would happen. And Jesus offered himself willingly as a sacrifice for the sins of all people. Even in his humble suffering, Jesus was ruling over the events of the day in order to accomplish the redemption of the world.

Matthew 26:30–28:10

Think of a time when you were discouraged because of disappointing events that were happening in your life. Describe how the reminder of Christ's work as Prophet, Priest, and King could have been a great source of encouragement at that time.

Luther

The devil came and led us into disobedience, sin, death, and all evil. So we fell under God's wrath and displeasure and were doomed to eternal damnation, just as we had merited and deserved. . . . [The eternal Son of God] came from heaven to help us. . . . He has delivered us poor, lost people from hell's jaws, has won us, has made us free, and has brought us again into the Father's favor and grace. He has taken us as his own property under his shelter and protection so that he may govern us by his righteousness, wisdom, power, life, and blessedness. (Large Catechism, II, par. 28-30)

Stricken, Smitten, and Afflicted (Stanzas 1,3)
Stricken, smitten, and afflicted, See him dying on the tree!
'Tis the Christ, by man rejected; Yes, my soul, 'tis he, 'tis he.
'Tis the long-expected Prophet, David's Son, yet David's Lord;
Proofs I see sufficient of it: 'Tis the true and faithful Word.

If you think of sin but lightly Nor suppose the evil great,
Here you see its nature rightly, Here its guilt may estimate.
Mark the sacrifice appointed; See who bears the awful load—
'Tis the Word, the Lord's Anointed, Son of Man and Son of God.

REDEMPTION

Christ's Work

The Bible tells us so much about Jesus, our Redeemer. But what would our lives be like without Jesus? If we did not know that Jesus had redeemed us from sin, death, and hell, how would we handle sickness and pain? Because God gave his only Son for us, he will love and care for us no matter what challenges we face (Romans 8:31,32). Jesus has shown us he loves us and knows even how many hairs we have on our heads. When we are afraid, has not Jesus promised to be with us always? Jesus promises to take us to heaven when we die. Where else can we find that sure hope except in the one who redeemed us?

The Second Article of the Apostles' Creed reminds us of the work Jesus came to do because he loves us.

Our Redemption

160. To appreciate fully the work Jesus accomplished for us, we must first understand what we were without him. **What was our spiritual condition by nature, without Jesus?**

> **Ephesians 2:1** You were *dead in your trespasses and sins.*
>
> **Romans 3:23** All have sinned and *fall short of the glory of God.*
>
> **Romans 7:18,19,21** I know that *good does not live in me,* that is, in my sinful flesh. The desire to do good is present with me, but I am not able to carry it out. So I fail to do the good I want to do. Instead, the evil I do not want to do, that is what I keep doing. So I find this law at work: When I want to do good, evil is present with me.
>
> **John 8:34** Jesus answered, "Amen, Amen, I tell you: Everyone who keeps committing sin is *a slave to sin.*"
>
> **Romans 5:12** Sin entered the world through one man and death through sin, *so also death spread to all people* because all sinned.
>
> **1 John 3:8** *The one who continues to sin is of the Devil,* because the Devil has been sinning from the beginning.

We are born spiritually dead. By nature we are slaves to sin, death, and the devil. The explanation of the Second Article summarizes this spiritual condition with the words "lost and condemned."

161. Christ's purpose in coming to earth and becoming a man was to free us from slavery to our sinful natures and the condemnation we deserve because of our guilt. **What did Jesus do in order to free us?**

Galatians 4:4,5 When the set time had fully come, God sent his Son to be born of a woman, so that he would be born under the law, in order *to redeem* those under the law, so that we would be adopted as sons.

Romans 5:19 Just as through the disobedience of one man the many became sinners, so also through the obedience of one man *the many will become righteous.*

Galatians 3:13 Christ *redeemed us* from the curse of the law by becoming a curse for us. As it is written, "Cursed is everyone who hangs on a tree."

1 Corinthians 15:3 I delivered to you as of first importance what I also received: that *Christ died for our sins* in accordance with the Scriptures.

1 John 2:2 He is the *atoning sacrifice for our sins,* and not only for ours but also for the whole world.

Romans 4:25 [Jesus our Lord] was handed over to death because of our trespasses and was raised to life *because of our justification.*

In order to free us, Christ kept God's law perfectly (active obedience), gave his life as the sacrifice for sin (passive obedience), and rose from the dead.

162. What do we call the work of Jesus in freeing us from slavery to sin, death, and the devil?

Hebrews 9:15 For this reason, he is the mediator of a new covenant. *A death took place as payment* for the trespasses committed under the first covenant, so that those who are called would receive the promised eternal inheritance.

Hebrews 9:12 He entered once into the Most Holy Place and obtained *eternal redemption,* not by the blood of goats and calves, but by his own blood.

A CLOSER LOOK

Ransom: A ransom is a payment given to free someone who is held captive. We sometimes hear the term when a person is being held hostage. His captors want something given to them in exchange for releasing the hostage, a ransom.

Jesus paid the ransom price necessary to free us from captivity to sin, death, and the devil.

We call Christ's work of ransoming all people from slavery to sin, death, and the devil **redemption.**

163. A ransom is often paid with money. However, gold or silver could not cover the cost to ransom our souls. **What ransom price did Jesus need to pay for our redemption?**

> **Matthew 20:28** The Son of Man did not come to be served, but to serve, and *to give his life as a ransom* for many.
>
> **Isaiah 53:5** It was because of our rebellion that he was *pierced.* He was *crushed* for the guilt our sins deserved. The punishment that brought us peace was upon him, and by *his wounds* we are healed.
>
> **1 Peter 1:18,19** You know that you were redeemed from your empty way of life handed down to you from your forefathers, *not with things that pass away,* such as silver or gold, *but with the precious blood of Christ,* like a lamb without blemish or spot.
>
> **Ephesians 1:7** In him we also have *redemption through his blood,* the forgiveness of sins, in keeping with the riches of his grace.
>
> **Revelation 1:5,6** . . . from Jesus Christ, the faithful witness, the firstborn from the dead, and the ruler of the kings of the earth. To him who loves us and has *freed us from our sins by his own blood* and made us a kingdom and priests to God his Father—to him be the glory and the power forever. Amen.

Christ suffered and died as the ransom payment for our redemption ("with his holy, precious blood and with his innocent suffering and death").

164. Why do we call Christ's blood holy and precious?

> **Hebrews 7:26,27** This is certainly the kind of high priest we needed: one who is holy, innocent, pure, separated from sinners, and exalted above the heavens. Unlike the other high priests, he does not need to offer sacrifices on a daily basis, first for his own sins and then for the sins of the people. In fact, *he sacrificed for sins once and for all when he offered himself.*
>
> **1 Peter 1:18,19** *You were redeemed* from your empty way of life handed down to you from your forefathers, not with things that pass away, such as silver or gold, but *with the precious blood of Christ,* like a lamb without blemish or spot.
>
> **1 John 1:7** If we walk in the light, just as he is in the light, we have fellowship with one another, and *the blood of Jesus Christ, his Son, cleanses us from all sin.*

Christ's blood is holy because it is the blood of God's perfect Son. It is precious because it paid the full ransom price for the sins of all people.

165. What does it mean that Christ's suffering and death were innocent?

2 Corinthians 5:21 God made him, *who did not know sin,* to become sin for us, so that we might become the righteousness of God in him.

Hebrews 4:15 We do not have a high priest who is unable to sympathize with our weaknesses, but one who has been tempted in every way, just as we are, *yet was without sin.*

166. What do we mean when we say that our Lord Jesus Christ "purchased and won me from all sins, from death, and from the power of the devil"?

"From all sins"

Colossians 2:13 When you were dead in your trespasses and the uncircumcision of your flesh, *God made you alive with Christ by forgiving us all our trespasses.*

John 8:34,36 Jesus answered, "Amen, Amen, I tell you: Everyone who keeps committing sin is *a slave to sin.* So if *the Son sets you free,* you really will be free."

Romans 8:1 There is now *no condemnation for those who are in Christ Jesus.*

Through his work of redemption, Christ paid the ransom price that frees us from the guilt of our sins and the punishment we deserve because of our sins.

"From death"

1 Corinthians 15:54,57 Death is swallowed up in victory. But thanks be to God, who gives us *the victory through our Lord Jesus Christ!*

John 11:25,26 Jesus said to her, "I am the resurrection and the life. Whoever believes in me will live, even if he dies. And *whoever lives and believes in me will never perish.* Do you believe this?"

2 Timothy 1:10 Our Savior Christ Jesus . . . *abolished death and brought life and immortality* to light through the gospel.

Our Lord Jesus Christ has freed us from the punishment of eternal death. Even though we will experience temporal death, we will rise to live forever. (See question 139 to review the three kinds of death.)

"From the power of the devil"

1 John 3:8 The one who continues to sin is of the Devil, because the Devil has been sinning from the beginning. This is why the Son of God appeared: *to destroy the works of the Devil.*

Genesis 3:15 I will put hostility between you and the woman, and between your seed and her seed. He will crush your head, and you will crush his heel.

Hebrews 2:14 Since the children share flesh and blood, he also shared the same flesh and blood, so that *through death he could destroy the one who had the power of death (that is, the Devil).*

Revelation 12:10,11 I heard a loud voice in heaven, saying: Now have come the salvation and the power and the kingdom of our God and the authority of his Christ, because *the accuser of our brothers has been thrown down,* the one who accuses them before our God day and night. They conquered him because of the blood of the Lamb and because of the word of their testimony. They did not love their lives in the face of death.

Christ's redemption has freed us from slavery to the devil's temptations and from the power of his accusations.

167. Christ has redeemed us from slavery to sin, death, and the devil. Yet it is obvious that we still experience the consequences of sin in pain and suffering and that we will still die. **In what way has Christ's redemption changed our attitude toward these things?**

Hebrews 12:6,11 *The Lord disciplines the one whom he loves,* and he corrects every son he accepts. No discipline seems pleasant when it is happening, but painful, yet later it yields a peaceful harvest of righteousness for those who have been trained by it.

1 Peter 1:6,7 Because of this you rejoice very much, even though now for a little while, if necessary, you have been grieved by various kinds of trials so that *the proven character of your faith*—which is more valuable than gold, which passes away even though it is tested by fire—may be found to result in praise, glory, and honor when Jesus Christ is revealed.

Romans 5:3,4 Not only this, but we also rejoice confidently in our sufferings, because we know that suffering produces patient endurance, and patient endurance produces tested character, and tested character produces hope.

Romans 8:35-37 What will separate us from the love of Christ? Will trouble or distress or persecution or famine or nakedness or danger or sword? Just as it is written: For your sake we are being put to death all day long. We are considered as sheep to be slaughtered. No, *in all these things we are more than conquerors* through him who loved us.

1 Thessalonians 4:13-18 (Paul comforts us with the truth that believers will waken from death to be with Jesus forever.)

Daniel 12:2 Many who are sleeping in the dusty ground *will awake,* some to everlasting life, and some to shame, to everlasting contempt.

1 Corinthians 15:57 Thanks be to God, *who gives us the victory* through our Lord Jesus Christ!

John 11:25,26 Jesus said to her, "I am the resurrection and the life. *Whoever believes in me will live, even if he dies.* And whoever lives and believes in me will never perish. Do you believe this?"

Christ's accomplished work of redemption assures us that God loves us. Because of his love, we understand that God uses our hardships to train us—for our blessing and his glory. The painful sting of despair has been removed even from death. For believers, death is the gate through which we enter the enjoyment of heaven.

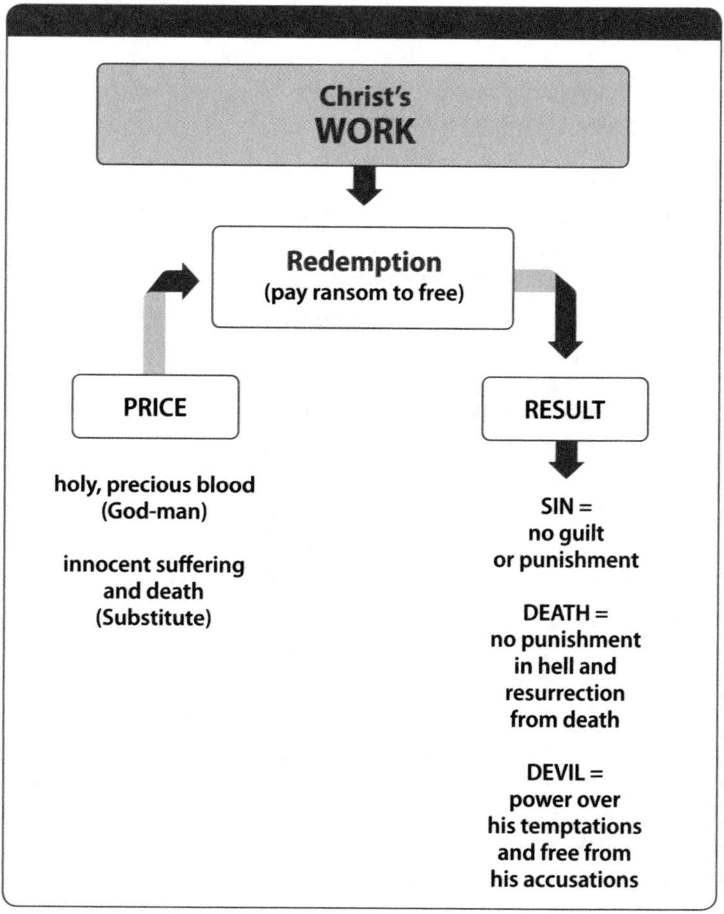

Christ's WORK

↓

Redemption
(pay ransom to free)

PRICE	**RESULT**
holy, precious blood (God-man) **innocent suffering and death (Substitute)**	**SIN = no guilt or punishment** **DEATH = no punishment in hell and resurrection from death** **DEVIL = power over his temptations and free from his accusations**

CONNECTIONS

Because we have grown accustomed to life in a world so corrupted by sin, it is hard for us to comprehend what life could have been like in the perfection of paradise. In Genesis chapter 3, we read of the fall into sin and the consequences that came as a result of sin. Those consequences are a daily reminder of how sin has destroyed the perfect relationship all of us could have enjoyed with God. Perhaps the most poignant reminder of how sin separates us from God is the way God removed Adam and Eve from the Garden of Eden. As you read the account of the fall into sin and its consequences, focus especially on God's promise that he would send a Savior to accomplish the work of redemption.

Genesis 3:1-24

Imagine that you are Adam or Eve and you were just removed from the perfect garden. What two or three things would be most on your mind as you face life in a sinful world?

Jesus has redeemed you by giving you freedom from sin, freedom from death, and freedom from the power of the devil. Choose one of those three freedoms. Explain how remembering that particular freedom helps you live in a sinful world.

Luther

He [Jesus Christ, the Lord of Life] has delivered us poor, lost people from hell's jaws, has won us, has made us free [Romans 8:1-2], and has brought us again into the Father's favor and grace. (Large Catechism, II, par. 30)

Jesus, Your Blood and Righteousness (Stanzas 1,3,4)

Jesus, your blood and righteousness
My beauty are, my glorious dress;
Mid flaming worlds, in these arrayed,
With joy shall I lift up my head.

Lord, I believe your precious blood,
Which at the very throne of God
Forever will for sinners plead,
For me—e'en for my soul—was shed.

Lord, I believe were sinners more
Than sands upon the ocean shore,
You have for all a ransom paid,
For all a full atonement made.

IMMANUEL

Christ's Humiliation and Exaltation

What kinds of things do you try to avoid in your life? Pain? Sickness? Poverty? Suffering? Embarrassment? Situations where your life would be in danger? Circumstances that you know would involve sacrificing something important to you?

Our strong desire to avoid anything unpleasant makes Jesus' work even more remarkable. During his life on earth, Jesus Christ, true God and true man, chose to endure the kinds of things we might go to great lengths to avoid. He did this in order to accomplish our salvation.

However, from the moment Jesus became alive in the tomb, things were different for him. Victory had been won. His time of sacrificing and enduring hardship was done.

In the Second Article, we confess important truths about Christ's life and work of salvation and important truths about what he did and is continuing to do now that his work has been accomplished. These truths describe Christ's humiliation and exaltation.

Christ's State of Humiliation

168. When we speak of Christ's *humiliation,* we aren't using the word as we commonly do, as if someone has done something embarrassing or worthy of shame. **What do we mean when we speak of Christ's humiliation?**

> **Philippians 2:6-8** Though [Christ Jesus] was by nature God, he did not consider equality with God as a prize to be displayed, but he *emptied himself by taking the nature of a servant. When he was born in human likeness,* and his appearance was like that of any other man, *he humbled himself and became obedient to the point of death*—even death on a cross.

> **2 Corinthians 8:9** You know the grace of our Lord Jesus Christ, that *although he was rich, yet for your sakes he became poor,* so that through his poverty you might become rich.

Jesus' life and work, from the time of his conception, were very different from what we would expect for the Son of God. He chose not to make full use of his divine powers. Instead, he voluntarily submitted to a very humble and lowly life that ended with death on a cross.

169. In what ways did Jesus humble himself?

Isaiah 7:14 The Lord himself will give a sign for all of you. Look! *The virgin will conceive and give birth to a son and name him Immanuel.*

Matthew 1:20 As he was considering these things, an angel of the Lord suddenly appeared to him in a dream and said, "Joseph, son of David, do not be afraid to take Mary home as your wife, because *the child conceived in her* is from the Holy Spirit."

Though he is God from eternity, Christ became human when, through the power of the Holy Spirit, he was conceived in the womb of a poor unmarried virgin named Mary.

Luke 2:6,7 While they were there, *the time came for her to give birth. And she gave birth to her firstborn son,* wrapped him in swaddling cloths, and laid him in a manger, because there was no room for them in the inn.

Luke 2:48-51 "Son, why have you treated us this way? See, your father and I have been anxiously looking for you." He said to them, "Why were you looking for me? Did you not know that I must be taking care of my Father's business?" They did not understand what he was telling them. *He went down with them and came to Nazareth. He was always obedient to them.* And his mother treasured up all these things in her heart.

Though he is true God who deserves all glory, he was born, wrapped in strips of cloth, and placed in a manger for his first bed. Though Christ possesses all power, he made himself dependent upon his parents. Though he has the right to rule all the world, he became obedient to his parents as a part of keeping God's law perfectly in our place.

Mark 15:1-20 (Jesus was taken before Pontius Pilate, where he was subjected to a trial; Jesus was flogged, mocked, spit on, crowned with thorns, and sentenced to crucifixion.)

Though he could have overwhelmed Pilate and the soldiers with his glory, walked away from them, or even destroyed them, Jesus willingly suffered their mistreatment in order to be our Savior.

Mark 15:22,24 They brought Jesus to the place called Golgotha, which means, "The place of a skull." *They crucified him.* And they divided his garments, casting lots for them to decide what each of them would take.

Though Christ could have destroyed all of the leaders of the people and the soldiers who played a part in his crucifixion, he willingly went to the cross to die for the sins of the world.

Mark 15:37 Jesus cried out with a loud voice and *breathed his last.*

Though Christ has power to give life and though he alone did not deserve to die, he willingly submitted to death in order to conquer death for us.

Isaiah 53:9 *They would have assigned him a grave with the wicked,* but he was given a grave with the rich in his death, because he had done no violence, and no deceit was in his mouth.

Mark 15:46 Joseph bought a linen cloth, took him down, and wrapped him in the linen cloth. He *laid him in a tomb* that had been cut out of rock, and he rolled a stone against the entrance of the tomb.

Though he is the Lord of life, Christ took his place in the grave as part of his plan to redeem us from sin, death, and the devil.

170. Why did Christ humble himself?

Mark 10:45 Even the Son of Man did not come to be served, but to serve, and *to give his life as a ransom for many.*

2 Corinthians 8:9 You know the grace of our Lord Jesus Christ, that although he was rich, *yet for your sakes he became poor,* so that through his poverty you might become rich.

Christ's State of Exaltation

171. What do we mean when we speak of Christ's exaltation?

John 17:5 *Now, Father, glorify me at your own side with the glory I had at your side before the world existed.*

Philippians 2:9,10 *God also highly exalted him* and gave him the name that is above every name, so that at the name of Jesus every knee will bow, in heaven and on earth and under the earth.

Hebrews 2:9 We look to Jesus (the one who was made lower than the angels for a little while, so that by God's grace he might taste death for everyone), now *crowned with glory and honor,* because he suffered death.

After Christ's work as our Redeemer was accomplished, he once again made full use of his divine power and glory.

172. How was Jesus exalted?

John 2:19 Jesus answered them, "Destroy this temple, and in three days I will raise it up again."

Mark 16:6 He said to them, "Do not be alarmed. You are looking for Jesus the Nazarene, who was crucified. *He has risen!* He is not here. See the place where they laid him."

John 10:17,18 *This is why the Father loves me, because I lay down my life so that I may take it up again.* No one takes it from me, but I lay it down on my own. I have the authority to lay it down, and I have the authority to take it up again. This is the commission I received from my Father.

Christ exercised the power he possessed as God and came to life just as he had said he would.

1 Peter 3:18,19 He was put to death in flesh but was made alive in spirit, in which *he also went and made an announcement to the spirits in prison.*

Colossians 2:15 *After disarming the rulers and authorities, he made a public display of them* by triumphing over them in Christ.

After Jesus came to life, he descended, body and soul, into hell to proclaim his victory to the souls there. Christ showed that the promise God had made in Eden, to crush the serpent's head, was fulfilled when he conquered death.

Acts 1:1-11 (After appearing to his disciples numerous times during a period of 40 days, which was visible and convincing proof that he had risen, Jesus gathered his disciples together. Before their eyes, he was taken up into the clouds. Two angels appeared and assured the disciples that Jesus would one day return in the same way they had seen him go into heaven.)

Mark 16:19 Then the Lord Jesus, after he had spoken to them, *was taken up into heaven* and *sat down at the right hand of God.*

Ephesians 1:19-22 How surpassingly great his power . . . which God worked in Christ when he raised him from the dead and *seated him at his right hand in the heavenly places, far above all rule, authority, power, and dominion,* and above every name that is given, not only in this age but also in the one to come. *God also placed all things under his feet and made him head over everything for the church.*

Christ ascended in the sight of the disciples so that all would know he had returned to the right hand of God in order to rule over all things.

Acts 17:31 *He has set a day on which he is going to judge the world in righteousness by the man he appointed.* He provided proof of this to everyone by raising him from the dead.

Revelation 1:7 *Look, he is coming with clouds, and every eye will see him, including those who pierced him. And all the nations of the earth will mourn because of him.* Yes. Amen.

Matthew 25:31,32 *When the Son of Man comes in his glory, and all the angels with him, he will sit on his glorious throne.* All the nations will be gathered in his presence, and he will separate them one from another, as a shepherd separates the sheep from the goats.

Christ will return to earth on the Last Day, when everyone will see him in his glory.

173. His exaltation reminds us of the precious promises that Jesus made and fulfilled. **What does the truth of Jesus' exaltation mean for us?**

Resurrection

Romans 4:25 He was handed over to death because of our trespasses and was *raised to life because of our justification.*

1 Corinthians 15:17 If Christ has not been raised, your faith is futile; you are still in your sins.

1 Peter 1:3 Blessed be the God and Father of our Lord Jesus Christ! By his great mercy *he gave us a new birth into a living hope through the resurrection of Jesus Christ from the dead.*

John 14:19 In a little while the world will see me no longer, but you will see me. *Because I live, you also will live.*

1 Corinthians 15:22,23 As in Adam they all die, so also *in Christ they all will be made alive.* But each in his own order: Christ as the firstfruits and then Christ's people, at his coming.

Christ's resurrection assures us that he is the Son of God, that our redemption is complete, and that we too will rise from the dead.

Descent Into Hell

1 Peter 3:18,19 He was put to death in flesh but was made alive in spirit, in which *he also went and made an announcement to the spirits in prison.*

Colossians 2:15 After disarming the rulers and authorities, he made a public display of them by triumphing over them in Christ.

Matthew 28:18 All authority in heaven and on earth has been given to me.

Christ's descent into hell assures us that he conquered Satan.

Ascension

John 14:2,3 In my Father's house are many mansions. If it were not so, I would have told you. I am going to prepare a place for you. And if I go and prepare a place for you, I will come again and take you to be with me, so that you may also be where I am.

1 John 2:1,2 My children, I write these things to you so that you will not sin. If anyone does sin, we have an Advocate before the Father: Jesus Christ, the Righteous One. He is the atoning sacrifice for our sins, and not only for ours but also for the whole world.

1 Timothy 2:5 There is one God and *one mediator between God and mankind, the man Christ Jesus.*

When Jesus' work on earth was done, it was time for him to return to his Father. Jesus' ascension assures us that he is preparing an eternal home for us. His ascension comforts us with the knowledge that he is pleading our cases before the Father.

Sitting at the Right Hand of God

Ephesians 1:19-22 How surpassingly great his power is for us who believe . . . as great as the working of his mighty strength, which God worked in Christ when he raised him from the dead and seated him at his right hand in the heavenly places, far above all rule, authority, power, and dominion, and above every name that is given, not only in this age but also in the one to come. *God also placed all things under his feet and made him head over everything for the church.*

Romans 8:28 We know that *all things work together for the good* of those who love God, for those who are called according to his purpose.

We are comforted that Christ is seated at the right hand of God because it assures us that Christ is ruling all things for our good.

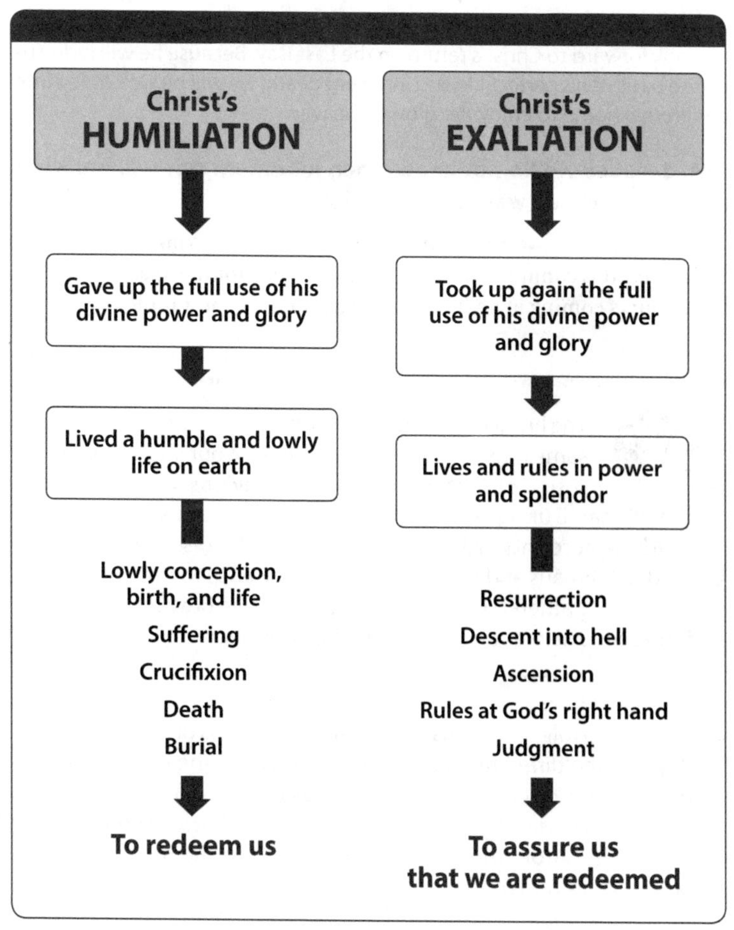

Christ's Return in Judgment

Luke 21:27,28 Then they will see the Son of Man coming in a cloud with power and great glory. But when these things begin to happen, stand up and lift up your heads, because your redemption is near.

Matthew 25:31-34 When the Son of Man comes in his glory, and all the angels with him, he will sit on his glorious throne. All the nations will be gathered in his presence, and he will separate them one from another, as a shepherd separates the sheep from the goats. He will put the sheep on his right and the goats on his left. Then the King will say to those on his right, "Come, you who are blessed by my Father, inherit the kingdom prepared for you from the foundation of the world."

Romans 8:1 *There is now no condemnation for those who are in Christ Jesus.*

We look forward to Christ's return on the Last Day. Because he will judge us on the basis of *his* perfect life and innocent death, we will be welcomed into our eternal home to enjoy the glory of heaven.

174. Because we do not know when judgment day will be, what attitude does God want us to have?

Matthew 24:42,44 *So be alert,* because you do not know on what day your Lord is coming. *You also need to be ready* for this reason: The Son of Man is coming at an hour when you do not expect him.

CONNECTIONS

The humiliation and exaltation of Jesus were part of the same master plan—the salvation of our souls. During Jesus' exaltation, it was very obvious that he was the winner. During Jesus' suffering, victory wasn't so obvious. Read the accounts of Jesus' appearance to the disciples on the road to Emmaus and his subsequent appearance to the disciples who were gathered behind locked doors. Note how Jesus comforted his disciples and overcame their doubts.

Luke 24:13-49
Those who followed Jesus had different reactions on Easter Sunday. List the different reactions, including both the reactions of the Emmaus disciples and the disciples gathered in Jerusalem. What did Jesus say to comfort them? How did Jesus show that he had risen from the grave? List reasons why the resurrection of Jesus is important to you.

Luther

He rose again from the dead, swallowed up and devoured death [1 Corinthians 15:54], and finally ascended into heaven and assumed the government at the Father's right hand [1 Peter 3:22]. He did these things so that the devil and all powers must be subject to him and lie at his feet [Hebrews 10:12-13] until finally, at the Last Day, He will completely divide and separate us from the wicked world, the devil, death, sin, and such [Matthew 25:31-46; 13:24-30,47-50]. (Large Catechism, II, par. 31)

He's Risen, He's Risen (Stanzas 1-3)

He's risen, he's risen, Christ Jesus, the Lord;
He opened death's prison, the incarnate Word.
Break forth, hosts of heaven, in jubilant song
And earth, sea, and mountain the praises prolong.

The foe was triumphant when on Calvary
The Lord of creation was nailed to the tree.
In Satan's domain did the hosts shout and jeer,
For Jesus was slain, whom the evil ones fear.

But short was their triumph; the Savior arose,
And death, hell, and Satan he vanquished, his foes.
The conquering Lord lifts his banner on high;
He lives, yes, he lives, and will nevermore die.

REDEEMED

"That I Should Be His Own"

Think of it. The eternal, all-knowing, and all-powerful God stepped into human history and since then things have never been the same. God took on human flesh. The God-man strapped on human sandals and walked and talked on earth. He lived a humble life. He didn't even have a place to call his home. He was willing to be hated and mistreated. He accepted a painful—and the most shameful—form of death: a cross. And then he rose from the dead. For such an incredible course of events, there must have been a reason. There was.

We Belong to Christ

175. The cost of our redemption was great. It cost Jesus his life. **Why did Jesus redeem us?**

> **1 Timothy 2:4** [God our Savior] wants all people to be saved and to come to the knowledge of the truth.
>
> **2 Corinthians 5:21** God made him, who did not know sin, to become sin for us, *so that we might become the righteousness of God* in him.
>
> **Revelation 5:9** They sang a new song, saying: You are worthy to take the scroll and to open its seals, because you were slain, and *you bought* us *for God* with your blood out of every tribe and language and people and nation.

176. Christ redeemed us so that we should be his own, both now and forever. **What is Christ's goal in making us his own?**

> **Luke 1:68,74,75** Blessed is the Lord, the God of Israel, because he has visited us and prepared redemption for his people . . . to grant deliverance to us from the hand of our enemies, *so that we are able to serve him* without fear, in holiness and righteousness before him all our days.
>
> **Romans 6:6** We know that our old self was crucified with him, to make our sinful body powerless, *so that we would not continue to serve sin.*
>
> **2 Corinthians 5:15** He died for all, so that those who live would *no longer live for themselves but for him, who died in their place* and was raised again.
>
> **Titus 2:14** [Jesus Christ] gave himself for us, to redeem us from all lawlessness and *to purify for himself a people who are his own chosen people, eager to do good works.*

1 Peter 2:9 You are a chosen people, a royal priesthood, a holy nation, the people who are God's own possession, so *that you may proclaim the praises of him who called you out of darkness into his marvelous light.*

Galatians 2:20 I have been crucified with Christ, and *I no longer live, but Christ lives in me.* The life I am now living in the flesh, I live by faith in the Son of God, who loved me and gave himself for me.

Christ made us his own so that we might be freed from slavery to sin to live instead for him ("live under him in his kingdom, and serve him in everlasting righteousness, innocence, and blessedness").

177. How is it possible that our service to God could be considered righteous, innocent, and blessed?

Isaiah 61:10 I will rejoice greatly in the LORD. My soul will celebrate because of my God, for he has clothed me in garments of salvation. *With a robe of righteousness he covered me, like* a bridegroom who wears a beautiful headdress like a priest, and like a bride who adorns herself with her jewelry.

Revelation 7:14 He said to me: These are the ones who are coming out of the great tribulation. *They have washed their robes and made them white in the blood of the Lamb.*

Titus 2:11-13 The grace of God has appeared, bringing salvation to all people. It *trains us to reject ungodliness and worldly lusts and to live self-controlled, upright, and godly lives* in this present age, while we wait for the blessed hope, that is, the glorious appearance of our great God and Savior, Jesus Christ.

Ephesians 4:24 *Put on the new self,* which has been created to be like God in righteousness and true holiness.

Colossians 3:17 Everything you do, whether in word or deed, *do it all in the name of the Lord Jesus, giving thanks to God the Father* through him.

John 12:1-8 (Mary anointed Jesus' feet with perfume as an expression of her love and gratitude.)

Jesus made us righteous by covering us with the robe of his righteousness. (He kept the law in our place and endured the punishment we deserve.) He raises up the new person within us who hates sin and who wants to live a godly life out of thanks to God.

178. Our hearts long for the day when we will be able to serve God without the struggles against our sinful nature. **When will we finally be able to serve in perfect and everlasting righteousness, innocence, and blessedness?**

2 Peter 3:13 According to his promise we look forward to *new heavens and a new earth, in which righteousness dwells.*

Revelation 7:14,15 He said to me: These are the ones who are coming out of the great tribulation. *They have washed their robes and made them white in the blood of the Lamb.* Because of this they are in front of the throne of God, and they *serve him day and night in his temple.* He who sits on the throne will spread his tent over them.

Revelation 14:4,5 They continually follow the Lamb wherever he goes. They were purchased from among mankind as firstfruits for God and the Lamb. And *no lie was found in their mouths. They are blameless.*

179. What gives us confidence that we will one day serve God in the perfection of heaven?

Job 19:25-27 I know that my Redeemer lives, and that at the end of time he will stand over the dust. Then, even after my skin has been destroyed, nevertheless, *in my own flesh I will see God.* I myself will see him. My own eyes will see him, and not as a stranger. My emotions are in turmoil within me.

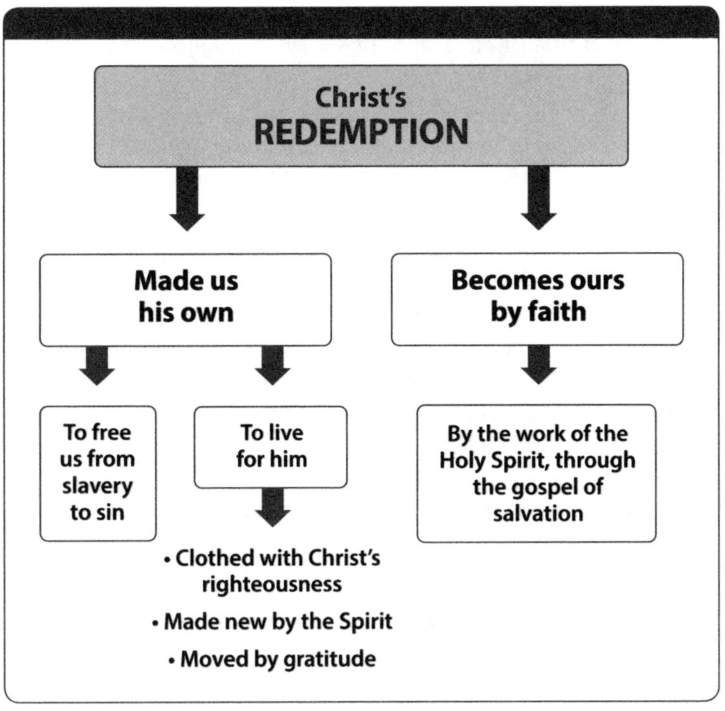

1 Corinthians 15:20 *Christ has been raised from the dead, the firstfruits of those who have fallen asleep.*

John 14:19 In a little while the world will see me no longer, but you will see me. *Because I live, you also will live.*

1 Corinthians 6:14 God raised up the Lord and *will also raise us up* by his power.

Philippians 3:20,21 Our citizenship is in heaven. We are eagerly waiting for a Savior from there, *the Lord Jesus Christ.* By the power that enables him to subject all things to himself, he *will transform our humble bodies to be like his glorious body.*

180. How does the redemption won for us by Christ become our own?

John 3:16 God so loved the world that he gave his only-begotten Son, that *whoever believes* in him shall not perish, but have eternal life.

Romans 10:4 *To everyone who believes,* Christ is the end of the law, resulting in righteousness.

Acts 16:30,31 Then he brought them outside and asked, "Sirs, what must I do to be saved?" They said, "*Believe* in the Lord Jesus and you will be saved, you and your household."

181. How do we come to believe in Jesus?

Romans 10:17 Faith comes from hearing the message, and the message comes through the word of Christ.

1 Corinthians 12:3 I am informing you that no one speaking by God's Spirit says, "A curse be upon Jesus," and no one can say, "Jesus is Lord," except by the Holy Spirit.

CONNECTIONS

When God works faith in a human heart, it changes that person. Before having faith, the person is a slave to sin. Everything the person wants, does, or says demonstrates that slavery. But the new heart is freed from this slavery, belongs to God, and desires to serve God. Zacchaeus was a tax collector who had been a slave to greed. Read how he changed when Jesus made Zacchaeus his own.

Luke 19:1-10

In what ways did Zacchaeus show that his heart was changed? We all struggle because of our sinful nature, but how does the message that you belong to Christ influence your attitude and actions?

Luther

The little word *Lord* means simply the same as *redeemer*. It means the One who has brought us from Satan to God, from death to life, from sin to righteousness, and who preserves us in the same. But all the points that follow in this article serve no other purpose than to explain and express this redemption. They explain how and by whom it was accomplished. They explain how much it cost Him and what He spent and risked so that He might win us and bring us under His dominion. (Large Catechism, II, par. 31)

Take My Life and Let It Be (Stanzas 1,5,6)

Take my life and let it be
Consecrated, Lord, to thee.
Take my moments and my days;
Let them flow in ceaseless praise.

Take my will and make it thine;
It shall be no longer mine.
Take my heart—it is thine own;
It shall be thy royal throne.

Take my love, my Lord, I pour
At thy feet its treasure store.
Take myself, and I will be
Ever, only, all for thee.

THE THIRD ARTICLE

Sanctification

I believe in the Holy Spirit; the holy Christian church, the communion of saints; the forgiveness of sins; the resurrection of the body; and the life everlasting. Amen.

What does this mean?

I believe that I cannot by my own thinking or choosing believe in Jesus Christ, my Lord, or come to him.

But the Holy Spirit has called me by the gospel, enlightened me with his gifts, sanctified and kept me in the true faith. In the same way he calls, gathers, enlightens, and sanctifies the whole Christian church on earth, and keeps it with Jesus Christ in the one true faith.

In this Christian church he daily and fully forgives all sins to me and all believers.

On the Last Day he will raise me and all the dead and give eternal life to me and all believers in Christ.

This is most certainly true.

SANCTIFICATION

The Work of the Holy Spirit

Jesus told his disciples that the time would come when he would no longer be with them visibly after his ascension. He comforted them by promising that he was going to send the Holy Spirit. From what Jesus told them, it was very obvious that the work the Holy Spirit would perform in their lives would be extremely important. As we think of what Jesus told his disciples, we find ourselves asking the questions: What would this important work be? Why is the work of the Holy Spirit so important to us today as well?

182. In the Third Article, we speak of the work of the Holy Spirit. **Who is the Holy Spirit?**

2 Corinthians 13:14 The grace of the Lord Jesus Christ, and the love of God, and the fellowship of the Holy Spirit be with you all.

Matthew 28:19 Go and gather disciples from all nations by baptizing them in the name of the *Father* and of the *Son* and of the *Holy Spirit.*

183. How does the Bible emphasize that the Holy Spirit is God?

Matthew 28:19 Go and gather disciples from all nations by baptizing them in the name of the Father and of the Son and of the *Holy Spirit.*

Acts 5:1-11 (Ananias lied to the members of the early church *and* to the Holy Spirit. See especially verses 3,4.) Peter said, "Ananias, why has Satan filled your heart to lie to the Holy Spirit and to keep back part of the proceeds of the land? Was it not yours before it was sold? And after it was sold, was not the money at your disposal? How could you plan such a thing in your heart? You have not lied to men but to *God.*"

1 Corinthians 3:16 Do you not know that you yourselves are God's temple, and that God's Spirit lives in you?

The Holy Spirit is called God.

Psalm 139:7,8 Where can I go from *your Spirit?* Where can I flee from your Presence? *If I go up to heaven, you are there.* If I make my bed in hell—*there you are!* (Omnipresent)

Hebrews 9:14 How much more will the blood of Christ, who through the *eternal Spirit* offered himself without blemish to God, cleanse our consciences from dead works, so that we worship the living God? (Eternal)

1 Corinthians 2:10 God revealed it to us through his Spirit. For the Spirit searches all things, even the depths of God. (Omniscient)

The Holy Spirit is described as having characteristics only God possesses.

Genesis 1:1,2 In the beginning, God created the heavens and the earth. The earth was undeveloped and empty. Darkness covered the surface of the deep, and the Spirit of God was hovering over the surface of the waters.

Titus 3:5 He saved us—not by righteous works that we did ourselves, but because of his mercy. He saved us through the washing of rebirth and the renewal by the *Holy Spirit.*

Romans 8:27 He who searches our hearts knows what the mind of the Spirit is, because the Spirit intercedes for the saints, according to God's will.

The Holy Spirit does work only God can do.

184. What is the focus of the work of the Holy Spirit?

1 Corinthians 12:3 No one can say, "Jesus is Lord," except by the Holy Spirit.

1 Timothy 2:4 [God our Savior] *wants all people to be saved* and to come to the knowledge of the truth.

1 Peter 2:9,11 You are a chosen people, a royal priesthood, a holy nation, the people who are God's own possession, so that you may proclaim the praises of him *who called you out of darkness* into his marvelous light. Dear friends, I urge you, as aliens and temporary residents in the world, to abstain from the desires of the sinful flesh, which war against your soul.

1 Corinthians 1:2 To the church of God in Corinth—those who have been sanctified in Christ Jesus, who are *called as saints*—along with all in every place who call on the name of our Lord Jesus Christ, their Lord and ours.

2 Timothy 1:9 [God] *saved us* and *called us with a holy calling,* not because of our works, but because of his own purpose and grace. This grace was given to us in Christ Jesus before time began.

The Holy Spirit works to bring us out of the darkness of unbelief to faith and to make us holy.

185. What is the work of the Holy Spirit called?

2 Thessalonians 2:13 We are always obligated to thank God for you, brothers, loved by the Lord, because God chose you from the beginning for salvation by the *sanctifying work* of the Spirit and faith in the truth.

1 Corinthians 6:11 Some of you were those types of people. But you were washed, you were *sanctified,* you were justified in the name of our Lord Jesus Christ and by the Spirit of our God.

The work of the Holy Spirit is called sanctification.

A CLOSER LOOK

The word *sanctification* means "to set apart." The Holy Spirit sets us apart from the unbelieving world by calling us to faith in Jesus. We are now holy and righteous in God's sight because we are clothed in Jesus' perfection. Furthermore, the Holy Spirit graciously sets us apart from the sinful behavior of the world around us by strengthening our faith (Colossians 3:10).

---

186. Why is the work of the Holy Spirit so important to us?

1 Corinthians 2:14 *An unspiritual person does not accept the truths taught by God's Spirit,* because they are foolishness to him, and he cannot understand them, because they are spiritually evaluated.

Ephesians 2:1 *You were dead in your trespasses and sins.*

Romans 8:7 *The mind-set of the sinful flesh is hostile to God,* since it does not submit to God's law, and in fact, it cannot.

1 Corinthians 12:3 I am informing you that no one speaking by God's Spirit says, "A curse be upon Jesus," and *no one can say, "Jesus is Lord," except by the Holy Spirit.*

187. How does the Holy Spirit call us to faith?

Acts 2:38 Peter answered them, "Repent and be *baptized,* every one of you, in the name of Jesus Christ for the forgiveness of your sins, and you will receive the gift of the Holy Spirit."

2 Thessalonians 2:13,14 We are always obligated to thank God for you, brothers, loved by the Lord, because God chose you from the beginning for salvation *by the sanctifying work of the Spirit and faith in the truth.* For this reason *he also called you through our gospel* so that you would obtain the glory of our Lord Jesus Christ.

2 Timothy 3:15 From infancy you have known *the Holy Scriptures, which are able to make you wise for salvation* through faith in Christ Jesus.

Romans 10:17 *Faith comes from hearing the message,* and the message comes through the word of Christ.

John 17:17 *Sanctify them by the truth. Your word is truth.*

Acts 10:1-48 (The Holy Spirit worked in the hearts of those in Cornelius' house through the gospel in the Word that they heard and through the gospel in Baptism.)

Matthew 26:26-28 While they were eating, Jesus took bread, blessed and broke it, and gave it to the disciples. He said, "Take, eat, this is my body." Then he took the cup, gave thanks, and gave it to them, saying, "Drink from it all of you, for this is my blood of the new testament, which is poured out for many for the forgiveness of sins."

The Holy Spirit works through the gospel in God's Word and the sacraments.

A CLOSER LOOK

Decision Theology

Can people decide, by the power of their own wills, to accept Jesus Christ as Lord and Savior?

Unfortunately, many today speak about faith in Christ as a personal decision. They believe that people must ultimately decide whether or not to accept what God has to say and whether or not to invite Jesus into their hearts.

The Bible doesn't teach this. Rather, it teaches that we are all by nature spiritually dead. Our human wills, in any spiritual sense, are also dead.

What is dead can't contribute toward becoming spiritually alive. Those who view faith as something brought about by a human decision are placing confidence for salvation in something other than God. Such misplaced confidence opens the door to uncertainty and doubt, leaving them to wonder if they truly believe or if they are sincere. We place our trust in God, who alone has the power to work the miracle of faith through the gospel.

---

188. Why do we say that the Holy Spirit deserves all credit for bringing us to faith?

1 Corinthians 12:3 I am informing you that no one speaking by God's Spirit says, "A curse be upon Jesus," and *no one can say, "Jesus is Lord," except by the Holy Spirit.*

Ephesians 2:8,9 It is by grace you have been saved, through faith—and *this is not from yourselves,* it is the gift of God—not by works, so that no one can boast.

189. In what different ways does the Bible describe the miracle the Holy Spirit works when he calls us to faith?

Conversion

Acts 3:19 Repent and *return* to have your sins wiped out.

Jeremiah 31:18 I have certainly heard Ephraim grieving: "You have disciplined me. I was disciplined like an untrained calf. Cause me to turn, and I will *turn,* because you are the LORD my God."

Psalm 51:13 I will teach rebels your ways, and sinners will *turn to you.*

Acts 11:21 The Lord's hand was with them, and a large number of people believed and *turned to the Lord.*

1 Peter 2:25 You were like sheep going astray, but you are *now returned* to the Shepherd and Overseer of your souls.

Acts 15:3 After they were sent on their way by the church, and as they passed through both Phoenicia and Samaria, they described in detail the conversion of the Gentiles and brought great joy to all the brothers.

Conversion is turning from unbelief to faith in God.

Rebirth

1 Peter 1:3,23 Blessed be the God and Father of our Lord Jesus Christ! By his great mercy he *gave us a new birth* into a living hope through the resurrection of Jesus Christ from the dead. For you have been *born again,* not from perishable seed but from imperishable, through the living and enduring word of God.

Titus 3:5 *He saved us*—not by righteous works that we did ourselves, but because of his mercy. He saved us *through the washing of rebirth* and the renewal by the Holy Spirit.

John 3:3,6 Jesus replied, "Amen, Amen, I tell you: *Unless someone is born from above, he cannot see the kingdom of God.*" Whatever is born of the flesh is flesh. Whatever is born of the Spirit is spirit.

Rebirth is being born again spiritually.

Quickening

Ephesians 2:4,5 God, because he is rich in mercy, because of the great love with which he loved us, *made us alive with Christ even when we were dead in trespasses.* It is by grace you have been saved!

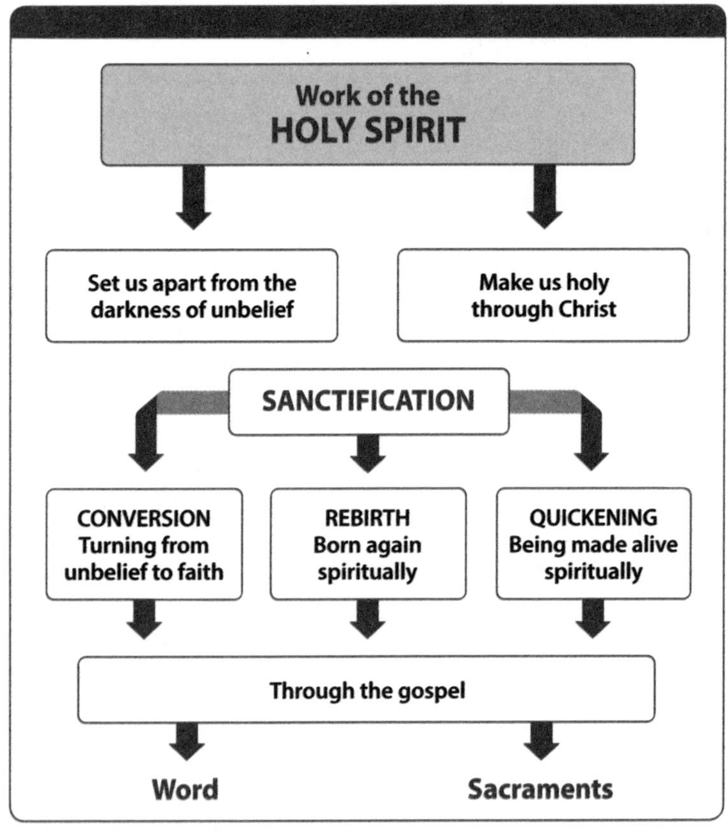

Colossians 2:13 When you were dead in your trespasses and the uncircumcision of your flesh, *God made you alive with Christ* by forgiving us all our trespasses.

Quickening is being made alive spiritually.

Election

The Bible shows that conversion is completely the work of God. That truth is tremendously comforting. If our conversion depended on us in any way, we would be filled with doubts about whether we could ever become a child of God. Those doubts could easily drive us to despair.

Another teaching of the Scriptures emphasizes that conversion is completely the work of God: the teaching of election. The Bible reveals that God elected (chose) us to be saved even before the world was created:

He chose us in Christ before the foundation of the world, so that we would be holy and blameless in his sight. In love he predestined us to be adopted as his sons through Jesus Christ. He did this in accordance with the good purpose of his will **(Ephesians 1:4,5).**

Paul, a servant of God and an apostle of Jesus Christ, for the faith of God's elect people and the knowledge of the truth that conforms to godliness . . . **(Titus 1:1).**

This truth of our election is so precious to us because we live in a world that is so damaged by sin. Things happen that frighten us, discourage us, and hurt us. We ourselves are weak. Our weakness can lead us to doubt our salvation. The teaching of election reminds us that our salvation depends completely on God, not on ourselves. We will be in heaven not because of our strength but because God graciously chose us to be his own before the world began. *In him we have also obtained an inheritance, because we were predestined according to the plan of him who works out everything in keeping with the purpose of his will* **(Ephesians 1:11).** *Those God foreknew, he also predestined to be conformed to the image of his Son, so that he would be the firstborn among many brothers* **(Romans 8:29).**

God's gracious choice took place before time began. In history, God brings that choice into effect through the work of the Holy Spirit, who creates and preserves saving faith through the gospel in Word and sacrament.

In a sense, the truth of election is like a magnifying glass that helps us see even more clearly that our salvation is *all* the result of God's grace. For that, we praise him.

He predestined us to be adopted as his sons through Jesus Christ. He did this in accordance with the good purpose of his will, and for the praise of his glorious grace, which he has graciously given us in the one he loves **(Ephesians 1:5,6).**

---

190. In the explanation to the Apostles' Creed, we confess that the Holy Spirit has "enlightened me with his gifts." *Enlighten* means "to give light to, to provide understanding by giving spiritual insight." **Why is the term *enlightened* used to describe the work of the Holy Spirit in our hearts?**

1 Peter 2:9 You are a chosen people, a royal priesthood, a holy nation, the people who are God's own possession, so that you may proclaim the praises of him *who called you out of darkness into his marvelous light.*

Ephesians 5:8 *You were once darkness, but now you are light in the Lord.* Walk as children of light.

2 Corinthians 4:4-6 *The god of this age has blinded the minds of the unbelievers,* to keep them from clearly seeing the light of the gospel of the glory of Christ, who is God's image. Indeed, we do not preach ourselves, but Jesus Christ as Lord, and ourselves as your servants for Jesus' sake. *For the God who said, "Light will shine out of darkness," is the same one who made light shine in our hearts to give us the light of the knowledge of the glory of God in the person of Jesus Christ.*

Acts 26:17,18 *I am sending you . . . to open their eyes, so that they may turn from darkness to light* and from the power of Satan to God, so that they may receive the forgiveness of sins and a place among those who are sanctified by faith in me.

Luke 10:23 Turning to the disciples, he said privately, *"Blessed are the eyes that see what you see!"*

The Holy Spirit opens the eyes of our hearts, which were spiritually blind, to see what God has done for us in Christ.

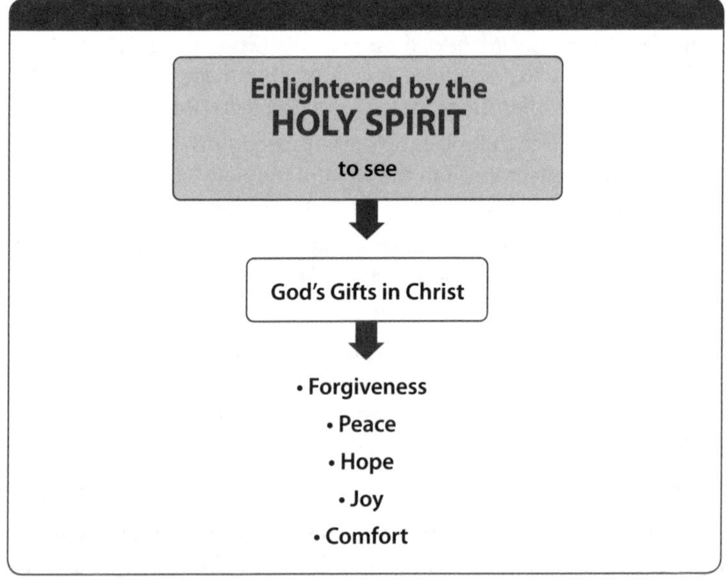

191. What gifts are we able to see clearly because of the Holy Spirit's work in our hearts?

1 Corinthians 12:3 I am informing you that no one speaking by God's Spirit says, "A curse be upon Jesus," *and no one can say, "Jesus is Lord," except by the Holy Spirit.*

John 17:3 *This is eternal life: that they may know you, the only true God, and Jesus Christ, whom you sent.*

Romans 8:16 *The Spirit himself joins our spirit in testifying that we are God's children.*

Ephesians 1:7 *In him we also have redemption through his blood, the forgiveness of sins,* in keeping with the riches of his grace.

Romans 15:13 May the God of hope *fill you with complete joy and peace as you continue to believe,* so that you overflow with hope by the power of the Holy Spirit.

Romans 5:1 Since we have been justified by faith, *we have peace with God* through our Lord Jesus Christ.

Isaiah 32:17 *The result of righteousness will be peace, and righteousness will bring lasting tranquility and security.*

Romans 8:24,25 Indeed, it was *for this hope we were saved.* But hope that is seen is not hope, because who hopes for what he already sees? But if we hope for something we do not see, we eagerly wait for it with patient endurance.

Luke 2:10 The angel said to them, "Do not be afraid. For behold, I bring you good news of *great joy,* which will be for all people."

Romans 5:2-4 Through him we also have obtained access by faith into this grace in which we stand. And *we rejoice confidently on the basis of our hope* for the glory of God. Not only this, but *we also rejoice confidently in our sufferings,* because we know that suffering produces patient endurance, and patient endurance produces tested character, and tested character produces hope.

Psalm 119:50 *This is my comfort in my suffering: that your saying gives me life.*

2 Corinthians 1:3,4 Blessed be the God and Father of our Lord Jesus Christ, the Father of mercies and God of all comfort, *who comforts us in all our trouble,* so that we can comfort those in any trouble with the same comfort with which we ourselves are comforted by God.

1 Peter 1:3,4 Blessed be the God and Father of our Lord Jesus Christ! *By his great mercy he gave us a new birth into a living hope through the resurrection of Jesus Christ from the dead,* into an inheritance that is undying, undefiled, and unfading, kept in heaven for you.

192. The Holy Spirit's work in our hearts doesn't stop after he creates our faith. **What ongoing work does the Holy Spirit do after our conversions?**

1 Thessalonians 2:13 We give thanks to God unceasingly, namely, when you received God's word, which you heard from us, you did not receive it as the word of men but as *the word of God (as it really is), which is now at work in you* who believe.

Isaiah 41:10 Do not fear, for I am with you. Do not be overwhelmed, for I am your God. *I will strengthen you. Yes, I will* help you. *I will uphold you* with my righteous right hand.

Ephesians 3:16 I pray that, according to the riches of his glory, *he would strengthen you with power through his Spirit* in your inner self.

Philippians 1:6 I am convinced of this very thing: that he who began a good work in you *will carry it on to completion* until the day of Christ Jesus.

1 Peter 1:5 Through faith *you are being protected by God's power* for the salvation that is ready to be revealed at the end of time.

1 Peter 5:10 After you have suffered a little while, the God of all grace, who called you into his eternal glory in Christ Jesus, *will himself restore, establish, strengthen, and support you.*

After the Holy Spirit sanctifies us at our conversions by setting us apart from the unbelieving world, he then continues to sanctify us by setting us apart more and more from sinful behaviors. He does this by strengthening our faith.

193. Why is the ongoing work of the Holy Spirit to keep us in the true faith so necessary?

1 Peter 5:8 Have sound judgment. Be alert. Your adversary, *the Devil, prowls around like a roaring lion, looking for someone to devour.*

Ephesians 6:11,12 Put on the full armor of God, so that you can stand against the schemes of the Devil. For our struggle is not against flesh and blood, but against the rulers, against the authorities, against the world rulers of this darkness, *against the spiritual forces of evil* in the heavenly places.

2 Corinthians 11:3 I am afraid that somehow, just as the serpent deceived Eve with his cunning, so also *your minds might be led astray* from a sincere and pure devotion to Christ.

1 John 2:15 *Do not love the world or the things in the world.* If anyone loves the world, the love of the Father is not in him.

Galatians 5:17 *The sinful flesh desires what is contrary to the spirit,* and the spirit what is contrary to the sinful flesh. In fact, these two continually oppose one another, so that you do not continue to do these things you want to do.

The devil, the world, and our own sinful flesh work to weaken and destroy our faith.

194. Because the new person within us understands the importance of the work of the Holy Spirit, what attitude do we as Christians properly display toward hearing the Word of God and using the sacraments?

Romans 1:16 *I am not ashamed of the gospel,* because it is the power of God for salvation to everyone who believes—to the Jew first, and also to the Greek.

Acts 2:42 *They continued to hold firmly to the apostles' teaching* and to the fellowship, to the breaking of the bread, and to the prayers.

John 8:47 *Whoever belongs to God listens to what God says.* The reason you do not listen is that you do not belong to God.

John 15:5 I am the Vine; you are the branches. The one who remains in me and I in him is the one who bears much fruit, because without me you can do nothing.

Matthew 13:1-9,18-23 (In the parable of the sower, Jesus describes the different ways people receive the Word of God. We want to be good soil.)

Revelation 1:3 Blessed is the one who reads the words of this prophecy and blessed are those who hear it and hold on to the things written in it, because the time is near.

Recognizing that the Holy Spirit works through the Word of God and the sacraments to create and strengthen faith, the new person within us desires to regularly hear, read, and study God's Word and to be faithful in our use of the sacraments.

CONNECTIONS

The Holy Spirit works through the sacraments and the Word of God to create and strengthen faith. That's why Baptism is so important for infants as well as adults. This also explains why it is important for us to hear and study God's Word regularly and to receive the Sacrament of Holy Communion often.

In the account of Philip and the Ethiopian, we see a clear example of how the Holy Spirit worked in one man's heart through God's Word and Baptism.

Acts 8:26-39

In what ways is the faith story of the Ethiopian eunuch similar to your own? In what ways is it different? The Ethiopian eunuch spent travel time reading God's Word. Consider ways that you might make the study of God's Word—that powerful tool of the Spirit—a bigger part of your own life.

Luther

Neither you nor I could ever know anything about Christ, or believe on him, and have him for our Lord, unless it were offered to us and granted to our hearts by the Holy Spirit through the preaching of the gospel [1 Corinthians 12:3; Galatians 4:6]. The work of redemption is done and accomplished. Christ has acquired and gained the treasure for us by his suffering, death, resurrection, and so on. But if the work remained concealed so that no one knew about it, then it would be useless and lost. So that this treasure might not stay buried but be received and enjoyed, God has caused the Word to go forth and be proclaimed. In the Word he has the Holy Spirit bring this treasure home and make it our own. Therefore, sanctifying is just bringing us to Christ so we receive this good, which we could not get ourselves [1 Peter 3:18]. (Large Catechism, II, par. 38)

Come, Holy Ghost, God and Lord (Stanza 1)

Come, Holy Ghost, God and Lord!
May all your graces be outpoured
On each believer's mind and heart;
Your fervent love to them impart.
Lord, by the brightness of your light
In holy faith your church unite
From ev'ry land and ev'ry tongue;
This to your praise, O Lord our God, be sung: Alleluia! Alleluia!

GOOD WORKS

Good Works and the Gifts of the Holy Spirit

Sometimes things happen that dramatically change our lives or change the way we think about things. Because of a car accident, a professional football player is never able to play again or earn the high wages other athletes earn. When a young boy visits his uncle, who is a missionary in a foreign country, the boy sees the extreme poverty that is a way of life for the people there. It forever changes his attitude about the many blessings he enjoys.

Perhaps something has happened to you that has changed your life or the way you think about the blessings you enjoy.

By working in our hearts, the Holy Spirit has dramatically changed our lives. This is reflected in the way we think about life and in the things we do.

The Gospel Reflected in Our Lives

195. What has changed in us as a result of the work of the Holy Spirit in our hearts?

2 Corinthians 5:17 *If anyone is in Christ, he is a new creation. The old has passed away. The new has come!*

Psalm 119:104,112 From your precepts I gain understanding. Therefore, *I hate every false road. I turn my heart to do your statutes, forever, right to the end.*

Psalm 40:8 *My God, I take pleasure in doing your will.* Your law is in my heart.

Titus 2:14 [Jesus Christ] gave himself for us, to redeem us from all lawlessness and *to purify for himself a people who are his own chosen people, eager to do good works.*

1 Thessalonians 4:7 *God did not call us for uncleanness, but in sanctification.*

Because the Holy Spirit has brought us to faith, our attitudes and desires have changed. Now we want to overcome sin and serve God with good works.

196. What are God's goals for those who are now Christians?

1 Thessalonians 5:23,24 *May the God of peace himself sanctify you completely,* and may your whole spirit, soul, and body *be kept blameless* at the coming of our Lord Jesus Christ. The one who calls you is faithful, and he will do it.

1 Thessalonians 4:3,4 Indeed, *this is God's will: that you be sanctified,* namely, that you keep yourselves away from sexual immorality. He wants each of you to learn to obtain a wife for yourself in a way that is holy and honorable.

Ephesians 1:18 I pray that *the eyes of your heart may be enlightened,* so that *you may know the hope* to which he has called you, just how rich his glorious inheritance among the saints is.

2 Peter 3:18 *Grow in the grace and knowledge of our Lord and Savior Jesus Christ.* To him be the glory, both now and forever. Amen.

1 Corinthians 6:9-11 (Paul pointed out that the Corinthians had been set apart from the wrongdoing so prevalent in their world.) Verse 11: *You were washed, you were sanctified,* you were justified in the name of our Lord Jesus Christ and by the Spirit of our God.

Ephesians 3:14-19 (Paul prays that God will strengthen those he has called to faith.)

Ephesians 2:10 We are God's workmanship, *created in Christ Jesus for good works,* which God prepared in advance so that we would walk in them.

God's goals for Christians are that we continue to be separated from the sins that characterize the unbelieving world, that we grow in faith, and that our lives be filled with good works.

197. Who alone is able to do works that are considered good by God?

Hebrews 11:6 *Without faith it is impossible to please God.* Indeed, it is necessary for the one who approaches God to believe that he exists and that he rewards those who seek him.

Galatians 2:20 I have been crucified with Christ, and I no longer live, but Christ lives in me. The life I am now living in the flesh, *I live by faith in the Son of God,* who loved me and gave himself for me.

Galatians 5:22-24 *The fruit of the spirit* is love, joy, peace, patience, kindness, goodness, faithfulness, gentleness, and self-control. Against such things there is no law. Those who belong to Christ Jesus have crucified the sinful flesh with its passions and desires.

Galatians 5:6 In Christ Jesus neither circumcision nor uncircumcision matters. Rather, it is *faith working through love* that matters.

Colossians 3:17 Everything you do, whether in word or deed, *do it all in the name of the Lord Jesus,* giving thanks to God the Father through him.

Mark 12:41-44 (Out of love for the Lord, a widow gave all that she had as an offering.)

Mark 14:3-9 (Mary poured expensive perfume over Jesus' head to express her gratitude and love for her Savior.)

Luke 19:1-10 (Zacchaeus showed his gratitude to Jesus by the things he did.)

Only a believer in Jesus can do works that God views as good.

198. What motivates a believer to do good works?

Romans 12:1 I urge you, brothers, *by the mercies of God,* to offer your bodies as a living sacrifice—holy and pleasing to God—which is your appropriate worship.

2 Corinthians 5:14,15 *The love of Christ compels us,* because we came to this conclusion: One died for all; therefore, all died. And *he died for all, so that those who live would no longer live for themselves but for him, who died in their place and was raised again.*

199. How does a believer know what works are truly good in God's sight?

Psalm 119:105 Your words are a lamp for my feet and a light for my path.

Psalm 119:9 How can a young man keep his path pure? *By guarding it with your words.*

Romans 12:2 Do not continue to conform to the pattern of this world, but be transformed by the renewal of your mind, *so that you test and approve what is the will of God*—what is good, pleasing, and perfect.

Luke 11:28 He said, "Even more blessed are those who *hear the word of God and keep it.*"

A CLOSER LOOK

Good works are the things believers do according to God's will, out of thanks to God for all he has done.

---

200. Even though we are saved through faith in Jesus, we still sin. **How is it possible that God can consider something done by a Christian, who still remains a sinner, to be truly good?**

1 John 1:9 If we confess our sins, he is faithful and just *to forgive us our sins and to cleanse us from all unrighteousness.*

1 Corinthians 6:11 Some of you were those types of people. But you were *washed,* you were *sanctified,* you were *justified* in the name of our Lord Jesus Christ and by the Spirit of our God.

Hebrews 11:6 *Without faith it is impossible to please God.* Indeed, it is necessary for the one who approaches God to believe that he exists and that he rewards those who seek him.

Galatians 2:20 I have been crucified with Christ, and I no longer live, but *Christ lives in me. The life I am now living* in the flesh, *I live by faith in the Son of God,* who loved me and gave himself for me.

John 15:5 I am the Vine; you are the branches. *The one who remains in me and I in him is the one who bears much fruit,* because without me you can do nothing.

Philippians 2:13 It is *God* who *is working in you, both to will and to work, for the sake of his good pleasure.*

Psalm 147:11 *The Lord is pleased with those who fear him, those who wait for his mercy.*

Romans 9:16 It does not depend on human desire or effort, but on God's mercy.

In his mercy, God delights in everything a believer does out of love for Jesus. God looks at us through Christ, whose righteousness covers our imperfection.

A CLOSER LOOK

Depending upon our callings in life (husband, wife, parent, child, employee, employer, etc.), we will have different opportunities to do works that God desires. See the biblical guidance God gives to those who serve in various roles as it is shown in the Table of Duties on pages 17-19.

---

201. Praising God, worshiping God, showing kindness to others, helping those who are in need—these are ways we all can do good works. The Bible also tells us that God gives each of us specific work to accomplish and that he gives each of us the unique gifts needed to do that work. **What are some of the unique gifts that the Holy Spirit has given to the members of the New Testament church?**

Romans 12:6-8 We have different gifts, according to the grace God has given us. If the gift is *prophecy,* do it in complete agreement with the faith. If it is *serving,* then serve. If it is *teaching,* then teach. If it is *encouraging,* then encourage. If it is *contributing,* be generous. If it is *leadership,* be diligent. If it is *showing mercy,* do it cheerfully.

Ephesians 4:11 *He himself gave the apostles, as well as the prophets, as well as the evangelists, as well as the pastors and teachers.*

1 Corinthians 12:8 *To one person a message of wisdom is given by the Spirit; to another, a message of knowledge, as the same Spirit provides it.*

202. What is the purpose of these gifts of the Holy Spirit?

Ephesians 4:11,12 He himself gave the apostles, as well as the prophets, as well as the evangelists, as well as the pastors and teachers, *for the purpose of training the saints for the work of serving, in order to build up the body of Christ.*

1 Corinthians 12:1,4-7 Now concerning spiritual gifts, brothers, I do not want you to be uninformed. There are various kinds of gifts, but the same Spirit. There are different kinds of ministries, and yet the same Lord. There are various kinds of activity, but the same God, who produces all of them in everyone. Each person is given a manifestation of the Spirit for the *common good.*

The Bible clearly shows the importance of the gifts that come to us from the Holy Spirit. God has prepared works of service for each Christian to perform. God equips each Christian for this work through the gifts given by the Holy Spirit. Though we all have different spiritual gifts, each of us has an important function to perform as part of the body of Christ.

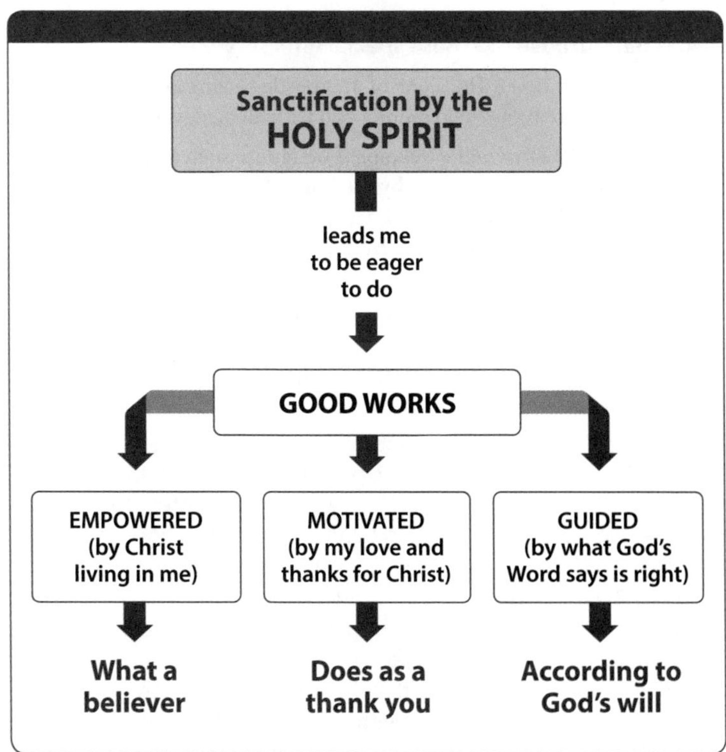

203. In the early years of the Christian church, the Holy Spirit gave some special, miraculous gifts. **What were some of those special gifts?**

1 Corinthians 12:8-10,28,30 To one person a message of wisdom is given by the Spirit; to another, a message of *knowledge,* as the same Spirit provides it; by the same Spirit, faith is given to someone else; and to another, the same Spirit gives *healing gifts.* Another is given *powers to do miracles;* another, *the gift of prophecy;* another, *the evaluating of spirits;* someone else, *different kinds of tongues;* and another, *the interpretation of tongues.* And God appointed in the church: first apostles, second prophets, third teachers; then *miracles,* healing gifts, helpful acts, leadership abilities, *kinds of tongues. Do all have healing gifts? Do all speak in tongues? Do all interpret?*

Acts 9:36-42 (Peter was given the power to raise Tabitha from the dead.)

Acts 3:1-11 (Peter healed a lame beggar, demonstrating that the power of God was behind his words.)

Acts 2:1-11 (On Pentecost the apostles were able to speak in many languages they had never known before.)

204. What purpose did these special gifts serve?

2 Corinthians 12:12 The signs of an apostle—signs and wonders and miracles—were performed among you with all perseverance.

Hebrews 2:3,4 How will we escape if we ignore such a great salvation? First the message was spoken by the Lord; then it was confirmed to us by those who heard him. *God also testified to it with signs and wonders, various miracles and gifts of the Holy Spirit,* according to his will.

A CLOSER LOOK

God gave special gifts, such as healing and miracles, to make it obvious that the message of salvation, proclaimed by the apostles and embraced by many Christians, was from God himself.

This purpose was especially important for the early New Testament church. The message the apostles proclaimed, which was confirmed many times by these special gifts, very soon was written down in the books of the New Testament. No additional confirmation was necessary. These Bible texts would serve as an ongoing standard by which truth could be judged.

God did not promise that these special spiritual gifts would always be given. Today when some Christians emphasize the need to experience some kind of special spiritual gift, they risk drawing attention away from the confirmed words of the apostles found in Holy Scripture. God has not promised to confirm his Word by miracles. Our certainty and joy do not come from outward signs but from the solid promises given to each and every one of us in the Bible. Those promises endure for all time, whether or not special signs are present.

CONNECTIONS

The work of the Holy Spirit in our hearts changes our lives. Because the Holy Spirit calls us out of darkness into light, we see everything differently. By nature we are selfish. We are concerned only about our own well-being. We work for things that will make our lives easier and more pleasurable. The work of the Holy Spirit in our hearts changes our focus. We want our lives to serve Jesus. We are more concerned about the well-being of those around us.

The change in attitude brought about by the Holy Spirit was demonstrated in the lives of the Christians in the Macedonian churches. They lived in extreme poverty and suffered persecution. Yet when an offering was being collected for needy Christians in Jerusalem, they gave very generously. The apostle Paul used their example to encourage other congregations, and us, to respond to God's love by generously sharing the blessings God had given to them.

2 Corinthians 8:1-9

Christians can be tempted to look at good works simply as something they must do. Explain how the example of the Macedonian Christians can be helpful when we struggle against such a temptation. Make a personal list of things you could do that would be helpful to someone else.

Lutheran Confessions

Furthermore, we teach that it is necessary to do good works. This does not mean that we merit grace by doing good works, but because it is God's will [Ephesians 2:10]. It is only by faith, and nothing else, that forgiveness of sins is apprehended. The Holy Spirit is received through faith, hearts are renewed and given new affections and then they are able to bring forth good works. Ambrose says: "Faith is the mother of a good will and doing what is right." Without the Holy Spirit people are full of ungodly desires. They are too weak to do works that are good in God's sight. (Augsburg Confession, XX, par. 27-31)

Come, Holy Ghost, Creator Blest (Stanzas 1,5,6)
Come, Holy Ghost, Creator blest,
And make our hearts your place of rest;
Come with your grace and heav'nly aid,
And fill the hearts which you have made.

Teach us to know the Father, Son,
And you, from both, as Three in One
That we your name may ever bless
And in our lives the truth confess.

Praise we the Father and the Son
And Holy Spirit, with them One,
And may the Son on us bestow
The gifts that from the Spirit flow!

THE CHURCH

The Family of Believers—the Holy Christian Church

What is a church? Is it a building? Is it a group of people who worship in one place? Is it a group of people who believe the same thing? The word *church* might be used when speaking of any of those. In the Third Article, we confess that we believe in the holy Christian church. What does that mean?

The Christian Church

205. What is the holy Christian church?

Ephesians 2:19-22 You are no longer foreigners and strangers, but you are fellow citizens with the saints and *members of God's household. You have been built on the foundation of the apostles and prophets, with Christ Jesus himself as the Cornerstone.* In him the whole building is joined together and grows into a holy temple in the Lord. In him you too are being built together into a dwelling place for God by the Spirit.

Acts 5:14 More and more believers in the Lord were added to their group, large numbers of both men and women.

Acts 2:46,47 Day after day, with one mind, they were devoted to meeting in the temple area, as they continued to break bread in their homes. They shared their food with glad and sincere hearts, as they continued praising God and being viewed favorably by all the people. Day after day the Lord added to their number those who were being saved.

The holy Christian church includes all people everywhere who believe in Christ Jesus as their Savior.

206. Why do we call the holy Christian church the *communion of saints*?

John 10:16 I also have other sheep that are not of this sheep pen. I must bring them also, and they will listen to my voice. Then *there will be one flock* and one shepherd.

Romans 12:5 Though we are many, we are one body in Christ, and individually members of one another.

Ephesians 5:23 Christ is the head of *the church, his body,* of which he himself is the Savior.

Ephesians 4:4 *There is one body* and one Spirit, just as also you were called in the one hope of your calling.

Communion means "having something in common" or "a coming together." The church is called the communion of saints because all believers are united by their common faith in Christ.

207. Who alone knows the members of the holy Christian church?

Luke 17:20,21 The Pharisees asked Jesus when the kingdom of God would come. Jesus answered them, "The kingdom of God is not coming in a way you can observe, nor will people say, 'Look, here it is!' or 'Look, there it is!' because *the kingdom of God is within you.*"

1 Samuel 16:7 The LORD said to Samuel, "Do not look at his appearance or at how tall he is, because I have rejected him. For the LORD does not look at things the way man does. For man looks at the outward appearance, but *the LORD looks at the heart.*"

2 Timothy 2:19 God's foundation stands firm, having this seal: *"The Lord knows those who are his,"* and "Let everyone who calls on the name of the Lord keep away from wickedness."

Only God can see faith in a person's heart. He alone knows the members of the holy Christian church (the *invisible church*).

208. Why is the invisible church—all believers everywhere—called *holy* and the communion of *saints*?

Ephesians 5:25-27 Husbands, love your wives, in the same way as Christ loved the church and gave himself up for her to make her holy, by *cleansing her with the washing of water in connection with the Word.* He did this so that he could present her to himself as a glorious church, having no stain or wrinkle or any such thing, but so that she would be holy and blameless.

Revelation 1:5,6 To [Jesus Christ] who loves us and has *freed us from our sins by his own blood* and made us a kingdom and priests to God his Father—to him be the glory and the power forever. Amen.

Romans 1:7 To all those loved by God who are in Rome, *called to be saints:* Grace to you and peace from God our Father and the Lord Jesus Christ.

1 Corinthians 1:2 To the church of God in Corinth—*those who have been sanctified in Christ Jesus, who are called as saints*—along with all in every place who call on the name of our Lord Jesus Christ, their Lord and ours.

209. The means the Holy Spirit used to call each of us to faith is the same means he uses to call, gather, enlighten, and sanctify all others in the holy Christian church: the gospel in God's Word and the sacraments. **Because the Holy Spirit works through the gospel, where only is the holy Christian church found?**

Isaiah 55:10,11 Just as the rain and the snow come down from the sky and do not return there unless they first water the earth, make it give birth, and cause it to sprout, so that it gives seed to the sower and bread to the eater, in the same way my word that goes out from my mouth will not return to me empty. Rather, it will accomplish whatever I please, and it will succeed in the purpose for which I sent it.

Matthew 18:20 Where two or three have gathered together in my name, there I am among them.

Matthew 28:19,20 Go and gather disciples from all nations by baptizing them in the name of the Father and of the Son and of the Holy Spirit, and by *teaching them to keep all the instructions I have given you.* And surely I am with you always until the end of the age.

John 8:31 Jesus said to the Jews who had believed him, "If you remain in my word, you are really my disciples."

The holy Christian church will be found only where the gospel is proclaimed and the sacraments are administered.

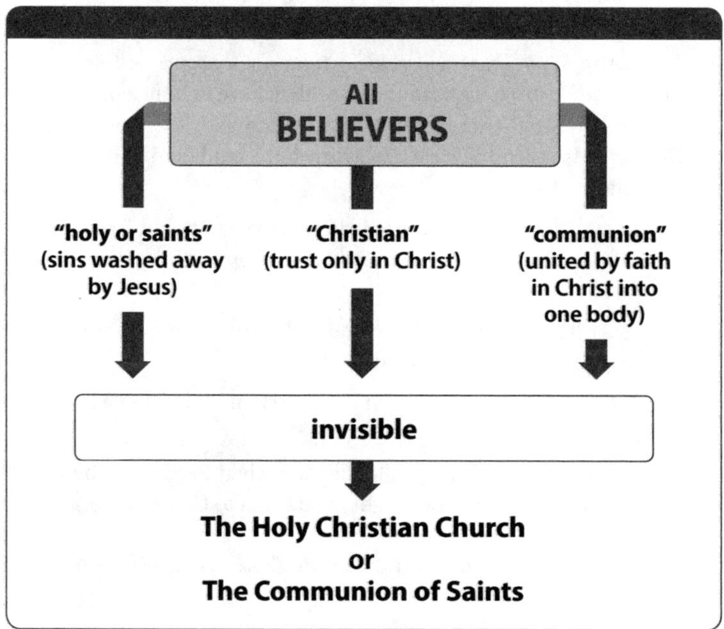

210. Why do we also call a group of people who gather together in one place to hear the gospel a *church* (visible church)?

Isaiah 55:11 In the same way my word that goes out from my mouth will not return to me empty. Rather, it will accomplish whatever I please, and it will succeed in the purpose for which I sent it.

Matthew 18:20 Where two or three have gathered together in my name, there I am among them.

We can see the people who come together to hear the gospel, so we call a group of people who come together to hear the gospel a visible church. We know that wherever the gospel is proclaimed, the Holy Spirit is at work creating faith. That doesn't mean every person who associates with a visible church is a believer, nor does it mean every visible church teaches all of God's truth faithfully.

211. God commands us to test every church. **What are we to examine as we evaluate different churches?**

Matthew 28:19,20 Go and gather disciples from all nations by baptizing them in the name of the Father and of the Son and of the Holy Spirit, and by *teaching them to keep all* the instructions I have given you. And surely I am with you always until the end of the age.

Acts 17:11 Now the Bereans were more noble-minded than the Thessalonians. They received the word very eagerly and examined the Scriptures every day to see if these things were so.

2 Timothy 4:3,4 *There will come a time when people will not put up with sound doctrine.* Instead, because they have itching ears, they will accumulate for themselves teachers in line with their own desires. They will also turn their ears away from the truth and will turn aside to myths.

1 John 4:1 Dear friends, do not believe every spirit, but *test the spirits* to see if they are from God, for many false prophets have gone out into the world.

John 8:31 Jesus said to the Jews who had believed him, "If you remain in my word, you are really my disciples."

Revelation 3:8-10 (Jesus praised the church in Philadelphia because it kept God's Word.)

Revelation 2:13-16 (Jesus faulted the church at Pergamum because it allowed false doctrine to be taught in addition to God's Word.)

212. When we find a church that passes God's test, what does God want us to do?

John 17:20,21 I am praying not only for them, but also for those who believe in me through their message. *May they all be one,* as you, Father, are in me and I am in you. May they also be one in us, so that the world may believe that you sent me.

1 Corinthians 1:10 Brothers, I am making an appeal to you using the name of our Lord Jesus Christ. I ask *that you all express the same view* *and not have any divisions among you,* but *that you be joined together* in the same mind and in the same judgment.

1 John 1:3 We are proclaiming what we have seen and heard also to you, so that *you may have fellowship with us.* Our fellowship is with the Father and his Son Jesus Christ.

We join in fellowship with those who hold to the truth. By declaring fellowship with them, we confess that our beliefs are the same and we participate with them in worshiping God and sharing the good news of Jesus.

213. How do we express the bond of fellowship with others who faithfully teach God's Word?

Hebrews 10:25 *Let us not neglect meeting together,* as some have the habit of doing. Rather, let us encourage each other, and all the more as you see the Day approaching.

1 Thessalonians 5:11 Encourage one another and build each other up, just as you are also doing.

Romans 1:11,12 I certainly long to see you, in order that I may deliver some spiritual gift to you, so that you are strengthened—that is, when I am with you, that we will be *mutually encouraged by each other's faith,* yours and also mine.

Ephesians 4:11-16 (God works through his servants so that we grow in strength and in unity with one another.)

We join in fellowship as we worship and study God's Word together so that together we grow stronger in our faith.

1 Corinthians 10:17 Because there is one bread, we, who are many, are *one body, for we all partake of the one bread.*

Acts 1:14 All of them kept *praying together* with one mind, along with the women, with Mary the mother of Jesus, and with his brothers.

Acts 2:42 They continued to hold firmly *to the apostles' teaching and to the fellowship,* to the *breaking of the bread,* and to *the prayers.*

1 Timothy 2:1-4,8 (Paul encourages Christians throughout the world *to join with one another to offer all kinds of prayers.*)

We join in fellowship as we pray together, go to the Lord's Supper together, and preach and teach the gospel together.

John 21:15 When they had eaten breakfast, Jesus asked Simon Peter, "Simon, son of John, do you love me more than these?" "Yes, Lord," he said, "you know that I care about you." Jesus told him, "Feed my lambs."

Psalm 78:4-7 We will not hide them from their descendants. We will *tell the next generation the praiseworthy deeds of the LORD,* his power, and the wonders that he has done. He set up testimony for Jacob. In

Israel he established the law. He commanded our fathers to make it known to their children. *Then the next generation would know it,* even the children not yet born. They would rise up and tell their children. Then they would put their confidence in God, and they would not forget the deeds of God, but they would keep his commands.

Joel 1:3 *Tell it to your children,* and let your children tell it to their children, and their children to the next generation.

Proverbs 22:6 Dedicate a child to the way he should go, and even when he becomes old, he will not turn away from it.

Christians join in fellowship as they work together to teach God's Word to their children.

We support parents in the teaching of their children in the home, and we also join with other Christians who faithfully hold to God's Word to provide Christian training in a variety of school settings.

Acts 13,14 especially 13:1-3 (A congregation of believers, guided by the Holy Spirit, sent Paul and Barnabas out to preach and teach the message of the gospel to others throughout the world. Acts 13 and 14 offer a record of Paul's first missionary journey.)

Matthew 28:19 Go and gather disciples from all nations by baptizing them in the name of the Father and of the Son and of the Holy Spirit.

Philippians 4:14-16 (The Philippians helped support Paul so he could devote his time to preaching the Word.)

We join in fellowship as we send out and support missionaries throughout the world.

A CLOSER LOOK

The word *synod* means "walking together." A synod is a group of congregations that unite in fellowship (walk together) to carry out the ministry opportunities God has placed in front of them. Training pastors, teachers, and staff ministers; conducting foreign mission work; and publishing materials that are faithful to God's Word are works of ministry that are more easily accomplished when congregations work together.

214. What does the Bible teach us to do when we discover visible churches or organizations that promote teachings contrary to God's Word?

2 Corinthians 6:14 *Do not be unequally yoked together with unbelievers.* For what partnership does righteousness have with lawlessness? Or what fellowship does light have with darkness?

Matthew 7:15,16 *Watch out for false prophets.* They come to you in sheep's clothing, but inwardly they are ravenous wolves. By their fruit you will recognize them. You do not gather grapes from thorn bushes or figs from thistles, do you?

2 Timothy 4:3 There will come a time when people will not put up with sound doctrine. Instead, because they have itching ears, they will accumulate for themselves teachers in line with their own desires.

Romans 16:17,18 I urge you, brothers, to *watch out for those who cause divisions and offenses contrary to the teaching that you learned, and keep away from them.* For such people are not serving Christ our Lord but their own appetites. By smooth talk and flattery, they seduce the hearts of the unsuspecting.

Galatians 1:8 If we or an angel from heaven would preach any gospel other than the one we preached to you—a curse on him!

Titus 3:10 Reject a divisive person after a first and second warning.

215. Why does the Bible command us to separate from those who do not faithfully teach God's Word?

John 17:17 Sanctify them by the truth. *Your word is truth.*

Psalm 119:30,31,103-105 I have chosen the way of truth. I accept your judgments. I cling to your testimonies, O Lord. Do not let me be put to shame. How sweet are your sayings to my taste, sweeter than honey to my mouth! From your precepts I gain understanding. Therefore, I hate every false road. Your words are a lamp for my feet and a light for my path.

John 14:6 Jesus said to him, "I am the Way and the Truth and the Life. No one comes to the Father, except through me."

John 8:31 Jesus said to the Jews who had believed him, "If you remain in my word, you are really my disciples."

Matthew 7:15 Watch out for false prophets. They come to you in sheep's clothing, but *inwardly they are ravenous wolves.*

2 Corinthians 11:3 I am afraid that somehow, just as the serpent deceived Eve with his cunning, so also *your minds might be led astray from a sincere and pure devotion to Christ.*

2 Timothy 2:16,17 As for pointless chatter, avoid it, for it will lead to an ever greater measure of godlessness, and *their message will spread like gangrene.*

Revelation 22:18,19 I give this warning to everyone who hears the words of the prophecy of this book: *If anyone adds to them, God will add to him the plagues that are written in this book. And if anyone takes away from the words of the book of this prophecy, God will take away his share in the Tree of Life* and in the Holy City, which are written in this book.

Titus 1:13,14 This testimony is true. For this reason, *correct them sharply so that they may be sound in the faith, not paying attention to Jewish myths or the commands of people who turn their backs on the truth.*

James 5:19,20 My brothers, if anyone among you wanders away from the truth and someone turns him back, let it be known that *the one who turns a sinner from the error of his way will save his soul from death and will cover a multitude of sins.*

Out of respect for God's truth, out of concern for our own souls, and out of love for the souls of others, we are to separate from those who do not faithfully teach God's Word.

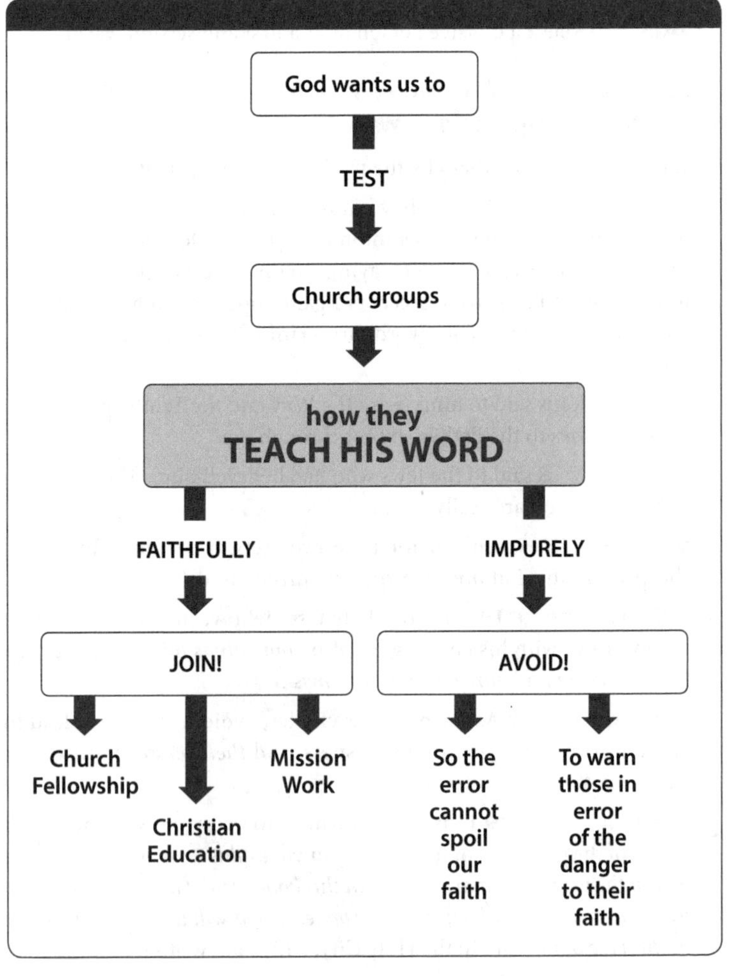

Confessions

Out of love for Christ, we want to honor him by joining together with those who faithfully teach his Word. We also want to avoid any kind of fellowship with those whose false teaching could weaken our faith or the faith of those around us. Because we can't see into the hearts of individual members of a church, we must test a church by examining what the church confesses and practices. We listen to what its pastor preaches, study its written statements of faith, and consider its practices.

The desire to remain faithful to God's Word has led the Lutheran church to adopt a number of confessional statements. They all were written at the time of the Reformation and were published together in *The Book of Concord.*

They include

1. the Small Catechism
2. the Large Catechism
3. the Augsburg Confession
4. the Apology of the Augsburg Confession
5. the Smalcald Articles
6. the Formula of Concord

CONNECTIONS

God's Word tells us, "Dear friends, do not believe every spirit, but test the spirits to see if they are from God, for many false prophets have gone out into the the world" (1 John 4:1). When we find groups that teach differently than God's Word teaches, God tells us to avoid them (Romans 16:17). But not practicing spiritual fellowship with those whose churches have false teaching may appear to some as unloving. We may certainly handle such circumstances in an unloving way because of our sinful flesh, but there is a way to honor God's truth and show love at the same time. Read the passage below and note the attitudes we are to have as Christians even when we are slandered for our faithfulness to the Lord.

1 Peter 3:8-17

Create a list of attitudes God asks you to have as you witness to others. Why will it be difficult to have such attitudes? Write a short prayer asking God to give you love for others and gentle respect in your conversations with those who believe differently.

Luther

I believe that there is upon earth a little holy group and congregation of pure saints, under one head, even Christ [Ephesians 1:22]. This group is called together by the Holy Spirit in one faith, one mind, and understanding, with many different gifts, yet agreeing in love, without sects or schisms [Ephesians 4:5-8,11]. I am also a part and member of this same group, a sharer and joint owner of all the goods it possess [Romans 8:17]. I am brought to it and incorporated into it by the Holy Spirit through having heard and continuing to hear God's Word [Galatians 3:1-2], which is the beginning of entering it. (Large Catechism, II, par. 51,52)

Lord, Keep Us Steadfast in Your Word (Stanzas 1-3)

Lord, keep us steadfast in your Word;
Curb those who by deceit or sword
Would seek to overthrow your Son
And to destroy what he has done.

Lord Jesus Christ, your pow'r make known,
For you are Lord of lords alone;
Defend your Christendom that we
May sing your praise eternally.

O Comforter of priceless worth,
Send peace and unity on earth.
Support us in our final strife,
And lead us out of death to life.

FORGIVENESS

We Are All Sinners

Have you ever felt so guilty that you couldn't eat or sleep? Perhaps you did something that hurt another person deeply and you feel horrible inside. Perhaps you committed a sin that only you know about and it continues to bother you.

At first, sin can seem so attractive. But after we commit the sin, we can so quickly become overwhelmed with guilt. Without the forgiveness of sins, our lives might be consumed with the burden of guilt and the certainty of the punishment we deserve.

We long for peace. We want to hear God tell us that our sins have been forgiven.

But can we be confident that this is true? In the Third Article we confess, "I believe in . . . the forgiveness of sins."

The Forgiveness of Sins

216. Why are all humans in need of God's forgiveness?

Matthew 22:37-39 Jesus said to him, "'*Love the Lord your God with all your heart, with all your soul, and with all your mind.*' This is the first and greatest commandment. The second is like it: 'Love your neighbor as yourself.'"

Matthew 5:48 So then, *be perfect, as your heavenly Father is perfect.*

1 Peter 1:16 It is written, *"Be holy, because I am holy."*

Romans 5:12 Just as sin entered the world through one man and death through sin, so also *death spread to all people because all sinned.*

Psalm 51:5 Certainly, *I was guilty when I was born.* I was sinful when my mother conceived me.

1 John 1:8 If we say we have no sin, we deceive ourselves, and the truth is not in us.

1 John 3:4 Everyone who commits sin also commits lawlessness. Sin is lawlessness.

Romans 7:18,19 Indeed, I know that good does not live in me, that is, in my sinful flesh. The desire to do good is present with me, but I am not able to carry it out. So I fail to do the good I want to do. Instead, *the evil I do not want to do, that is what I keep doing.*

Psalm 143:2 Do not bring charges against your servant, because *no one living can be righteous before you.*

We owe God perfect obedience, but we are born corrupted by original sin and keep sinning every day. We deserve eternal punishment.

217. We have no reason to expect anything from God but his judgment. **What has God revealed about himself that gives us hope?**

Psalm 86:15 You, Lord, are a compassionate and gracious God, slow to anger, abounding in mercy and faithfulness.

Isaiah 43:25 I, yes I, am he. I blot out your rebellious deeds for my own sake, and I will not remember your sins.

John 3:16 God so *loved the world.*

218. What did our gracious God do to overturn the judgment against our sin?

Galatians 4:4,5 When the set time had fully come, *God sent his Son* to be born of a woman, so that he would be born under the law, in order *to redeem those under the law,* so that we would be adopted as sons.

John 1:29 The next day, John saw Jesus coming toward him and said, "Look! The Lamb of God, *who takes away the sin of the world!*"

1 John 2:2 He is the atoning sacrifice for our sins, and not only for ours but also *for the whole world.*

2 Corinthians 5:19 *God was in Christ reconciling the world* to himself, not counting their trespasses against them. And he has entrusted to us the message of reconciliation.

Romans 5:18 Just as one trespass led to a verdict of condemnation for all people, so also one righteous verdict led to *life-giving justification for all people.*

Ephesians 1:7 In him *we also have redemption through his blood, the forgiveness of sins,* in keeping with the riches of his grace.

Titus 3:5-7 He saved us—not by righteous works that we did ourselves, but because of his mercy. He saved us through the washing of rebirth and the renewal by the Holy Spirit, whom he poured out on us abundantly through Jesus Christ our Savior, so that, having been justified by his grace, *we might become heirs in keeping with the hope of eternal life.*

God reconciled the whole world to himself, that is, he declared the whole world not guilty.

219. How is it possible that God, who is holy and just, would declare sinners righteous?

Isaiah 53:5,6 It was because of our rebellion that he was pierced. He was crushed for the guilt our sins deserved. *The punishment that brought us* *peace was upon him,* and by his wounds we are healed. We all have gone astray like sheep. Each of us has turned to his own way, *but the LORD has charged all our guilt to him.*

Romans 4:25 *[Jesus our Lord] was handed over to death because of our trespasses* and was raised to life because of our justification.

2 Corinthians 5:21 *God made him, who did not know sin, to become sin for us,* so that we might become the righteousness of God in him.

Romans 3:23-25 All have sinned and fall short of the glory of God and are justified freely by his grace through the redemption that is in Christ Jesus, whom God publicly displayed as the atonement seat through faith in his blood.

God can declare sinners righteous without violating his justice because he declared Jesus to be guilty of every sin that has ever been or will ever be committed. God made the only one who was without sin to be sin for us. On the cross, Jesus was punished for every sin. Because of the cross, the entire world has been declared to be not guilty. This is true, not because people believe it but because it truly happened (universal/objective justification).

220. Why doesn't everyone receive the blessings that Christ won for every person on the cross?

Philippians 3:18,19 To be sure, *many walk as enemies of the cross of Christ.* I told you about them often, and now I am saying it while weeping. Their end is destruction, their god is their appetite, and their glory is in their shame. *They are thinking only about earthly things.*

Romans 2:12 All people who have sinned without law will also perish without law, and all the people who have sinned in connection with law will be judged by law.

Matthew 22:1-14 (Jesus compared the kingdom of heaven to a wedding banquet prepared by a king. Those who were invited refused to come, so the king sent his servants into the streets to invite others. One of the guests, however, refused to wear the wedding clothes that were provided for him.)

Romans 10:3 Since they were ignorant of the righteousness from God and *sought to establish their own righteousness,* they did not submit to the righteousness from God.

Galatians 5:4 You who are trying to be declared righteous by the law are completely separated from Christ. You have fallen from grace.

Hebrews 10:26 If we deliberately keep on sinning after we have received the full knowledge of the truth, there no longer remains any sacrifice for sins.

Romans 3:23-25 All have sinned and fall short of the glory of God and are justified freely by his grace through the redemption that is in Christ Jesus, whom God publicly displayed as the atonement seat *through faith* in his blood.

Many people reject God's gracious gift of righteousness because they feel that they don't need to have righteousness or they believe that they have lived a righteous-enough life to make God happy with them. When humans reject the truth of what Christ did, they separate themselves from the forgiveness Christ won for them.

221. What means does the Holy Spirit use to bring Christ's forgiveness to our hearts?

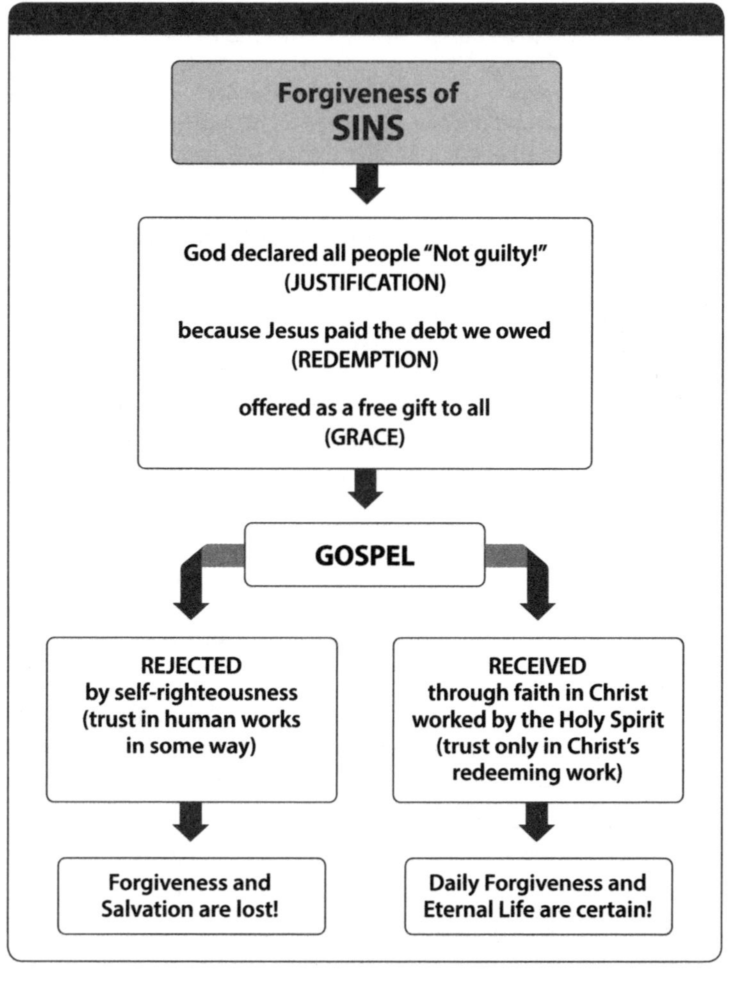

Romans 1:16 I am not ashamed of *the gospel,* because it *is the power of God for salvation* to everyone who believes—to the Jew first, and also to the Greek.

Acts 2:38 Peter answered them, "Repent and be *baptized,* every one of you, in the name of Jesus Christ *for the forgiveness of your sins,* and you will receive the gift of the Holy Spirit."

Matthew 26:26-28 While they were eating, Jesus took bread, blessed and broke it, and gave it to the disciples. He said, "Take, eat, this is my body." Then he took the cup, gave thanks, and gave it to them, saying, "Drink from it all of you, for this is my blood of the new testament, *which is poured out for many for the forgiveness of sins.*"

222. How do we receive the forgiveness of sins that God declared for all people?

Ephesians 2:8,9 It is by grace you have been saved, *through faith*—and this is not from yourselves, it is the gift of God—not by works, so that no one can boast.

Romans 3:22,28 This righteousness from God comes through *faith* in Jesus Christ to all and over all who believe. In fact, there is no difference. For we conclude that *a person is justified by faith* without the works of the law.

Romans 4:5 To the person who does not work but believes in the God who justifies the ungodly, his *faith is credited to him as righteousness.*

Romans 1:17 In the gospel a righteousness from God is revealed *by faith, for faith,* just as it is written, "The righteous will live by faith."

Genesis 15:6 Abram believed in the LORD, and the LORD credited it to him as righteousness.

Galatians 3:26,27 *You are all sons of God through faith* in Christ Jesus. Indeed, as many of you as were baptized into Christ have been clothed with Christ.

Acts 10:43 All the prophets testify about him that, through his name, *everyone who believes in him receives forgiveness of sins.*

We receive the benefits of what Christ did for the world when the Holy Spirit works the gift of faith in our hearts. We believe the objective truth, that God has declared the whole world justified because of Jesus' sacrifice. The personal possession of forgiveness by faith in Jesus is called *subjective justification.*

A CLOSER LOOK

There are two basic approaches to religion in the world. One approach claims that humans are able to contribute something toward their salvation, to offer a level of righteousness that God will accept. The other approach, the Bible's, recognizes that there is nothing we can offer to God by our own strength that could make him less angry—not to mention happy—with us. Our forgiveness—our status of being righteous in the sight of God—depends completely on God's grace in Christ. This truth is at the heart of our salvation: "There is salvation in no one else, for there is no other name under heaven given to people by which we must be saved" (Acts 4:12).

---

223. Why can we be certain that our sins have been forgiven?

John 1:29 The next day, John saw Jesus coming toward him and said, "Look! The Lamb of God, *who takes away the sin of the world!*"

1 John 2:2 He is the atoning sacrifice for our sins, and not only for ours but also *for the whole world.*

1 Timothy 4:10 It is for this reason that we work hard and are insulted: because we have put our hope in the living God, who is *the Savior of all people,* especially of those who believe.

2 Corinthians 5:19 *God was in Christ reconciling the world to himself,* not counting their trespasses against them. And he has entrusted to us the message of reconciliation.

Romans 3:23,24 All have sinned and fall short of the glory of God and are *justified freely by his grace through the redemption that is in Christ Jesus.*

Titus 3:7 *Having been justified by his grace, we might become heirs in keeping with the hope of eternal life.*

We are certain that our sins have been forgiven because God tells us that Jesus paid for the sins of the entire world. We are part of the world. Since Jesus paid the price for all sins, he surely paid for our sins.

CONNECTIONS

Sometimes feelings of guilt just won't leave us alone. Our consciences trouble us, leading us to ask how true Christians could do the things we have done. We wonder if God will really forgive us. At such times, the clear promises of the Bible comfort us. God has taken away all the sins of all the world. As you read the account of the crucifixion of Jesus, remember that Jesus was paying for the guilt of your sin. Note especially the thief who was crucified with Jesus. By his own admission, he had done evil things and deserved to be crucified. Yet, in the last minutes of his life, the Holy Spirit gave him faith to believe that Jesus is the innocent Son of God, his Savior, and that his sins were forgiven.

Luke 23:26-43

Explain how you might use the account of the thief on the cross to bring comfort to someone struggling with guilt. Imagine now that this person has heard your words, but they have objections to what you are saying. What might those objections be? How might they call into question the comfort you are sharing? How can you respond?

Luther

But the purpose of this prayer ["Dear Father, forgive us our trespasses"] is that we may recognize and receive such forgiveness. The flesh in which we daily live is of such a nature that it neither trusts nor believes God. It is ever active in evil lusts and devices, so that we sin daily in word and deed, by what we do and fail to do. By this the conscience is thrown into unrest, so that it is afraid of God's wrath and displeasure. So it loses the comfort and confidence derived from the gospel. Therefore, it is always necessary that we run here and receive consolation to comfort the conscience again. (Large Catechism, III, par. 88,89)

Chief of Sinners Though I Be (Stanzas 1,3,5)

Chief of sinners though I be, Jesus shed his blood for me,
Died that I might live on high,
Lives that I might never die.
As the branch is to the vine, I am his and he is mine!

Only Jesus can impart Comfort to a wounded heart:
Peace that flows from sin forgiv'n,
Joy that lifts the soul to heav'n,
Faith and hope to walk with God In the way that Enoch trod.

Strengthen me, O gracious Lord, By your Spirit and your word.
When my wayward heart would stray,
Keep me in the narrow way;
Grace in time of need supply While I live and when I die.

RESURRECTION

Eternal Life

Christians and unbelievers have very different views of death. For both, death is the cause of sorrow. When a loved one dies, it hurts deeply, whether one is a Christian or not. We all grieve. Yet, there is a difference.

The apostle Paul explained the difference in a letter he wrote to the Thessalonians: Unbelievers have no hope. Christians can grieve, but Christians also have hope (1 Thessalonians 4:13,14).

We confess the reason for this hope in the words of the Third Article: "I believe in . . . the resurrection of the body; and the life everlasting."

The Resurrection of the Body

224. What happens when humans die?

Ecclesiastes 12:7 The dust goes back into the ground—just as it was before, and the spirit goes back to God who gave it.

John 11:39 Martha, the dead man's sister, told him, "Lord, by this time there will be an odor, because it has been four days."

Hebrews 9:27,28 Just as it is appointed for people to die only once and *after this comes the judgment,* so also Christ was offered only once to take away the sins of many, and he will appear a second time—without sin—to bring salvation to those who are eagerly waiting for him.

Luke 23:43 Jesus said to him, "Amen I tell you: *Today you will be with me in paradise.*"

Luke 16:22,23 The beggar died, and the angels carried him to Abraham's side. The rich man also died and was buried. In hell, where he was in torment, he lifted up his eyes and saw Abraham far away and Lazarus at his side.

At death the soul and body separate. The body decays. The soul is either in hell or with God in heaven.

225. The judgment verdict, pronounced individually at the time of death, will be announced publicly before all on the Last Day—judgment day. On that day, every person who has ever lived will face God in judgment. **What are the signs that this final day could happen at any moment?**

Matthew 24:3-12; Luke 21:10-12,25,26 (Jesus told about signs of turmoil that would take place on earth, which are general reminders that the end of the world is coming.)

Matthew 24:36 *No one knows when that day and hour will be,* not the angels of heaven, not even the Son, but only the Father.

2 Corinthians 6:2 He says: At a favorable time I listened to you, and in the day of salvation I helped you. Look, now is the favorable time! See, *now is the day of salvation!*

Matthew 25:1-13 (Jesus told a parable to emphasize the urgency of being prepared for the Last Day.)

Matthew 24:14 *This gospel of the kingdom will be proclaimed throughout the whole world* as a testimony to all nations, and then the end will come.

John 20:31 *These are written that you may believe* that Jesus is the Christ, the Son of God, and that by believing you may have life in his name.

We don't know when the Last Day will come. However, God points to signs all around us, reminding us that the day is fast approaching: wars and famines and persecution and false prophecy. While evil things like these are occurring, something wonderful is also taking place—the gospel is being proclaimed so that we might be prepared for the Last Day with faith in our hearts and so that others may come to faith in Jesus.

226. What will happen on judgment day?

2 Peter 3:10,12 The day of the Lord will come like a thief. On that day the heavens will pass away with a roar, the elements will be dissolved as they burn with great heat, and the earth and what was done on it will be burned up. . . . That day will cause the heavens to be set on fire and destroyed, and the elements to melt as they burn with great heat.

Daniel 12:2 Many who are sleeping in the dusty ground will awake, some to everlasting life, and some to shame, to everlasting contempt.

1 Thessalonians 4:16,17 The Lord himself will come down from heaven with a loud command, with the voice of an archangel, and with the trumpet call of God, and the dead in Christ will rise first. Then we who are alive, who are left, will be caught up in the clouds together with them, to meet the Lord in the air. And so we will always be with the Lord.

Matthew 25:31-46 (Jesus describes judgment day. He will come in glory. From his throne, he will invite believers to receive the glories of heaven.) Verse 34: *Come, you who are blessed by my Father, inherit the kingdom prepared for you from the foundation of the world.* (To those who rejected him, his words will proclaim judgment.) Verse 41: *Depart from me, you who are cursed, into the eternal fire, which is prepared for the Devil and his angels.*

Millennialism

At the time of Jesus' ministry on earth, many people were looking for a Messiah to be a dynamic leader who would rule over a powerful earthly kingdom. Many Christians today mistakenly look forward to a similar age of prosperity and peace on earth, when the church will enjoy tremendous power and success and the troubles of this world—crime, poverty, disease, and war—will be overcome. Some believe that Jesus himself will visibly rule over this earthly kingdom. Some speak of a rapture, when Jesus will snatch believers from the earth before a period of worldwide suffering (called the *tribulation*). They believe this will precede the time of Christ's rule.

Because some people misinterpret several references in the book of Revelation, many believe the period of prosperity will last for one thousand years. This false belief is called millennialism, which is derived from the Latin term *mille* ("one thousand").

Millennialism overlooks clear teachings of Scripture: Christ's kingdom is not a kingdom of earthly rule. Also, the Bible predicts only one mass resurrection of the dead, the resurrection on the Last Day. Finally, Scripture does not speak of an intermediate return of Christ; there will be no time when those who are alive will have a second chance to come to repentance.

227. What will judgment day be like for unbelievers?

Luke 21:26 People [will be] fainting from fear and expectation of the things coming on the world, for the powers of *the heavens will be shaken.*

Jude 14,15 Look, the Lord is going to come with tens of thousands of his holy ones, *to execute judgment* against all of them and to convict every soul concerning all their ungodly deeds, which they did in an ungodly way, and concerning all the harsh words that ungodly sinners spoke against him.

Mark 16:16 Whoever believes and is baptized will be saved, but *whoever does not believe will be condemned.*

Matthew 25:41,46 Then he will say to those on his left, *"Depart from me, you who are cursed, into the eternal fire, which is prepared for the Devil and his angels."* And they will go away to eternal punishment, but the righteous to eternal life.

Matthew 22:10-13 (Jesus describes the end for those who expect to stand in judgment without wearing the garment of righteousness he has provided for them.) Verse 13: *Tie him hand and foot and throw him into the outer darkness where there will be weeping and gnashing of teeth.*

2 Thessalonians 1:9 Such people will receive *a just penalty: eternal destruction* away from the presence of the Lord and from his glorious strength.

Revelation 20:15 If anyone's name was not found written in the Book of Life, he was thrown into the Lake of Fire.

228. How will the day be different for believers?

Matthew 25:34,46 Then the King will say to those on his right, *"Come, you who are blessed by my Father, inherit the kingdom prepared for you from the foundation of the world."* And they will go away to eternal punishment, but *the righteous to eternal life.*

1 Thessalonians 4:17 Then we who are alive, who are left, will be caught up in the clouds together with them, to meet the Lord in the air. And so we will always be with the Lord.

Psalm 16:11 You have made known to me the path of life, fullness of joy in your presence, *pleasures at your right hand forever.*

229. What does the Bible tell us about heaven, the final home of believers?

John 11:25,26 Jesus said to her, "I am the resurrection and the life. Whoever believes in me *will live,* even if he dies. And whoever lives and believes in me *will never perish.* Do you believe this?"

1 Corinthians 2:9 As it is written: What no eye has seen and no ear has heard and no human mind has conceived—that is what God has prepared for those who love him.

Revelation 14:13 I heard a voice from heaven say, "Write: Blessed are the dead who die in the Lord from now on." "Yes," says the Spirit, "because *they will rest from their labors,* for their works follow them."

Revelation 21:3,4 From the throne I heard a loud voice that said, "Look! *God's dwelling is with people.* He will dwell with them, and they will be his people. God himself will be with them, and he will be their God. *He will wipe away every tear from their eyes. There will be no more death or sorrow or crying or pain,* because the former things have passed away."

Revelation 7:15-17 Because of this they are in front of the throne of God, and they serve him day and night in his temple. He who sits on the throne will spread his tent over them. They will never be hungry or thirsty ever again. The sun will never beat upon them, nor will any scorching heat, for *the Lamb at the center of the throne will be their shepherd.* He will lead them to springs of living water. And God will wipe away every tear from their eyes.

Hebrews 4:9,10 There remains a *Sabbath rest* for the people of God. For the one who enters God's rest also rests from his own work, just as God rested from his work.

Colossians 3:4 When Christ, who is your life, appears, then *you also will appear with him in glory.*

Revelation 21:22-26 I did not see a temple in the city, because the Lord God Almighty and the Lamb are its temple. The city does not need the sun or the moon to shine on it, because the glory of God has given it light, and the Lamb is its lamp. The nations will walk by its light, and the kings of the earth will bring their glory into it. There is no day when its gates will be shut, for there will be no night in that place. They will bring the glory and the honor of the nations into it.

230. What will our bodies be like after our resurrection?

John 5:28,29 Do not be amazed at this, for a time is coming when all who are in their graves will hear his voice and will come out. Those who have done good will rise to live, but those who have practiced evil will rise to be condemned.

Isaiah 26:19 Your dead ones will live. *Their dead bodies will rise.* Wake up and sing for joy, you who dwell in the dust, because your dew will glisten like morning light, and the earth will give up the spirits of the dead.

Job 19:25-27 I know that my Redeemer lives, and that at the end of time he will stand over the dust. Then, even after my skin has been destroyed, nevertheless, *in my own flesh I will see God. I myself will see him.* My own eyes will see him, and not as a stranger. My emotions are in turmoil within me.

1 Corinthians 15:42-44,50-53 (Our bodies are devastated by sin in this life, but they will be raised in glory.)

Philippians 3:21 By the power that enables [our Lord Jesus Christ] to subject all things to himself, *he will transform our humble bodies to be like his glorious body.*

1 Corinthians 15:42-44 That is the way the resurrection of the dead will be. What is sown is perishable; *it is raised imperishable.* It is sown in dishonor; it is raised in glory. It is sown in weakness; it is raised in power. It is sown as a natural body; it is *raised as a spiritual body.* If there is a natural body, there is also a spiritual body.

231. What truth gives me confidence that I will rise to eternal life?

1 Corinthians 15:3-8,12-22 (God gave many witnesses of Christ's resurrection. Christ's resurrection gives the assurance that we too will rise.)

2 Timothy 2:11 This saying is trustworthy: *Indeed, if we have died with him, we will also live with him.*

John 11:25 Jesus said to her, *"I am the resurrection and the life. Whoever believes in me will live, even if he dies."*

John 14:19 In a little while the world will see me no longer, but you will see me. *Because I live, you also will live.*

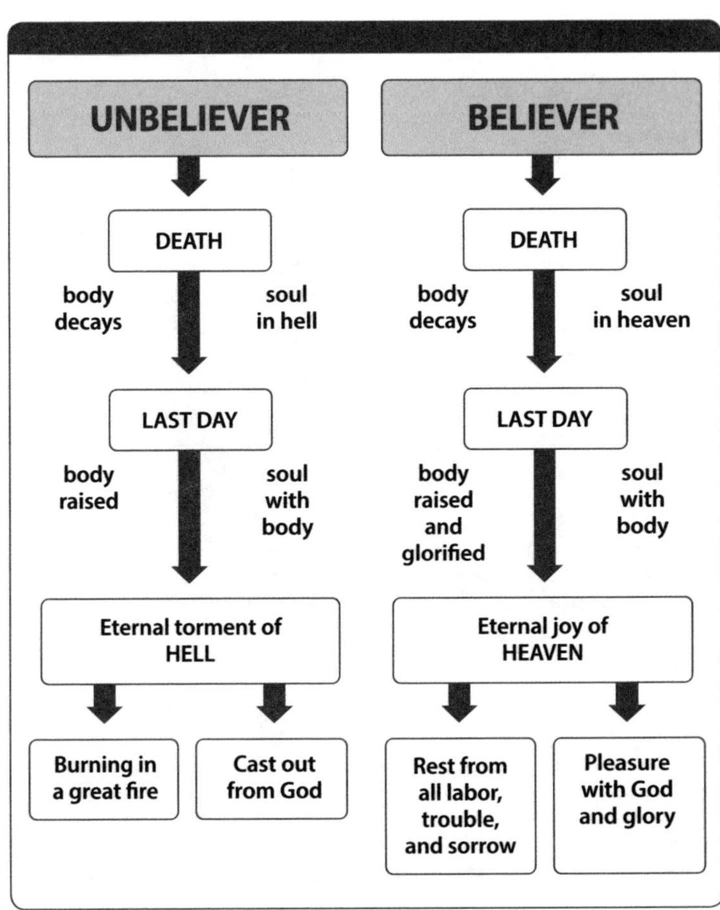

CONNECTIONS

When a fellow Christian dies, we experience both grief and hope. But isn't grief evidence of weakness? Shouldn't we be strong and not shed a tear? The account of Jesus at the tomb of Lazarus puts death and tears into perspective.

John 11:1-6,17-44

Because Jesus is the perfect God-man, we know that his tears did not come from a lack of faith. How would you describe the difference between pure tears and the grief that comes from spiritual weakness? Jesus raised Lazarus, but Lazarus eventually died again. With that in mind, explain what lasting comfort Jesus' raising of Lazarus gives to Christians.

Luther

While sanctification has begun and is growing daily, we expect that our flesh will be destroyed and buried with all its uncleanness. Then we will come forth gloriously and arise in a new, eternal life of entire and perfect holiness. For now we are only half pure and holy. So the Holy Spirit always has some reason to continue His work in us through the Word. He must daily administer forgiveness until we reach the life to come. At that time there will be no more forgiveness, but only perfectly pure and holy people. We will be full of godliness and righteousness, removed and free from sin, death, and all evil, in a new, immortal, and glorified body. (Large Catechism, II, par. 57-58)

I Know That My Redeemer Lives (Stanzas 1,2,7)

I know that my Redeemer lives;
What comfort this sweet sentence gives!
He lives, he lives, who once was dead;
He lives, my everliving Head!

He lives triumphant from the grave;
He lives eternally to save.
He lives all-glorious in the sky;
He lives exalted there on high.

He lives and grants me daily breath;
He lives, and I shall conquer death.
He lives my mansion to prepare;
He lives to bring me safely there.

A NEW CREATION

The Life of a Christian Is a Life of Struggle

When we think of all God has done for us, our hearts overflow with gratitude. We want to fear, love, and trust in God above all things. We want to thank, praise, serve, and obey our heavenly Father. We want our lives to be expressions of appreciation for all God's gifts to us: the Father created us, Jesus redeemed us by his blood, and the Holy Spirit has called us to faith by the gospel. By God's grace we do love and serve our Savior, yet we still remain sinners and still struggle with temptations. Why does this struggle continue? Where can we find strength for this struggle?

The New Self Against the Old Adam

232. How does the Bible describe those the Holy Spirit has brought to faith?

> **2 Corinthians 5:17,18** If anyone is in Christ, *he is a new creation.* The old has passed away. *The new has come!* And all these things are from God, who reconciled us to himself through Christ and gave us the ministry of reconciliation.
>
> **Colossians 3:9,10** Do not lie to each other since you have put off the old self with its practices, and *put on the new self,* which is continually being renewed in knowledge, according to the image of its Creator.
>
> **Romans 7:22** *I certainly delight in God's law according to my inner self.*

We are a new creation, totally different from what we were by nature. Our new self finds its delight in the salvation won by Jesus. Our new self delights in God's law. Speaking through the apostle Paul, God teaches us that this new self is what we really are by faith. We do see sin in our lives, but Paul says, "Now it is no longer I who am doing it, but it is sin living in me" (Romans 7:17).

233. Because of what the Lord has done for each of us, the "real me" loves to live for Jesus. At the same time, we are troubled by our many sinful desires, which often lead to sinful acts. **Why do we have these sinful desires?**

> **Romans 5:12** Just as *sin entered the world through one man* and death through sin, so also death spread to all people because all sinned.
>
> **John 3:6** Whatever is born of the flesh is flesh. Whatever is born of the Spirit is spirit.

Psalm 51:5 Certainly, *I was guilty when I was born.* I was sinful when my mother conceived me.

Romans 7:18 I know that *good does not live in me, that is, in my sinful flesh.* The desire to do good is present with me, but I am not able to carry it out.

Genesis 8:21 The LORD smelled the pleasant aroma. The LORD said in his heart, "I will never again curse the soil anymore because of man, for the thoughts he forms in his heart are evil from his youth. Neither will I ever again strike every living thing, as I have done."

Mark 7:21,22 In fact, from within, out of people's hearts, come evil thoughts, sexual sins, theft, murder, adultery, greed, wickedness, deceit, unrestrained immorality, envy, slander, arrogance, and foolishness.

A CLOSER LOOK

Through Adam's fall, sin entered the world. As a result, all people are by nature conceived and born as sinners. We each have a sinful nature. Because this nature has been passed down to us from Adam, we call it the old Adam. It is also called the old self.

234. In what ways does our sinful nature show itself to be our enemy?

Romans 7:15 I do not understand what I am doing, *because I do not keep doing what I want. Instead, I do what I hate.*

Romans 7:18,19 I know that good does not live in me, that is, in my sinful flesh. The desire to do good is present with me, but I am not able to carry it out. So I fail to do the good I want to do. Instead, *the evil I do not want to do, that is what I keep doing.*

Romans 7:21-24 I find this law at work: When I want to do good, evil is present with me. I certainly delight in God's law according to my inner self, but I see a different law at work in my members, waging war against the law of my mind and taking me captive to the law of sin, which is present in my members. What a miserable wretch I am! Who will rescue me from this body of death?

Galatians 5:17 *The sinful flesh desires what is contrary to the spirit,* and the spirit what is contrary to the sinful flesh. In fact, these two continually oppose one another, so that you do not continue to do these things you want to do.

Galatians 5:19-21 The works of the sinful flesh are obvious: sexual immorality, impurity, complete lack of restraint, idolatry, sorcery, hatred, discord, jealousy, outbursts of anger, selfish ambition, dissensions, heresies, envy, murders, drunkenness, orgies, and things similar to these. I warn you, just as I also warned you before, that *those who continue to do such things will not inherit the kingdom of God.*

Our sinful nature leads us into all sorts of sin, with the ultimate goal that we would abandon our faith.

235. When we see sinful desires and words and actions in our lives, we might be tempted to think that we don't need to be bothered by them because God loves us anyway. **What does God want us as Christians to understand when we see the wickedness of our own sinful flesh?**

Luke 18:10-14 (In the parable of the Pharisee and the tax collector, Jesus shows the reaction believers will have when they contemplate the sin in their lives. The reaction is exemplified by the words of the tax collector.) Verse 13: However the tax collector stood at a distance and would not even lift his eyes up to heaven, but was beating his chest and saying, *"God, be merciful to me, a sinner!"*

Psalm 38:18 I declare my guilt, and I am troubled by my sin.

Luke 15:21 The son said to him, "Father, I have sinned against heaven and in your sight. *I am no longer worthy to be called your son.*"

Psalm 51:4,17 *Against you, you only, have I sinned, and I have done this evil in your eyes.* So you are justified when you sentence me. You are blameless when you judge. The sacrifices God wants are a broken spirit. A broken and crushed heart, O God, you will not despise.

Romans 7:24 What a miserable wretch I am! Who will rescue me from this body of death?

2 Corinthians 7:10 *Godly sorrow* produces repentance, which leads to salvation, leaving no regret. On the other hand, worldly sorrow produces death.

God wants us Christians to understand that we deserve God's judgment because of the wickedness of our sinful flesh.

236. When we see the struggle within ourselves and know that all sin deserves God's judgment, we may be tempted to despair. **How does God bring us comfort when we struggle?**

Romans 7:24,25 What a miserable wretch I am! Who will rescue me from this body of death? I thank God through Jesus Christ our Lord! So then, I myself serve the law of God with my mind, but with my sinful flesh I serve the law of sin.

Matthew 11:28-30 Come to me all you who are weary and burdened, and I will give you rest. Take my yoke upon you and learn from me, because I am gentle and humble in heart, and you will find rest for your souls. For my yoke is easy and my burden is light.

Ephesians 2:3-5 Formerly, we all lived among them in the passions of our sinful flesh, as we carried out the desires of the sinful flesh and its thoughts. Like all the others, we were by nature objects of God's wrath. But *God, because he is rich in mercy, because of the great love with which he loved us, made us alive with Christ even when we were dead in trespasses.* It is by grace you have been saved!

Ephesians 2:8,9 It is by grace you have been saved, through faith—and this is not from yourselves, it is the gift of God—not by works, so that no one can boast.

Romans 4:22-25 This is why "it was credited to him as righteousness." Now the statement *"it was credited to him" was not written for him alone, but also for us* to whom it would be credited, namely, to us who believe in the one who raised our Lord Jesus from the dead. He was handed over to death because of our trespasses and was raised to life because of our justification.

Through his Word, God assures us that our sins have been paid for by Jesus our Lord.

237. What important role does this gospel comfort play as we struggle against our sinful nature?

Romans 12:1 I urge you, brothers, *by the mercies of God,* to offer your bodies as a living sacrifice—holy and pleasing to God—which is your appropriate worship.

2 Corinthians 5:14,15 *The love of Christ compels us,* because we came to this conclusion: One died for all; therefore, all died. And he died for all, so that those who live would no longer live for themselves but for him, who died in their place and was raised again.

Colossians 2:6,7 *Just as you received Christ Jesus as Lord, continue to walk in him,* by being rooted and built up in him, and strengthened in the faith just as you were taught, while you overflow in faith with thanksgiving.

Colossians 3:15,16 Let the peace of Christ control your hearts, to which you were also called, in one body. And be thankful. Let the word of Christ dwell in you richly, as you teach and admonish one another with all wisdom, singing psalms, hymns, and spiritual songs, with gratitude in your hearts to God.

Ephesians 5:8 You were once darkness, but *now you are light in the Lord. Walk as children of light.*

Galatians 2:20 I have been crucified with Christ, and I no longer live, but *Christ lives in me. The life I am now living in the flesh, I live by faith in the Son of God, who loved me and gave himself for me.*

Romans 7:22 I certainly delight in God's law according to my inner self.

John 15:5 I am the Vine; you are the branches. *The one who remains in me and I in him is the one who bears much fruit,* because without me you can do nothing.

Philippians 3:14 I press on toward the goal, for the prize of the upward call of God in Christ Jesus.

God's grace in Christ gives us the reason and the power to fight our sinful flesh. We are eager to turn away from sin and turn toward righteousness.

238. As Christians we will remain both old Adam and new self for the rest of our earthly lives. **How does that reality influence the way we live our lives?**

1 Corinthians 10:12 Let him who thinks he stands *be careful that he does not fall.*

1 Corinthians 10:13 No testing has overtaken you except ordinary testing. But God is faithful. He will not allow you to be tested beyond your ability, but *when he tests you, he will also bring about the outcome* that you are able to bear it.

Ephesians 6:13-17 Take up the full armor of God, so that you will be able to take a stand on the evil day and, after you have done everything, to stand. Stand, then, with the belt of truth buckled around your waist, with the breastplate of righteousness fastened in place, and with the readiness that comes from the gospel of peace tied to your feet like sandals. At all times hold up the shield of faith, with which you will be able to extinguish all the flaming arrows of the Evil One. Also take the helmet of salvation and the sword of the Spirit, which is the word of God.

We recognize that life is a spiritual struggle, one for which we need to be constantly on guard and equipped with God's powerful weapons.

Psalm 51:4,17 Against you, you only, have I sinned, and I have done this evil in your eyes. So you are justified when you sentence me. You are blameless when you judge. *The sacrifices God wants are a broken spirit. A broken and crushed heart, O God, you will not despise.*

Romans 7:24,25 What a miserable wretch I am! Who will rescue me from this body of death? I thank God through Jesus Christ our Lord! So then, I myself serve the law of God with my mind, but with my sinful flesh I serve the law of sin.

2 Corinthians 7:10 *Godly sorrow produces repentance,* which leads to salvation, leaving no regret. On the other hand, worldly sorrow produces death.

Acts 3:19 Therefore *repent* and return to have your sins wiped out.

1 John 1:9 *If we confess our sins,* he is faithful and just to forgive us our sins and to cleanse us from all unrighteousness.

Romans 1:17 In the gospel a righteousness from God is revealed by faith, for faith, just as it is written, "The righteous will live by faith."

Romans 3:23,24 All have sinned and fall short of the glory of God and are justified freely by his grace through the redemption that is in Christ Jesus.

The Holy Spirit leads us to repent regularly of our sins and then rejoice in the good news of forgiveness.

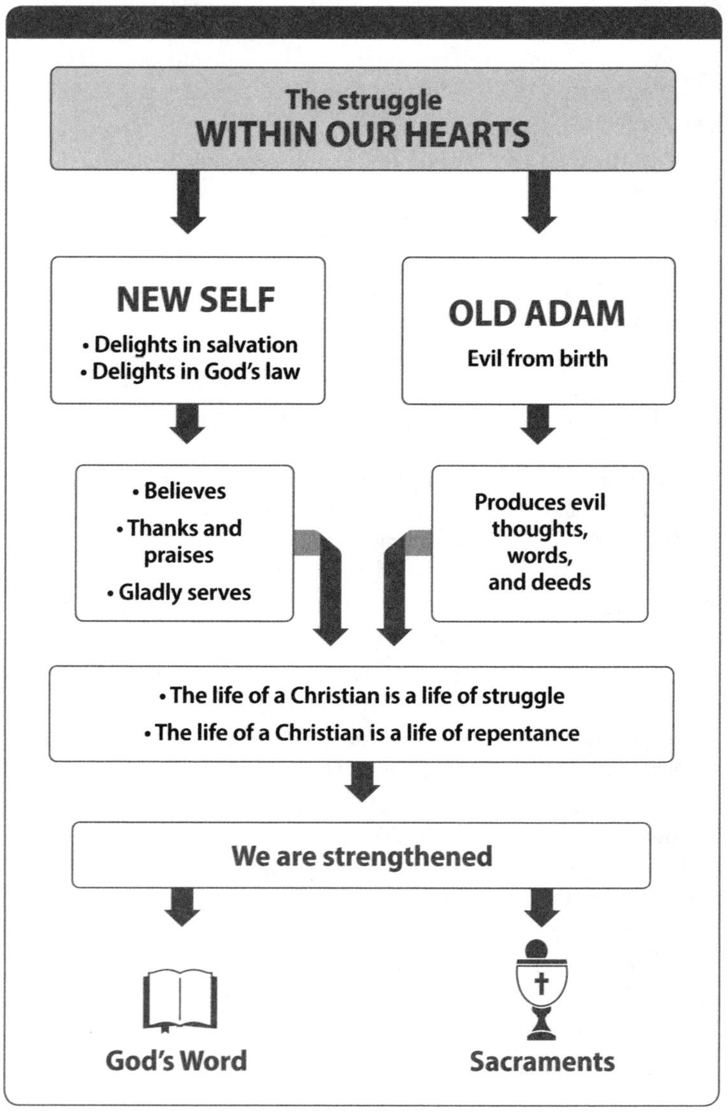

Repentance

Repentance is a change of heart about sin. It includes sorrow over sin, the desire to stop sinning, and faith in the forgiveness won for us by Jesus, which then motivates us to avoid sin and serve God.

Philippians 3:14 I press on toward the goal, for the prize of the upward call of God in Christ Jesus.

Romans 10:17 Faith comes from hearing the message, and the message comes through the word of Christ.

John 20:31 These are written that you may believe that Jesus is the Christ, the Son of God, and that by believing you may have life in his name.

John 8:31,32 Jesus said to the Jews who had believed him, "If you remain in my word, you are really my disciples. You will also know the truth, and the truth will set you free."

Titus 3:5 He saved us—not by righteous works that we did ourselves, but because of his mercy. He saved us through the washing of rebirth and the renewal by the Holy Spirit.

Matthew 26:26-28 While they were eating, Jesus took bread, blessed and broke it, and gave it to the disciples. He said, "Take, eat, this is my body." Then he took the cup, gave thanks, and gave it to them, saying, "Drink from it all of you, for this is my blood of the new testament, which is poured out for many for the forgiveness of sins."

We treasure the Word of God and the sacraments because they are the tools God uses to give us forgiveness and to motivate and strengthen us for the fight against sin.

CONNECTIONS

Christians today struggle with their sinful natures. The believers mentioned in the Bible did too. As we learn about the challenges they faced, we learn important lessons about our own weaknesses and to whom we must turn for strength. Peter was one of Jesus' chosen apostles and had spent a lot of time learning from Jesus. Yet Peter also gave in to his sinful nature. As you read about how he denied knowing Jesus, consider the lessons you can learn about your own struggle with your sinful nature.

Matthew 26:31-35,69-75

Explain how Peter's confident promise to Jesus was both good and bad. Consider this account together with what happened later (John 21:15-17). How can this incident in Peter's life serve as both a warning and an encouragement to you as you struggle with your own sinful nature?

Lutheran Confessions

When people are born again through the Spirit of God and set free from the law (that is, liberated from its driving powers and driven by the Spirit of Christ), they live according to the unchanging will of God, as comprehended in the law, and do everything, insofar as they are reborn, from a free and merry spirit. . . . However, since believers in this world are not perfectly renewed—the old creature clings to them down to the grave—the battle between spirit and flesh continues in them. Therefore, they indeed desire to perform the law of God according to their inner person, but the law in their members struggles against the law of their mind [Romans 7:23]. (Formula of Concord, SD, VI, par. 17, 18)

My Song Is Love Unknown (Stanzas 1,2)

My song is love unknown, My Savior's love to me,
Love to the loveless shown That they might lovely be.
Oh, who am I That for my sake
My Lord should take Frail flesh and die?

He came from his blest throne Salvation to bestow,
But such disdain! So few The longed-for Christ would know!
But oh, my friend, My friend indeed,
Who at my need His life did spend!

LORD'S PRAYER

Psalm 141:2 describes prayer as incense that rises to God.

PRAYER

Teach Us to Pray

Christians rejoice when God speaks to them in his Word, the Bible. It is God's voice assuring believers of his love.

Comforted and assured, Christians love to speak to God in return. The two-year-old child loves to fold his hands and pray to Jesus. The elderly grandmother treasures being able to bow her head and whisper her prayers to the Lord.

Because we consider prayer to be such a privilege, we want to know how to pray properly. With Jesus' disciples, we plead, "Lord, teach us to pray."

The Privilege of Prayer

239. What is prayer?

Psalm 19:14 May the *speech from my mouth and the thoughts in my heart* be pleasing to you, O Lord, my Rock and my Redeemer.

Psalm 62:8 Trust in him at all times, you people. *Pour out your hearts* before him. God is a refuge for us.

Psalm 73:25,26 Who else is there for me in heaven? And besides you, I desire no one else on earth. My flesh and my heart fail, but God is the rock of my heart and my portion forever.

Psalm 9:10 *Those who know your name will trust in you,* for you, O Lord, have not forsaken those who seek you.

Psalm 28:7 The Lord is my strength and my shield. In him *my heart trusts,* and I am helped.

Psalm 121:2 My help comes from the Lord, the Maker of heaven and earth.

Genesis 18:16-33 (Abraham spoke from his heart, pleading on behalf of Sodom.)

Philippians 4:6 Do not worry about anything, but in everything, by prayer and petition, with thanksgiving, let your requests be made known to God.

Prayer is speaking to God from the heart as a natural response of faith and an expression of our trust in the power and love of God.

240. What has God revealed about himself that encourages us to come to him in prayer?

Genesis 17:1 When Abram was ninety-nine years old, the LORD appeared to Abram and said to him, "*I am God Almighty.* Walk before me and be blameless."

Deuteronomy 33:27 *The everlasting God is a dwelling place,* and his eternal arms are under you.

Jeremiah 31:3 The LORD appeared to me from a distance, saying: *I have loved you with an everlasting love.* I have drawn you with mercy.

Exodus 34:6,7 The LORD, the LORD, the *compassionate and gracious* God, slow to anger, and overflowing with mercy and truth, maintaining mercy for thousands, *forgiving guilt and rebellion and sin.*

John 11:25,26 I am the resurrection and the life. Whoever believes in me will live, even if he dies. And whoever lives and believes in me will never perish.

Romans 8:34 Christ Jesus, who died and, more than that, was raised to life, is the one who is at God's right hand and who *is also interceding for us!*

In his Word, God has revealed that he is the almighty, eternal God whose love for us will never end. He has demonstrated the depth of his love by redeeming us from the power of sin and death and by forgiving our sins.

241. Why is trust in the true God the foundation of our prayers?

Numbers 23:19 God is not a man, that he should lie, nor a son of man, that he changes his mind. Does he say something, and then not carry it out? Does he speak, and then not bring it about?

Joshua 21:45 Not one promise out of all the good promises that the LORD had promised to the house of Israel failed. They all came true!

Romans 12:2 Do not continue to conform to the pattern of this world, but be transformed by the renewal of your mind, so that you test and approve what is the will of God—what is good, pleasing, and perfect.

1 John 5:14 This is the confidence that we have before him: that if we ask anything according to his will, he hears us.

James 1:6-8 Let him ask in faith, without doubting, because the one who doubts is like a wave of the sea, blown and tossed by the wind. In fact, that person should not expect that he will receive anything from the Lord. He is a double-minded man, unstable in all his ways.

2 Corinthians 1:20 As many promises as God has made, they have always been "Yes" in him. For that reason we also say "Amen" through him to the glory of God.

Psalm 119:105 Your words are a lamp for my feet and a light for my path.

John 17:17 Sanctify them by the truth. Your word is truth.

Our prayers are expressions of trust that all God has said in his Word is true and that he will keep the promises he has made in his Word. We entrust our lives to him.

242. To whom only do we pray?

Psalm 65:2 *You who hear prayer,* to you all mortals will come.

Isaiah 42:8 I am the LORD; that is my name. I will not give my glory to another, nor my praise to idols.

1 John 5:20,21 We know that the Son of God has come and has given us understanding so that we may know him who is true. And we are in *him who is true,* in his Son, Jesus Christ. *He is the true God* and eternal life. Dear children, guard yourselves from idols.

Jeremiah 10:10 *The LORD is the true God.* He is the living God, the eternal King.

Revelation 22:8,9 When I heard and saw them, I bowed down to worship at the feet of the angel who showed me these things. But he said to me, "Do not do it! I am a fellow servant with you and your brothers the prophets, and also with those who hold on to the words of this book. *Worship God!*"

Acts 14:8-18 (After healing a man who was lame, Paul and Barnabas had to restrain the people from honoring them as gods.)

A CLOSER LOOK

Some people pray to individuals who have died—individuals like Mary, other saints, or even family members—believing that those who are dead can do something about the challenges the living face on earth. God has never told us that those who have died can hear anything spoken to them by the living. Instead, God commands and invites us to go directly to him for all of our needs. When we place our confidence in someone other than God, we sin against the First Commandment.

243. Why does God only hear the prayers of Christians?

Isaiah 1:15 When you spread out your hands, I will hide my eyes from you. Indeed, even though you make many prayers, I will not hear.

1 Peter 3:12 *The eyes of the Lord are on the righteous,* and his ears are open to their requests. But the face of the Lord is against those who do evil.

Isaiah 59:2 It is your guilt that has separated you from your God, and your sins have hidden God's face from you, so that he does not hear.

Ephesians 1:7 In him we also have redemption through his blood, the forgiveness of sins.

Galatians 3:26 You are all sons of God through faith in Christ Jesus.

Hebrews 11:6 *Without faith it is impossible to please God.*

John 16:23 Amen, Amen, I tell you: *Whatever you ask the Father in my name, he will give you.*

Psalm 145:18,19 The LORD is near to all who call on him, to all who call on him in truth. He grants the desire of those who fear him. He hears their cry and saves them.

1 Kings 18:25-39 (On Mount Carmel God showed the people that he is the only true God who can answer prayer.)

Sin is a barrier between humans and God. When Christians, by faith in Jesus, enjoy the blessings of the forgiveness of sins, they gain access to God in prayer.

244. What confidence do we have whenever we pray for something that God has promised?

John 16:23 Amen, Amen, I tell you: *Whatever you ask the Father in my name, he will give you.*

Matthew 7:7,8 Keep asking, and it will be given to you. Keep seeking, and you will find. Keep knocking, and it will be opened for you. For everyone who asks receives, and everyone who seeks finds, and to the one who knocks, it will be opened.

245. What confidence do we have when our prayers include a request for something God hasn't specifically promised?

Matthew 7:9-11 Who among you, if his son asks him for bread, would give him a stone? Or who, if his son asks for a fish, would give him a snake? Then if you know how to give good gifts to your children, even though you are evil, *how much more will your Father in heaven give good gifts to those who ask him!*

Romans 8:28,32 We know that *all things work together for the good of those who love God,* for those who are called according to his purpose. Indeed, he who did not spare his own Son, but gave him up for us all—how will he not also graciously give us all things along with him?

Matthew 6:10 Your kingdom come. Your will be done on earth as it is in heaven.

A CLOSER LOOK

So that our prayers always reflect God's will, we use his Word as our guide when we pray. However, God's Word doesn't tell us what his will is for every detail of our lives. For example, we may pray that God heal a loved one who is sick, but it may be his will to use that sickness to bring that person to the blessings of eternal life in heaven. When God's Word doesn't tell us what his will is for a given situation, we often close our prayers with the words "if it is your will" or "but let your will be done." This too is an expression of our faith, since we are confessing that only God knows what is best for us. As we pray in this way, we know that God will give us exactly what we have asked for, namely, that his will shall be done.

---

246. What kinds of prayers does God invite us to bring to him?

1 Thessalonians 5:17 *Pray without ceasing.*

1 Timothy 2:1,2 First of all, then, I urge that *petitions, prayers, intercessions, and thanksgivings be made for all people,* for kings and all those who are in authority, in order that we might live a quiet and peaceful life in all godliness and dignity.

Psalm 51:3,4 I admit my rebellious acts. My sin is always in front of me. Against you, you only, have I sinned, and I have done this evil in your eyes.

Psalm 51:9 Hide your face from my sins. Erase all my guilty deeds.

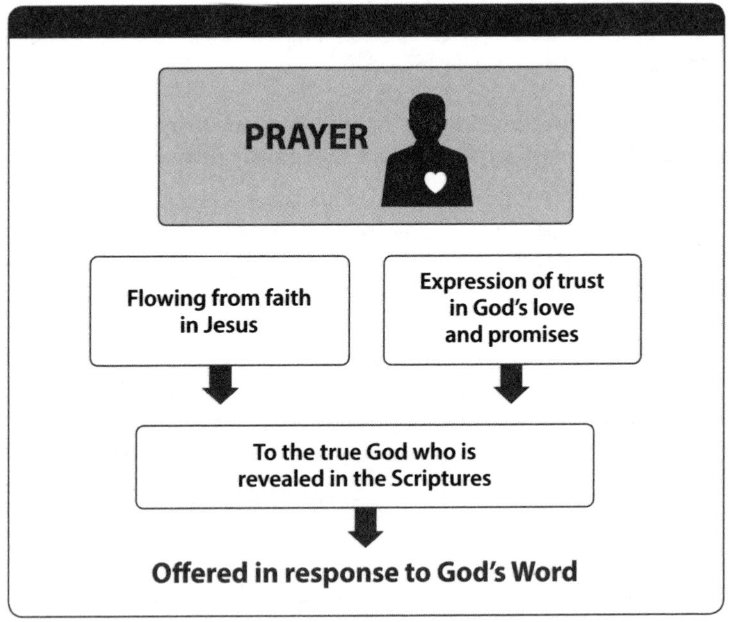

Psalm 138:1 I will thank you with all my heart.

Psalm 136:1 *Give thanks to the* Lord, for he is good. For his mercy endures forever.

1 Chronicles 29:13 Now, our God, we are thanking you and praising your glorious name.

Philippians 4:6 Do not worry about anything, but *in everything,* by prayer and petition, with thanksgiving, let your requests be made known to God.

Ephesians 6:18 *At every opportunity, pray in the Spirit with every kind of prayer and petition.* Stay alert for the same reason, always persevering in your intercession for all the saints.

Matthew 5:44 I tell you, love your enemies and *pray for those who persecute you.*

Matthew 6:11 *Give us today our daily bread.*

1 Timothy 2:8 *I want the men in every place to pray.*

God invites us to share with him whatever is on our hearts and our minds. He clearly shows us that he wants us to be in regular communication with him. We are to pray continually, confessing our sins and submitting requests concerning the challenges that face us. We are to pray concerning our own well-being, but also concerning the well-being of others—even those who treat us as enemies. We can pray about physical needs, but he teaches us to pray especially about spiritual needs. Then, as we survey the goodness of God so evident in our lives, we can offer prayers of thanksgiving.

CONNECTIONS

We often face problems or challenges that are impossible for us to solve on our own. By God's grace, we know we aren't on our own. God is with us. He has power to take care of us and invites us to pray for his help. Through prayer, we are able to bring the concerns of our hearts to the only, true, almighty, and loving God.

Daniel found himself in a seemingly impossible situation. A law had been passed that for 30 days everyone could pray only to the king. Daniel knew that to do so would dishonor God, so he continued to pray to the Lord as he always had. As you read the account of Daniel, you will see how God protected Daniel and showed himself to be the true and only God.

Daniel 6:1-23

When Daniel found out that the king's decree had been published, he shared words of prayer and offered "praise before his God" (v. 10). What do you think Daniel might have said in his prayers? The Lord encourages us to give thanks in all circumstances of our lives (1 Thessalonians 5:18), just as Daniel did. Think of a challenging situation you are facing or have faced. Think of three prayers of thanks that you might offer at the time of such a challenge.

Luther

We should be more encouraged and moved to pray because God has also added a promise and declared that it shall surely be done for us as we pray. He says in Psalm 50:15, "Call upon Me in the day of trouble, I will deliver you." And Christ says in the Gospel of St. Matthew, "Ask, and it will be given to you; . . . for everyone who asks receives" (7:7-8). Such promises certainly ought to encourage and kindle our hearts to pray with pleasure and delight. For He testifies with his own Word that our prayer is heartily pleasing to Him. Furthermore, it shall certainly be heard and granted, in order that we may not despise it or think lightly of it and pray based on chance. (Large Catechism, III, par. 19-20)

What a Friend We Have in Jesus (Stanza 1)

What a friend we have in Jesus,
All our sins and griefs to bear!
What a privilege to carry
Ev'rything to God in prayer!
Oh, what peace we often forfeit,
Oh, what needless pain we bear,
All because we do not carry
Ev'rything to God in prayer!

THE ADDRESS

Our Father in heaven.

What does this mean?

With these words God tenderly invites us to believe that he is our true Father and that we are his true children, so that we may pray to him as boldly and confidently as dear children ask their dear father.

OUR FATHER

We Address God as Our Father

When do you pray? How often? What do you pray for? How do you pray? We want to pray properly, and so did Jesus' disciples. They said to Jesus, "Lord, teach us to pray" (Luke 11:1). So Jesus gave his disciples of all times a very special prayer, which we call the Lord's Prayer. Every part of this prayer is worthy of our study. Every sentence is filled with spiritual treasures. The first words of this familiar prayer remind us of the privilege that is ours. We bring our prayers to our loving heavenly Father.

247. Why is it proper for us to call God our Father?

Malachi 2:10 Don't we all have one Father? *Hasn't one God created us?*

2 Corinthians 6:18 *I will be your Father,* and you will be my sons and daughters, says the Lord Almighty.

Galatians 4:4,5 When the set time had fully come, God sent his Son to be born of a woman, so that he would be born under the law, in order to redeem those under the law, *so that we would be adopted as sons.*

Galatians 4:6 Because you are sons, God sent the Spirit of his Son into our hearts to shout, "*Abba*, Father!"

Psalm 103:13 As a father has compassion on his children, *so the LORD has compassion on those who fear him.*

We call God our Father because he created us and adopted us into his family through Christ's redemption. Our heavenly Father loves us and cares deeply for us.

248. What does God do for us as our Father?

1 John 3:1 See the kind of love the Father has given us that *we should be called children of God,* and that is what we are!

1 Peter 1:23 You have been born again, not from perishable seed but from imperishable, *through the living and enduring word of God.*

Philippians 1:6 *He who began a good work in you will carry it on to completion* until the day of Christ Jesus.

1 Peter 1:17 *If you call on the Father who judges impartially, according to the work of each person,* conduct yourselves during the time of your pilgrimage in reverence.

Proverbs 3:12 *The Lord warns the one he loves* as a father warns a son with whom he is pleased.

Psalm 145:15,16 The eyes of all look eagerly to you, and you give them their food at the proper time. *He opens his hand, and he satisfies the desire of every living thing.*

John 16:23 Amen, Amen, I tell you: *Whatever you ask the Father in my name, he will give you.*

Isaiah 43:1,2 This is what the Lord says, the Lord who created you, O Jacob, the Lord who formed you, O Israel. Do not be afraid, because I have redeemed you. I have called you by name. You are mine. *When you cross through the waters, I will be with you. When you cross the rivers, they will not sweep you away. When you walk through fire, you will not be burned, and the flame will not set you on fire.*

249. What makes our heavenly Father different from earthly fathers?

Genesis 17:1 I am God Almighty.

Deuteronomy 32:4 He is a faithful God. He does no wrong. Righteous and upright is he.

Psalm 27:10 If my father and my mother abandoned me, the Lord would take me in.

Hebrews 12:10 They disciplined us for a little while, according to what seemed best to them, but *God disciplines us for our good, so that we may have a share in his holiness.*

James 1:17 Every good act of giving and every perfect gift is from above, coming down from the Father of the lights, who does not change or shift like a shadow.

250. With the Lord's Prayer, we bring many requests to God. **As we make those requests, why is it comforting for us to remember that God is our Father?**

Psalm 91:9,10 Yes, you LORD are *my refuge!* If you make the Most High *your shelter,* evil will not overtake you. Disaster will not come near your tent.

Romans 8:32 He who did not spare his own Son, but gave him up for us all—how will he not also *graciously give us all things along with him?*

Matthew 7:9-11 Who among you, if his son asks him for bread, would give him a stone? Or who, if his son asks for a fish, would give him a snake? Then if you know how to give good gifts to your children, even though you are evil, *how much more will your Father in heaven give good gifts to those who ask him!*

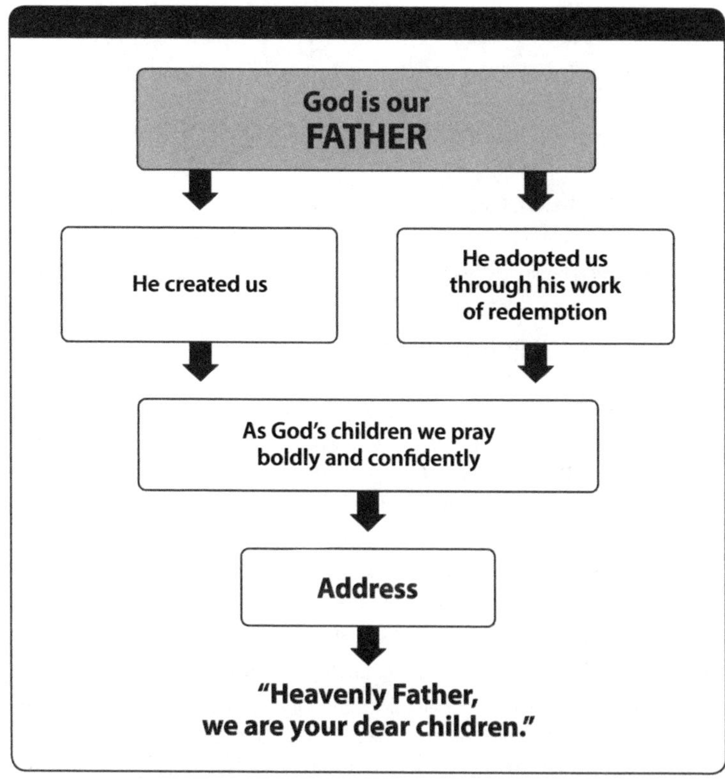

251. What attitude does God invite us to have as we pray the petitions of the Lord's Prayer?

Ephesians 3:12 In him *we can freely approach God with confidence* through faith in him.

James 1:6 Let him *ask in faith,* without doubting, because the one who doubts is like a wave of the sea, blown and tossed by the wind.

Romans 8:15 You did not receive a spirit of slavery so that you are afraid again, but you received the Spirit of adoption by whom we call out, "*Abba,* Father!"

Hebrews 4:16 Let us *approach the throne of grace with confidence,* so that we may receive mercy and find grace to help in time of need.

Genesis 18:1-5,16-33 (Abraham prayed boldly on behalf of his nephew Lot and the city of Sodom.)

252. What are we confessing when we acknowledge that our Father is in heaven?

Ephesians 4:6 . . . one God and Father of all, who is over all, and through all, and in us all.

Isaiah 6 (When he commissioned Isaiah as his prophet, God gave Isaiah a glimpse of heaven. Isaiah saw the Lord seated on his throne, in power and glory. Isaiah witnessed the honor and glory the angels were attributing to God.)

Psalm 115:3 Our God is in the heavens. *He does everything that pleases him.*

Haggai 2:8 The silver is mine and the gold is mine, declares the LORD of Armies.

Psalm 124:8 Our help is in the name of the LORD, the Maker of heaven and earth.

Psalm 139:7-10 Where can I go from your Spirit? Where can I flee from your Presence? If I go up to heaven, you are there. If I make my bed in hell—there you are! I rise on the wings of dawn. I settle on the far side of the sea. *Even there your hand guides me, and your right hand holds on to me.*

Acts 17:24 The God who made the world and everything in it is the Lord of heaven and earth and does not live in temples made with hands.

Ephesians 3:20 Now to *him, who is able,* according to the power that is at work within us, *to do infinitely more than we can ask or imagine . . .*

From heaven, God reigns over all things in glory. By addressing our Father in heaven, we are confessing his greatness, power, and glory. Because he possesses all things, we are acknowledging that he is the one who can answer our prayers.

A CLOSER LOOK

We begin the address (and the entire prayer) with the word *our.* That word reminds us that we are all members of the family of God, brothers and sisters through Christ's redemption, who pray with one another and for one another.

Our safety, our health, our well-being, our prosperity, our faith—none of those things is the result of our own strength, ingenuity, or decision. Each is the work and blessing of God. God wants us to come to him in prayer, as a child comes to his loving father. He encourages us to acknowledge that he is the source of all good things and to ask for the things we need. Jacob gave us a prayer model. At a time when it seemed that Jacob's life and the lives of his descendants were in danger, Jacob struggled with God and wouldn't let go of God. He prayed with confidence in God's power and in God's desire to bless him.

Genesis 32:9-12,22-31

Jacob boldly held on to God and wouldn't let him go because he knew the promises God had made to him. God has made many promises to us as well. Imagine a situation where you are tempted to worry and to be afraid. Think of a promise of God that would be comforting in that moment. Now compose a prayer that mentions that promise.

Luther

["Father"] is indeed a friendly, sweet, intimate, and warmhearted word. To speak the words "Lord" or "God" or "Judge" would not be nearly as gracious and comforting to us. The name "Father" is part of our nature and is sweet by nature. That is why it is the most pleasing to God, and why no other name moves him so strongly to hear us. With this name we likewise confess that we are the children of God, which again stirs his heart mightily; for there is no lovelier sound than that of a child speaking to his father. (LW 42:22)

Our Father, Who From Heaven Above (Stanza 1)

Our Father, who from heav'n above
Bids all of us to live in love
As members of one family
And pray to you in unity,
Teach us no thoughtless words to say,
But from our inmost heart to pray.

THE FIRST PETITION
Hallowed be your name.

What does this mean?
God's name is certainly holy by itself, but we pray in this petition that we too may keep it holy.

How is God's name kept holy?
God's name is kept holy when his Word is taught in its truth and purity and we as children of God lead holy lives according to it. Help us to do this, dear Father in heaven! But whoever teaches and lives contrary to God's Word dishonors God's name among us. Keep us from doing this, dear Father in heaven!

GOD'S NAME
Help Us Honor God's Name

When you are a part of a family, your actions—good and bad—can affect the reputation of your family. By God's grace, we are part of God's family. Our actions, then, can affect what other people think when they hear the name of God. How can God's name best be honored? What do we mean when we pray, "Hallowed be your name"?

A CLOSER LOOK

Hallow means to value something as holy, that is, pure and perfect; to set it apart as special; and to live so others might realize it is holy in our lives.

253. What is God's name?

Genesis 17:1 I am God Almighty.

Isaiah 42:8 *I am the Lord;* that is my name. I will not give my glory to another, nor my praise to idols.

Exodus 34:5-7 The Lord came down in the cloud. He took his stand there with Moses and proclaimed the name of the Lord. . . . "The Lord, the Lord, the compassionate and gracious God, slow to anger, and overflowing with mercy and truth, maintaining mercy for thousands, forgiving guilt and rebellion and sin. He will by no means clear the guilty. He calls their children and their children's children to account for the guilt of the fathers, even to the third and the fourth generation."

John 17:6,8 I revealed your name to the men you gave me out of the world. . . . *I gave them the words you gave me.*

2 Corinthians 13:14 The grace of the Lord Jesus Christ, and the love of God, and the fellowship of the Holy Spirit be with you all.

Psalm 9:10 *Those who know your name will trust in you,* for you, O LORD, have not forsaken those who seek you.

God's name is his titles and everything else he has revealed about himself in his Word.

254. What special connection do we have with God's name?

Numbers 6:27 They will *put my name on the Israelites,* and I will bless them.

Isaiah 43:1 This is what the LORD says, the LORD who created you, O Jacob, the LORD who formed you, O Israel. Do not be afraid, because I have redeemed you. I have called you by name. *You are mine.*

Matthew 28:19 Go and gather disciples from all nations by *baptizing them in the name* of the Father and of the Son and of the Holy Spirit.

Romans 10:13 Everyone *who calls on the name of the Lord* will be saved.

Ephesians 2:19 You are no longer foreigners and strangers, but you are fellow citizens with the saints and *members of God's household.*

Galatians 3:26,27 *You are all sons of God* through faith in Christ Jesus. Indeed, as many of you as were baptized into Christ have been clothed with Christ.

God places his holy name on us when he calls us to faith through the means of grace.

255. God's name is holy in and of itself. When we pray "hallowed be your name," we aren't saying that we can change or add to the essence of his name. We are asking, rather, that God work in us so that we treat his name as special, that is, keep it holy in our lives. **In what ways do we keep God's name holy in our lives?**

Jeremiah 23:28 Let the prophet who has a dream tell his dream. But *let the one who has my word speak my word faithfully.*

Deuteronomy 4:2 *Do not add to the word that I am commanding you, and do not subtract from it,* so that you keep the commandments of the LORD your God that I am commanding you.

1 Chronicles 16:8 Give thanks to the LORD. *Call on his name. Make known his deeds among the peoples.*

2 Samuel 22:50 I will thank you among the nations, LORD. *To your name I will make music.*

Psalm 9:11 Make music for the LORD, who is seated in Zion. *Proclaim his deeds among the peoples.*

2 Timothy 4:1-5 (God urges us to be faithful in proclaiming his Word.)

We treat God's name as special when we teach his Word faithfully.

Ezra 10:11 So now, give praise to the LORD, the God of your fathers, and do his will.

Ephesians 4:1 As a prisoner in the Lord, therefore, I urge you to *walk in a manner worthy of the calling with which you have been called.*

Matthew 5:16 In the same way *let your light shine in people's presence,* so that they may see your good works and glorify your Father who is in heaven.

1 Corinthians 6:20 You were bought at a price. Therefore *glorify God with your body.*

1 Corinthians 10:31 Whether you eat or drink, or do anything else, *do everything to the glory of God.*

2 Corinthians 3:3 It is clear that *you are a letter from Christ,* delivered by us, written not with ink but with the Spirit of the living God, not on stone tablets but on tablets that are hearts of flesh.

Galatians 5:22,23 The fruit of the spirit is love, joy, peace, patience, kindness, goodness, faithfulness, gentleness, and self-control.

Titus 2:14 [Jesus Christ] gave himself for us, to redeem us from all lawlessness and *to purify for himself a people who are his own chosen people,* eager to do good works.

We treat God's name as special when we honor him with our good works.

256. As we recognize our own weaknesses, what promises from God give us confidence as we look forward to doing good works?

Ephesians 2:10 We are God's workmanship, created in Christ Jesus for good works, *which God prepared in advance so that we would walk in them.*

Philippians 2:13 It is God who is working in you, both to will and to work, for the sake of his good pleasure.

Even as we do these things, we acknowledge that it is God's power that works this good in us.

257. How is God's name dishonored?

Exodus 20:7 The LORD will not permit anyone *who misuses his name* to escape unpunished.

Jeremiah 23:31 Indeed, *I am against the prophets,* declares the LORD, *who use their own tongues to say, "This is what the LORD declares!"*

Malachi 1:6; 2:7,8 (The priests dishonored God's name by teaching things that were contrary to the Word of God.)

2 Peter 2:1,2 *There will be false teachers among you.* They will secretly bring in destructive heresies, even denying the Master who bought them, bringing swift destruction on themselves. Many will follow their depraved ways, and because of them the way of the truth will be blasphemed.

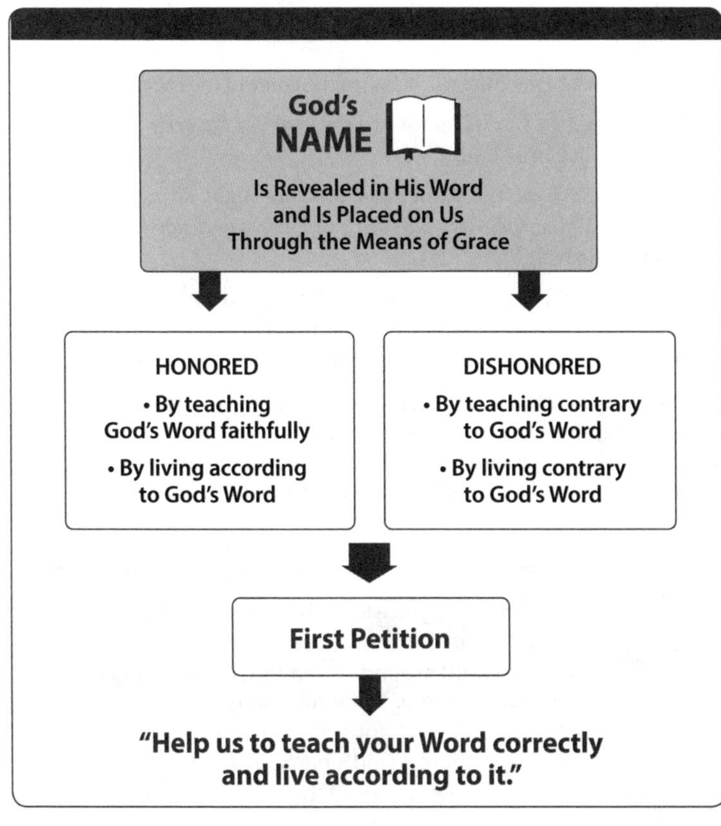

Matthew 7:15 Watch out for *false prophets.* They come to you in sheep's clothing, but inwardly they are ravenous wolves.

God's name is dishonored when his Word is distorted or not taught faithfully.

Romans 2:23,24 You who boast in the law *bring shame on God by breaking the law.* Yes, as it is written, *"God's name is blasphemed among the Gentiles because of you."*

Ezekiel 36:23 I will sanctify *my great name,* which has been profaned among the nations, which *you profaned among them.* Then the nations will know that I am the LORD, declares the LORD God, when I reveal myself as holy in front of their eyes through you.

God's name is dishonored when people live contrary to God's Word.

258. As children of God, why are we eager to honor God's name?

Acts 4:12 There is salvation in no one else, for *there is no other name under heaven given to people by which we must be saved.*

Matthew 16:26 What will it benefit a person if he gains the whole world, but forfeits his soul? Or what can a person give in exchange for his soul?

Romans 10:13 Everyone who calls on the name of the Lord will be saved.

Philippians 3:14 I press on toward the goal, *for the prize of the upward call of God* in Christ Jesus.

Matthew 5:16 In the same way let your light shine in people's presence, so that *they may see your good works and glorify your Father* who is in heaven.

Matthew 18:6 If anyone causes one of these little ones who believe in me to sin, it would be better for him to have a huge millstone hung around his neck and to be drowned in the depths of the sea.

God has given his name for our salvation. That truth is more important to us than anything else on earth. We will study and teach his Word faithfully so that God's name will always be on us and so that others also come to his name. We will live our lives so that our actions don't turn others away from God.

CONNECTIONS

God's amazing grace leads believers to want to honor his name. That isn't always easy to do. Our sinful flesh and the world around us tempt us to do things that would dishonor God's name. Three men were threatened with execution if they didn't bow down to an image made of gold. Discover how they honored God's name in spite of the threat to their lives, and see how God used them to bring even greater honor to his name throughout the land.

Daniel 3:1-29
God's enemies threatened the three men with death. Read verses 16-18 again. The three men did not know what God planned to do. What was most important to them? Think of

a personal situation in which doing or saying the right thing could be unpopular. In what different ways could this event from the book of Daniel be encouraging to you?

Luther

Now, here is a great need that we ought to be more concerned about. This name should have its proper honor; it should be valued holy and grand as the greatest treasure and holy thing that we have. As godly children we should pray that God's name, which is already holy in heaven, may also be and remain holy with us upon earth and in all the world.

"But how does it become holy among us?" Answer, as plainly as it can be said: "When both our doctrine and life are godly and Christian." Since we call God our Father in this prayer, it is our duty always to act and behave ourselves as godly children, that He may not receive shame, but honor and praise from us. (Large Catechism, III, par. 38-39)

Our Father, Who From Heaven Above

Your name be hallowed. Help us, Lord,
In purity to keep your Word,
That to the glory of your name
We walk before you free from blame.
Let no false doctrine us pervert;
All poor, deluded souls convert.

Not Unto Us (Stanzas 1,2)

Not unto us, not unto us be glory, Lord;
Not unto us but to your name be praise;
Not unto us but to your name all honor be giv'n
For matchless mercy, forgiveness, and grace.

Amazing grace—that chose us ere the worlds were made;
Amazing grace—that sent your Son to save;
Amazing grace—that robed us in your righteousness
And taught our lips to sing glory and praise.

THE SECOND PETITION

Your kingdom come.

What does this mean?

God's kingdom certainly comes by itself even without our prayer, but we pray in this petition that it may also come to us.

How does God's kingdom come?

God's kingdom comes when our heavenly Father gives his Holy Spirit, so that by his grace we believe his holy Word and lead a godly life now on earth and forever in heaven.

GOD'S KINGDOM

Believe His Word and Lead a Godly Life

What is ruling your heart? Who or what is in charge of your life? Many things want to control what you do, think, and say. The love for material wealth wants to control your decisions. A love for pleasure wants to dictate what you do. Yes, the sinful flesh is eager to rule your heart so that you serve only yourself.

When we pray the Second Petition, we are asking God to do something about those desires that wish to control us—to do something very important both in our hearts and in the hearts of others.

259. What does God tell us about his kingdom?

Colossians 1:13,14 The Father rescued us from the domain of darkness and *transferred us into the kingdom of the Son he loves,* in whom we have redemption, the forgiveness of sins.

Colossians 3:15,16 Let *the peace of Christ control your hearts. . . .* Let the word of Christ dwell in you richly.

Luke 17:20,21 The Pharisees asked Jesus when the kingdom of God would come. Jesus answered them, "The kingdom of God is not coming in a way you can observe, nor will people say, 'Look, here it is!' or 'Look, there it is!' because *the kingdom of God is within you.*"

Romans 14:17 *The kingdom of God* does not consist of eating and drinking, but of *righteousness and peace and joy in the Holy Spirit.*

John 3:5 Jesus answered, "Amen, Amen, I tell you: Unless someone is born of water and the Spirit, he cannot enter the kingdom of God!"

John 18:36,37 Jesus replied, "*My kingdom is not of this world.* If my kingdom were of this world, my servants would fight so that I would not be handed over to the Jews. But now my kingdom is not from here." "You are a king then?" Pilate asked. Jesus answered, "I am, as you say, a king. For this reason I was born, and for this reason I came into the world, to testify to the truth. *Everyone who belongs to the truth listens to my voice.*"

The kingdom of God is Christ's rule in our hearts through his Word.

260. How does God's kingdom come to us?

Romans 14:9 For this reason he died, rose, and lived, to be Lord of both the dead and the living.

Mark 1:15 "The time is fulfilled," he said. "The kingdom of God has come near! *Repent, and believe in the gospel.*"

1 Corinthians 12:3 I am informing you that no one speaking by God's Spirit says, "A curse be upon Jesus," and *no one can say, "Jesus is Lord," except by the Holy Spirit.*

Romans 5:5 *God's love has been poured out into our hearts* by the Holy Spirit, who was given to us.

Romans 9:16 So then, it does not depend on human desire or effort, but on God's mercy.

Romans 1:16 I am not ashamed of the gospel, because *it is the power of God for salvation* to everyone who believes.

Matthew 28:19,20 Go and gather disciples from all nations by baptizing them in the name of the Father and of the Son and of the Holy Spirit, and by teaching them to keep all the instructions I have given you. And surely I am with you always until the end of the age.

Titus 2:14 [Jesus Christ] gave himself for us, *to redeem us* from all lawlessness and *to purify for himself a people who are his own chosen people,* eager to do good works.

God's kingdom comes as the Holy Spirit works and strengthens faith in our hearts through the means of grace.

261. What are we praying for when we ask that God's kingdom come to us?

Matthew 11:28-30 *Come to me* all you who are weary and burdened, and I will give you rest. Take my yoke upon you and learn from me, because I am gentle and humble in heart, and you will find rest for your souls. For my yoke is easy and my burden is light.

John 8:31,32 If you *remain in my word,* you are really my disciples. You will also know the truth, and the truth will set you free.

We are praying that God would keep us in our faith and trusting in the gospel promises.

2 Corinthians 5:15,17 He died for all, *so that those who live would no longer live for themselves but for him, who died in their place and was raised again.* So then, if anyone is in Christ, he is a new creation. The old has passed away. The new has come!

Galatians 2:20 I have been crucified with Christ, and I no longer live, but Christ lives in me. *The life I am now living in the flesh, I live by faith in the Son of God,* who loved me and gave himself for me.

Colossians 3:3,4 You died, and your life is hidden with Christ in God. When *Christ, who is your life,* appears, then you also will appear with him in glory.

We are praying that God reign in our hearts through his Word so that we live to his honor and glory.

262. God's kingdom already has a stronghold in Christian hearts. Why, then, do we continue to pray that God's kingdom come?

1 Corinthians 10:12 Let him who thinks he stands be careful *that he does not fall.*

2 Peter 3:17,18 Dear friends, since you already know these things, be on your guard so that you do not fall from your own firm position by being led astray through the error of the wicked. Instead *grow in the grace and knowledge of our Lord and Savior Jesus Christ.* To him be the glory, both now and forever. Amen.

Mark 9:24 I do believe. *Help me with my unbelief!*

Ephesians 6:12 Our struggle is not against flesh and blood, but against the rulers, against the authorities, against the world rulers of this darkness, against the spiritual forces of evil in the heavenly places.

1 Peter 5:8 Have sound judgment. Be alert. *Your adversary, the Devil, prowls around* like a roaring lion, *looking for someone to devour.*

Romans 7:21,23 I find this law at work: When I want to do good, evil is present with me. But *I see a different law at work in my members, waging war against the law of my mind and taking me captive to the law of sin, which is present in my members.*

We pray for God's kingdom to come because another kingdom—that of the devil, the world, and our sinful flesh—is trying to dislodge God's throne from our hearts.

Matthew 28:19 Go and *gather disciples from all nations* by baptizing them in the name of the Father and of the Son and of the Holy Spirit.

John 10:16 I also have other sheep that are not of this sheep pen. *I must bring them also,* and they will listen to my voice. Then there will be one flock and one shepherd.

We pray for God's kingdom to come to those who are not yet part of the kingdom through faith.

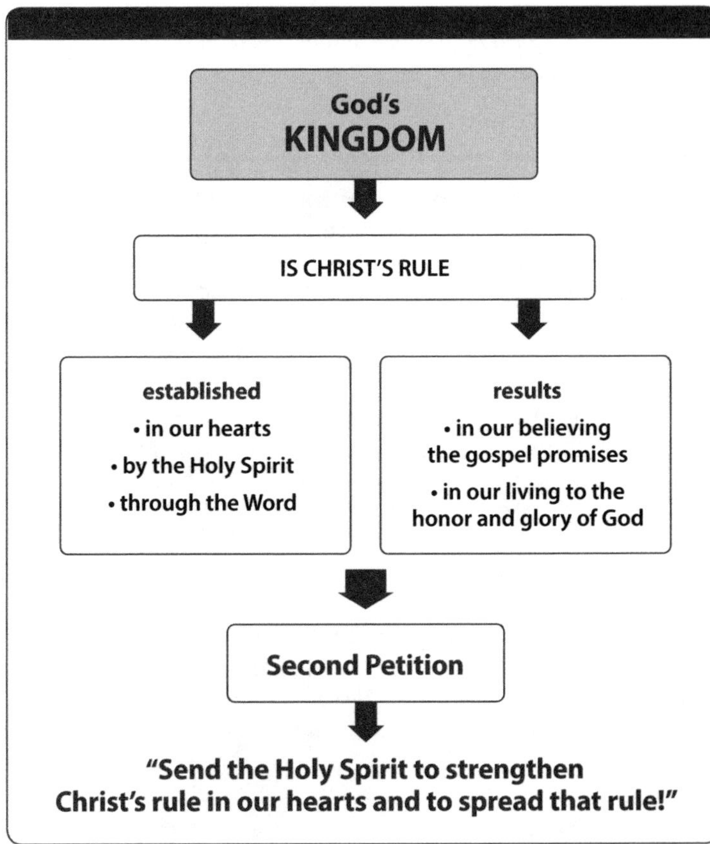

263. What role do regular worship, the study of God's Word, the Lord's Supper, and Baptism play in God's kingdom coming to us?

Isaiah 52:7 How beautiful on the mountains are the feet of *a herald, who proclaims peace and preaches good news,* who proclaims salvation, who says to Zion, "Your God is king!"

Romans 10:17 *Faith comes from hearing* the message, and the message comes through the word of Christ.

Matthew 26:26-28 While they were eating, Jesus took bread, blessed and broke it, and gave it to the disciples. He said, "Take, eat, this is my body." Then he took the cup, gave thanks, and gave it to them, saying, "Drink from it all of you, for this is my blood of the new testament, which is poured out for many *for the forgiveness of sins.*"

Ephesians 6:16,17 At all times *hold up the shield of faith,* with which you will be able to extinguish all the flaming arrows of the Evil One. Also *take the helmet of salvation* and *the sword of the Spirit,* which is the word of God.

CONNECTIONS

When someone's heart is not ruled by Jesus, there are eternal consequences. For this reason, we work together with other members of our church to send missionaries both to foreign countries and to new places in our own country. In our personal lives, we pray for chances to share Jesus with those we know, people whose hearts are still ruled by something else.

Christians long ago wanted to share Jesus too. Christians in the city of Antioch sent out two missionaries, Paul and Barnabas. These missionaries were ready to give up everything, working hard so that God's kingdom might come to others as well.

Acts 13:1-12; 14:1-7

List some sacrifices Paul and Barnabas made in order to share Jesus with more people. What sorts of things can make it hard for Christians to share Jesus with others today? Imagine that a friend tells you that he or she is scared to tell someone about Jesus. How would you encourage this friend?

Luther

We pray that the kingdom may come to those who are not yet in it, and, by daily growth that it may come to us who have received it, both now and hereafter in eternal life. All this is nothing other than saying, "Dear Father, we pray, give us first Your Word, so that the Gospel may be preached properly throughout the world. Second, may the Gospel be received in faith and work and live in us, so that through the Word and the Holy Spirit's power [Romans 15:18-19], Your kingdom may triumph among us. And we pray that the devil's kingdom be put down [Luke 11:17-20], so that he may have no right or power over us [Luke 10:17-19; Colossians 1], until at last his power may be utterly destroyed. So sin, death, and hell shall be exterminated [Revelation 20:13-14]. Then we may live forever in perfect righteousness and blessedness" [Ephesians 4:12-13]. (Large Catechism, III, par. 53-54)

Our Father, Who From Heaven Above

Your kingdom come, we humbly pray,
That Christ may rule in us today
And that your Holy Spirit bring
Still more to worship Christ as King.
Break Satan's pow'r, defeat his rage;
Preserve your Church from age to age.

Spread, Oh, Spread the Mighty Word (Stanzas 1,6)

Spread, oh, spread the mighty Word;
Spread the kingdom of the Lord
Ev'rywhere his breath has giv'n
Life to beings meant for heav'n.

Lord of harvest, grant anew,
Joy and strength to work for you,
Till the gath'ring nations all
See your light and heed your call.

THE THIRD PETITION
Your will be done on earth as in heaven.

What does this mean?
God's good and gracious will certainly is done without our prayer, but we pray in this petition that it may be done among us also.

How is God's will done?
God's will is done when he breaks and defeats every evil plan and purpose of the devil, the world, and our sinful flesh, which try to prevent us from keeping God's name holy and letting his kingdom come. And God's will is done when he strengthens and keeps us firm in his Word and in the faith as long as we live. This is his good and gracious will.

GOD'S WILL

May Your Will Be Done

Disasters bring suffering. Personal loss brings pain. People around us may ridicule God's Word. Christians often experience an inner struggle—a battle with their own sinful desires as they long to do the will of God.

Such challenges can be a big part of life, but Christians are not left without hope. We have a gracious and powerful God who is working in our lives and who invites us to pray the Third Petition with confidence. What are we asking of him when we pray, "Your will be done on earth as in heaven"?

264. What is God's will?

2 Timothy 4:2 *Preach the word.*

Mark 16:15 He said to them, "Go into all the world and *preach the gospel to all creation.*"

Jeremiah 23:28 Let the prophet who has a dream tell his dream. But let the one who has *my word speak my word faithfully.*

2 Timothy 4:1-5 (God urges us to be faithful in proclaiming his Word.)

God's will is that we hallow his name by faithfully teaching and preaching his Word.

1 Timothy 2:3,4 This is good and pleasing in the sight of God our Savior, *who wants all people to be saved* and to come to the knowledge of the truth.

John 6:40 *This is the will of my Father: that everyone* who sees the Son and believes in him *may have eternal life.* And I will raise him up on the Last Day.

John 20:31 *These are written that you may believe* that Jesus is the Christ, the Son of God, and that by believing you may *have life in his name.*

1 Timothy 4:16 *Pay close attention to yourself and to the doctrine.* Persevere in them, because by doing this *you will save both yourself and those who listen to you.*

God's will is that as we teach and preach his Word, his kingdom will come and more souls will be saved for eternal life.

2 Peter 3:18 *Grow* in the grace and knowledge of our Lord and Savior Jesus Christ.

1 Timothy 6:11,12 Pursue righteousness, godliness, faith, love, perseverance, and gentleness. Fight the good fight of faith. *Take hold of eternal life,* to which you were called and about which you made your good confession in the presence of many witnesses.

1 Timothy 4:8 Bodily training is beneficial to an extent, but *godliness is beneficial in all things,* because it holds promise both for life now and for the life to come.

1 Thessalonians 4:1,3 Beyond this, brothers, just as you received instruction from us about how you are to walk so as to please God (as indeed you are doing), we ask and urge you in the Lord Jesus that you do so even more. Indeed, *this is God's will: that you be sanctified,* namely, that you keep yourselves away from sexual immorality.

Colossians 1:9,10 We also have not stopped praying for you. We keep asking that you would be filled with the knowledge of his will . . . *so that you might live in a way that is worthy of the Lord. Our goal is that you please him by bearing fruit in every kind of good work and by growing in the knowledge of God.*

God's will is that through his Word, we will grow in faith to serve him and one another more and more.

Luke 10:38-42 (Jesus commended Mary for choosing to listen to his Word, the one thing that is needed.)

Psalm 1:1-3 How blessed is the man who does not walk in the advice of the wicked, who does not stand on the path with sinners, and who does not sit in a meeting with mockers. But *his delight is in the teaching of the*

Lord, and on his teaching he meditates day and night. He is like a tree planted beside streams of water, which yields its fruit in season, and its leaves do not wither. Everything he does prospers.

Psalm 119:37 Keep my eyes from looking at worthless things. *Give me life according to your ways.*

Psalm 122:1 I rejoiced with those who said to me, *"Let us go to the house of the Lord."*

1 Timothy 6:20 Guard what has been entrusted to you, turning away from godless, empty talk and the contradictions of what is falsely called "knowledge."

Matthew 13:44-46 (Jesus told two brief parables to emphasize that the kingdom of God is our greatest treasure.)

God's will for us is that we recognize his Word and the kingdom that comes through his Word as our greatest treasures.

265. God's will is done. We know that is true. In the explanation of this petition, Luther distinguishes between the way the will of God is done in heaven and the way it is done on earth. **How is God's will done in heaven?**

Psalm 103:20 Bless the Lord, you *his angels, you strong warriors who obey his word* by listening to what he says.

Matthew 18:10 See to it that you do not look down on one of these little ones, because I tell you that their angels in heaven always see the face of my Father who is in heaven.

In heaven, where there is no sin, God's will is done perfectly by the angels.

266. On earth, God's will meets opposition. **Who opposes God's will here on earth?**

1 Peter 5:8 Your adversary, *the Devil,* prowls around like a roaring lion, looking for someone to devour.

Matthew 4:1-11 (The devil tried to lead Jesus into sin so that he could not be our savior.)

1 Thessalonians 2:18 We wanted to come to you . . . but Satan *hindered us.*

James 4:4 Whoever wants to be a friend of *the world* makes himself an enemy of God.

2 Timothy 3:1-5 In the last days there will be terrible times. For people will be lovers of themselves, lovers of money, boastful, arrogant, blasphemous, disobedient to their parents, ungrateful, unholy, unloving, not able to reconcile with others, slanderous, without self-control, savage, haters of what is good, treacherous, reckless, puffed up with conceit, lovers of pleasure rather than lovers of God, holding to an outward form of godliness but denying its power. *Turn away from such people.*

2 Timothy 4:3,4 There will come a time when *people will not put up with sound doctrine.* Instead, because they have itching ears, they will accumulate for themselves teachers in line with their own desires. They will also turn their ears away from the truth and will turn aside to myths.

Galatians 5:17 *The sinful flesh* desires what is contrary to the spirit, and the spirit what is contrary to the sinful flesh. In fact, these two continually oppose one another, so that you do not continue to do these things you want to do.

Romans 7:18 I know that *good does not live in me, that is, in my sinful flesh.* The desire to do good is present with me, but I am not able to carry it out.

Romans 8:8 Those who are in the sinful flesh cannot please God.

James 1:14,15 Each person is tempted when he is dragged away and enticed *by his own desire.* Then when desire has conceived, it gives birth to sin. And sin, when it is full grown, gives birth to death.

Joshua 7 (Achan was overcome by the desires of his sinful flesh.)

267. How is God's will done for us as we experience the spiritual struggles of life on earth?

1 John 3:8 This is why the Son of God appeared: *to destroy the works of the Devil.*

John 16:33 I have told you these things, so that you may have peace in me. In this world you are going to have trouble. But be courageous! *I have overcome the world.*

Romans 6:6 We know that *our old self was crucified with him, to make our sinful body powerless,* so that we would not continue to serve sin.

God's will is done when he defeats the evil plans of the devil, the world, and our sinful flesh.

2 Thessalonians 3:3 The Lord is faithful. *He will establish you and protect you* from the Evil One.

1 Corinthians 1:8 [Our Lord] will also *keep you strong until the end,* so that you will be blameless on the day of our Lord Jesus Christ.

1 Peter 1:4,5 . . . an inheritance that is undying, undefiled, and unfading, kept in heaven for you. *Through faith you are being protected by God's power* for the salvation that is ready to be revealed at the end of time.

1 Corinthians 10:13 No testing has overtaken you except ordinary testing. But God is faithful. He will not allow you to be tested beyond your ability, but when he tests you, *he will also bring about the outcome that you are able to bear it.*

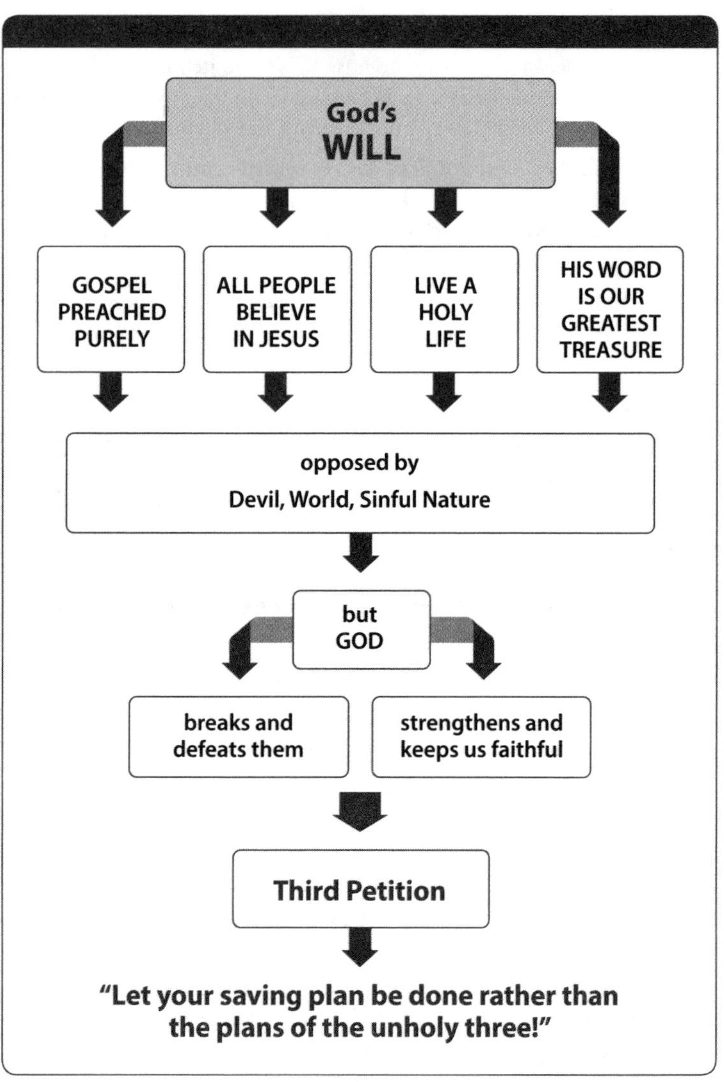

1 Peter 5:10 The God of all grace, who called you into his eternal glory in Christ Jesus, *will himself restore, establish, strengthen, and support you.*

Philippians 1:6 He who began a good work in you will carry it on to completion until the day of Christ Jesus.

Ephesians 6:10-18 (God provides the armor we need to resist the devil's attacks.)

James 4:7 Resist the Devil, and he will flee from you.

God's will is done on earth when he strengthens us and keeps us faithful to his Word.

Hebrews 13:21 May [the God of peace] equip you with every good thing *to do his will, as he works in us what is pleasing in his sight* through Jesus Christ. To him be glory forever and ever. Amen.

Psalm 86:12 I will thank you, O Lord my God, with all my heart, and *I will glorify your name forever.*

1 Corinthians 10:31 Whether you eat or drink, or do anything else, *do everything to the glory of God.*

God's will is done on earth when we hallow his name by our words and actions.

CONNECTIONS

Satan and the world will always seek to oppose God's will in the world. Christianity is openly ridiculed. Christians sometimes are openly persecuted and even killed. Sin is defended and promoted as if it were our right to do whatever we want. Christians can easily become discouraged. However, it is comforting to remember that when Jesus rose from the dead, he won the victory over Satan and the world. As long as the world exists, God's will continues to be done. Read about the opposition Christianity faced shortly after Jesus ascended. The Christians in Jerusalem were persecuted to the point that they had to flee to other cities and countries. Discover how God used that seeming victory of Satan to bring about great victories for the faith.

Acts 6:8-15; 7:51–8:8; 11:19-21

What blessings did God bring even as enemies were working so hard to hurt the church? We may not immediately see the blessings God is bringing during hard times, but we know his good and gracious will is getting done. Think of yourself suffering persecution in some way today. What blessings can God bring to you through that kind of suffering?

Luther

No one can believe how the devil opposes and resists these prayers. He cannot allow anyone to teach or to believe rightly. It hurts him beyond measure to have his lies and abominations exposed. . . . Therefore, he chafes and rages as a fierce enemy with all his power and might. He marshals all his subjects and in addition, enlists the world and our own flesh as his allies. . . . So he provokes the world against us, fans and stirs the fire, so that he may hinder and drive us back, cause us to fall, and again bring us under his power . . . so there is just as great a need, as in all the other petitions, that we pray without ceasing, "Dear Father, Your will be done, not the devil's will or our enemies' or anything that would persecute and suppress Your holy Word or hinder your kingdom." (Large Catechism, III, par. 62,63,65,67]

Our Father, Who From Heaven Above (Stanza 4)

Your gracious will on earth be done
Just as in heav'n around your throne,
That patiently we may obey
Throughout our lives all that you say.
Curb sinful flesh and ev'ry ill
That sets itself against your will.

Jesus, Lead Us On (Stanzas 1,2)

Jesus, lead us on Till our rest is won;
And although the way be cheerless,
We will follow, calm and fearless.
Guide us by your hand
To our fatherland.

If the way be drear, If the foe be near,
Let not faithless fears o'ertake us;
Let not faith and hope forsake us,
For through many a woe
To our home we go.

THE FOURTH PETITION

Give us today our daily bread.

What does this mean?

God surely gives daily bread without our asking, even to all the wicked, but we pray in this petition that he would lead us to realize this and to receive our daily bread with thanksgiving.

What, then, is meant by daily bread?

Daily bread includes everything that we need for our bodily welfare, such as food and drink, clothing and shoes, house and home, land and cattle, money and goods, a godly spouse, godly children, godly workers, godly and faithful leaders, good government, good weather, peace and order, health, a good name, good friends, faithful neighbors, and the like.

DAILY BREAD

Everything We Need

Where do all the things we need for daily living come from? Someone might answer, "We earn money to buy things from a store." If we think a little more, we realize that all things in a store come from factories or farms. We have the money to buy these things because we work for a paycheck.

Our paychecks, as well as the places that produce or sell things, certainly play a role in getting us our daily bread. But when Jesus teaches us to pray for physical blessings, he points our eyes in a very different direction. Where do all the things we need come from?

268. What is meant by daily bread?

Psalm 37:25,26 I was a young man. Now I am old. But *I have never seen a righteous person forsaken or his children begging for bread.* Every day he is gracious and lends. His children will be blessed.

Deuteronomy 10:18 He carries out justice for the fatherless and widows. He loves the alien who dwells among you and *gives him food and clothing.*

Psalm 145:15,16 The eyes of all look eagerly to you, and you give them their food at the proper time. He opens his hand, and *he satisfies the desire of every living thing.*

Deuteronomy 8:18 Remember that the LORD your God is the one who *gives you the ability to produce wealth.*

Psalm 34:7 *The Angel of the LORD* camps around those who fear him, and he *delivers them.*

Psalm 68:6 *God causes the lonely to dwell together as a household.*

Romans 13:1 Everyone must submit to the governing authorities. For no authority exists except by God, and *the authorities that do exist have been established by God.*

Leviticus 26:6 *I will give peace in the land so that* you may lie down without anyone frightening you.

Daily bread includes everything God gives for our bodily welfare.

269. For what purposes does God give us our daily bread?

Psalm 145:15 The eyes of all look eagerly to you, and you give them their food at the proper time.

Philippians 4:19 My God will *fully supply your every need.*

Acts 14:17 He did not leave himself without testimony of the good he does. He gives you rain from heaven and crops in their seasons. *He fills you with food and fills your hearts with gladness.*

2 Corinthians 9:8,11 God is able to make all grace overflow to you, so that in all things, at all times, having all that you need, *you will overflow in every good work.* You will be made rich in every way so that you may be generous in every way, which produces thanksgiving to God through us.

1 Timothy 5:8 If anyone does not *provide for his own family,* and especially for his own household, he has denied the faith and is worse than an unbeliever.

James 2:15,16 If a brother or sister needs clothes and lacks daily food and one of you tells them, "Go in peace, keep warm, and eat well," but does not give them what their body needs, what good is it?

2 Corinthians 8:7 See that you also *overflow in this gracious gift.*

Proverbs 3:9 *Honor the LORD with your wealth,* with the firstfruits from your entire harvest.

1 Corinthians 16:2 On the first day of every week, each of you is to *set something aside in keeping with whatever he gains, saving it up at home.*

Proverbs 14:31 A person who oppresses the poor insults his Maker, but one who is gracious to the needy honors him.

God gives us daily bread in order to provide for our physical needs and to provide us with a means to honor him and serve others.

270. To whom does God give daily bread?

Matthew 5:45 He makes his sun to rise on the evil and the good and sends rain *on the righteous and the unrighteous.*

Psalm 145:15,16 *The eyes of all look eagerly to you,* and you give them their food at the proper time. He opens his hand, and he satisfies the desire of every living thing.

271. If God gives daily bread to all creatures, why does he teach us to pray this petition?

Deuteronomy 8:17,18 You might say in your heart, "My ability and the power of my hand have earned this wealth for me." But then you are to *remember that the LORD your God is the one who gives you the ability to produce wealth,* to confirm his covenant that he promised to your fathers with an oath, as he does to this day.

James 1:17 *Every good act of giving and every perfect gift is from above,* coming down from the Father of the lights, who does not change or shift like a shadow.

Psalm 92:1 It is good to *give thanks to the LORD.*

Matthew 6:25-34 (God teaches us to trust that he will provide for us by pointing to the birds of the air and the flowers of the field, which he adorns with beauty.)

1 Peter 5:7 Cast all your anxiety on him, because he cares for you.

Philippians 4:6 Do not worry about anything, but in everything, by prayer and petition, with thanksgiving, *let your requests be made known to God.*

Through this petition, God reminds us that everything we receive for our physical well-being comes from him. Therefore, we receive these blessings with grateful hearts and bring all our needs to him in prayer.

272. What does God teach us by inviting us to ask for *daily* bread?

James 4:15 It is better for you to say, "If it is the Lord's will, we will live, and we will do this or that."

Luke 14:28-30 Which of you, if he wants to build a tower, does not first sit down and count the cost to see if he has enough to complete it? Otherwise, when he has laid a foundation and is not able to finish, everyone who sees it will begin to ridicule him, saying, "This fellow began to build, but was not able to finish."

1 Timothy 6:8 If we have food and clothing, *with these we will be satisfied.*

Luke 12:15 Watch out and *be on guard against all greed,* because a man's life is not measured by how many possessions he has.

Matthew 6:25-34 (By pointing to the birds of the air and the flowers of the field, which he adorns with beauty, God teaches us not to worry but, rather, to trust that he will provide what we need for each day.)

1 Timothy 6:17 Instruct those who are rich in this present age not to be arrogant or to put their hope in the uncertainty of riches, but rather in God, who richly supplies us with all things for our enjoyment.

Although God encourages us to plan carefully and humbly for the future, he invites us to ask for daily bread in order to remind us to be content and to trust him to give us all that we need for each day.

273. What attitude does God want us to have regarding the way we use the physical blessings he has given to us?

Psalm 24:1 *The earth is the Lord's* and everything that fills it, the world and all who live in it.

Matthew 6:33,34 *Seek first the kingdom of God and his righteousness,* and all these things will be given to you as well. So do not worry about tomorrow, for tomorrow will care for itself. Each day has enough trouble of its own.

2 Corinthians 9:8 God is able to make all grace overflow to you, so that in all things, at all times, having all that you need, you will *overflow in every good work.*

Luke 12:15-21 (Jesus warned against the desire to heap up blessings for our own pleasure rather than using our blessings to his glory and for the benefit of his kingdom.)

1 Corinthians 4:2 It is required of stewards that they *be found faithful.*

Luke 6:38 *Give, and it will be given to you.* A good measure pressed down, shaken together, and running over will be poured into your lap. In fact, the measure with which you measure will be measured back to you.

2 Corinthians 8:1-15 (The Macedonian churches considered it a great blessing to be able to give of their own blessings in order to help fellow Christians.)

2 Corinthians 9:7 Each one should give as he has determined in his heart, not reluctantly or under pressure, for *God loves a cheerful giver.*

Matthew 25:14-30 (Jesus told a parable about a king. Before leaving on an extended journey, the king entrusted his servants with bags of money, expecting them to put the money to good use while he was gone. Through the parable, Jesus teaches us to use what he has given us wisely and faithfully.)

Luke 16:9 I tell you, make friends for yourselves with unrighteous *mammon,* so that when it runs out, they will welcome you into the eternal dwellings.

God wants us to be faithful managers of all the blessings he has given us, generously and cheerfully placing him first in all we do.

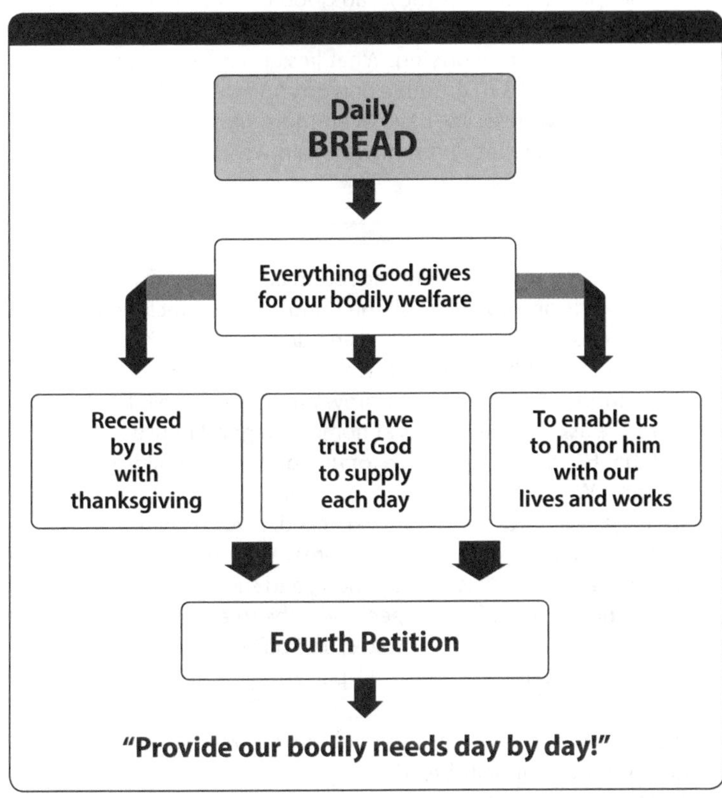

CONNECTIONS

When we forget that everything we have for our physical well-being comes from God, we can easily become dissatisfied or worry that we won't have enough. By teaching us to pray for our daily bread, God reminds us that he is the one who provides for us and that we can trust he will give us what we need each day.

When the nation of Israel left Egypt, the people were afraid that they wouldn't survive. Their fears quickly turned to complaining and rebellion against God. God showed both his patience and his power—he was able to provide daily bread for this huge community of people.

Exodus 16

The people of Israel felt they had good reason to doubt God. Describe a time in your life when you found yourself complaining against God or worrying. What lies about God does Satan tell us that lead us to grumble or worry? As we rejoice in God's patient forgiveness, we have even more reason to trust and give thanks. In what different ways can we express thanks to God for our daily bread?

Luther

On this topic anyone might indeed make a long prayer. With many words one could list all the things that are included, like when we ask God to give us food and drink, clothing, house and home, and health of body. Or when we ask that He cause the grain and fruit of the field to grow and mature well. Furthermore, we ask that he help us at home with good housekeeping and that He give and preserve for us a godly wife, children, and servants. We ask that He cause our work, trade, or whatever we are engaged in to prosper and succeed, favor us with faithful neighbors and good friends, and other such things. Likewise, we ask that He give wisdom, strength, and success to emperors, kings, and all estates, and especially to the rulers of our country and to all counselors, magistrates, and officers. Then they may govern well. (Large Catechism, III, par. 76-77)

Our Father, Who From Heaven Above (Stanza 5)

Give us today our daily bread,
And let us all be clothed and fed.
From hardship, war, and earthly strife,
From sickness, famine, spare our life.
Let selfishness and worry cease
That we may live in godly peace.

Praise God, From Whom All Blessings Flow

Praise God, from whom all blessings flow;
Praise him, all creatures here below;
Praise him above, ye heav'nly host;
Praise Father, Son, and Holy Ghost!

THE FIFTH PETITION

Forgive us our sins, as we forgive those who sin against us.

What does this mean?

We pray in this petition that our Father in heaven would not look upon our sins or because of them deny our prayers; for we are worthy of none of the things for which we ask, neither have we deserved them, but we ask that he would give them all to us by grace; for we daily sin much and surely deserve nothing but punishment.

So we too will forgive from the heart and gladly do good to those who sin against us.

FORGIVENESS

Don't Deny Our Prayers Because of Our Sin

Our sins separate us from God (Isaiah 59:2). God has every reason to be angry with us because of our sins, yet he invites us to ask him for his forgiveness. He is ready to forgive because of the work of his Son, Jesus.

The words and actions of others sometimes separate us from them. The hurt we feel can lead to hard feelings and even a desire for revenge. In the Fifth Petition, God invites us to ask him to forgive our sins and then, forgiven, we ask him to help us forgive others.

274. What do we confess about ourselves when we pray the Fifth Petition?

Psalm 51:4 *Against you, you only, have I sinned,* and I have done this evil in your eyes.

Romans 3:10,12 There is *no one who is righteous, not even one.* They all turned away; together they became useless. There is no one who does what is good; there is not even one.

Psalm 143:2 Do not bring charges against your servant, because *no one living can be righteous before you.*

Genesis 32:10 *I am not worthy* of even a bit of all the mercy and all the faithfulness that you have shown to your servant.

Romans 6:23 The wages of sin is death.

Because we sin every day by our thoughts, words, and deeds, we don't deserve to have God answering our prayers and giving us what we want or need. Instead, we deserve eternal punishment.

275. What are we asking when we pray this petition?

Psalm 51:1,2,9 *Be gracious to me,* God, according to your mercy. Erase my acts of rebellion according to the greatness of your compassion. Scrub me clean from my guilt. Purify me from my sin. Hide your face from my sins. Erase all my guilty deeds.

Psalm 51:11 *Do not cast me from your presence.* Do not take your Holy Spirit from me.

Psalm 19:12 Who can recognize his own errors? *Declare me innocent of hidden sins.*

Psalm 130:3,4 If you, Lord, kept a record of guilt, O Lord, who could stand? *But with you there is pardon.*

Luke 18:13 God, be merciful to me, a sinner!

Psalm 25:18 See my affliction and my trouble, and *take away all my sins.*

We are asking that God not hold our sins against us but, in his mercy, forgive us.

Psalm 55:1,2 *Turn your ear to my prayer,* O God. Do not hide from my plea for mercy. Pay attention to me and answer me. I am troubled in my thoughts and I groan.

Psalm 66:20 Blessed be God, who *has not turned aside my prayer* or turned aside his mercy from me!

Psalm 69:16 Answer me, Lord, for your mercy is good. *According to your great compassion, turn to me.*

We are asking God for mercy, so he would not deny our prayers because of our sins.

276. Why can we be confident that this petition will be granted?

Matthew 11:28 *Come to me* all you who are weary and burdened, and I will give you rest.

Revelation 1:5 To him who loves us and has freed us from our sins by his own blood . . .

Psalm 103:12 As distant as the east is from the west, *so far has he removed our rebellious acts from us.*

Jeremiah 31:34 I will forgive their guilt, and *I will remember their sins no more.*

Matthew 9:2 Take heart, son! *Your sins are forgiven.*

Acts 10:43 Through his name, everyone who believes in him receives forgiveness of sins.

1 John 1:9 If we confess our sins, *he is faithful and just to forgive us our sins and to cleanse us from all unrighteousness.*

Matthew 26:28 This is my blood of the new testament, which is poured out for many *for the forgiveness of sins.*

God accomplished our forgiveness by sending his Son to take the guilt of our sins upon himself on a cross. He forgives us through his Word and through the Sacraments.

277. What blessings are ours because we have the forgiveness of sins?

Romans 5:1 Since we have been justified by faith, *we have peace with God* through our Lord Jesus Christ.

Isaiah 61:10 *I will rejoice greatly in the Lord.* My soul will celebrate because of my God, for he has clothed me in garments of salvation. With a robe of righteousness he covered me.

Hebrews 9:14 How much more will the blood of Christ, who through the eternal Spirit offered himself without blemish to God, *cleanse our consciences* from dead works, so that we worship the living God?

278. We treasure the forgiveness of sins. **What are we eager to do when others sin against us?**

Colossians 3:13 *Forgive, just as Christ forgave you.*

Matthew 18:21,22 "Lord, how many times must I forgive my brother when he sins against me? As many as seven times?" Jesus said to him, "Not seven times, but I tell you as many as seventy-seven times."

Matthew 18:23-35 (Jesus used a parable to show that it is incomprehensible that we would refuse to forgive others if we have been forgiven all of our sins. See verses 32 and 33.) I forgave you all that debt when you begged me to. Should you not have had mercy on your fellow servant just as I had mercy on you?

Ephesians 4:32 Be kind and compassionate to one another, *forgiving one another,* just as God in Christ has forgiven us.

Luke 6:36 *Be merciful, just as your Father is merciful.*

279. In what way does this petition provide the foundation for all of our requests to God?

Psalm 32:5 I acknowledged my sin to you, and I did not cover up my guilt. I said, "I will confess my rebellion to the LORD," *and you forgave the guilt of my sin.*

1 Peter 3:12 *The eyes of the Lord are on the righteous,* and his ears are open to their requests.

Psalm 69:16 Answer me, LORD, for your mercy is good. According to your great compassion, turn to me.

Psalm 66:20 Blessed be God, who *has not turned aside my prayer or turned aside his mercy from me!*

Isaiah 30:19 When he hears you, he will answer you.

Without the forgiveness of sins, we would have no right to pray to God or expect that he would hear our prayers.

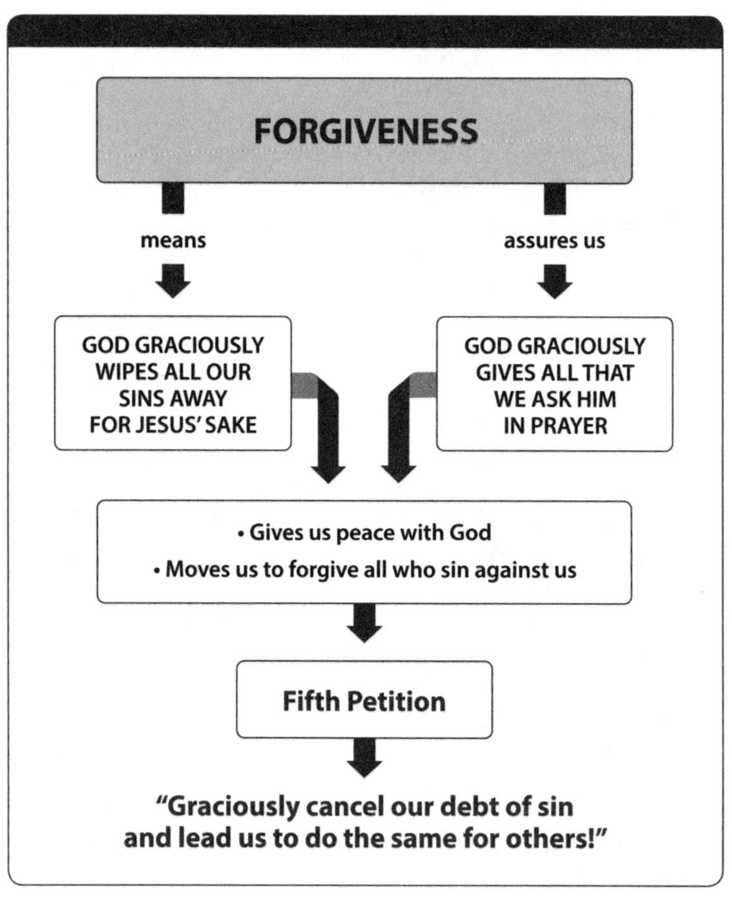

The forgiveness God has graciously given us empowers us to change the way we react when others sin against us. Joseph was mistreated in so many ways by others. Joseph's brothers hated him. When they saw the opportunity to make some money, they sold him as a slave. It's not hard to imagine that Joseph would have been determined to get revenge. Instead, he stands as an example for us of one who forgave those who mistreated him.

Genesis 50:15-21

From an earthly point of view, why could it have been very hard for Joseph to forgive his brothers? Consider a situation where it might be hard for you to forgive others for the way they treated you. How might the Holy Spirit use the account of Joseph to help you in that situation?

Luther

It is, therefore, the intent of this petition that God would not regard our sins and hold up to us what we daily deserve. But we pray that He would deal graciously with us and forgive, as He has promised, and so grant us a joyful and confident conscience to stand before Him in prayer [Hebrews 10:22]. For where the heart is not in a right relationship with God, or cannot take such confidence, it will not dare to pray anymore. Such a confident and joyful heart can spring from nowhere else than the certain knowledge of the forgiveness of sin [Psalm 32:1-2; Romans 4:7-8]. (Large Catechism, III, par. 92)

Our Father, Who From Heaven Above (Stanza 6)

Forgive our sins, Lord, we implore,
That they may trouble us no more;
We, too, will gladly those forgive
Who hurt us by the way they live.
Help us in our community
To serve each other willingly.

I Am Trusting You, Lord Jesus (Stanzas 1-3)

I am trusting you, Lord Jesus, Trusting only you,
Trusting you for full salvation, Free and true.

I am trusting you for pardon; At your feet I bow,
For your grace and tender mercy Trusting now.

I am trusting you for cleansing In the crimson flood,
Trusting you who made me holy By your blood.

THE SIXTH PETITION

Lead us not into temptation.

What does this mean?

God surely tempts no one to sin, but we pray in this petition that God would guard and keep us, so that the devil, the world, and our flesh may not deceive us or lead us into false belief, despair, and other great and shameful sins; and though we are tempted by them, we pray that we may overcome and win the victory.

TEMPTATION

Keep Us From Temptation

Because we love God, we want to serve and obey him. Yet the battle against sin does not let up. Temptations assault us every day. What can we do? How can we serve God and avoid sin? How can we avoid hurting others, bringing disgrace and unnecessary suffering into our lives, and even jeopardizing our faith? We are so weak.

God alone is strong. He alone has power to help us in our struggle against sin. Therefore, we pray the Sixth Petition with all earnestness: "Lead us not into temptation."

280. What is temptation?

Genesis 3:1-13 (The devil tempted Adam and Eve to rebel against God.)

James 1:14,15 Each person is tempted when *he is dragged away and enticed by his own desire.* Then when desire has conceived, *it gives birth to sin. And sin,* when it is full grown, *gives birth to death.*

Galatians 1:6,7 I am amazed that you are *so quickly deserting the one who called you* in the grace of Christ, for a different gospel, which is really not another gospel at all. There are, however, some who are trying to disturb you by perverting the gospel of Christ.

Temptations are the attempts of our spiritual enemies to lure us away from God and his truth.

281. Who are these spiritual enemies that attempt to lure us away from God?

Revelation 12:9 *The great dragon* was thrown down—*the ancient serpent, the one called the Devil and Satan,* the one who leads the whole inhabited earth astray.

1 John 2:15,16 *Do not love the world or the things in the world.* If anyone loves the world, the love of the Father is not in him. For everything in the world—*the lust of the flesh, the desire of the eyes, boasting about material possessions—is not from the Father but from the world.*

2 Peter 2:18 By uttering arrogant, empty words, they use the depraved lusts of the flesh *to seduce* those who are barely escaping from those who live in error.

Romans 7:18 I know that *good does not live in me, that is, in my sinful flesh.* The desire to do good is present with me, but I am not able to carry it out.

Mark 7:21,22 *From within, out of people's hearts,* come evil thoughts, sexual sins, theft, murder, adultery, greed, wickedness, deceit, unrestrained immorality, envy, slander, arrogance, and foolishness.

282. What are the goals of these enemies when they entice us with temptations?

Matthew 7:15 Watch out for *false prophets.* They come to you in sheep's clothing, but inwardly they are *ravenous wolves.*

Matthew 24:11 *Many false prophets will appear and deceive many people.*

Romans 1:25 Such people have *traded the truth about God for the lie,* worshipping and serving the creation rather than the Creator.

John 8:44 You belong to your father, the Devil, and you want to do your father's desires. He was a murderer from the beginning and did not remain standing in the truth, because there is no truth in him. Whenever he lies, he speaks from what is his, because he is a liar and the father of lying.

2 Thessalonians 2:9,10 The coming of the lawless one will be in accordance with the work of Satan, with every kind of miracle, that is, *with false signs and wonders, and with every kind of unrighteousness that deceives* those who are perishing.

2 Peter 2:1 There were false prophets also among the people, just as there will be false teachers among you. They will secretly bring in *destructive heresies,* even denying the Master who bought them, bringing swift destruction on themselves.

Jeremiah 8:8 How can you say, "We are wise, and the law of the LORD is with us," when in reality the lying pen of the scribes has changed it into a lie?

Galatians 5:7 You were running well! Who cut in on you, so that you are no longer persuaded by the truth?

The devil, the world, and our sinful nature try to deceive us and lead us into false belief.

Matthew 27:3-5 (After Satan enticed him to betray Jesus, Judas despaired of forgiveness.)

2 Corinthians 2:7 You should rather forgive and comfort him, or else such a person could be *overwhelmed* by excessive sorrow.

2 Corinthians 4:8 We are hard pressed on every side, yet *not crushed;* perplexed, yet *not despairing.*

The devil, the world, and our sinful nature tempt us to fall into despair.

Proverbs 1:10 My son, if sinners lure you, *do not go along with them.*

1 Timothy 6:9,10 Those who want to get rich fall into temptation and a trap and many foolish and harmful desires, which plunge them into complete destruction and utter ruin. For *the love of money is a root of all sorts of evils.* By striving for money, some have wandered away from the faith and have pierced themselves with many pains.

Philippians 3:19 Their end is destruction, their god is their appetite, and their glory is in their shame. They are thinking only about earthly things.

Matthew 26:69-75 (In the courtyard of the high priest, Peter was seduced by fear of the world to deny Christ.)

2 Samuel 12:9 (David's sinful nature tempted him to commit adultery and murder.)

The devil, the world, and our sinful nature tempt us to fall into great and shameful sins.

283. Who is responsible when we give in to temptation?

James 1:13 Let no one say when he is tempted, "I am being tempted by God," because God cannot be tempted by evil, and *he himself tempts no one.*

James 1:14,15 *Each person* is tempted when he is dragged away and enticed *by his own desire.* Then when desire has conceived, it gives birth to sin. And sin, when it is full grown, gives birth to death.

284. The Bible tells us that God never tempts anyone to sin. **What, then, are we asking when we pray that our Father in heaven lead us not into temptation?**

Matthew 26:41 *Watch and pray,* so that you do not enter into temptation. The spirit is willing, but *the flesh is weak.*

2 Thessalonians 3:3 The Lord is faithful. *He will establish you and protect you* from the Evil One.

1 Peter 1:5 Through faith you are being protected by God's power for the salvation that is ready to be revealed at the end of time.

Philippians 4:7 The peace of God, which surpasses all understanding, will *guard your hearts and your minds in Christ Jesus.*

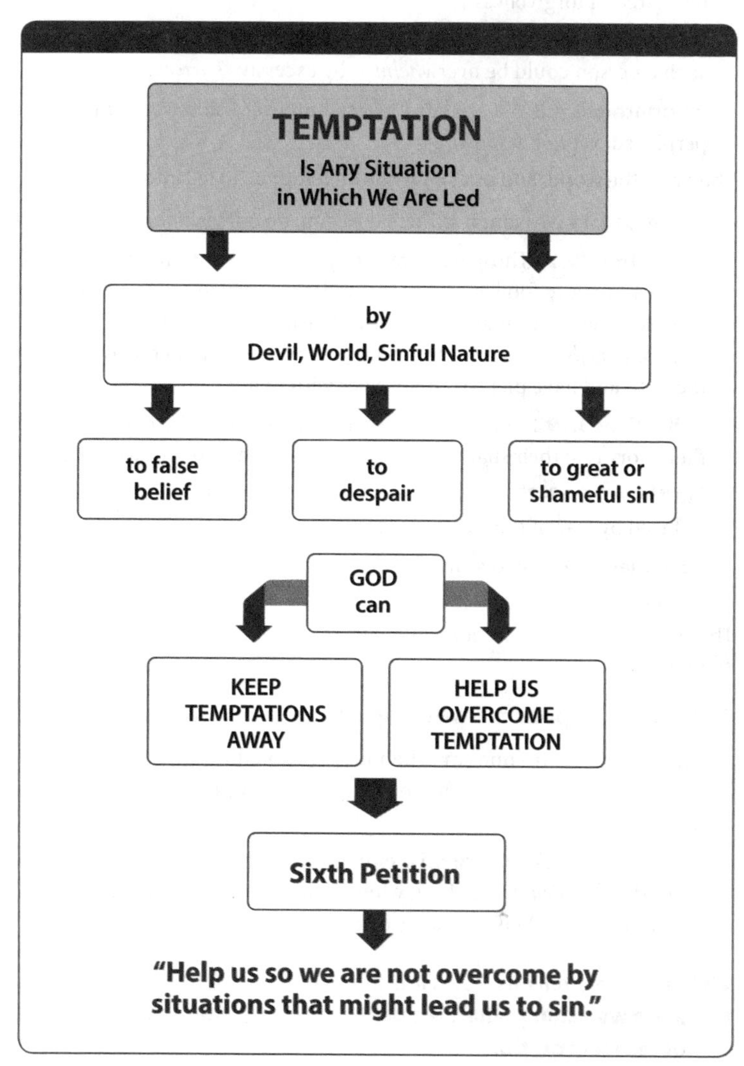

In this petition we ask our Father in heaven to guard and keep us from temptation.

Luke 22:31,32 Simon, Simon, pay attention: Satan has asked to have you all, so that he may sift you as wheat. But I prayed for you, Simon, *that your faith may not fail.* And when you have returned to me, strengthen your brothers.

Ephesians 6:11,13,17 Put on the full armor of God, *so that you can stand against the schemes of the Devil.* For this reason, take up the full armor of God, so that you will be able to take a stand on the evil day and, after you have done everything, to stand. Also take the helmet of salvation and the sword of the Spirit, which is the word of God.

1 Corinthians 10:12,13 Let him who thinks he stands be careful that he does not fall. No testing has overtaken you except ordinary testing. But God is faithful. *He will not allow you to be tested beyond your ability,* but when he tests you, he will also bring about the outcome that you are able to bear it.

Hebrews 4:15 We do not have a high priest who is unable to sympathize with our weaknesses, but one who has been tempted in every way, just as we are, yet was without sin.

Hebrews 2:18 Because he suffered when he was tempted, *he is able to help those who are being tempted.*

Hebrews 12:1,2 *Let us get rid of every burden and the sin that so easily ensnares us,* and let us run with patient endurance the race that is laid out for us. Let us keep our eyes fixed on Jesus, who is the author of our faith and the one who brings it to its goal.

1 Corinthians 9:25-27 Everyone who competes in the games exercises self-control in all things. They do it to receive a perishable victor's wreath, but we do it for an imperishable one. That is why there is nothing aimless about the way I run. There is no pummeling of the air in the way I box. Instead *I hit my body hard and make it my slave* so that, after preaching to others, I myself will not be rejected.

With this petition we ask our Father in heaven to strengthen and preserve us when we face temptation so that we may overcome and win the victory.

CONNECTIONS

The world can put a lot of pressure on us to sin. If we resist, we might experience consequences. People may ridicule us. A friend may desert us. Family members may accuse us of betraying them. We certainly need God to help us resist temptation.

Read about how Joseph resisted the temptation to commit adultery and the consequences he experienced.

Genesis 39:6-20

What can we learn from Joseph that will help us when we face temptation? Think of a specific temptation you might face sometime in the future. What consequences might come if you say no to that temptation? What Bible truths can help you be ready to accept those consequences?

Luther

This is and will ever remain a life of trials.

Therefore we do not say, "Spare us the trial," but, "Do not lead us into it." It is as if we were to say, "We are surrounded on all sides by trials and cannot avoid them; however, dear Father, help us so that we do not fall prey to them and yield to them and thus be overcome and vanquished." He who gives way to them sins and becomes captive to sin, as St. Paul declares [Romans 7:23].

Thus, as Job asserts, this life is nothing but combat and struggle against sin. (LW 42:71)

Our Father, Who From Heaven Above (Stanza 7)

Into temptation lead us not.
When evil foes against us plot
And vex our souls on ev'ry hand,
Oh, give us strength that we may stand
Firm in the faith, a mighty host,
Through comfort of the Holy Ghost.

God's Own Child, I Gladly Say It (Stanza 3)

Satan, hear this proclamation: I am baptized into Christ!
Drop your ugly accusation; I am not so soon enticed.
Now that to the font I've traveled,
All your might has come unraveled,
And, against your tyranny, God, my Lord, unites with me!

THE SEVENTH PETITION

But deliver us from evil.

What does this mean?

In conclusion, we pray in this petition that our Father in heaven would deliver us from every evil that threatens body and soul, property and reputation, and finally when our last hour comes, grant us a blessed end and graciously take us from this world of sorrow to himself in heaven.

Deliver Us From Evil

The world is filled with all kinds of evils. We see pain, suffering, and sorrow in the lives of others. We experience days of sorrow and difficulty. Whenever we or other people consider these evils, we might be tempted to wonder whether there is a God. "How could a loving God permit such things to happen?" we ask. It's a difficult question to answer. We might even begin to wonder whether praying "deliver us from evil" does any good.

God most certainly is a loving God, and he invites us to pray "deliver us from evil" because he has promised to do just that.

285. What is meant by evil?

Romans 8:22 We know that all of creation is groaning *with birth pains* right up to the present time.

Psalm 36:4 *He plots deception even on his bed.* He sets out on a path that is not good. He does not reject wrong.

Psalm 119:153 *See my affliction* and deliver me, because I have not forgotten your law.

Psalm 38:7 Even my back burns with pain. My whole body is unhealthy.

Jeremiah 10:19 Woe to me because of *my wound! My injury is severe!* But I said, "Yes, this is my suffering, and I must bear it."

Jeremiah 14:14 Then the LORD said this to me: *Those prophets are prophesying lies in my name, but* I did not send them. I did not command them, and I did not speak to them. They are prophesying a false vision to you and providing worthless omens—something from their own imagination.

Evil includes all the bad things associated with life on earth, such as pain, suffering, hurtful actions, and false teaching.

286. What is the cause of all evil in the world?

Genesis 3:16-19,24 (Pain and suffering, hurt relationships, difficult working conditions, death, and loss of fellowship with God all came as the result of sin.)

Romans 6:23 The *wages of sin* is death.

Matthew 15:19 *Out of the heart* come evil thoughts, murders, adulteries, sexual sins, thefts, false testimonies, and blasphemies.

287. What are some of the effects of evil in our lives?

Psalm 31:9-13 Be merciful to me, LORD, for I am in distress. My eye grows weak with sorrow—my soul and my body too. Yes, *my life is consumed by grief*, and my years by groaning. My strength fails because of my guilt, and my bones grow weak. *Because of all my foes, I am a disgrace,* especially to my neighbors. I am dreaded by those who know me. Those who see me on the street flee from me. I have been forgotten like a dead man, gone from memory. *I have become like a broken pot.* Yes, I hear the slander of many. There is terror on every side. When they conspire together against me, they plot to take my life.

Acts 14:22 We must go through many troubles on our way to the kingdom of God.

Romans 8:17 Now if we are children, we are also heirs—heirs of God and fellow heirs with Christ, since *we suffer with him,* so that we may also be glorified with him.

Job 1:13-19; 2:7,11-13; 17:1; 19:13-20 (Job's suffering included the *loss of his property and his children, serious illness, and the loss of respect and friendship.)*

Psalm 42:3 My tears have been food for me day and night, while people are saying to me all day, "Where is your God?"

Ecclesiastes 4:1 *I looked again, and I saw all the acts of oppression* being done under the sun. Just look at the tears of the oppressed, who have no one to comfort them!

Psalm 119:69 *The arrogant have smeared me with lies.* I guard your precepts with all my heart.

Psalm 5:9 Nothing reliable comes out of their mouth. From within them comes destruction. Their throat is an open grave. With their tongue they flatter.

The evil in this world brings about all kinds of physical and emotional suffering and distress: sicknesses, famines, natural disasters, wars and hostility, damaged reputations, and spiritual dangers.

288. In what ways does God answer our prayers to rescue us from evils that threaten our bodies and souls, properties and reputations?

Psalm 121:7,8 The LORD will watch to keep you from all harm. *He will watch over your life.* The LORD will watch over your going and your coming from now to eternity.

Psalm 91:9,10 Yes, you LORD are my refuge! If you make the Most High your shelter, *evil will not overtake you. Disaster will not come near your tent.*

Our Father in heaven may keep evil from us.

Romans 8:28 We know that *all things work together for the good of those who love God,* for those who are called according to his purpose.

2 Corinthians 4:17 Our momentary, light trouble *produces for us an eternal weight of glory* that is far beyond any comparison.

Romans 5:3-5 We also rejoice confidently in our sufferings, because we know that *suffering produces patient endurance, and patient endurance produces tested character, and tested character produces hope.* And hope will not put us to shame, because God's love has been poured out into our hearts by the Holy Spirit, who was given to us.

2 Corinthians 1:3,4 Blessed be the God and Father of our Lord Jesus Christ, . . . who comforts us in all our trouble, *so that we can comfort those in any trouble* with the same comfort with which we ourselves are comforted by God.

When our Father in heaven allows evil to touch our lives, he promises to work good through it.

Deuteronomy 8:5 Know in your heart that just as a man disciplines his son, so *the LORD your God disciplines you.*

Proverbs 3:12 The LORD warns the one he loves as a father warns a son with whom he is pleased.

Hebrews 12:6 The Lord *disciplines* the one whom he loves, and he *corrects* every son he accepts.

2 Corinthians 7:9,10 Now I rejoice, not because you were made to feel sorrow, but because this sorrow resulted in repentance. Yes, you were made sorry in a godly way. So you were not harmed in any way by us. In fact, godly sorrow produces repentance, which leads to salvation, leaving no regret. On the other hand, worldly sorrow produces death.

Our Father in heaven may use evil to discipline us or to lead us to repentance.

2 Corinthians 12:9 He said to me, *"My grace is sufficient for you, because my power is made perfect in weakness."* Therefore I will be glad to boast all the more in my weaknesses, so that the power of Christ may shelter me.

Psalm 94:17-19 Unless the LORD had been my helper, my soul would soon have dwelt in silence. *When I said, "My foot has slipped," your mercy, LORD, upheld me. When my worries within me were many, your comfort brought joy to my soul.*

1 Peter 5:10 After you have suffered a little while, the God of all grace, who called you into his eternal glory in Christ Jesus, *will himself restore, establish, strengthen, and support you.*

2 Thessalonians 3:3 The Lord is faithful. *He will establish you and protect you from the Evil One.*

Matthew 10:24,25 A disciple is not above his teacher, nor is a servant above his master. *It is enough for the disciple to be like his teacher and the servant like his master.* If the master of the house was called Beelzebul, how much more the members of his household!

Matthew 5:11,12 Blessed are you when people insult you and persecute you and falsely say all kinds of evil against you because of me. Rejoice and be glad, because great is your reward in heaven. In fact, that is how they persecuted the prophets who were before you.

When our Father in heaven allows evil to touch our lives, he strengthens us and encourages us so that we are able to bear the evil.

A CLOSER LOOK

Theology of the Cross

If God is on the side of Christians, shouldn't Christians have trouble-free lives? It can be tempting to wish for that—how wonderful it would be to have lives free from pain or sorrow, lives of glory!

We look forward to that kind of life in eternity. But life is different here. Jesus has told us that as we follow him on this earth, we can expect to share in his cross. We can expect to have troubles and hardships even *because* we are Christians. So does that mean that God doesn't love us? Not at all. Remember, God accomplished our salvation through the suffering of his Son. God has promised to bring blessing through our sufferings too.

God's ultimate purpose for the crosses we endure in life is to turn us back to Christ's cross and the promises of his unfailing love and sure deliverance. While we are here on earth, God strengthens us through the gospel. At life's end, when our journey here is finished, God promises to take us from this world of sorrow and trouble to heaven.

289. What final deliverance from evil do we ask the Lord to bring to us?

Philippians 1:23 *I have the desire to depart and be with Christ,* which is better by far.

Revelation 21:4 He will *wipe away every tear* from their eyes. There will be no more death or sorrow or crying or pain, because the former things have passed away.

2 Timothy 4:18 The Lord will rescue me from every evil work and will *bring me safely into his heavenly kingdom.*

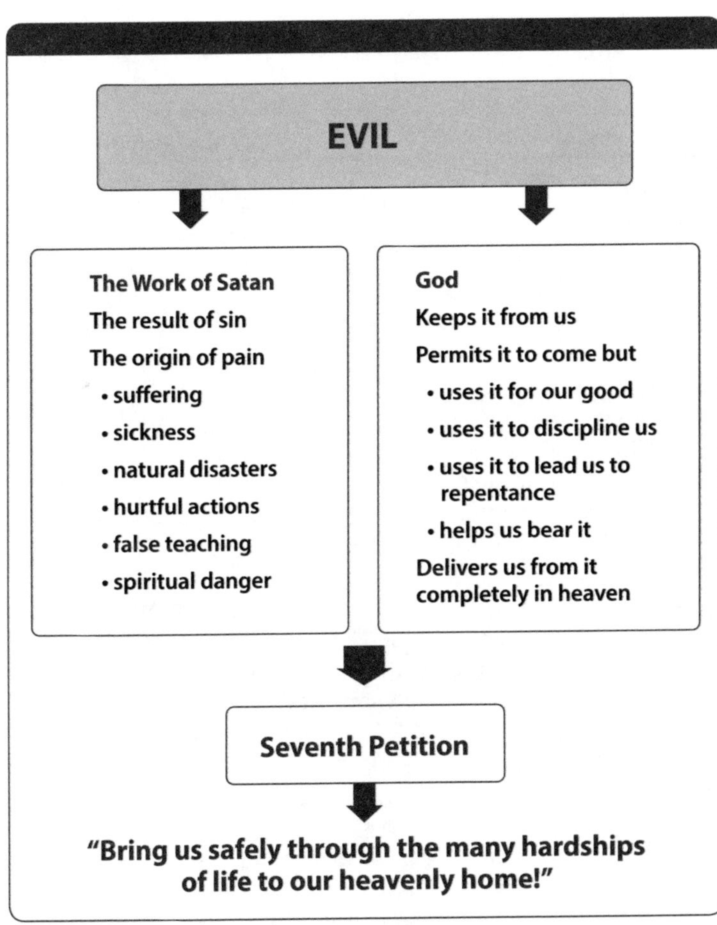

290. What is our Christian response as we see the evil in the world?

Psalm 42:5 Why are you so depressed, O my soul? Why so disturbed within me? *Hope in God,* for I will again praise him for salvation from his presence.

Psalm 85:8 *I will hear what the true God, the LORD, will say.* He indeed speaks peace to his people.

Psalm 73:25,26 Who else is there for me in heaven? And besides you, I desire no one else on earth. My flesh and my heart fail, but *God is the rock of my heart and my portion forever.*

Romans 8:18 I conclude that our sufferings at the present time are not worth comparing with the glory that is going to be revealed to us.

Psalm 146:3,5 Do not trust in human helpers, in a mortal man who cannot save you. *Blessed is everyone who has the God of Jacob as his help. His hope is in the LORD his God.*

CONNECTIONS

Evil comes in many different forms. Sometimes because someone has sinned against us, we experience pain and suffering. When someone sins against us, we can be tempted to be angry, but we can also be tempted to despair. We may feel that God has abandoned us. We may wonder why God has allowed this sin, which has hurt us so deeply.

Joseph endured tremendous suffering because of his brothers' sin. From his experience, we learn that there is never reason to despair when we are suffering because of someone else's evil. Instead, we know that God is working behind the scenes to accomplish what is best for us eternally.

Genesis 45:5-9; 50:20

Genesis 50:20 tells us what God intended through all Joseph's suffering. Make a list of all the blessings God brought about through the sale of Joseph into slavery in Egypt. In what different ways can God work for good through the difficulties you experience?

Luther

[An upright man] says, "Dear Father, evil and pain oppress me. I suffer much distress and discomfort. I am afraid of hell. Deliver me from these, but only if this is to your honor and glory and if it agrees with your divine will. If not, then your will, and not mine, be done [Luke 22:42]. Your divine honor and will are dearer to me than my own ease and comfort, both now and eternally." Now that is a pleasing and good prayer and is certain to be heard in heaven. (LW 42:75)

Our Father, Who From Heaven Above (Stanza 8)
From evil, Lord, deliver us;
The times and days are perilous.
Redeem us from eternal death,
And, when we yield our dying breath,
Console us, grant us calm release,
And take our souls to you in peace.

THE DOXOLOGY

For the kingdom, the power, and the glory are yours now and forever. Amen.

What does this mean?

We can be sure that these petitions are acceptable to our Father in heaven and are heard by him, for he himself has commanded us to pray in this way and has promised to hear us. Therefore we say, "Amen. Yes, it shall be so."

AMEN

Confident That God Answers

Imagine that you are asking another person for something. Can that person give you what you want? Does that person want to give you what you ask? Receiving what you ask for depends on the other person's ability and desire to help.

In the Lord's Prayer, we ask God for many important things. The final words of praise—the Doxology—explain why we are confident that God will answer our prayer.

291. Why are we confident that these petitions are acceptable to our Father in heaven?

Matthew 6:9 *Therefore pray like this:* "Our Father in heaven, hallowed be your name."

Luke 11:2 *[Jesus] said to them, "When you pray, say,* 'Our Father in heaven, hallowed be your name. Your kingdom come.'"

We are confident that these petitions are acceptable to God because Jesus commanded us to pray in this way.

292. Why can we be confident that our Father in heaven will hear and answer our petitions?

Matthew 7:7,8 *Keep asking, and it will be given to you. Keep seeking, and you will find. Keep knocking, and it will be opened for you.* For everyone who asks receives, and everyone who seeks finds, and to the one who knocks, it will be opened.

John 14:13,14 *I will do whatever you ask in my name* so that the Father may be glorified in the Son. If you ask me for anything in my name, I will do it.

Romans 8:32 He who did not spare his own Son, but gave him up for us all—*how will he not also graciously give us all things along with him?*

1 John 5:14,15 This is the confidence that we have before him: that if we ask anything according to his will, he hears us. And if we know that he hears us—whatever we ask—we also know that we receive the things we have asked from him.

We are confident that he hears and answers our petitions because he promises to give us whatever we ask in Jesus' name.

Matthew 19:26 With God all things are possible.

Matthew 8:27 The men were amazed, saying, "What kind of a man is this? *Even the wind and the sea obey him!*"

Ephesians 3:20,21 Now *to him, who is able, according to the power that is at work within us, to do infinitely more than we can ask or imagine,* to him be the glory in the church and in Christ Jesus throughout all generations, forever and ever! Amen.

Exodus 16 (The Lord miraculously provided manna and quail for the people to eat.)

Psalm 78:24 He rained down manna for them to eat, and he gave them the grain of heaven.

Psalm 29:2 *Ascribe to the LORD the glory of his name.* Bow down to the LORD in the splendor of holiness.

Psalm 18:3 I call to the LORD, who is worthy of praise, and *I am saved* from my enemies.

Revelation 5:12 Worthy is the Lamb who was slain to receive power and riches and wisdom and strength and honor and glory and blessing.

We can be confident that he hears and answers our petitions because he rules over everything, possesses all power, and is worthy of our glory and praise.

A CLOSER LOOK

Why do we say these words?

The words of the Doxology are a very appropriate ending to the Lord's Prayer. They confess our confidence in God, who answers our prayers. Similar words were spoken by David in 1 Chronicles 29:11, as he gave praise to God in prayer. There is some uncertainty as to whether Jesus himself included those words when teaching his disciples how to pray in Matthew 6. Whatever the case, many Christians for centuries have joyfully concluded the Lord's Prayer with this confident confession of praise.

293. Why do we conclude our prayers with the word *Amen*?

James 1:6,7 Let him ask in faith, *without doubting*, because the one who doubts is like a wave of the sea, blown and tossed by the wind. In fact, that person should not expect that he will receive anything from the Lord.

Psalm 20:7 Some rely on chariots, and some on horses, but *we rely on the name of the Lord our God.*

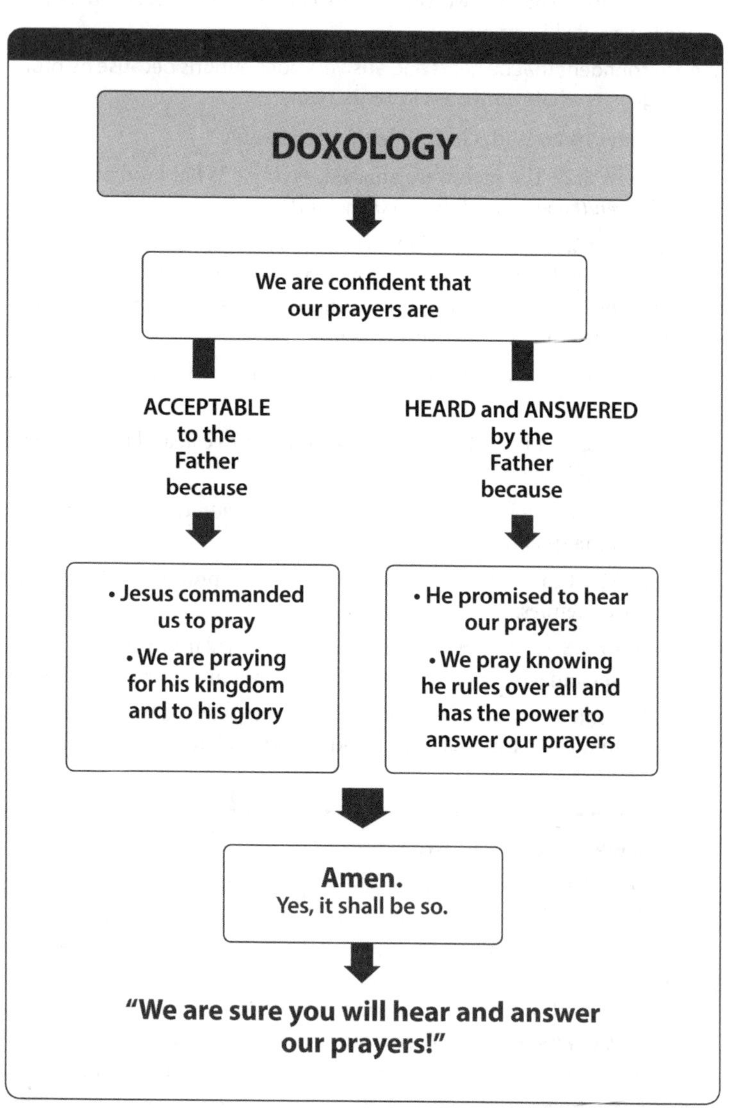

2 Samuel 7:28 LORD God, you are God. *Your words are truth.* You have promised this good thing to your servant.

Nehemiah 8:6 Ezra blessed the LORD, the great God, and all the people answered, "Amen! Amen!" while they lifted up their hands and then knelt and bowed down with their faces to the ground.

Psalm 62:8 *Trust in him at all times,* you people. Pour out your hearts before him. God is a refuge for us.

Psalm 13:5 *I trust in your mercy.* My heart rejoices in your salvation.

Psalm 121:1,2 I lift up my eyes to the mountains. Where does my help come from? *My help comes from the LORD, the Maker of heaven and earth.*

Psalm 73:25,26 *Who else is there for me in heaven?* And besides you, I desire no one else on earth. My flesh and my heart fail, but God is the rock of my heart and my portion forever.

Amen means "Yes! It shall be so." We use the word *Amen* because we are not doubting but firmly believing that our Father in heaven will hear and answer our prayers.

CONNECTIONS

When we praise God at the close of the Lord's Prayer, we are expressing confidence that God is going to give us exactly what we pray for because he has invited us to pray for these things. We are praising him before we have even seen his answer.

Many years ago, God promised King Jehoshaphat that he would be victorious in battle without even having to fight. As the army marched out the next day, the king ordered some of his men to lead the soldiers and to do something amazing.

---

2 Chronicles 20:1-30

In what different ways did Jehoshaphat and his people show their trust in the Lord? The various petitions of the Lord's Prayer are connected to promises God has made to you. Choose petitions of the Lord's Prayer and list the promises God has given in connection with those requests. (If you struggle with one, look back to that petition's explanation to find the answer.) Then rejoice that God keeps every one of his promises to you too.

Luther

The little word "Amen" means the same as truly, verily, certainly. It is a word uttered by the firm faith of the heart. It is as though you were to say, "O my God and Father, I have no doubt that you will grant the things for which I petitioned, not because of my prayer, but because of your command to me to request them and because of your promise to hear me. I am convinced, O God, that you are truthful, that you cannot lie. It is not the worthiness of my prayer, but the certainty of your truthfulness that leads me to believe this firmly. I have no doubt that my petition will become and be an Amen." (LW 42:77)

Our Father, Who From Heaven Above (Stanza 9)

Amen, that is, it shall be so.
Make strong our faith that we may know
That we may doubt not but believe
What here we ask we shall receive.
Thus in your name and at your Word
We say, "Amen. Oh, hear us, Lord!"

MEANS OF GRACE

God's Means for Blessing Us

The Christian life is full of challenges. In the Lord's Prayer, we place all of our challenges into the hands of our gracious and powerful God, confident that he will give us everything we need to face them. But how does God help us in our spiritual struggles? How does he give us the strength to overcome temptation, doubt, and despair?

The *means of grace* is the tool that equips us for our struggles. It gives spiritual life to the dead, provides spiritual strength to those who are alive in Christ, and preserves God's children for eternal life in heaven.

A Unique Treasure

294. The blessings God brings through the means of grace are needed by everyone. **What is the natural spiritual condition of all people?**

Isaiah 59:2 *It is your guilt that has separated you from your God, and* your sins have hidden God's face from you, so that he does not hear.

Ephesians 2:1,2 *You were dead in your trespasses and sins,* in which you formerly walked when you followed the ways of this present world. You were following the ruler of the domain of the air, the spirit now at work in the people who disobey.

1 Corinthians 2:14 An unspiritual person does not accept the truths taught by God's Spirit, because they are foolishness to him, and he cannot understand them, because they are spiritually evaluated.

Romans 8:7 The mind-set of the sinful flesh is *hostile to God,* since it does not submit to God's law, and in fact, it cannot.

295. What has God graciously done for the entire world?

Isaiah 53:5 It was because of our rebellion that he was pierced. He was crushed for the guilt our sins deserved. The punishment that brought us peace was upon him, and *by his wounds we are healed.*

John 1:29 Look! The Lamb of God, who takes away the sin of the world!

2 Corinthians 5:19,21 *God was* in Christ *reconciling the world to himself,* not counting their trespasses against them. And he has entrusted to us the message of reconciliation. God made him, who did not know sin, to become sin for us, so that we might become the righteousness of God in him.

Romans 3:23,24 All have sinned and fall short of the glory of God and are *justified freely by his grace through the redemption that is in Christ Jesus.*

Romans 5:18,19 Just as one trespass led to a verdict of condemnation for all people, so also one righteous verdict led to life-giving justification for all people. For just as through the disobedience of one man the many became sinners, so also *through the obedience of one man the many will become righteous.*

1 John 2:2 He is the atoning sacrifice for our sins, and not only for ours but also for the whole world.

296. How do I receive the blessings of this grace?

Ephesians 2:8,9 It is *by grace* you have been saved, through faith—and this is not from yourselves, *it is the gift of God*—not by works, so that no one can boast.

Romans 3:28 We conclude that a person is justified by faith without the works of the law.

297. As we learned earlier, faith is not something that we accomplish. **What is the power that creates faith in our hearts?**

Romans 1:16,17 *I am not ashamed of the gospel,* because *it is the power of God* for salvation to everyone who believes—to the Jew first, and also to the Greek. *For in the gospel a righteousness from God is revealed* by faith, for faith, just as it is written, "The righteous will live by faith."

2 Thessalonians 2:14 *He also called you through our gospel* so that you would obtain the glory of our Lord Jesus Christ.

The very message that we are saved through the perfect life and innocent death of Jesus—the gospel—is God's power to create faith in our hearts.

298. Through what means does God apply the power of the gospel to human hearts?

Romans 10:17 *Faith comes from hearing* the message, and the message comes through the word of Christ.

2 Timothy 3:15 From infancy you have known *the Holy Scriptures, which are able to make you wise for salvation through faith in Christ Jesus.*

1 Corinthians 1:21 Since the world through its wisdom did not know God, God in his wisdom decided to save those who believe, through the foolishness of the preached message.

Acts 2 (Through the Word and Baptism, a multitude of people are brought to faith.)

Acts 8:26-39 (The Ethiopian received forgiveness through faith as he heard the Word and was baptized.)

Titus 3:5 *He saved us*—not by righteous works that we did ourselves, but because of his mercy. He saved us *through the washing of rebirth and the renewal by the Holy Spirit.*

1 Peter 3:21 *Corresponding to that, baptism now saves you*—not the removal of dirt from the body but the guarantee of a good conscience before God through the resurrection of Jesus Christ.

Matthew 26:26-28 While they were eating, *Jesus took bread,* blessed and broke it, and gave it to the disciples. He said, *"Take, eat, this is my body." Then he took the cup,* gave thanks, and gave it to them, saying, *"Drink from it all of you, for this is my blood of the new testament, which is poured out for many for the forgiveness of sins."*

1 Corinthians 11:23-26 I received from the Lord what I also delivered to you: *The Lord Jesus,* on the night when he was betrayed, *took bread,* and when he had given thanks, he broke it and said, *"This is my body, which is for you. Do this in remembrance of me."* In the same way, *after the meal, he also took the cup, saying, "This cup is the new testament in my blood. Do this, as often as you drink it, in remembrance of me."* For as often as you eat this bread and drink the cup, you proclaim the Lord's death until he comes.

God uses the gospel in his Word, in Baptism, and in the Lord's Supper to reach souls with his grace.

A CLOSER LOOK

Means of Grace

The means of grace is defined as "the gospel in Word and sacraments." The gospel—the good news of sins forgiven in Jesus—can be proclaimed through spoken words. We see an example of this in Acts 13:26-43, where Paul preaches the good news in the community of Pisidian Antioch. The gospel can also come to human hearts through the sacraments—Baptism and Holy Communion—where the Word of God is attached to visible elements.

Sacraments

The word *sacrament* means "a sacred action." Sacraments have three characteristics:

1. A sacrament is a sacred act that Christ instituted or established for Christians to do.
2. A sacrament is a sacred act that includes the use of earthly elements (water, bread, and wine) connected with God's Word.
3. A sacrament is a sacred act through which Christ offers, gives, and seals the forgiveness of sins and, so also, life and salvation.

The two sacraments are Baptism and the Lord's Supper. Note how the three characteristics of a sacrament are found in each.

Baptism

Matthew 28:18,19 Jesus approached and spoke to them saying, "All authority in heaven and on earth has been given to me. *Therefore go and gather disciples from all nations by baptizing them in the name of the Father and of the Son and of the Holy Spirit."*

1 Peter 3:20,21 God's patience was waiting in the days of Noah while the ark was being built. In this ark a few, that is, eight souls, were saved by water. And corresponding to that, *baptism now saves you*—not the removal of dirt from the body but the guarantee of a good conscience before God through the resurrection of Jesus Christ.

Lord's Supper

1 Corinthians 11:23-25 *I received from the Lord* what I also delivered to you: *The Lord Jesus,* on the night when he was betrayed, *took bread,* and when he had given thanks, he broke it and said, "This is my body, which is for you. Do this in remembrance of me." *In the same way, after the meal, he also took the cup,* saying, "This cup is the new testament in my blood. *Do this,* as often as you drink it, in remembrance of me."

Matthew 26:26-28 While they were eating, *Jesus took bread, blessed and broke it,* and gave it to the disciples. He said, "Take, eat, this is my body." *Then he took the cup, gave thanks, and gave it to them,* saying, "Drink from it all of you, for this is my blood of the new testament, which is poured out *for many for the forgiveness of sins."*

---

299. The gospel is God's power to create faith—to bring unbelievers from spiritual death to spiritual life. But the gospel doesn't stop being important once someone has been brought to faith. **Why is the means of grace—the gospel in Word and sacraments—so important for Christians?**

Isaiah 40:1 *Comfort, comfort* my people, says your God.

Ephesians 1:17 The God of our Lord Jesus Christ, the glorious Father, will give you the Spirit of *wisdom* and revelation in knowing Christ fully.

2 Peter 3:18 *Grow in the grace* and knowledge of our Lord and Savior Jesus Christ. To him be the glory, both now and forever. Amen.

Psalm 40:8 My God, I take pleasure in doing your will. Your law is in my heart.

Psalm 119:9 How can a young man keep his path pure? By *guarding it with your words.*

John 15:5 I am the Vine; you are the branches. The one who remains in me and I in him is the one who *bears much fruit*, because without me you can do nothing.

Galatians 5:24,25 Those who belong to Christ Jesus have crucified the sinful flesh with its passions and desires. If we live by the spirit, let us also walk in step with it.

300. Because of the great, saving power of the gospel in Word and sacraments, what attitude does God want us to have toward the means of grace?

Psalm 119:105 Your words are a lamp for my feet and a light for my path.

Psalm 119:81 My soul is worn out, as I wait for your salvation. I wait confidently for your word.

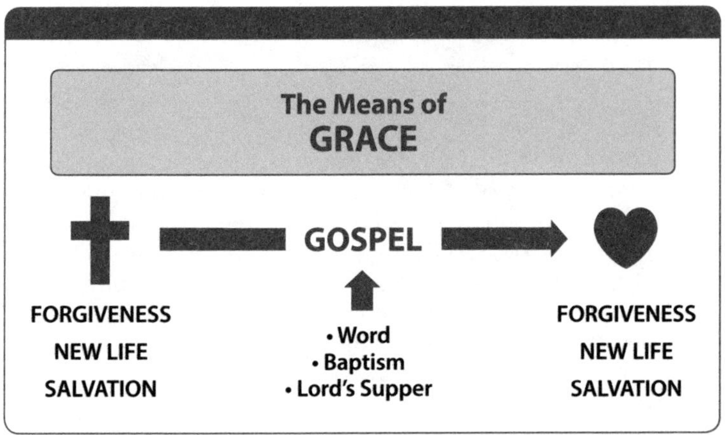

Psalm 119:97 How I love your laws! I meditate on them all day long.

Luke 10:38-42 (Mary cherished the opportunity to listen to the words of Jesus.)

Acts 8:26-39 (As soon as the Ethiopian learned about Jesus and about Baptism, he desired to be baptized immediately.)

Acts 16:25-34 (The jailer and his family were baptized in the middle of the night.)

Acts 2:42 They continued to hold firmly to the apostles' teaching and to the fellowship, to the breaking of the bread, and to the prayers.

1 Corinthians 11:25 In the same way, after the meal, he also took the cup, saying, "This cup is the new testament in my blood. Do this, as often as you drink it, in remembrance of me."

Romans 4:7 Blessed are those whose lawless deeds are forgiven and whose sins are covered.

CONNECTIONS

The means of grace—the gospel in Word and sacraments—has changed your life and continues to be a blessing for you. You want others to have those same blessings. As you read the account of Lydia, think about people you know to whom you would like to bring the gospel.

Acts 16:11-15

What different tools, or means, did the Holy Spirit use to change Lydia's heart? How does God make clear that it was his gracious power that brought Lydia to faith in Jesus? How can this account help you as you think about a friend or relative who doesn't currently believe in Jesus?

Luther

So today the Word itself, Baptism, and the Lord's Supper are our morning stars to which we turn our eyes as certain indications of the Sun of grace. For we can definitely assert that where the Lord's Supper, Baptism, and the Word are found, Christ, the remission of sins, and life eternal are found. On the other hand, where these signs of grace are not found, or where they are despised by men, not only grace is lacking but also foul errors will follow. (*What Luther Says,* Ewald M. Plass, p. 914, par. 2862)

The Church's One Foundation (Stanzas 1,2)

The Church's one foundation Is Jesus Christ, her Lord;
She is his new creation By water and the Word.
From heav'n he came and sought her To be his holy bride;
With his own blood he bought her, And for her life he died.

Elect from ev'ry nation, Yet one o'er all the earth;
Her charter of salvation: One Lord, one faith, one birth.
One holy name she blesses, Partakes one holy food,
And to one hope she presses, With ev'ry grace endued.

The shell, water, and dove remind us of Christ's baptism and the work of the Holy Spirit in our own baptisms.

THE INSTITUTION OF BAPTISM

First: *What is Baptism?*
Baptism is not just plain water, but it is water used by God's command and connected with God's Word.

What is that word of God?
Christ our Lord says in the last chapter of Matthew, "Go and make disciples of all nations, baptizing them in the name of the Father and of the Son and of the Holy Spirit."

BAPTISM

A Very Special Day

Can you remember the day of your baptism? Those who were baptized as infants may remember seeing pictures and hearing stories about that day. Those who were baptized when they were older may clearly recall the sensation of water and the sound of the powerful words.

The day of a person's baptism is a very special day. God's Word will show us what baptism is and why our baptisms are important.

301. When we speak of the *institution* of Baptism, we are pointing to the time when Jesus established Baptism as a sacred act to be followed by the church. **When did God institute the Sacrament of Baptism?**

> **Matthew 28:18-20** *Jesus* approached and *spoke to them saying,* "All authority in heaven and on earth has been given to me. *Therefore go and gather disciples from all nations by baptizing* them in the name of the Father and of the Son and of the Holy Spirit, and by teaching them to keep all the instructions I have given you. And surely I am with you always until the end of the age."

After his resurrection, Jesus met with the apostles on a mountain in Galilee where he commanded them to make disciples by baptizing people of all nations and teaching them God's Word.

302. What does the word *baptize* mean?

> **Mark 7:3,4** The Pharisees and all the Jews do not eat unless they scrub their hands with a fist, holding to the tradition of the elders. When

they come from the marketplace, they do not eat unless they *wash*. And there are many other traditions they adhere to, such as the *washing* of cups, pitchers, kettles, and dining couches.

The word *baptize,* as used in New Testament times, means "to apply water in various ways: immerse, wash, pour, or sprinkle."

A CLOSER LOOK

Special water is not required for Baptism. Jesus was baptized in the Jordan River. As Philip was teaching an Ethiopian the gospel of Jesus, they happened on a source of water and the Ethiopian asked to be baptized.

When the prison doors were miraculously opened for Paul and Silas (Acts 16:16-34), they had a chance to teach the jailer and his family about Jesus. In the middle of the night, Paul and Silas baptized the jailer's family. They all simply used the water that was available to them.

303. Why do we say that the Sacrament of Baptism is not just plain water?

Matthew 28:19 [Jesus commanded,] "Therefore go and gather disciples from all nations by *baptizing them in the name of the Father and of the Son and of the Holy Spirit.*"

Ephesians 5:25,26 Husbands, love your wives, in the same way as Christ loved the church and gave himself up for her to make her holy, by cleansing her with the *washing of water in connection with the Word.*

Baptism is not simply plain water but water used by God's command and connected with God's Word.

304. What does Jesus mean when he commands us to baptize in the name of the triune God?

Numbers 6:27 They will put my name on the Israelites, and I will bless them.

Galatians 3:27 As many of you as were baptized into Christ *have been clothed with Christ.*

1 Corinthians 12:13 *By one Spirit we all were baptized into one body,* whether Jews or Greeks, whether slaves or free people, and we were all caused to drink one Spirit.

Ephesians 2:19 You are no longer foreigners and strangers, *but you are fellow citizens with the saints and members of God's household.*

The authority and power behind Baptism come from the one true God, the triune God. Through Baptism, the triune God puts his name on us and makes us members of his family.

305. What is Jesus teaching us when he commands us to baptize "all nations"?

Acts 2:38 Peter answered them, "Repent and be baptized, *every one of you,* in the name of Jesus Christ for the forgiveness of your sins, and you will receive the gift of the Holy Spirit."

1 Corinthians 1:16 *I also baptized the household* of Stephanas.

Acts 16:15 When *she and her household were baptized,* she urged us, "If you consider me a believer in the Lord, come and stay at my house."

Acts 16:33 At the same hour of the night, he took them and washed their wounds. Without delay, *he and all his family* were baptized.

God wants all people to benefit from the blessings that Baptism brings.

306. Why is it important that little children also are baptized?

Matthew 28:19 Go and *gather disciples from all nations* by baptizing them in the name of the Father and of the Son and of the Holy Spirit.

Acts 2:38,39 Peter answered them, "Repent and be baptized, every one of you, in the name of Jesus Christ for the forgiveness of your sins, and you will receive the gift of the Holy Spirit. *For the promise is for you and for your children* and for all who are far away, as many as the Lord our God will call."

Little children are a part of "all nations" and, therefore, are included among those Jesus commands to be baptized.

Psalm 51:5 Certainly, I was guilty when I was born. I was sinful when my mother conceived me.

Ephesians 2:3 Formerly, we all lived among them in the passions of our sinful flesh, as we carried out the desires of the sinful flesh and its thoughts. Like all the others, *we were by nature objects of God's wrath.*

John 3:5,6 Jesus answered, "Amen, Amen, I tell you: *Unless someone is born of water and the Spirit, he cannot enter the kingdom of God! Whatever is born of the flesh is flesh. Whatever is born of the Spirit is spirit.*"

Little children are by nature sinful and deserve God's punishment. They must be born again by the Holy Spirit working through the gospel.

Mark 10:13-16 Some people began bringing little children to Jesus so that he would touch them. But the disciples rebuked them. When Jesus saw this, he was indignant. He said, "*Let the little children come to me!* Do not hinder them, *because the kingdom of God belongs to such as these.* Amen I tell you: Whoever will not receive the kingdom of God like a little child will never enter it." And he took the little children in his arms, laid his hands on them, and blessed them.

Matthew 18:6 If anyone causes *one of these little ones who believe in me* to sin, it would be better for him to have a huge millstone hung around his neck and to be drowned in the depths of the sea.

Luke 18:15-17 People were bringing even their babies to Jesus, so that he would touch them. When the disciples saw this, they began to rebuke them. But Jesus invited them, saying, "Let the little children come to me, and do not hinder them, for *the kingdom of God belongs to such as these.* Amen I tell you: *Whoever does not receive the kingdom of God like a little child will never enter it.*"

Jesus invites little children to be brought to him and points to their faith. The Holy Spirit is able to work faith in the hearts of children.

307. Why are adults instructed before being baptized?

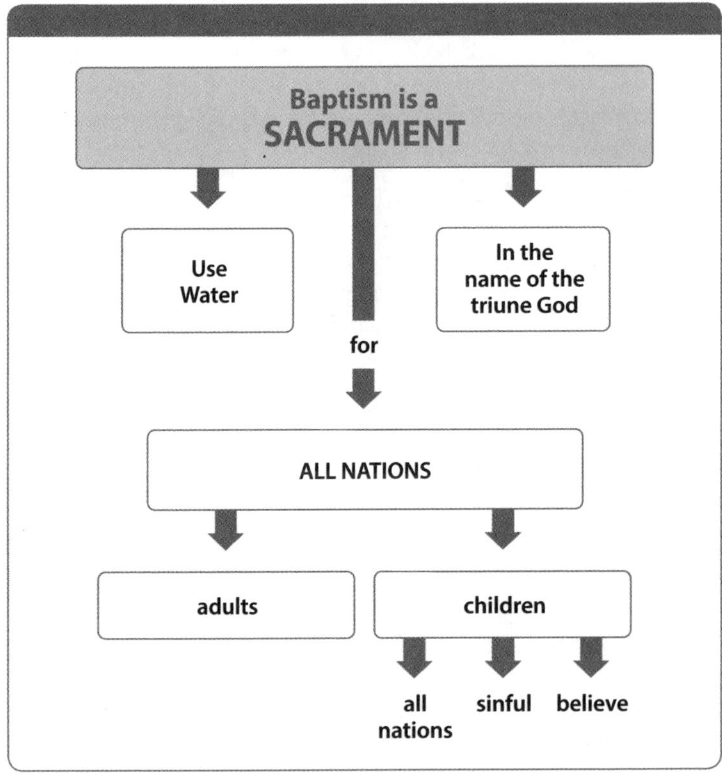

Acts 2:38,39,41 Peter answered them, "Repent and be baptized, every one of you, in the name of Jesus Christ for the forgiveness of your sins, and you will receive the gift of the Holy Spirit. For the promise is for you and for your children and for all who are far away, as many as the

Lord our God will call." *Those who accepted his message were baptized,* and that day about three thousand people were added.

Acts 16:29-34 (The jailer at Philippi was taught about Jesus and then was baptized.)

Acts 8:26-39 (Philip taught the Ethiopian about Jesus and about Baptism. Then the Ethiopian was baptized.)

Before baptizing adults, we teach them about Jesus and about Baptism, following the model given in the Scriptures.

A CLOSER LOOK

The Pastor Baptizes

Baptism is Christ's institution for the holy Christian church. This means that any believer has the right to baptize. However, God also instructs us to do everything in an orderly way (1 Corinthians 14:40). In the interest of good order, when a congregation calls a pastor, the congregation asks him to do the baptizing. As the shepherd of the congregation, he will see to it that those under his care are baptized.

Emergency Baptism

In the case of an emergency, when an unbaptized person is in danger of dying and the pastor is not present, any Christian can and should administer Baptism. The important thing is that Baptism is done as Jesus commanded, using water connected with God's Word. Apply water to the person and say, "I baptize you in the name of the Father and of the Son and of the Holy Spirit."

If there is time, you may include a Bible reading (for example, Luke 18:15-17), the Lord's Prayer, and/or another prayer.

Sponsors or Witnesses

The custom of choosing sponsors for a baby dates back hundreds of years. Though it is a fine custom and has value, it isn't commanded by God and so is not necessary for Baptism.

The parents ask the sponsor to be concerned about the spiritual well-being of the child. The sponsor can pray for the child and encourage him or her to be faithful in hearing God's Word. They can remind the child of his or her baptism and the importance of Baptism. If the parents should die while the child is young, the sponsor can help look after the spiritual needs of the child and make every attempt to see that the child is brought up in the true faith.

It is evident from this description that we would ask to be sponsors for our children only people with whom we share spiritual fellowship.

If parents want to have a friend or family member who does not share the same confession of faith join them at the baptism, that person would serve as a witness rather than as a sponsor.

CONNECTIONS

God's children have a high regard for Baptism. This can be shown in different ways. The Sacrament is often part of the regular church service, done in front of the entire congregation. A special decorative baptismal font, which holds the water for Baptism, can be used. Guests may come from far away. It's obvious that what takes place at Baptism is important.

The Bible tells of a man and his family who were baptized in the middle of the night. For them, there was no formal church service or decorative font and there were no specially invited guests. But there was no question that Baptism was very important for them.

Acts 16:16-40

In what ways did the jailer at Philippi show how much he treasured Jesus and the blessings Jesus brings through Baptism? Do you know the date of your baptism? Think of ways you could celebrate the anniversary of your baptism, ways that would remind you of the importance of this Sacrament.

Luther

Let us not doubt that Baptism is divine. It is not made up or invented by people. For as surely as I can say, "No one has spun the Ten Commandments, the Creed, and the Lord's Prayer out of his head; they are revealed and given by God Himself," so also I can boast that Baptism is no human plaything, but it is instituted by God Himself. . . . It is of the greatest importance that we value Baptism as excellent, glorious, and exalted. We contend and fight for Baptism chiefly because the world is now so full of sects arguing that Baptism is an outward thing and that outward things are of no benefit. But let Baptism be a thoroughly outward thing. Here stand God's Word and command, which institute, establish, and confirm Baptism. What God institutes and commands cannot be an empty thing. (Large Catechism, IV, par. 6-8)

God's Own Child, I Gladly Say It (Stanzas 1,2)

God's own child, I gladly say it:
I am baptized into Christ!
He, because I could not pay it,
Gave my full redemption price.
Do I need earth's treasures many?
I have one worth more than any
That brought me salvation free,
Lasting to eternity!

Sin, disturb my soul no longer:
I am baptized into Christ!
I have comfort even stronger:
Jesus' cleansing sacrifice.
Should a guilty conscience seize me
Since my baptism did release me
In a dear forgiving flood,
Sprinkling me with Jesus' blood?

THE BLESSINGS OF BAPTISM

Second: *What does Baptism do for us?*

Baptism works forgiveness of sin, delivers from death and the devil, and gives eternal salvation to all who believe this, as the words and promises of God declare.

What are these words and promises of God?

Christ our Lord says in the last chapter of Mark, "Whoever believes and is baptized will be saved, but whoever does not believe will be condemned."

BAPTISM
The Blessings

What is the most valuable gift your parents ever gave you? Many people measure value according to how much something costs. But there is something parents can do for a child that costs them nothing, yet it is God's way of giving that child everything. God's gift of Baptism brings incredible blessings.

308. What blessings does God give through Baptism?

Acts 2:38 Peter answered them, "Repent and be baptized, every one of you, in the name of Jesus Christ *for the forgiveness of your sins,* and you will receive the gift of the Holy Spirit."

Acts 22:16 Now what are you waiting for? Get up, be baptized, and *wash away your sins,* calling on his name.

Through Baptism, God forgives sins.

Romans 6:3-5 Do you not know that all of us who were baptized into Christ Jesus were baptized into his death? We were therefore buried with him by this baptism into his death, so that just as he was raised from the dead through the glory of the Father, *we too would also walk in a new life.* For if we have been united with him in the likeness of his death, *we will certainly also be united with him in the likeness of his resurrection.*

Hebrews 2:14,15 Since the children share flesh and blood, he also shared the same flesh and blood, so *that through death he could destroy the one who had the power of death (that is, the Devil)* and free those who were held in slavery all their lives by the fear of death.

Colossians 1:13 *The Father rescued us from the domain of darkness* and transferred us into the kingdom of the Son he loves.

Through Baptism, God delivers from death and the power of the devil.

Mark 16:16 *Whoever believes and is baptized will be saved, but whoever does not believe will be condemned.*

1 Peter 3:21 Baptism *now saves you*—not the removal of dirt from the body but the guarantee of a good conscience before God through the resurrection of Jesus Christ.

Titus 3:5 *He saved us*—not by righteous works that we did ourselves, but because of his mercy. He saved us *through the washing of rebirth and the renewal by the Holy Spirit.*

Through Baptism, God gives eternal salvation.

309. Jesus won forgiveness of sins, life, and salvation for us on a cross. **Why do we say that Baptism *works* these blessings?**

Galatians 3:27 As many of you as were baptized into Christ have been *clothed with Christ.*

Romans 6:3,5 Do you not know that all of us who were *baptized into Christ Jesus* were baptized into his death? For if we have been *united with him in the likeness of his death,* we will certainly also *be united with him in the likeness of his resurrection.*

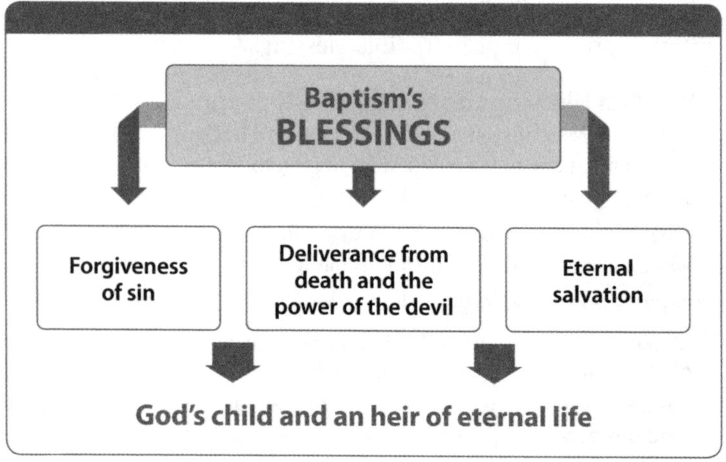

1 Corinthians 6:11 *You were washed, you were sanctified, you were justified* in the name of our Lord Jesus Christ and *by the Spirit of our God.*

1 Peter 3:21 Baptism now *saves you*—not the removal of dirt from the body but the guarantee of a good conscience before God *through the resurrection of Jesus Christ.*

Through Baptism, we are joined to Christ's death and resurrection. Through Baptism, we receive the benefits of all that Christ has done. It is for this reason that Baptism is a means of grace.

310. What comfort does my baptism give me?

Galatians 3:26,27 You are all sons of God through faith in Christ Jesus. Indeed, as many of you as were baptized into Christ have been clothed with Christ.

Titus 3:5-7 *He saved us*—not by righteous works that we did ourselves, but because of his mercy. He saved us *through the washing of rebirth and the renewal by the Holy Spirit,* whom he poured out on us abundantly through Jesus Christ our Savior, so that, having been justified by his grace, *we might become heirs in keeping with the hope of eternal life.*

CONNECTIONS

God's gift of Baptism brings incredible blessing. To help us better understand what is happening in Baptism, God compares baptismal waters to the waters of the flood.

This might seem strange—the waters of the flood destroyed so much. But the waters of the flood did something else as well.

Genesis 7:6–8:5,15-22

The floodwaters not only destroyed—what else did they do? In 1 Peter 3:20,21, the Holy Spirit says, "In [the ark] only a few people, eight in all, were saved through water, and this water symbolizes baptism that now saves you also." Explain how the flood can be a helpful picture as you think about your own baptism.

Luther

The power, work, profit, fruit, and purpose of Baptism is this—to save [1 Peter 3:21]. For no one is baptized in order that he may become a prince, but, as the words say, that he "be saved." We know that to be saved is nothing other than to be delivered from sin, death, and the devil [Colossians 1:13-14]. It means to enter into Christ's kingdom [John 3:5], and to live with Him forever. (Large Catechism, IV, par. 24-25)

God's Own Child, I Gladly Say It (Stanza 3)

Satan, hear this proclamation:
I am baptized into Christ!

Drop your ugly accusation;
I am not so soon enticed.
Now that to the font I've traveled,
All your might has come unraveled,
And, against your tyranny
God, my Lord, unites with me!

THE POWER OF BAPTISM

Third: ***How can water do such great things?***

It is certainly not the water that does such things, but God's Word which is in and with the water and faith which trusts this Word used with the water.

For without God's Word the water is just plain water and not Baptism. But with this Word it is Baptism, that is, a gracious water of life and a washing of rebirth by the Holy Spirit.

Where is this written?

Saint Paul says in Titus, chapter 3, "[God] saved us through the washing of rebirth and renewal by the Holy Spirit, whom he poured out on us generously through Jesus Christ our Savior, so that, having been justified by his grace, we might become heirs having the hope of eternal life. This is a trustworthy saying."

BAPTISM
The Power

God tells us that Baptism works incredible miracles: It gives forgiveness, life, and salvation. How can Baptism do those things? There certainly is nothing special about the water. When baptisms happen today, they do not need water from the Jordan River in Israel. The water just comes out of a faucet. The words that are used might seem so simple: "I baptize you in the name of the Father and of the Son and of the Holy Spirit." Yet Baptism does work incredible miracles. We now consider the power that is behind Baptism.

311. Baptism works forgiveness of sins, delivers from death and the devil, and gives eternal salvation. **Why is Baptism able to offer and give such great blessings?**

> **John 3:5,6** Amen, Amen, I tell you: *Unless someone is born of water and the Spirit,* he cannot enter the kingdom of God! Whatever is born of the flesh is flesh. *Whatever is born of the Spirit is spirit.*

Acts 2:38 Peter answered them, "Repent and be baptized, every one of you, in the name of Jesus Christ for the forgiveness of your sins, and you will receive *the gift of the Holy Spirit.*"

Titus 3:5 He saved us—not by righteous works that we did ourselves, but because of his mercy. He saved us through the washing of rebirth and the renewal *by the Holy Spirit.*

312. Without the work of the Holy Spirit, the water would be just plain water and not Baptism. **What does the Holy Spirit use to work through Baptism?**

Ephesians 5:25,26 Husbands, love your wives, in the same way as Christ loved the church and gave himself up for her to make her holy, by cleansing her with the *washing of water in connection with the Word.*

1 Peter 1:23 You have been born again, not from perishable seed but from imperishable, *through the living and enduring word of God.*

313. What does the Holy Spirit do through the Word of God connected with the water in Baptism?

Ephesians 2:8,9 It is by grace you have been saved, through faith—and this is not from yourselves, it is the gift of God—not by works, so that no one can boast.

1 Corinthians 12:3 No one can say, "Jesus is Lord," except by the Holy Spirit.

1 Peter 3:21 Corresponding to that, baptism now saves you—not the removal of dirt from the body but the *guarantee of a good conscience before God* through the resurrection of Jesus Christ.

Galatians 3:26,27 You are all sons of God through faith in Christ Jesus. Indeed, *as many of you as were baptized into Christ have been clothed with Christ.*

Mark 16:16 *Whoever believes and is baptized will be saved, but whoever does not believe will be condemned.*

Through the Word of God in Baptism, the Holy Spirit saves us by creating or strengthening faith. As we then trust God's promises, we are children of God—clothed with Christ and heirs of eternal life.

314. Why is Baptism called a gracious water of life and a washing of rebirth?

Ephesians 2:1 *You were dead* in your trespasses and sins.

John 3:3-5 Jesus replied, "Amen, Amen, I tell you: Unless someone is *born from above,* he cannot see the kingdom of God." Nicodemus said to him, "How can a man be born when he is old? He cannot enter a second time into his mother's womb and be born, can he?" Jesus answered, "Amen, Amen, I tell you: *Unless someone is born of water and the Spirit, he cannot enter the kingdom of God!*"

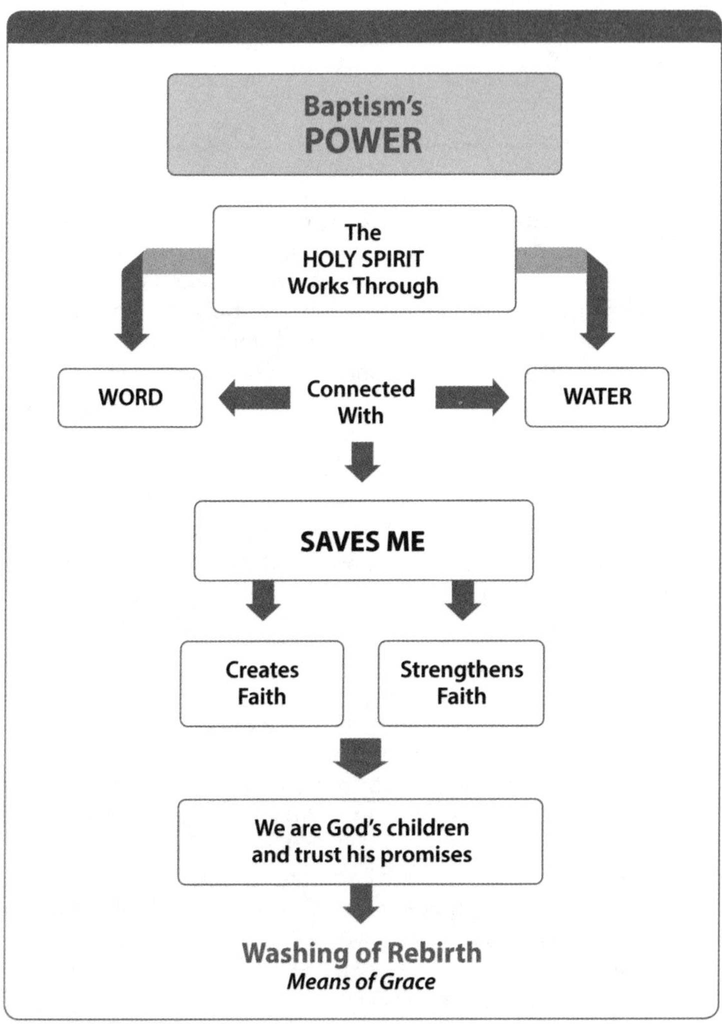

Titus 3:5-7 He saved us—not by righteous works that we did ourselves, but because of his mercy. He saved us through the *washing of rebirth* and the renewal by the Holy Spirit, whom he poured out on us abundantly through Jesus Christ our Savior, so that, having been justified by his grace, we might become heirs in keeping with the hope of eternal life.

Romans 6:4,8 We were therefore buried with him by this baptism into his death, so that just as he was raised from the dead through the glory of the Father, we too would also walk in a new life. And *since we died with Christ, we believe that we will also live with him.*

Baptism is a gracious water of life and a washing of rebirth; by creating and strengthening faith, Baptism brings life—gives new birth—to those who were spiritually dead.

CONNECTIONS

God's Word is powerful; yet, so often, God dresses his Word in what might seem to be very humble clothing. Baptism is a wonderful example of that—powerful, yet humble looking. Such a contrast can present a challenge for humans. We most often value the powerful rather than the humble, so we don't always recognize or appreciate the power in God's Word. A high ranking military official of long ago faced that same challenge.

---

2 Kings 5:1-14

Naaman was not being baptized, but his attitude toward the command of Elisha was similar to the attitude some can have toward Baptism. What lessons do you think Naaman learned through his healing experience? In what ways can the lessons from this account help shape our attitude toward Baptism?

Luther

Here you see again how highly and preciously we should value Baptism, because in it we receive such an unspeakable treasure. This also proves that it cannot be ordinary, mere water. For mere water could not do such a thing. But the Word does it and, . . . so does the fact that God's name is included in Baptism. Where God's name is, there must also be life and salvation [Psalm 54:1]. So Baptism may certainly be called a divine, blessed, fruitful, and gracious water. Such power is given to Baptism by the Word that it is a washing of new birth, as St. Paul also calls it in Titus 3:5. (Large Catechism, IV, par. 26-27)

God's Own Child, I Gladly Say It (Stanzas 4,5)

Death, you cannot end my gladness:
I am baptized into Christ!
When I die, I leave all sadness

To inherit paradise!
Though I lie in dust and ashes
Faith's assurance brightly flashes:
Baptism has the strength divine
To make life immortal mine.

There is nothing worth comparing
To this lifelong comfort sure!
Open-eyed my grave is staring:
Even there I'll sleep secure.
Though my flesh awaits its raising,
Still my soul continues praising:
I am baptized into Christ;
I'm a child of paradise!

THE MEANING OF BAPTISM FOR OUR DAILY LIFE

Fourth: *What does baptizing with water mean?*

Baptism means that the old Adam in us should be drowned by daily contrition and repentance, and that all its evil deeds and desires be put to death. It also means that a new person should daily arise to live before God in righteousness and purity forever.

Where is this written?

Saint Paul says in Romans, chapter 6, "We were . . . buried with [Christ] through baptism into death in order that, just as Christ was raised from the dead through the glory of the Father, we too may live a new life."

BAPTISM

The Meaning for Life

How long has it been since you were baptized? You may not remember the day, but maybe you have a certificate testifying to your baptism. Perhaps you can remember the day. Whether you remember it or not, it was a special day. It has lasting significance for you. You have forgiveness, life, and salvation because of your baptism. Your baptism has also given you a new birth so that you can turn away from sin and serve Jesus every day of your life.

315. What change did the Holy Spirit bring about in my life through my baptism?

Romans 8:7 *The mind-set of the sinful flesh is hostile to God,* since it does not submit to God's law, and in fact, it cannot.

1 Corinthians 2:14 *An unspiritual person does not accept the truths taught by God's Spirit,* because they are foolishness to him, and he cannot understand them, because they are spiritually evaluated.

Ephesians 2:4,5 God, because he is rich in mercy, because of the great love with which he loved us, *made us alive with Christ even when we were dead in trespasses.* It is by grace you have been saved!

Romans 6:1-4 What shall we say then? Shall we keep on sinning so that grace may increase? Absolutely not! We died to sin. How can we go on living in it any longer? Or do you not know that all of us who were baptized into Christ Jesus were baptized into his death? *We were therefore buried with him by this baptism into his death,* so that just as he was raised from the dead through the glory of the Father, *we too would also walk in a new life.*

Ephesians 4:22-24 As far as your former way of life is concerned, . . . take off the old self, which is corrupted by its deceitful desires, . . . be renewed continually in the spirit of your mind, and . . . *put on the new self, which has been created to be like God in righteousness and true holiness.*

In my baptism, God made me spiritually alive. He gave me a *new self,* a new person that loves the Lord and seeks to avoid sin.

316. What new attitude characterizes the new person within each of us?

2 Corinthians 5:17 If anyone is in Christ, *he is a new creation.* The old has passed away. The new has come!

2 Corinthians 5:14,15 The love of Christ compels us, because we came to this conclusion: One died for all; therefore, all died. And he died for all, so that *those who live would no longer live for themselves but for him,* who died in their place and was raised again.

Romans 6:6 We know that our old self was crucified with him, to make our sinful body powerless, so *that we would not continue to serve sin.*

Psalm 119:104,112 From your precepts I gain understanding. Therefore, *I hate every false road.* I turn my heart to do your statutes, forever, right to the end.

Titus 2:14 [Jesus Christ] gave himself for us, to redeem us from all lawlessness and to purify for himself a people who are his own chosen people, *eager to do good works.*

Psalm 40:8 My God, I take pleasure in doing your will. *Your law is in my heart.*

The new person in each of us is eager to do what pleases the Lord.

317. In what ways does the old Adam battle against the new person within us?

Galatians 5:17 *The sinful flesh desires what is contrary to the spirit,* and the spirit what is contrary to the sinful flesh. In fact, these two continually oppose one another, so that you do not continue to do these things you want to do.

Genesis 8:21 *The thoughts he forms in his heart are evil from his youth.*

Romans 7:19 I fail to do the good I want to do. Instead, *the evil I do not want to do, that is what I keep doing.*

Romans 7:22-25 I certainly delight in God's law according to my inner self, but I see a different law at work in my members, waging war against the law of my mind and taking me captive to the law of sin, which is present in my members. What a miserable wretch I am! Who will rescue me from this body of death? I thank God through Jesus Christ our Lord! So then, I myself serve the law of God with my mind, but *with my sinful flesh I serve the law of sin.*

318. In what way does Baptism equip us to battle the old Adam in our daily lives?

Romans 6:2-4,6 We died to sin. How can we go on living in it any longer? Or do you not know that all of us who were baptized into Christ Jesus were baptized into his death? We were therefore buried with him by this baptism into his death, so that just as he was raised from the dead through the glory of the Father, we too would also walk in a new life. *We know that our old self was crucified with him, to make our sinful body powerless,* so that we would not continue to serve sin.

Romans 6:12,13 Do not let sin reign in your mortal body so that you obey its desires. Do not offer the members of your body to sin as tools of unrighteousness. Instead, offer yourselves to God as those who are alive from the dead, and offer the members of your body to God as tools of righteousness.

In our baptisms, we were set free from slavery to sin. Our baptisms, then, have worked in us a hatred of sin, so we wish daily to put to death—to drown—our sinful nature and all of its evil desires.

A CLOSER LOOK

Daily we are tempted. Sometimes we stumble and fall into sin. It's a struggle to live as a Christian. As a result, the life of a Christian is marked by contrition and repentance. Contrition is God-given sorrow over sin and recognition that we deserve his punishment for our sinful actions. Repentance is a God-given change of mind that sees sin as an enemy and trusts God's gracious promise of forgiveness. Each day we confess our failures and sins and turn to God for his precious forgiveness. Baptism reminds us that our sins have been paid for by Jesus; we are washed and cleansed. Through Baptism, God has made us his dear children and his promises give us the strength to serve him—turning away from sin so that we can live as his children.

319. How do we drown the sinful nature in our daily lives?

Psalm 51:17 The sacrifices God wants are a broken spirit. *A broken and crushed heart,* O God, you will not despise.

Psalm 51:4 Against you, you only, have I sinned, and I have done this evil in your eyes. So you are justified when you sentence me. You are blameless when you judge.

Psalm 38:18 I declare my guilt, and I am troubled by my sin.

Luke 15:21 The son said to him, "*Father, I have sinned* against heaven and in your sight. I am no longer worthy to be called your son."

Job 42:6 I despise myself. I *repent* in dust and ashes.

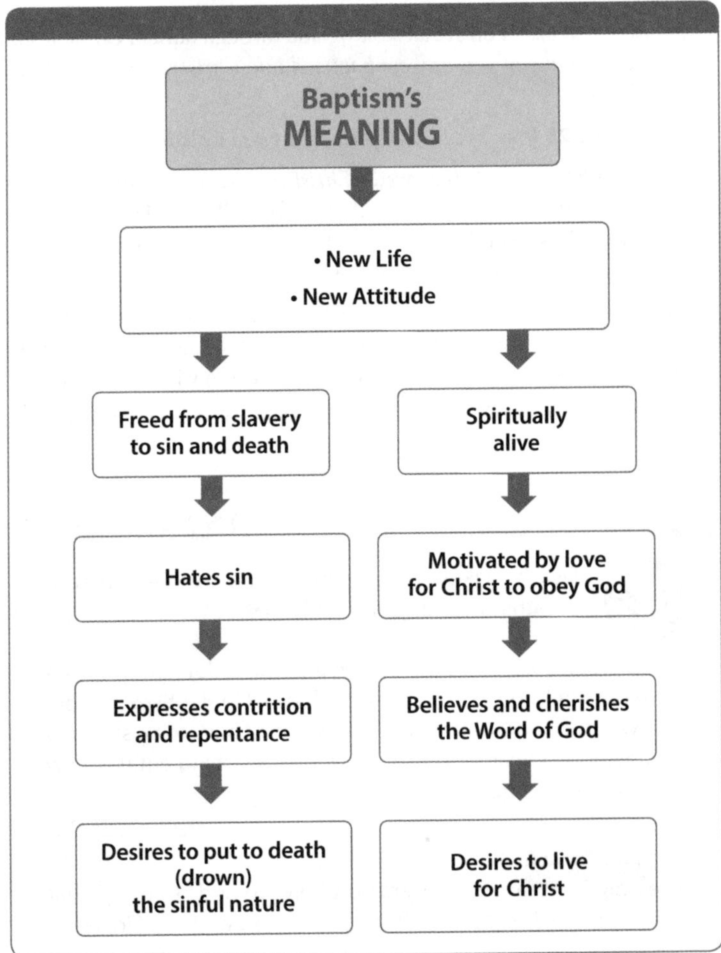

Ezekiel 18:30 Repent and turn away from all your rebellious acts, so that you will not set out a stumbling block that makes you guilty.

Matthew 3:8 Produce fruit in keeping with repentance!

Luke 15:10 I tell you, there is joy in the presence of the angels of God over one sinner who *repents.*

Revelation 2:5 Remember, therefore, the state from which you have fallen! *Repent and do the works you did at first.*

We drown the sinful nature—put off the old Adam—through daily contrition and repentance.

320. How does Baptism strengthen the new person within us for Christian living every day of our lives?

Galatians 3:26,27 You are all sons of God through faith in Christ Jesus. Indeed, *as many of you as were baptized into Christ have been clothed with Christ.*

Galatians 5:25 *If we live by the spirit, let us also walk in step with it.*

2 Corinthians 5:14,15 *The love of Christ compels us,* because we came to this conclusion: One died for all; therefore, all died. And he died for all, so that those who live would no longer live for themselves but for him, who died in their place and was raised again.

Colossians 2:6,7 *Just as you received Christ Jesus as Lord, continue to walk in him,* by being rooted and built up in him, and strengthened in the faith just as you were taught, while you overflow in faith with thanksgiving.

Baptism's promise of forgiveness, life, and salvation motivates us to give thanks to the Lord with our entire lives.

CONNECTIONS

Death makes things stop. When we die, we stop breathing, talking, and walking.

By nature, we were all slaves to sin and the sinful nature within us. What could put a stop to such slavery? In Baptism, our old self was crucified with Jesus so that we don't have to be slaves to sin anymore. We are dead to sin. Now, something entirely new comes to life—a new life, a new self.

Romans 6:1-14

The Holy Spirit says that we are now "alive to God." List ways that a person's life is different after he or she is baptized. Sin keeps surfacing in our lives. How can our baptisms play an important part in our daily struggles with sin?

Luther

[Baptism's power and work] is nothing other than putting to death the old Adam and affecting the new man's resurrection after that [Romans 6:4-6]. Both of these things must take place in us all our lives. So a truly Christian life is nothing other than a daily Baptism, once begun and ever to be continued. For this must be done without ceasing, that we always keep purging away whatever belongs to the old Adam. Then what belongs to the new man may come forth. (Large Catechism, IV, par. 65)

All Christians Who Have Been Baptized (Stanzas 4,5)

In Baptism we now put on Christ—Our shame is fully covered
With all that he once sacrificed And freely for us suffered.
For here the flood of his own blood
Now makes us holy, right, and good
Before our heav'nly Father.

O Christian, firmly hold this gift And give God thanks forever!
It gives the power to uplift In all that you endeavor.
When nothing else revives your soul,
Your baptism stands and makes you whole
And then in death completes you.

THE KEYS

Christ gives his church two keys: the power to forgive sins and the power to refuse to forgive sins.

THE KEYS

First: *What is the use of the keys?*

The use of the keys is that special power and right which Christ gave to his church on earth: to forgive the sins of penitent sinners but refuse forgiveness to the impenitent as long as they do not repent.

Where is this written?

The holy evangelist John writes in chapter 20, "[Jesus] breathed on [his disciples] and said, 'Receive the Holy Spirit. If you forgive anyone his sins, they are forgiven; if you do not forgive them, they are not forgiven.' "

KEYS

Use of the Keys

Keys can open doors, and keys can lock doors. Those who possess keys also possess a great deal of responsibility. They need to know when a door should be unlocked and when it should be shut tight. God gives believers in Jesus the keys to open and close the door of heaven. It might not seem right that God should give these keys to people. How can humans ever handle this responsibility?

Christians do have an amazing privilege and responsibility. Thankfully, God tells us exactly how to use the keys to the kingdom of heaven.

321. What are the keys?

Matthew 16:19 I will give you the keys of the kingdom of heaven. *Whatever you bind on earth* will be bound in heaven, and *whatever you loose on earth* will be loosed in heaven.

Matthew 18:18 Amen I tell you: Whatever you bind on earth will be bound in heaven, and whatever you loose on earth will be loosed in heaven.

John 20:23 *Whenever you forgive people's sins,* they are forgiven. *Whenever you do not forgive them,* they are not forgiven.

2 Corinthians 5:18-20 All these things are from God, who reconciled us to himself through Christ and gave us the ministry of reconciliation. That is, God was in Christ reconciling the world to himself, not counting their trespasses against them. And he has *entrusted to us the message of reconciliation.* Therefore, we are ambassadors for Christ, inasmuch as God is making an appeal through us. We urge you, on Christ's behalf: Be reconciled to God.

The keys are the special power and right given to Christians to forgive sins or to refuse to forgive sins. The power and right to forgive sins is the loosing key. It opens the door to heaven, declaring the person free from the guilt and punishment of sin. The power and right to refuse to forgive sins is the binding key. It locks the door of heaven, binding the person to the guilt and condemnation of his or her sin.

322. To whom has God given the special power and right to use these keys?

John 20:19,21-23 On the evening of that first day of the week, *the disciples were together* behind locked doors because of their fear of the Jews. Jesus came, stood among them, and said to them, "Peace be with you! . . . *Just as the Father has sent me, I am also sending you.*" After saying this, he breathed on them and said, "Receive the Holy Spirit. Whenever you forgive people's sins, they are forgiven. Whenever you do not forgive them, they are not forgiven."

1 Peter 2:7,9 Therefore, for *you who believe,* this is an honor. But for those who do not believe: The stone which the builders rejected has become the cornerstone. But *you are a chosen people, a royal priesthood,* a holy nation, the people who are God's own possession, so that you may proclaim the praises of him who called you out of darkness into his marvelous light.

Christ has given to all Christians (the church) the special power and right to forgive sins or to refuse to forgive sins.

323. How valid and certain is the use of the keys by believers?

John 20:23 Whenever you forgive people's sins, *they are forgiven.* Whenever you do not forgive them, *they are not forgiven.*

Luke 17:3 Watch yourselves. "If your brother sins, rebuke him. If he repents, forgive him."

Matthew 18:18 Amen I tell you: Whatever you bind on earth will be bound in heaven, and whatever you loose on earth will be loosed in heaven.

The use of the keys by believers is as valid and certain in heaven also, as if Christ, our dear Lord, dealt with us himself.

324. When does God want us to use the loosing key?

1 John 1:9 *If we confess our sins, he is faithful and just to forgive* us our sins and to cleanse us from all unrighteousness.

Acts 3:19 *Repent* and return *to have your sins wiped out.*

Psalm 51:17 The sacrifices God wants are a broken spirit. *A broken and crushed heart, O God, you will not despise.*

Luke 15:10 I tell you, *there is joy in the presence of the angels of God over one sinner who repents.*

Luke 18:13,14 The tax collector stood at a distance and would not even lift his eyes up to heaven, but was beating his chest and saying, "God, be merciful to me, a sinner!" I tell you, this man went home justified rather than the other, because everyone who exalts himself will be humbled, but the one who humbles himself will be exalted.

Jesus commands us to forgive the sins of those who repent.

325. Why does Jesus want us to use the loosing key?

Psalm 38:2-4,8,18,21,22 (King David's guilt crushed his soul. He longed for the comfort and relief of the forgiveness of sins.)

Psalm 51:2,3,11,12 Scrub me clean from my guilt. Purify me from my sin. For I admit my rebellious acts. My sin is always in front of me. Do not cast me from your presence. Do not take your Holy Spirit from me. Restore to me the joy of your salvation. Sustain me with a willing spirit.

2 Corinthians 2:7 You should rather forgive and comfort him, *or else such a person could be overwhelmed by excessive sorrow.*

Psalm 51:8 Let me hear joy and gladness. *Let the bones you have crushed celebrate.*

Jesus wants us to use the loosing key to comfort those who repent and to assure them that their sins are forgiven.

326. When does God want us to use the binding key?

1 John 1:8,10 *If we say we have no sin, we deceive ourselves,* and the truth is not in us. If we say we have not sinned, we make him out to be a liar, and his Word is not in us.

Luke 18:10-14 (Because the Pharisee did not repent, he had no forgiveness.)

Matthew 18:15-18 (If someone refuses to repent, we are to treat that person like an unbeliever.)

John 20:23 Whenever you forgive people's sins, they are forgiven. *Whenever you do not forgive them,* they are not forgiven.

Jesus commands us to refuse to forgive the sins of those who do not repent.

327. Why does Jesus command us to use the binding key?

Galatians 5:21 I also warned you before, that those who continue to do such things will not inherit the kingdom of God.

Hebrews 10:26,27 If we deliberately keep on sinning after we have received the full knowledge of the truth, there no longer remains any sacrifice for sins. Instead, *there is a certain fearful expectation of judgment* and a raging fire that is going to consume the enemies of God.

1 Corinthians 5:13 Remove the wicked man from among yourselves.

1 Corinthians 5:5 Hand such a man over to Satan for the destruction of the flesh, so that the spirit may be saved on the day of the Lord Jesus.

Matthew 18:15 If your brother sins against you, go and show him his sin just between the two of you. *If he listens to you, you have regained your brother.*

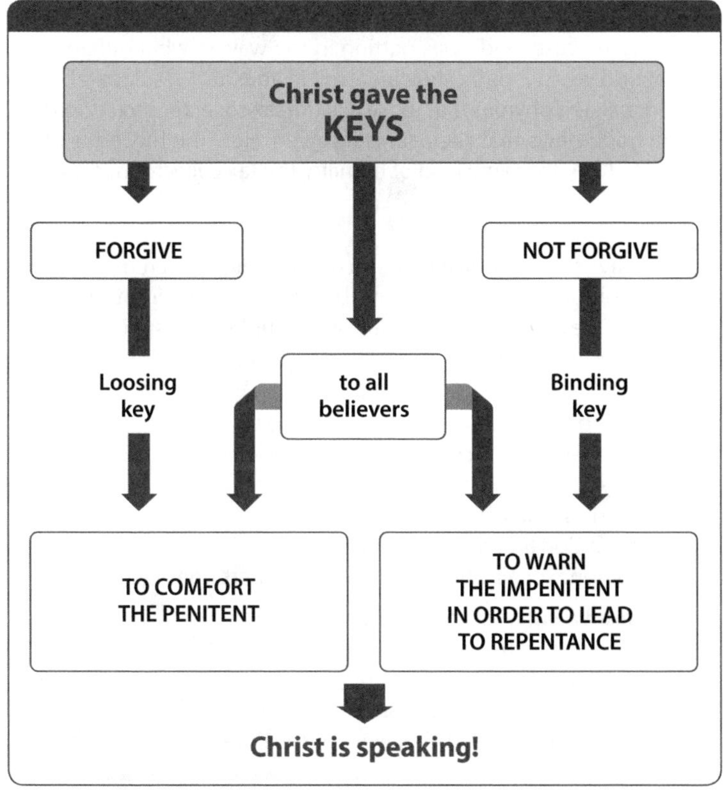

Luke 15:10 I tell you, *there is joy in the presence of the angels of God over one sinner who repents.*

Jesus wants us to use the binding key in the hope that the declaration of God's judgment will lead the unrepentant sinner to repent and receive the forgiveness of sins.

CONNECTIONS

Some people don't believe that their sins are serious or even that they have sinned. Others are driven to despair when they think of their sins. Jesus has given the keys to the church in order to address the spiritual needs of both kinds of people. He once told a parable that helps us better understand when to use the binding key and when to use the loosing key.

Luke 18:9-14

Jesus' parable makes it obvious that those like the Pharisee *should not* be given assurance that their sin is forgiven. In the Pharisee's case, pride was getting in the way. In what different ways do you see pride showing itself in your life? Jesus' parable also makes it obvious that those like the tax collector *should* hear the good news that their sin is forgiven. How might God lead you to have the same kind of humility the tax collector had?

Luther

God gave the key which binds so that we might not remain too confident in our sins, arrogant, barbarous, and without God; and the key which looses, that we should not despair in our sins. (LW 40:325ff)

Jesus Sinners Does Receive (Stanzas 1,2)

Jesus sinners does receive;
Oh, may all this saying ponder
Who in sin's delusions live
And from God and heaven wander.
Here is hope for all who grieve—Jesus sinners does receive.

We deserve but grief and shame,
Yet his words, rich grace revealing,
Pardon, peace, and life proclaim;
Here their ills have perfect healing
Who with humble hearts believe—Jesus sinners does receive.

THE PUBLIC USE OF THE KEYS

Second: ***How does a Christian congregation use the keys?***
A Christian congregation with its called servant of Christ uses the keys in accordance with Christ's command by forgiving those who repent of their sin and are willing to amend, and by excluding from the congregation those who are plainly impenitent that they may repent. I believe that when this is done, it is as valid and certain in heaven also, as if Christ, our dear Lord, dealt with us himself.

Where is this written?
Jesus says in Matthew, chapter 18, "Whatever you bind on earth will be bound in heaven, and whatever you loose on earth will be loosed in heaven."

Public Use of the Keys

Believers are naturally concerned about the souls of others. They rejoice when someone comes to faith in Jesus and are sad when someone strays away from Jesus. They thank God for giving all Christians the binding and loosing keys. When Christians gather in groups with other Christians, they call spiritual shepherds to partner with them and to lead them in their use of the keys. Together, God's people announce God's warnings and God's comfort.

328. Why do Christians gather together in congregations?

Hebrews 10:24,25 Let us also consider carefully *how to spur each other on* to love and good works. Let us *not neglect meeting together,* as some have the habit of doing. Rather, let us *encourage each other,* and all the more as you see the Day approaching.

Acts 2:42 They continued to hold firmly to the apostles' teaching and to the fellowship, to the breaking of the bread, and to the prayers.

2 Peter 3:18 *Grow in the grace and knowledge of our Lord and Savior Jesus Christ.* To him be the glory, both now and forever. Amen.

329. How do members of a Christian congregation use the keys to encourage one another?

Colossians 3:16 Let the word of Christ dwell in you richly, as you *teach and admonish one another* with all wisdom, singing psalms, hymns, and spiritual songs, with gratitude in your hearts to God.

Galatians 5:19-21 The works of the sinful flesh are obvious: sexual immorality, impurity, complete lack of restraint, idolatry, sorcery, hatred, discord, jealousy, outbursts of anger, selfish ambition, dissensions, heresies, envy, murders, drunkenness, orgies, and things similar to these. *I warn you,* just as I also warned you before, that those who continue to do such things will not inherit the kingdom of God.

John 20:23 *Whenever you forgive people's sins,* they are forgiven. *Whenever you do not forgive them,* they are not forgiven.

2 Corinthians 2:7 *You should rather forgive and comfort him,* or else such a person could be overwhelmed by excessive sorrow.

330. How does God guide Christian congregations as they use the keys publicly?

Matthew 18:20 Where two or three have gathered together in my name, *there I am among them.*

Ephesians 4:11,12 *He himself gave the apostles, as well as the prophets, as well as the evangelists, as well as the pastors and teachers,* for the purpose of training the saints for the work of serving, in order to build up the body of Christ.

Titus 1:5 The reason I left you in Crete was so that you would set in order the things that were left unfinished and *appoint elders* in every city, as I directed you.

Acts 14:23 *They had elders elected* for them in every church, and with prayer and fasting they entrusted them to the Lord, in whom they believed.

1 Timothy 5:17 *The elders who lead* well should be considered worthy of double honor, especially the ones who work hard in the word and doctrine.

Matthew 16:19 *I will give you the keys of the kingdom of heaven.* Whatever you bind on earth will be bound in heaven, and whatever you loose on earth will be loosed in heaven.

God provides Christian congregations with leaders who are to faithfully guide the affairs of the congregation. Preaching and teaching God's Word is one of the most important ways that they lead their congregations.

Spiritual Leaders

All Christians have the same rights and responsibilities, but God determined that spiritual leaders in the church (the office of the public ministry) will serve in the name of the members of the church to help Christians carry out their work. As it works in practical terms, Christians gathered together have the right to choose those who will help them grow and work together. Individual Christians may not assume positions of public leadership and ministry unless the other Christians ask or call them to do so. In addition, God gives Christians the freedom to implement specific roles of ministry that will meet their spiritual needs and then to call those who will work among them. For example, a congregation calls one or more pastors to take the lead in preaching and teaching God's Word. A congregation may also call staff ministers, vicars, evangelists, teachers, and others to lead them in service to God. Consider what the early church did in Jerusalem as an example: "Brothers, carefully select from among you seven men with good reputations, who are full of the Holy Spirit and wisdom. We will put them in charge of this service" (Acts 6:3).

331. What qualifications has God established for those who serve in the public ministry?

Titus 1:5-9 Appoint elders in every city, as I directed you. Such a man is to be *blameless, the husband of only one wife,* and to have believing children who are not open to a charge of wild living or disobedience. Indeed an overseer, since he is God's steward, must be blameless, *not arrogant, not quick-tempered, not a drunkard, not violent, not eager for dishonest gain.* Instead, he must be *hospitable, loving what is good, self-controlled, upright, devout,* and *disciplined.* He must *cling to the trustworthy message as it has been taught,* so that he will be able both to encourage people by the sound teaching and also to correct those who oppose him.

1 Peter 5:2 *Shepherd God's flock* that is among you, serving as overseers, not grudgingly but willingly, as God desires, not because you are greedy for money but because you are *eager to do it.*

Acts 20:28 Always keep watch over yourselves and over the whole flock in which the *Holy Spirit has placed you as overseers, to shepherd the church of God,* which he purchased with his own blood.

332. Who may serve as pastors (shepherds) in congregations?

1 Timothy 3:2-7 It is necessary, then, for the overseer to be above reproach, the husband of only one wife, temperate, self-controlled, respectable, hospitable, able to teach, not a drunkard, not a violent man but gentle, not quarrelsome, not a lover of money. It is necessary that he manage his own household well, with all dignity making sure that his children obey him. (If a man does not know how to manage his own household, how will he take care of God's church?) He must not be a recent convert, or he might become conceited and fall into the same condemnation as the Devil. In addition, he must have a good reputation with those outside the church, so that he may not fall into disgrace and the Devil's trap.

1 Corinthians 4:2 It is required of stewards that they *be found faithful.*

It is necessary that those who serve as pastors in congregations possess the qualifications God has established for that position.

1 Timothy 2:11-13 A woman should learn in a quiet manner with full submission. And I do not permit a woman to teach or to have authority over a man. Instead, she is to continue in a quiet manner. For Adam was formed first, then Eve.

1 Corinthians 14:34,37 Women are to keep silent in the churches, for they are not permitted to speak. Instead they are to be subordinate, as also the Law says. If anyone thinks he is a prophet or spiritual person, let him recognize that the things I write to you are the Lord's commands.

Because our pastors serve in a position of spiritual leadership over both men and women, God has directed the church to call men to serve as pastors.

Acts 20:28 Always keep watch over yourselves and over the whole flock in which the Holy Spirit has placed you as overseers, *to shepherd the church of God,* which he purchased with his own blood.

Acts 14:23 *They had elders elected for them in every church,* and with prayer and fasting they entrusted them to the Lord, in whom they believed.

Those whom the Holy Spirit has appointed (called) through the congregation may serve as pastors.

A CLOSER LOOK

Qualifications for Leaders

When God established the office of the public ministry, he gave Christians great freedom in determining the forms such leadership would take. As we consider the qualifications required of those who serve in our office of pastor, we recognize that those in other offices of the public ministry are also to honor these qualifications.

---

333. What are some ways in which a pastor serves the congregation that has called him?

1 Corinthians 4:1 This is the way a person should think of us: *as servants of Christ and stewards of God's mysteries.*

1 Timothy 4:13 Until I come, devote yourself to the *reading of Scripture, to encouraging, and to teaching.*

2 Timothy 4:2,3 *Preach the word.* Be ready whether it is convenient or not. Correct, rebuke, and encourage, with all patience and teaching. For there will come a time when people will not put up with sound doctrine. Instead, because they have itching ears, they will accumulate for themselves teachers in line with their own desires.

Mark 16:15 *He said to them, "Go into all the world and preach the gospel to all creation."*

Luke 24:47 Repentance and forgiveness of sins *will be preached in his name to all nations,* beginning from Jerusalem.

2 Timothy 4:5 Keep a clear head in every situation. Bear hardship. *Do the work of an evangelist.* Fulfill your ministry.

Isaiah 52:7 How beautiful on the mountains are the feet of *a herald, who proclaims peace and preaches good news, who proclaims salvation,* who says to Zion, "Your God is king!"

James 5:14 Is anyone among you sick? He should call the elders of the church, and they should pray over him, anointing him with oil in the name of the Lord.

2 Corinthians 1:3,4 Blessed be the God and Father of our Lord Jesus Christ, the Father of mercies and God of all comfort, *who comforts us in all our trouble, so that we can comfort those in any trouble* with the same comfort with which we ourselves are comforted by God.

The pastor serves the congregation by leading the members in public worship, preaching and teaching God's law and gospel, and counseling and encouraging the members with God's Word.

1 Corinthians 14:40 Let all things be done decently and in good order.

Matthew 28:19 Go and gather disciples from all nations by *baptizing* them in the name of the Father and of the Son and of the Holy Spirit.

1 Corinthians 11:24,25 When he had given thanks, he broke it and said, "This is my body, which is for you. *Do this* in remembrance of me." In the same way, after the meal, he also took the cup, saying, "This cup is the new testament in my blood. *Do this,* as often as you drink it, in remembrance of me."

The pastor serves the congregation by administering the sacraments in an orderly way.

Ephesians 4:11,12 He himself gave the apostles, as well as the prophets, as well as the evangelists, as well as the pastors and teachers, *for the* *purpose of training the saints for the work of serving, in order to build up the body of Christ.*

The pastor serves the members of the congregation by training them with the Word of God, equipping them to serve their Savior.

334. How will the congregation with its called shepherd use the binding key?

Matthew 18:15-18 If your brother sins against you, go and show him his sin just between the two of you. If he listens to you, you have regained your brother. But if he will not listen, take one or two others along with you, so that "every matter may be established by the testimony of two or three witnesses." If he refuses to listen to them, tell it to the church. And, if he refuses to listen even to the church, then treat him as an unbeliever or a tax collector. Amen I tell you: Whatever you bind on earth will be bound in heaven, and whatever you loose on earth will be loosed in heaven.

1 Corinthians 5:4,5,13 When you are gathered together, and my spirit is there, along with the power of our Lord Jesus, hand such a man over to Satan for the destruction of the flesh, so that the spirit may be saved on the day of the Lord Jesus. God will judge the people outside the church. "Remove the wicked man from among yourselves."

1 Timothy 5:20 *In the presence of everyone, rebuke* the ones who persist in sin, so that *the rest may be afraid.*

The congregation together with its pastor will use the binding key to exclude from the congregation those who are obviously impenitent—with the goal that they repent and receive forgiveness (church discipline).

A CLOSER LOOK

Excommunication

Out of love for the souls of those who demonstrate a lack of repentance for their sin, Jesus commands the church to carry out church discipline. In Matthew 18:15-18, Jesus explains how to demonstrate this loving concern for lost souls. He says that if someone has sinned against you, you are to talk to the person privately to point out the sin. If the person listens and repents, you have won the person over. If the person refuses to listen or repent, you are to take one or two others with you to impress upon the person the seriousness of his or her sin. If the person still refuses to listen, you are then to take the matter to the leaders of the church. If the impenitent refuses to listen to the leaders of the church, then God commands the congregation to treat the person as an unbeliever. Removing the person from the Christian congregation is not intended to harm the sinning individual. Rather, Christians pray that such a severe rebuke will highlight the seriousness of sin and ultimately lead the individual to repentance and restoration.

335. How will the congregation with its called shepherd use the loosing key?

2 Corinthians 2:6-8,10 This punishment inflicted on such a person by the majority is enough, so that instead *you should rather forgive and comfort him,* or else such a person could be overwhelmed by excessive sorrow. For that reason, I urge you to reaffirm your love for him. *If you forgive anyone anything, I do too.* To be sure, if I have forgiven anything, I have forgiven it in the presence of Christ for your sake.

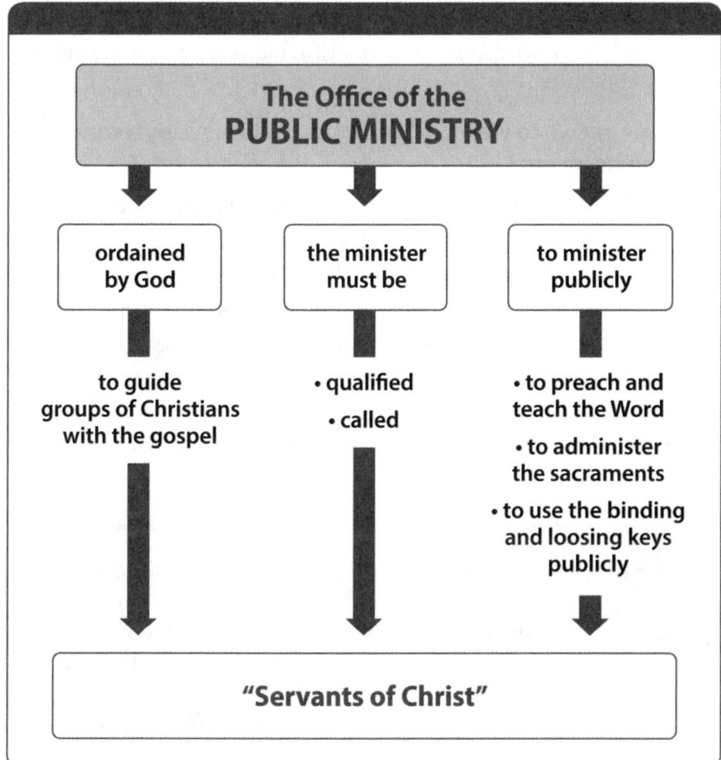

They will use the loosing key to announce forgiveness to the person under church discipline who repents of his or her sin and will welcome the person back into the fellowship of the congregation.

Acts 26:18 You are to open their eyes, so that they may turn from darkness to light and from the power of Satan to God, so that they may receive the forgiveness of sins and a place among those who are sanctified by faith in me.

They will use the loosing key to announce forgiveness to those who were formerly unbelievers but have now repented of their sins.

Isaiah 40:1,2 Comfort, comfort my people, says your God. *Speak to the heart* of Jerusalem and call out to her. Her warfare really is over. *Her guilt is fully paid for.* Yes, she has received from the LORD's hand double for all her sins.

1 Thessalonians 2:11,12 You know that we treated each of you as a father deals with his own children: encouraging, comforting, and urging you to live lives worthy of God, who is calling you into his kingdom and glory.

The congregation asks its pastor to use the loosing key to announce forgiveness publicly in its worship services, as well as individually to those offering a private confession.

336. How are we to view the public use of the keys by a congregation with its pastor?

1 Corinthians 4:1 This is the way a person should think of us: *as servants of Christ* and stewards of God's mysteries.

Matthew 18:15-20 (Jesus gave the church the authority to forgive the sins of the penitent and to refuse to forgive the sins of the impenitent.)

Luke 10:16 *Whoever listens to you listens to me.* Whoever rejects you rejects me. And whoever rejects me rejects the one who sent me.

The public use of the keys by a congregation with its called pastor is as valid and certain in heaven also, as if Christ, our dear Lord, dealt with us himself.

CONNECTIONS

When a Christian congregation rebukes someone who is straying from the faith, the words can seem so harsh. But Christian love sometimes does hard things out of love for the person's soul and with trust that God knows what is best.

Christians in Corinth needed to do something hard like this. In their case, the ending was very happy.

---

1 Corinthians 5:1-4; 2 Corinthians 2:3-11

After the rebuke was spoken, the Holy Spirit created sorrow in the heart of the sinner. What temptations can Satan bring to someone who is feeling very bad because of a sin? Based on

Paul's words in 2 Corinthians chapter 2, what might we say to a friend who has been brought to repentance?

Luther

The key which binds is the power or office to punish the sinner who refuses to repent by means of a public condemnation and separation from the rest of Christendom. The loosing key is the power or office to absolve the sinner who makes confession and is converted from sins, promising again eternal life. To bind and to loose clearly is nothing else than to proclaim and to apply the gospel. For what is it to loose if not to announce the forgiveness of sins before God? What is it to bind, except to withdraw the gospel and to declare the retention of sins? (LW 40:325ff)

Jesus Sinners Does Receive (Stanzas 1,3)

Jesus sinners does receive;
Oh, may all this saying ponder
Who in sin's delusions live
And from God and heaven wander.
Here is hope for all who grieve—Jesus sinners does receive.

Sheep that from the fold did stray
Are not by the Lord forsaken;
Weary souls who lost their way
Are by Christ, the shepherd, taken
In his arms that they may live—Jesus sinners does receive.

CONFESSION

First: *What is confession?*

Confession has two parts. The one is that we confess our sins; the other, that we receive absolution or forgiveness from the pastor as from God himself, not doubting but firmly believing that our sins are thus forgiven before God in heaven.

Second: *What sins should we confess?*

Before God we should plead guilty of all sins, even those we are not aware of, as we do in the Lord's Prayer.

But before the pastor we should confess only those sins which we know and feel in our hearts.

Third: *How can we recognize these sins?*

Consider your place in life according to the Ten Commandments. Are you a father, mother, son, daughter, employer, or employee? Have you been disobedient, unfaithful, or lazy? Have you hurt anyone by word or deed? Have you been dishonest, careless, wasteful, or done other wrong?

Fourth: *How will the pastor assure a penitent sinner of forgiveness?*

He will say, "By the authority of Christ, I forgive you your sins in the name of the Father and of the Son and of the Holy Spirit. Amen."

CONFESSION

Confession and Absolution

An old Scottish proverb says, "Confession is good for the soul." Many people believe that proverb is true in a general way. Admitting a wrong can bring a measure of inner peace and help restore relationships with others.

When God speaks about confession, he is not simply interested in restoring earthly relationships or giving emotional peace. Sin has the power to break our relationships with God. Confession is important for our souls.

337. The word *confess* means to admit a wrong. The first part of confession is that we admit we are sinners who deserve to be punished for our sin. **Why do we confess our sins?**

Psalm 51:1 *Be gracious to me, God,* according to your mercy. Erase my acts of rebellion according to the greatness of your compassion.

Psalm 32:3,5 *When I kept silent, my bones wasted away as I groaned all day long.* I acknowledged my sin to you, and I did not cover up my guilt. I said, "I will confess my rebellion to the LORD," and you forgave the guilt of my sin.

1 John 1:8,9 If we say we have no sin, we deceive ourselves, and the truth is not in us. *If we confess our sins, he is faithful and just to forgive us our sins* and to cleanse us from all unrighteousness.

Luke 18:13 The tax collector stood at a distance and would not even lift his eyes up to heaven, but was beating his chest and saying, *"God, be merciful to me, a sinner!"*

James 5:16 *Confess your sins to one another.*

We confess our sins because God commands us to and because we long for forgiveness.

338. What do we acknowledge in our confessions to God?

Psalm 51:5 Certainly, *I was guilty when I was born.* I was sinful when my mother conceived me.

Isaiah 64:6 *All of us have become like something unclean,* and all our righteous acts are like a filthy cloth. All of us have withered like a leaf, and our guilt carries us away like the wind.

James 2:10 Whoever keeps the whole law but stumbles in one point *has become guilty of breaking all of it.*

Isaiah 59:12 Our rebellious deeds are many before you, and *our sins testify against us.* Our rebellious deeds are with us, and as for our guilty deeds, we are aware of them.

Psalm 19:12 *Who can recognize his own errors?* Declare me innocent of hidden sins.

Romans 6:23 The wages of sin is death, but the undeserved gift of God is eternal life in Christ Jesus our Lord.

Romans 7:24 What a miserable wretch I am! Who will rescue me from this body of death?

We confess not only what we do but what we are. We were born with a sinful nature that continues to cause us to sin daily in thought, word, and deed. Our sins deserve eternal punishment.

339. How does God lead us to confess our sins?

Romans 3:20 No one will be declared righteous in his sight by works of the law, for *through the law we become aware of sin.*

Romans 7:7 *I would not have recognized sin except through the law.* For example, I would not have known about coveting if the law had not said, "You shall not covet."

Psalm 38:3,6,18 There is no health in my flesh because of your rage. There is no wellness in my bones because of my sin. I am drooping. I am completely bent over. All day long I go around mourning. So I declare my guilt, and *I am troubled by my sin.*

God's law makes us aware of our sins—each of us according to our place in life, whether we are a father, mother, son, daughter, employer, or employee. It points out if we have been disobedient, unfaithful, or lazy; if we have hurt anyone with our words or by our actions; if we have been dishonest, careless, wasteful, or committed any other wrongs. The law makes us aware of the punishment we deserve because of our sins.

340. Confession has a second part. **When God has led us to confess our sins, what announcement does he then make?**

2 Samuel 12:1-13 (When David confessed his sins, Nathan announced that God had forgiven his sins.)

Luke 7:48 Jesus said to [the sinful woman], *"Your sins have been forgiven."*

Matthew 9:2 [Jesus] said to the paralyzed man, "Take heart, son! *Your sins are forgiven.*"

Hebrews 8:12 I will be merciful in regard to their unrighteousness, and I will not remember their sins any longer.

341. When does the pastor regularly proclaim this comforting announcement?

Psalm 32:5 I acknowledged my sin to you, and I did not cover up my guilt. I said, "I will confess my rebellion to the LORD," and *you forgave the guilt of my sin.*

John 20:21-23 Jesus said to them again, "Peace be with you! Just as the Father has sent me, *I am also sending you.*" After saying this, he breathed on them and said, "Receive the Holy Spirit. Whenever you forgive people's sins, they are forgiven. Whenever you do not forgive them, they are not forgiven."

Our pastor regularly announces this gospel comfort in our worship services when he says, "As a called servant of Christ and by his authority, I forgive you all your sins in the name of the Father and of the Son and of the Holy Spirit."

Confession

When Martin Luther originally spoke about confession, he was describing a practice that began, but did not end, with admitting sins. Luther envisioned that Christians would go to their spiritual shepherds, privately admit sins, and receive the assurance of forgiveness. With this practice in mind, we understand why the question "What is confession?" can be answered in two parts: It is confessing sin *and* receiving the forgiveness of sins.

342. When is it beneficial to confess our sins privately to our pastor?

Psalm 32:4 Day and night your hand was heavy on me. *My moisture was dried up by the droughts of summer.*

Psalm 38:4 *My guilt has gone over my head.* Like a heavy burden, it is too heavy for me.

Psalm 51:3 I admit my rebellious acts. *My sin is always in front of me.*

We may privately confess our sins to the pastor at any time. We may seek the comforting gospel promise of forgiveness particularly when sins continue to trouble our consciences.

343. How should we receive the announcement of forgiveness from the pastor?

Matthew 16:19 I will give you the keys of the kingdom of heaven. Whatever you bind on earth will be bound in heaven, and whatever you loose on earth *will be loosed in heaven.*

We receive absolution—forgiveness—from the pastor as from God himself, not doubting but firmly believing that our sins are forgiven before God in heaven.

A CLOSER LOOK

Private Confession

Although Luther focused on private confession to one's spiritual shepherd, he didn't mean to imply that confessing sins to a Christian spouse or parent or friend was less important or less biblical. Rather, he was attempting to help people properly understand what had been the practice for many years, namely, confessing sins to one's priest.

Although it isn't mandatory, going to our spiritual shepherd to confess sins and receive absolution can continue to be a blessing today. We are grateful for our pastor's knowledge of Scripture and his ability to bring comfort through the words of God.

344. When does God want us to confess our sins to a fellow Christian?

James 5:16 *Confess your sins to one another* and pray for one another.

Matthew 5:23,24 If you are about to offer your gift at the altar, and there you remember that your brother has something against you, leave your gift there in front of the altar and go. *First be reconciled to your brother.* Then come and offer your gift.

Luke 15:11-21 (The lost son came to realize the extent of his sin against his father and confessed his sin.)

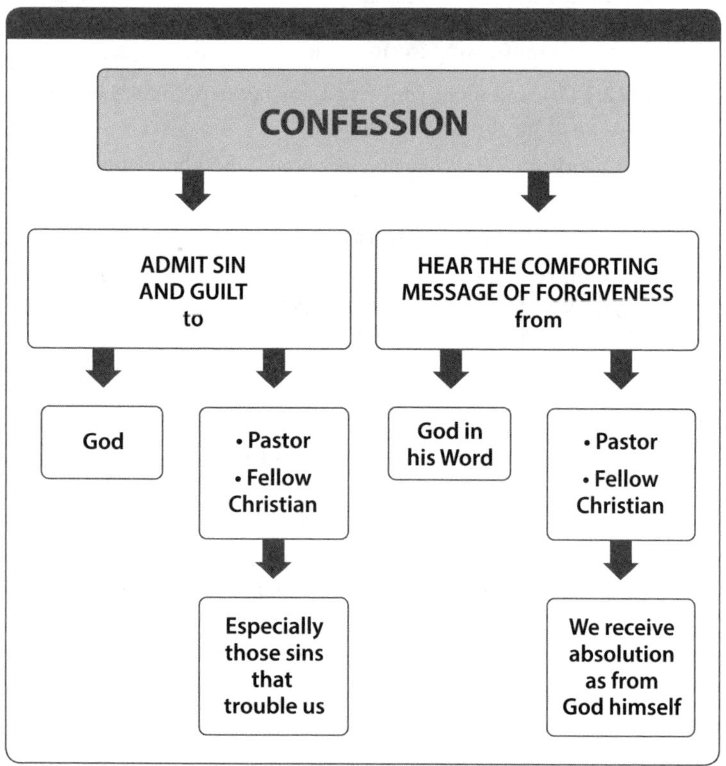

345. How are we to receive the announcement of forgiveness from our fellow Christian?

John 20:21-23 Jesus said to them again, "Peace be with you! Just as the Father has sent me, *I am also sending you.*" After saying this, he breathed on them and said, "Receive the Holy Spirit. Whenever you forgive people's sins, they are forgiven. Whenever you do not forgive them, they are not forgiven."

Matthew 16:19 I will give you the keys of the kingdom of heaven. Whatever you bind on earth will be bound in heaven, and whatever you loose on earth will be loosed in heaven.

We receive absolution—the declaration of forgiveness—from a fellow Christian as from God himself, not doubting but firmly believing that our sins are forgiven before God in heaven.

CONNECTIONS

We can come up with many reasons not to confess a sin. Our pride gets in the way. We imagine the bad things that might happen once the truth gets out. We are ashamed.

Our sinful flesh works hard to keep us from admitting our wrongs, but God commands us to confess—and not because he wants to hurt us! Rather, God longs to bring great blessings to us, as is evident in Jesus' parable about a son and his father.

Luke 15:11-32

How did God bring the young man to his senses so that he was willing to confess his sins to his father? How does God bring us to our senses about sin and lead us to confess? The reaction of the father in the parable is a picture of how our heavenly Father deals with our sin. How is the love God shows us similar to the love shown by the father in the story?

Luther

As to the current practice of private confession, I am heartily in favor of it. . . .

It is useful, even necessary, and I would not have it abolished. Indeed, I rejoice that it exists in the church of Christ for it is a cure without equal for distressed consciences. (LW 36:30ff)

From Depths of Woe I Cry to You (Stanzas 1,2)

From depths of woe I cry to you;
Lord, hear me, I implore you.
Bend down your gracious ear to me;
My prayer let come before you.
If you kept record of my sin
And held against me what I've been,
How could I stand before you?

Your love and grace alone avail
To blot out my transgression.
The best and holiest deeds must fail
To break sin's dread oppression.
Before you none can boasting stand,
But all must fear your strict demand
And live alone by mercy.

THE LORD'S SUPPER

Christ gives us his body and blood under bread and wine.

THE INSTITUTION OF HOLY COMMUNION

First: *What is the Sacrament of Holy Communion?*

It is the true body and blood of our Lord Jesus Christ under the bread and wine, instituted by Christ for us Christians to eat and to drink.

Where is this written?

The holy evangelists Matthew, Mark, Luke, and the apostle Paul tell us: Our Lord Jesus Christ, on the night he was betrayed, took bread; and when he had given thanks, he broke it and gave it to his disciples, saying, "Take and eat; this is my body, which is given for you. Do this in remembrance of me."

Then he took the cup, gave thanks, and gave it to them, saying, "Drink from it, all of you; this is my blood of the new covenant, which is poured out for you for the forgiveness of sins. Do this, whenever you drink it, in remembrance of me."

LORD'S SUPPER

A Blessed and Important Meal

The night when Jesus first instituted the Lord's Supper was packed with drama. With his disciples, Jesus celebrated the Passover meal, which recalled God's dramatic rescue of the Jews from Egypt. Judas was there but would disappear, only to reappear in the Garden of Gethsemane with betrayal on his lips. In the darkness of the garden, Jesus was arrested and led off to his trial before the Jewish leaders and, later, Pilate. The next day he was crucified.

During the meal, Jesus knew all this was about to happen. Yet on this night, Jesus was thinking of his disciples and us. He began something new, placing on the lips of his dearest friends the very body and blood that would soon be given and shed for the forgiveness of the sins of the world. Clearly this gift of the Lord's Supper was incredibly special. It mattered to Jesus. It mattered for his disciples. It matters to us.

Other Names

The Lord's Supper is also known as the Sacrament of the Altar, the Lord's Table, Communion, Holy Communion, the Breaking of Bread, and the Eucharist.

346. When instituting the Lord's Supper, Jesus took earthly elements—bread and wine, gave thanks to God, and gave the bread and wine to the disciples. **What did Jesus say the disciples were receiving along with the bread and wine?**

Matthew 26:26-29 While they were eating, Jesus took bread, blessed and broke it, and gave it to the disciples. He said, "Take, eat, *this is my body.*" Then he took the cup, gave thanks, and gave it to them, saying, "Drink from it all of you, for *this is my blood* of the new testament, which is poured out for many for the forgiveness of sins. I tell you that I will not drink of this fruit of the vine from now until that day when I drink it new with you in my Father's kingdom."

Mark 14:22-24 While they were eating, Jesus took bread. When he had blessed it, he broke it and gave it to them, saying, *"Take it. This is my body."* Then he took the cup, gave thanks, and gave it to them. They all drank from it. He said to them, "*This is my blood of the new testament,* which is poured out for many."

347. What, then, do we receive in the Lord's Supper?

Mark 14:22,24 This is my body. . . . This is my blood.

1 Corinthians 10:16 The cup of blessing that we bless, is it not a *communion of the blood of Christ?* The bread that we break, is it not a *communion of the body of Christ?*

1 Corinthians 11:29 If anyone eats and drinks in an unworthy way because he *does not recognize the Lord's body,* he eats and drinks judgment on himself.

God's Word clearly teaches that the Lord's Supper is a special supper through which we receive Jesus' body and blood in, with, and under the bread and wine.

348. How is it possible for Jesus to actually give his body and blood to all who receive this sacrament?

Psalm 33:6 *By the word of the LORD the heavens were made.* By the breath of his mouth he made the whole army of stars.

Hebrews 4:12 *The word of God* is living and active, sharper than any double-edged sword. It penetrates even to the point of dividing soul and spirit, joints and marrow, even being able to judge the ideas and thoughts of the heart.

Matthew 8:8 The centurion answered, "Lord, I am not worthy for you to come under my roof. But only say the word, and my servant will be healed."

Matthew 28:18 Jesus approached and spoke to them saying, "*All authority* in heaven and on earth has been *given to me.*"

A CLOSER LOOK

False Beliefs

Representation. Not all Christians believe what the Bible says about the bread and wine and the body and blood in the Sacrament. Some see the bread and wine as symbols and signs. They say that the bread merely represents the body of Christ and that the wine merely represents the blood of Christ. They see the celebration of the Lord's Supper as merely a *remembrance* of what Christ did on the cross rather than as a way for God to *give* us what Jesus won for us on the cross: the forgiveness of sins.

In the Lord's Supper, we do remember what Christ did, but there is more. Scripture plainly teaches that we receive Christ's true body and blood, the very price paid for our forgiveness. Jesus said so, and he has the power to give his body and blood even if we do not understand how this can be. So the Lord's Supper is a means of grace, a tool God uses to bring his gift of forgiveness, life, and salvation to individual hearts.

Transubstantiation. This is the view held by the Catholic Church. It teaches that the earthly elements turn into body and blood and are no longer bread and wine. First Corinthians 10:16 makes it clear that the bread and body and the wine and blood all exist in the Sacrament. God says that the cup is "a participation in," or a sharing in (a communion with), the blood and that the bread is a sharing in the body. Those who receive the Lord's Supper, then, receive four things: bread and wine and body and blood.

The Catholic Church believes that in the Lord's Supper, the priest is resacrificing Jesus in order to turn away God's wrath. The Catholic Church believes this repeated sacrifice of Jesus benefits not only those who partake of the Sacrament but also those who are dead and are not yet completely purified.

The Bible teaches that sin and its consequences were paid for once and for all time when Christ died on the cross (Hebrews 7:27; 9:28). No additional sacrifice is necessary. Also, the Bible teaches that forgiveness given in the Sacrament is full and complete—Christians are not described as "partly purified" so that they might be in need of additional help after death. Rather, the forgiveness given in the Lord's Supper is total—"the blood of Jesus, his Son, cleanses us from all sin" (1 John 1:7).

---

349. When did Jesus institute this special Supper?

Luke 22:1,7-14,17-23,39-54 (Jesus instituted this special Supper when the disciples were celebrating their last Passover with him, just hours before his betrayal and arrest.)

1 Corinthians 11:23,25 I received from the Lord what I also delivered to you: The Lord Jesus, *on the night when he was betrayed,* took bread. In the same way, after the meal, he also took the cup.

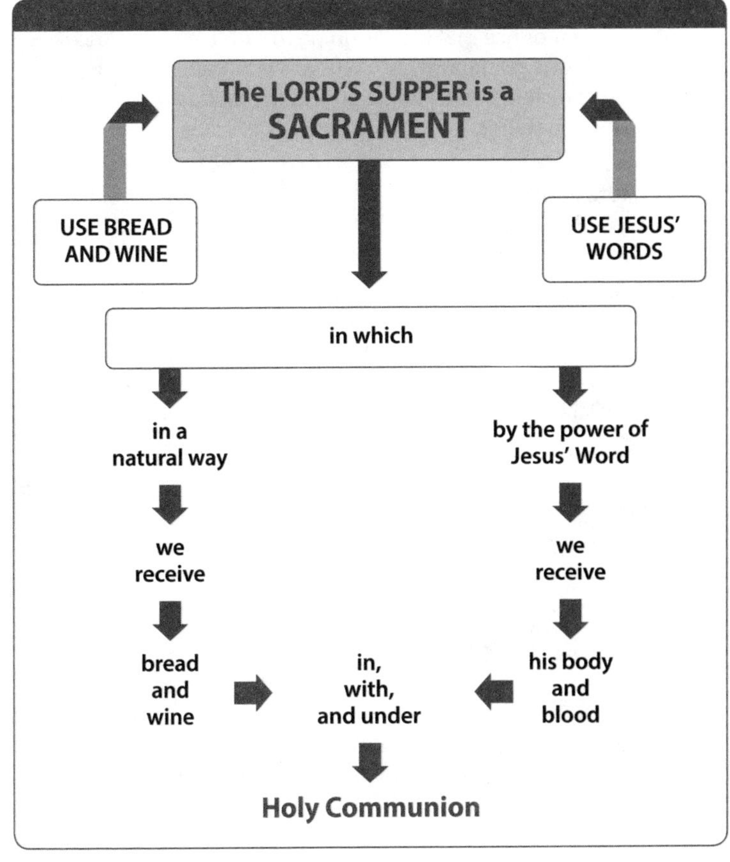

350. For whom did Jesus institute his Supper?

Matthew 26:26,27 While they were eating, Jesus took bread, blessed and broke it, and gave it *to the disciples.* He said, "Take, eat, this is my body." Then he took the cup, gave thanks, and *gave it to them,* saying, "Drink from it *all of you.*"

1 Corinthians 11:26,27 *As often as you eat* this bread and drink the cup, *you* proclaim the Lord's death until he comes. *Therefore whoever eats* the bread or drinks the cup of the Lord in an unworthy manner will be guilty of sinning against the Lord's body and blood.

In this extraordinary meal, Jesus gives his true body and blood in, with, and under the bread and wine. This blessing is for Christians of all times.

CONNECTIONS

So many things were happening that night. Imagine being one of Jesus's closest friends and hearing him announce that he was going to suffer. Imagine knowing that he was going away, that he was no longer going to be with you as he had been. Imagine learning that one of your own number was a traitor.

This was a challenging night. But Jesus gave his friends the perfect gift to address the challenge.

Luke 22:1,7-14,17-23,39-54

Jesus instituted his Supper on the same night he was betrayed—the evening before his crucifixion. In what different ways could the Lord's Supper have been an encouragement to the disciples during those difficult hours? Explain how the Lord's Supper can be a special encouragement to you in challenging times.

Luther

"Now, what is the Sacrament of the Altar?"

Answer, "It is the true body and blood of our Lord Jesus Christ, in and under the bread and wine, which we Christians are commanded by Christ's Word to eat and to drink."

Just as we have said that Baptism is not simple water, so here also we say that though the Sacrament is bread and wine, it is not mere bread and wine, such as are ordinarily served at the table [1 Corinthians 10:16-17]. But this is bread and wine included in, and connected with, God's Word. (Large Catechism, V, par. 8-9)

What Is This Bread? (Stanzas 1,2)

What is this bread?
Christ's body risen from the dead:
This bread we break.
This life we take
Was crushed to pay for our release.
Oh, taste and see—the Lord is peace.

What is this wine?
The blood of Jesus shed for mine;
The cup of grace
Brings his embrace
Of life and love until I sing!
Oh, taste and see—the Lord is King.

THE BLESSINGS OF HOLY COMMUNION

Second: ***What blessing do we receive through this eating and drinking?***

That is shown us by these words: "Given" and "poured out for you for the forgiveness of sins."

Through these words we receive forgiveness of sins, life, and salvation in this sacrament.

For where there is forgiveness of sins, there is also life and salvation.

LORD'S SUPPER

Eternal Blessings

Christians recognize the importance of the Lord's Supper. When they face serious surgery, Christians crave the assurance that they are at peace with God. When Christian soldiers face the dangers of battle, they know the importance of God's forgiveness. When Christians sense that death is fast approaching, they yearn for the personal comfort Jesus gives them with his body and blood in the Sacrament. When Christians are physically incapable of attending worship services, they cherish opportunities to have the pastor bring the Lord's Supper to them privately. Yes, Christians long for the blessings God offers in the Lord's Supper, especially in times of trouble.

All Christians are always facing fearful enemies—sin and guilt. We know that death can come at any moment. We long for the peace that comes from the forgiveness of sins, so it is no surprise that Christians treasure the blessings of the Lord's Supper.

351. What blessing did Jesus promise to give through the Sacrament?

Matthew 26:28 This is my blood of the new testament, which is poured out for many *for the forgiveness of sins.*

Luke 22:19,20 He took bread, and when he had given thanks, he broke it and gave it to them, saying, "This is my body, which is *given for you.*

Do this in remembrance of me." In the same way, he took the cup after the supper, saying, "This cup is the new testament in my blood, which is being *poured out for you.*"

Revelation 1:4,5 *Grace to you and peace . . .* from Jesus Christ, the faithful witness, the firstborn from the dead, and the ruler of the kings of the earth. To him who loves us and has *freed us from our sins by his own blood . . .*

In the Lord's Supper, God gives us the forgiveness of sins.

A CLOSER LOOK

Covenant

A covenant is a solemn agreement, especially one in which God promises to bless and to save. The *old covenant* was the one God made with the nation of Israel at Mount Sinai. As part of his agreement with Israel, he gave the Israelites laws that governed their diets, their worship, and other aspects of their lives. These laws reminded them that they were different from the nations around them—that they were God's chosen people. These laws also showed the people that they were sinners. The *new covenant* is God's solemn agreement signed in Jesus' blood. It is meant for all people. God promises that he has forgiven our sins because of the blood Jesus shed when he died for us.

Hebrews 9:15 [Christ] is the mediator of *a new covenant.* A death took place as payment for the trespasses committed under the first covenant, that those who are called would receive the promised eternal inheritance.

352. How did Jesus accomplish the forgiveness of sins?

Isaiah 53:6 We all have gone astray like sheep. Each of us has turned to his own way, but *the LORD has charged all our guilt to him.*

Ephesians 1:7 In him *we also have redemption through his blood,* the forgiveness of sins, in keeping with the riches of his grace.

1 Peter 2:24 *He himself carried our sins* in his body on the tree so that we would be dead to sins and alive to righteousness. By his wounds you were healed.

2 Corinthians 5:21 *God made him, who did not know sin, to become sin for us,* so that we might become the righteousness of God in him.

A CLOSER LOOK

A Means of Grace

The Bible shows us that the Lord's Supper is a sacrament. The Lord's Supper was instituted by Jesus. He commanded the use of earthly elements, bread and wine, and attached the promise of the forgiveness of sins. It is, therefore, a means of grace for us and all Christians.

1 Corinthians 11:23-25 I received from the Lord what I also delivered to you: *The Lord Jesus,* on the night when he was betrayed, *took bread,* and when he had given thanks, he broke it and said, "This is my body, which is for you. *Do this* in remembrance of me." In the same way, after the meal, he also *took the cup,* saying, "This cup is the new testament in my blood. *Do this,* as often as you drink it, in remembrance of me."

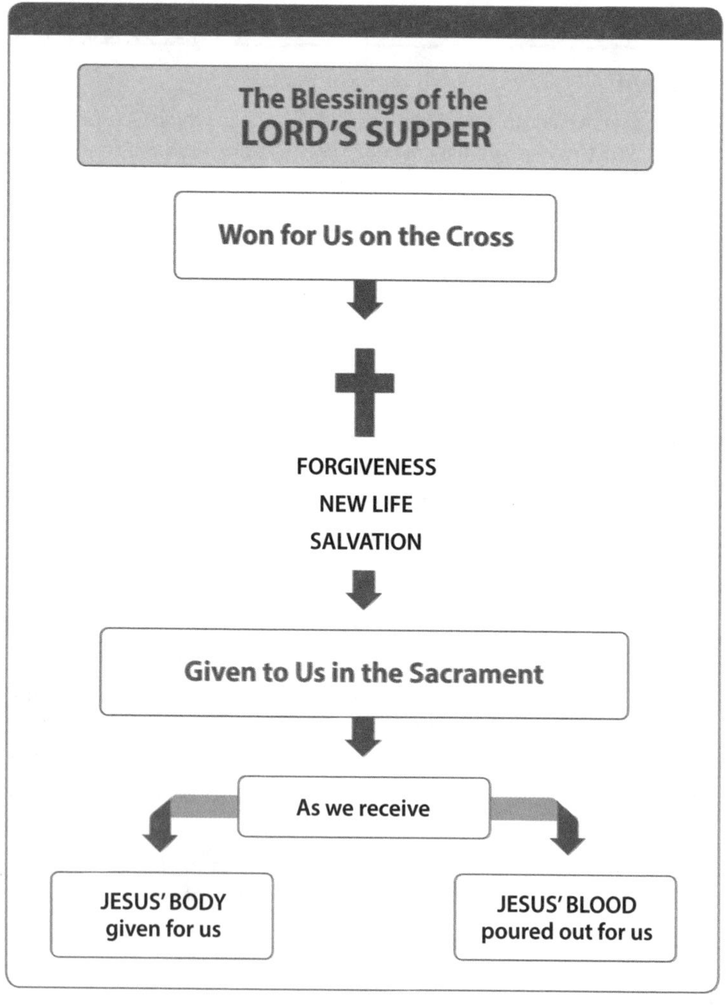

Matthew 26:28 This is my blood of the new testament, which is poured out for many for the *forgiveness of sins.*

We often speak of this sacrament as Jesus' last will and testament. On the night before he died, he bequeathed (legal term often used in a will), or set aside for distribution at his death, forgiveness through his body and blood to all believers.

---

353. What further blessings are ours because of the forgiveness of sins?

Romans 5:9 Since we have now been justified by his blood, it is even more certain that *we will be saved* from God's wrath *through him.*

Romans 6:22,23 Now, since you were set free from sin and have become slaves to God, you have your fruit resulting in sanctification—and the final result is *eternal life.* For the wages of sin is death, but *the undeserved gift of God is eternal life in Christ Jesus our Lord.*

1 Peter 2:24,25 He himself carried our sins in his body on the tree so that we would *be dead to sins* and *alive to righteousness.* By his wounds you were healed. For you were like sheep going astray, but you are now returned to the Shepherd and Overseer of your souls.

354. In our church services, the pastor proclaims forgiveness to the entire congregation. **What makes receiving the Sacrament so very comforting as well?**

Luke 22:19,20 He took bread, and when he had given thanks, he broke it and gave it to them, saying, "This is my body, which is given *for you.* Do this *in remembrance of me.*" In the same way, he took the cup after the supper, saying, "This cup is the new testament in my blood, which is being poured out *for you.*"

1 Corinthians 11:23-25 I received from the Lord what I also *delivered to you:* The Lord Jesus, on the night when he was betrayed, took bread, and when he had given thanks, he broke it and said, "This is my body, which is *for you.* Do this *in remembrance of me.*" In the same way, after the meal, he also took the cup, saying, "This cup is the new testament in my blood. Do this, as often as you drink it, *in remembrance of me.*"

In the Lord's Supper, God gives forgiveness, life, and salvation in a very personal and individual way.

CONNECTIONS

In 1 Corinthians 5:7, we are told that Jesus Christ is our Passover lamb. How appropriate, then, that the Lord's Supper was instituted in the middle of a Passover celebration.

Just as the body and blood of Jesus would bring about salvation, so many years before the blood of Passover lambs brought about an amazing rescue.

Exodus 12:1-30

The Old Testament Passover celebration was a shadow of things to come (Colossians 2:17). Explain how the following pictured so well our Savior, the Passover lamb to come.

- Male lamb without blemish or defect
- Blood smeared on the sides and top frames of the doors
- Households with blood on the door frames spared from death that night

---

Luther

Now examine further the effectiveness and benefits that really caused the Sacrament to be instituted. This is its most necessary part, so that we may know what we should seek and gain there. This is plain and clear from the words just mentioned, "This is my body and blood, given and shed for you for the forgiveness of sins." Briefly, that is like saying, "For this reason we go to the Sacrament: there we receive such a treasure by and in which we gain forgiveness of sins. . . ." On this account it is indeed called a food of souls, which nourishes and strengthens the new man. (Large Catechism, V, par. 20-23)

What Is This Bread? (Stanzas 4,5)

Yet is God here?
Oh, yes! By Word and promise clear.
In mouth and soul
He makes us whole—
Christ, truly present in this meal.
Oh, taste and see—the Lord is real.

Is this for me?
I am forgiven and set free!
I do believe
That I receive
His very body and his blood.
Oh, taste and see—the Lord is good.

THE POWER OF HOLY COMMUNION

Third: ***How can eating and drinking do such great things?***

It is certainly not the eating and drinking that does such things, but the words "Given" and "poured out for you for the forgiveness of sins."

These words are the main thing in this sacrament, along with the eating and drinking.

And whoever believes these words has what they plainly say, the forgiveness of sins.

LORD'S SUPPER

Saving Power

Bread and wine don't look powerful. Some might wonder whether anything impressive can really be happening in the Lord's Supper. Usually when something is powerful, we can sense it. We can tell when an athlete is strong; we watch his performance in awe. We can feel when a rocket thunders into the sky. We shake when a bolt of lightning strikes close to our home.

But bread and wine? Of themselves, they would have no great power. But there is something that changes all that and gives humble eating and drinking power beyond imagination.

355. How do we know that we receive the great blessings of forgiveness, life, and salvation through eating and drinking in the Sacrament?

Matthew 26:28 This is my blood of the new testament, which is poured out for many for the forgiveness of sins.

Luke 22:19,20 He took bread, and when he had given thanks, he broke it and gave it to them, saying, "This is my body, which is given for you. Do this in remembrance of me." In the same way, he took the cup after the supper, saying, "This cup is the new testament in my blood, which is being poured out for you."

Romans 5:9 Since we have now been justified by his blood, it is even more certain that we will be saved from God's wrath through him.

Romans 6:22,23 Now, since you were set free from sin and have become slaves to God, you have your fruit resulting in sanctification—and the final result is eternal life. For the wages of sin is death, but the undeserved gift of God is eternal life in Christ Jesus our Lord.

We have absolute confidence that the Lord's Supper gives all of these blessings because the powerful Word of God is in the Sacrament and works through the Sacrament.

356. How do we know that God's Word is powerful and that it is able to give us these blessings?

Romans 1:16 I am not ashamed of *the gospel,* because it *is the power of God* for salvation to everyone who believes—to the Jew first, and also to the Greek.

Psalm 33:6 *By the word of the LORD the heavens were made.* By the breath of his mouth he made the whole army of stars.

Matthew 8:8 The centurion answered, "Lord, I am not worthy for you to come under my roof. But only *say the word,* and *my servant will be healed.*"

Mark 4:36-39 Leaving the crowd behind, the disciples took him along in the boat, just as he was. Other small boats also followed him. A great windstorm arose, and the waves were splashing into the boat, so that the boat was quickly filling up. Jesus himself was in the stern, sleeping on a cushion. They woke him and said, "Teacher, don't you care that we are about to drown?" Then he got up, rebuked the wind, and said to the sea, *"Peace! Be still!" The wind stopped, and there was a great calm.*

John 11:17-44 (Jesus raised Lazarus from the dead by commanding him to come out of the tomb.)

Romans 10:17 *Faith* comes from hearing the message, and the message comes through *the word of Christ.*

357. What does the Word of God accomplish in the Lord's Supper?

Matthew 26:28 This is my blood of the new testament, which is poured out for many *for the forgiveness of sins.*

Romans 10:17 *Faith* comes from hearing the message, and the message comes through *the word of Christ.*

Hebrews 11:1 Faith is being sure about what we hope for, being convinced about things we do not see.

Romans 4:20,21 He did not waver in unbelief with respect to God's promise, but *he grew strong in faith,* giving glory to God and being fully convinced that God was able to do what he had promised.

Through his Word in the Lord's Supper, Jesus promises to give us his body and blood for the forgiveness of our sins. Through these same divine words, Jesus strengthens our faith, giving us trust in his promises and making the blessings of the Sacrament our own.

358. Because of the power of God's Word, what is the Lord's Supper?

1 Corinthians 10:16 The cup of blessing that we bless, is it not *a communion of the blood of Christ?* The bread that we break, is it not a *communion of the body of Christ?*

Matthew 26:28 This is my blood of the new testament, which is poured out for many for *the forgiveness of sins.*

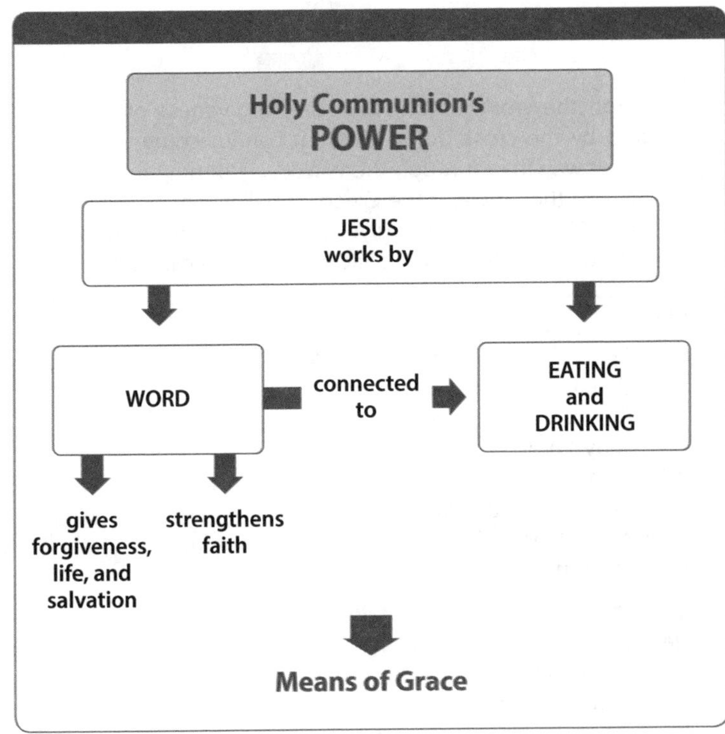

The Lord's Supper is a sacred act that Christ instituted. Through it we receive his body and blood in, with, and under the earthly elements of bread and wine. Through this sacrament, the Lord gives us the forgiveness of sins, life, and salvation (means of grace).

The Lord's Supper may not look powerful, but it certainly is. This is how God so often works—he attaches a powerful promise to something seemingly humble. Many years ago, God did exactly this in the middle of a wilderness.

Numbers 21:4-9

How was it possible that a bronze serpent on a pole saved those who looked to it?

Imagine that a friend asks you, "How can eating a small piece of unleavened bread and drinking a small swallow of wine help us?" How might you use the account of the bronze serpent as part of your response?

Luther

Although the work is done and the forgiveness of sins is secured by the cross [John 19:30], it cannot come to us in any other way than through the Word. . . . But now the entire gospel and the article of the Creed—I believe in . . . the holy Christian Church, . . . the forgiveness of sins, and so on—are embodied by the Word in this Sacrament and presented to us. (Large Catechism, V, par. 30-31)

Lord Jesus Christ, You Have Prepared (Stanzas 5,6)

Though reason cannot understand,
Yet faith this truth embraces:
Your body, Lord, is ev'rywhere
At once in many places.
I leave to you how this can be;
Your Word alone suffices me;
I trust its truth unfailing.

Lord, I believe what you have said;
Help me when doubts assail me.
Remember that I am but dust,
And let my faith not fail me.
Your supper in this vale of tears
Refreshes me and stills my fears
And is my priceless treasure.

THE RECEPTION OF HOLY COMMUNION

Fourth: *Who, then, is properly prepared to receive this sacrament?*

Fasting and other outward preparations may serve a good purpose, but he is properly prepared who believes these words: "Given" and "poured out for you for the forgiveness of sins."

But whoever does not believe these words or doubts them is not prepared, because the words "for you" require nothing but hearts that believe.

LORD'S SUPPER

True Preparation

Fancy dinners bring out the best in their guests. Those invited put on the nicest clothes, carefully check their appearance, and make sure that they are prepared in every way for the special meal.

The Lord's Supper is indeed a special meal. Christians want to know, "How can I best be prepared to attend the Lord's great Supper?"

359. Why is it important that we are properly prepared to receive the Lord's Supper?

> **1 Corinthians 11:27,28** *Whoever eats* the bread *or drinks* the cup of the Lord *in an unworthy manner* will be guilty of *sinning against the Lord's body and blood.* Instead, let a person examine himself and after doing so, let him eat of the bread and drink from the cup.

We want to be properly prepared so that we do not sin by receiving the body and blood of Jesus in an unworthy manner (failing to recognize that we receive the body and blood of Jesus in, with, and under the bread and wine in the Sacrament or failing to believe that it is "given and shed for us" for forgiveness).

360. How might fasting or other outward preparations help us prepare to receive the Lord's Supper?

Leviticus 23:26-32 (God commanded his people to do no work and to deny themselves—Jewish practice included fasting—so that they would focus on the meaning of the Day of Atonement.)

Exodus 19:10 (God commanded an outward action—that his people wash their clothes—as a way for them to show respect for their holy God.)

Fasting or other outward preparations can help us prepare for the Lord's Supper when those actions help us focus on the meaning of the Sacrament and display honor for God.

361. What, however, is at the heart of being properly prepared to receive the Lord's Supper?

Luke 22:19,20 He took bread, and when he had given thanks, he broke it and gave it to them, saying, "This is *my body,* which is given *for you.* Do this in remembrance of me." In the same way, he took the cup after the supper, saying, "This cup is the new testament in *my blood,* which is being poured out *for you.*"

Matthew 26:28 This is my blood of the new testament, which is poured out for many *for the forgiveness of sins.*

Jesus said that the *body* and *blood* received in the Sacrament were given and shed *for you* for the forgiveness of sins. When we come to the Lord's Table trusting that we receive the true body and blood of Jesus sacrificed on the cross for us for the forgiveness of sins, we are prepared.

362. Why are we careful about whom we invite to receive the Lord's Supper?

1 Corinthians 11:27,29 Whoever eats the bread or drinks the cup of the Lord in an unworthy manner will be guilty of sinning against the Lord's body and blood. For if anyone eats and drinks in an unworthy way because he does not recognize the Lord's body, he *eats and drinks judgment on himself.*

We are careful about whom we invite to receive the Lord's Supper because we do not want others to bring God's judgment on themselves by receiving the Sacrament in an unworthy manner.

363. Whom does God want us to invite to the Lord's Supper?

1 John 1:8,9 *If we say we have no sin,* we deceive ourselves, and the truth is not in us. *If we confess our sins,* he is faithful and just to forgive us our sins and to cleanse us from all unrighteousness.

Matthew 18:15-18 (We are to withhold forgiveness from those who refuse to repent of their sins.)

Hebrews 10:26 *If we deliberately keep on sinning* after we have received the full knowledge of the truth, there no longer remains any sacrifice for sins.

God wants us to invite to the Lord's Supper only repentant sinners.

1 Corinthians 11:24,26,29 When he had given thanks, he broke it and said, "This is my body, which is for you. *Do this in remembrance of me.*" For as often as you eat this bread and drink the cup, you proclaim the Lord's death until he comes. For if anyone eats and drinks in an unworthy way *because he does not recognize* the Lord's body, he eats and drinks judgment on himself.

Hebrews 5:13; 6:1 Everyone who lives on milk is not acquainted with the word of righteousness, because he is still an infant. Therefore, *leaving the beginning discussion of Christ,* let us press on toward matters that require greater maturity, not laying again the foundation of repentance from dead works, of faith in God.

God wants us to invite to the Lord's Supper only those who are instructed so that they know the meaning of Christ's death and understand that Jesus' body and blood are really present.

1 Corinthians 11:28 Let a person examine himself and after doing so, let him eat of the bread and drink from the cup.

God wants us to invite to the Lord's Supper only those who are able to examine themselves. (This is another reason individuals are instructed in God's Word prior to receiving the Sacrament. For the same reason, a person who isn't able to understand what is being received—for example, a person in a coma or someone suffering from an advanced stage of dementia—will not be given the Lord's Supper.)

2 John 10 If someone comes to you and does not bring this teaching, do not receive him into your house. Do not even wish him well.

1 Corinthians 10:17 Because there is one bread, we, who are many, are one body, for we all partake of the one bread.

God wants us to give the Lord's Supper only to those who are one with us in what we believe and teach. (See question 213.)

364. Why will we want to receive Communion often?

Romans 7:19 I fail to do the good I want to do. Instead, the evil I do not want to do, that is what I keep doing.

Mark 9:24 The child's father immediately cried out and said with tears, "I do believe. *Help me with my unbelief!*"

Isaiah 42:3 A bent reed he will not break, and a dimly burning wick he will not snuff out. He will faithfully bring forth a just verdict.

Hebrews 4:15,16 We do not have a high priest who is unable to sympathize *with our weaknesses,* but one who has been tempted in every way, just as we are, yet was without sin. So let us approach the throne of grace with confidence, so that we may receive mercy and find grace to help in time of need.

We struggle every day against our sinful flesh and need God's assistance to overcome our weakness in faith.

Matthew 11:28 Come to me *all you who are weary and burdened,* and I will give you rest.

Matthew 26:28 This is my blood of the new testament, which is poured out for many for the forgiveness of sins.

Romans 4:7 Blessed are those whose lawless deeds are *forgiven and whose sins are covered.*

God gives us the forgiveness of sins in the Lord's Supper, providing us with freedom from guilt and strengthening our faith.

2 Corinthians 5:14,15 The love of Christ compels us, because we came to this conclusion: One died for all; therefore, all died. And he died for all, so that *those who live would no longer live for themselves but for him, who died in their place and was raised again.*

Colossians 2:6,7 Just as you received Christ Jesus as Lord, continue to *walk in him,* by being rooted and built up in him, and strengthened in the faith just as you were taught, while you overflow in faith with thanksgiving.

Receiving God's forgiving love in the Sacrament empowers us to live godly lives of thanksgiving.

1 Corinthians 11:26 As often as you eat this bread and drink the cup, you proclaim the Lord's death until he comes.

Hebrews 10:23-25 Let us hold on firmly to the confession of our hope without wavering, since he who promised is faithful. Let us also consider carefully how to *spur each other on* to love and good works. Let us not neglect meeting together, as some have the habit of doing. Rather, *let us encourage each other,* and all the more as you see the Day approaching.

When we receive the Lord's Supper and publicly proclaim the Lord's death together with others, we are encouraging one another in our Christian faith.

A CLOSER LOOK

Closed or Close Communion

Receiving the Lord's Supper is an act that expresses our faith. The apostle Paul also tells us that when we take the Lord's Supper with others, we are declaring that we are all one in faith—we believe the same things.

1 Corinthians 10:17 Because there is one loaf, we, who are many, are one body, for we all share the one loaf.

We express this truth by practicing *close* or *closed* Communion. We might refer to it as "close" Communion because we only commune with those who are united with us in faith. We may also say that we practice "closed" Communion to indicate that the Lord's Supper is closed to those who believe and teach differently. Whichever term is used, the practice of communing only with those who share a common faith is according to God's command and testifies to our desire to be faithful to God's Word.

Open Communion is practiced by many denominations today. In these churches, any Christians may come to the Lord's Table, no matter what they believe and teach.

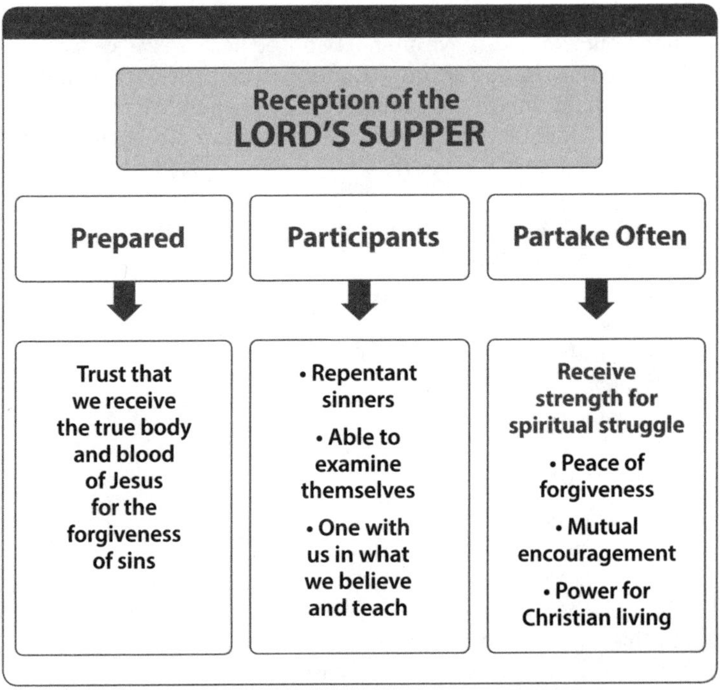

Reception of the LORD'S SUPPER

Prepared	Participants	Partake Often
Trust that we receive the true body and blood of Jesus for the forgiveness of sins	• Repentant sinners • Able to examine themselves • One with us in what we believe and teach	Receive strength for spiritual struggle • Peace of forgiveness • Mutual encouragement • Power for Christian living

CONNECTIONS

The Lord's Supper is an amazing miracle. What a privilege it is to be invited to such a feast!

As we come to this feast, we want to be prepared. The heart of our preparation focuses on one thing—joy-filled confidence in the promises of God. Many years ago, a young man prepared for a big event. His preparation was carefully thought through, and for him too there was one key focus.

---

1 Samuel 17:1-10,32-52

What different things did David do to prepare for his battle with Goliath? Explain why the truth expressed in 1 Samuel 17:37 was more important for David's preparation than anything else he did. In what ways can David's example help us as we prepare to receive the Lord's Supper?

Luther

It is the highest art to know that our Sacrament does not depend upon our worthiness. We are not baptized because we are worthy and holy. Nor do we go to Confession because we are pure and without sin. On the contrary, we go because we are poor, miserable people. We go exactly because we are unworthy. (Large Catechism, V, par. 61)

Soul, Adorn Yourself With Gladness (Stanzas 7,8)

Jesus, Sun of life, my Splendor,
Jesus, Friend of friends most tender,
Jesus, Joy of my desiring,
Fount of life, my soul inspiring—
At your feet I cry, my Maker:
Let me be a fit partaker
Of this blessed food from heaven
For our good, your glory, given.

Jesus, Lord of life, I pray you,
Let me gladly here obey you.
By your love I am invited;
Be your love with love requited.
By this supper let me measure,
Lord, how vast and deep love's treasure.
Through the gift of grace you give me
As your guest in heav'n receive me.

CHRISTIAN QUESTIONS

For those preparing to receive the Lord's Supper

1. **Do you believe that you are a sinner?**
   Yes, I believe that I am a sinner.

2. **How do you know this?**
   I know this from the Ten Commandments, which I have not kept.

3. **Are you sorry for your sins?**
   Yes, I am sorry that I have sinned against God.

4. **What have you deserved from God because of your sins?**
   I deserve his wrath and displeasure, temporal death, and eternal damnation.

5. **Are you convinced that you are saved?**
   Yes, such is my confidence.

6. **In whom, then, do you trust?**
   I trust in my dear Lord Jesus Christ.

7. **Who is Jesus Christ?**
   Jesus Christ is the Son of God, true God and man.

8. **How many Gods are there?**
   There is only one God, but there are three persons: Father, Son, and Holy Spirit.

9. **What has Christ done for you that you trust in him?**
   He died for me and shed his blood for me on the cross for the forgiveness of sins.

10. **Did the Father also die for you?**
    He did not; for the Father is God only, the Holy Spirit likewise. But the Son is true God and true man. He died for me and shed his blood for me.

11. How do you know this?

I know this from the holy gospel and from the words of the Sacrament of Holy Communion.

12. Which are those words?

Our Lord Jesus Christ, on the night he was betrayed, took bread; and when he had given thanks, he broke it and gave it to his disciples, saying, "Take and eat; this is my body, which is given for you. Do this in remembrance of me" (NIV).

Then he took the cup, gave thanks, and gave it to them, saying, "Drink from it, all of you; this is my blood of the new covenant, which is poured out for you for the forgiveness of sins. Do this, whenever you drink it, in remembrance of me" (NIV).

13. Do you believe, then, that the true body and blood of Christ are in the Sacrament?

Yes, I believe it.

14. What moves you to believe this?

I am moved to believe this by the words of Christ, "Take and eat; this is my body. . . . Drink from it, all of you; this is my blood of the new covenant" (NIV).

15. What does Christ want you to do when you eat his body and drink his blood in the Lord's Supper?

Christ wants me to remember and proclaim his death and the pouring out of his blood as he taught me: "Do this, whenever you drink it, in remembrance of me" (NIV).

16. Why does Christ want you to remember and proclaim his death?

He wants me to do this so that (1) I learn to believe that no creature could make satisfaction for my sins, but only Christ, who is true God and man, could and did do that; (2) I learn to look with terror upon my sins and regard them as great indeed; (3) I find joy and comfort in Christ alone and believe that I have salvation through faith in him.

17. What moved him to die and make a complete payment for your sins?

He was moved to do this by his great love for his Father and for me and other sinners, as the Scriptures teach (John 14:31; Romans 5:8; Galatians 2:20; Ephesians 5:2).

18. Finally, why do you desire to receive Holy Communion?

I desire to do this so that I learn to believe that Christ out of great love died for *my* sins and that I also learn of him to love God and my neighbor.

19. What admonishes and moves you to receive Holy Communion frequently?

The command and the promise of Christ my Lord admonishes and moves me. Also, the burden of sin that lies heavy upon me causes me to feel a hunger and thirst for Holy Communion.

20. But what can a person do if he or she is not aware of the burden of sin and does not feel hunger and thirst for Holy Communion?

To such a person no better advice can be given than that, in the first place, the person put his hand into his bosom and feel whether he still has flesh and blood, and that he by all means believes what the Scriptures say about this (Galatians 5:17,19-21; Isaiah 64:6; Romans 7:18).

Secondly, that he look around to see whether he is still in the world and keep in mind that there will be no lack of sin and trouble, as the Scriptures say (John 15:18-25; Matthew 24:9-13; Acts 14:22).

Thirdly, that person will certainly have the devil also about him. With his lying and murdering, day and night, the devil will let him have no peace. So the Scriptures picture the devil (John 8:44; 1 Peter 5:8; Ephesians 6:10-12; 2 Timothy 2:26).

21. What can you do if you are sick and are unable to come to Holy Communion?

Then I can send for my pastor to pray with me and to give me Holy Communion privately.

22. When is the proper time to do this?

The time to do this is not only when death is at hand, but earlier before all physical and mental power is gone.

23. Why would you want to do this?

I would want to do this to receive the assurance through Holy Communion that my sins are forgiven and that salvation is mine.

GLOSSARY

Abba The word for "father" in the language of the Jews.

Abortion The killing of an unborn child.

Abound To be plentiful; to exist in large numbers or amounts.

Absolution The announcement after a confession of sins that God has forgiven our sins because Jesus died for them. Absolution may be spoken publicly in a worship service or privately to an individual.

Abstain To hold oneself back from doing something; to do without.

Acknowledge To recognize the authority or claims of someone; to approve of someone or something; to accept.

Active Obedience of Christ Christ's fulfillment of the law by keeping all the commandments perfectly for all sinners.

Address The first words of the Lord's Prayer, indicating to whom the prayer is spoken.

Admonish To warn against or point out a sin.

Adultery Sexual intercourse with someone other than the person to whom one is married. A person commits adultery in the heart with impure words or thoughts in respect to sexual matters.

Advent The season of the church year in which we celebrate the coming of Christ into the world as a man and look forward to Christ's second coming.

Alien Stranger; foreigner.

Alienate To estrange; to make a stranger of.

Amen "Yes, it shall be so!" A word used at the end of a prayer to express confidence that the prayer will be heard and answered.

Angel Messenger; a bodiless spirit created by God to serve him.

Anguish Agony; intense pain or distress.

Anoint To pour oil on to show that someone or something is being set aside for the service of God.

Apology Defense. *The Apology* is a booklet written by Melanchthon to defend the Augsburg Confession.

Apostle One of the special men personally chosen and sent out by Christ to preach the gospel.

Arrogance Haughtiness; pride.

Ascension Christ's visible return to heaven 40 days after his resurrection.

Atone To make a payment to remove the guilt of sin so that God will no longer be angry.

Atonement A payment offered to remove the guilt of sin so that God and sinful humans are reconciled (see *Vicarious Atonement* and Questions 26 and 156).

Attribute A quality that is characteristic of a person.

Authority The power and right to do something.

Baal The name of a false god of the Canaanites.

Baptism The Sacrament in which water is used in the name of the triune God to bring us into the family of God.

Baptize To use water by immersing, washing, pouring, or sprinkling.

Believe 1. To accept as true; 2. to trust or rely upon.

Betray 1. To hand over (a friend to an enemy); 2. to reveal (a secret).

Bible God's written Word; a collection of 66 books inspired by God.

Binding Key The power and right given by Christ to his church to refuse to forgive the sins of those who are impenitent.

Bishop An overseer; a church leader who watches over a congregation.

Blaspheme To speak of God in an evil or disrespectful way.

Blessing 1. Any good thing given by God; 2. the words that promise good things to be given by God.

Born Again Converted; having begun the new life in Christ (see *Rebirth* and Question 189).

Call (Divine) The request or invitation a person receives from a congregation or other group of Christians to serve in the public ministry (see Questions 331-333 and the narrative following Question 330).

Catechism A book of instruction in the form of questions and answers.

Centurion A Roman army officer in command of about one hundred soldiers.

Ceremonial Law The portion of the Law of Moses that instructed the Israelites how to worship God (see the narrative following Question 12). Since the time of Christ, God no longer requires that his church keep this part of the law.

Chaplain A minister who takes care of the spiritual needs of people in a special setting (e.g., the armed forces, health institutions).

Christ Anointed; the name of Jesus that refers to his office. In Hebrew the word for "the Anointed" is *Messiah.*

Christian 1. Belonging to Christ (adjective); 2. one who trusts in Christ alone for salvation (noun).

Church 1. All those everywhere who believe in Jesus as the Savior (same as holy Christian church, invisible church, communion of saints); 2. a group of people who come together to hear the gospel (visible church, congregation, church body); 3. a building where Christians gather to worship.

Church Fellowship The sharing of worship and church work through which people express their unity of faith (see *Fellowship* and Question 213).

Circumcision The cutting off of the foreskin of the male sex organ, which made an Old Testament man a member of God's family and obligated him to keep the Old Testament law.

Civil Law The portion of the Law of Moses that governed the Israelites as a nation. Since the time of Christ, God no longer requires that his church keep this part of the law.

Code A collection of laws.

Commend 1. To praise for a job well done; 2. to entrust or hand over to someone for safekeeping.

Commune To receive the Lord's Supper (see *Communion*).

Communicant Someone who receives the Lord's Supper (see *Communion*).

Communion A coming together or having something in common. The church is called the communion of saints because all believers are united by the faith in Christ they have in common. The Lord's Supper is called Holy Communion because in it Christians are joined to the Lord and thus also to one another (see *Church; Holy Communion*).

Compassion Sorrow for another's distress and a desire to help.

Conceive 1. To think or imagine; 2. to become pregnant.

Concord Agreement; harmony.

Condemn To judge someone guilty of sin and deserving of punishment.

Confess 1. To admit that one has sinned; 2. to tell what one believes.

Confession 1. An admission of sin; 2. a statement of faith (see the narrative following Question 215).

Confirmation A ceremony following instruction in which Christians confess their faith and are acknowledged as sufficiently instructed to receive Holy Communion.

Conform To do something in a way that has been determined by someone else.

Conformity Becoming or acting like someone else in his or her way of thinking and doing.

Congregation A group of Christians who unite for the public worship of God.

Conscience The voice God places in us that bears witness to his law (see Question 13).

Consecrate To set aside for special use in the church.

Consolation Comfort.

Conspire To plot together.

Contempt Scorn; the feeling that someone or something is bad or worthless.

Contrition Fear and sorrow caused by a knowledge of one's sin.

Conversion Turning from unbelief to faith in Christ (see Question 189).

Convert To turn from unbelief to faith in Christ.

Corrupt 1. To spoil or make bad (verb); 2. morally bad or rotten (adjective).

Covenant A solemn agreement, especially one in which God promises to bless and save; a contract.

Covet To desire something that God does not want us to have (see Question 91).

Crave To desire intensely.

Create To bring into existence; to make.

Creation 1. The act of making; 2. that which is made.

Credit To list on the plus side of an account. Faith in Christ is credited to the sinner as righteousness, thus cancelling the debt of sin.

Creed A statement of what a person or group of people believes and teaches (see narrative before Question 118).

Crucify To put to death by hanging on a cross.

Curse To use God's name to wish evil on someone or something.

Damnation Everlasting punishment in hell; separation from God.

Deacon Servant; someone chosen by a congregation to serve in the church.

Debauchery Giving in to sinful sexual desires to an extreme degree.

Deceive To lead into sin or error by telling lies.

Decree A command made by a ruler.

Defile To make unclean or impure.

Delusion A false belief or opinion.

Demon A fallen angel. The demons are led by Satan in war against God and his believers. The demons are also called devils (see Question 137).

Desertion The act of abandoning or leaving when one should stay; especially, the act of abandoning one's marriage partner.

Despair The sin of losing all hope in God's goodness.

Detest To hate; to dislike intensely.

Devil 1. The leader of the fallen angels and chief enemy of God. The devil's name is Satan. 2. Any fallen angel. The devils are also called demons (see Question 137).

Discern To recognize.

Disciple One who follows in order to learn; frequently used of the Twelve who followed Jesus most closely during his ministry. It can also be used of any Christian.

Discipline A rebuke and/or punishment given in love to a wrongdoer to turn that person away from any further sinning (see Questions 55, 56, and 334).

Discord Disagreement; lack of harmony.

Dismay Fear or discouragement in the face of trouble.

Dissension Quarreling; strong disagreement.

Distort To twist so as to misrepresent the truth.

Divination The attempt to learn hidden things or predict the future by using supernatural power.

Divine Of God; having to do with God.

Divisive Causing division or disagreement.

Divorce To end a marriage officially in a court of law.

Doctrine A teaching.

Dominion Rule; the power of a lord to govern.

Doxology An expression of praise to God.

Easter The festival of the church year on which we celebrate the resurrection of Jesus. As a matter of church tradition, Easter is the first Sunday after the first full moon on or after March 21.

Elder A man who is given certain spiritual responsibilities in a congregation.

Element A part of a whole. The water in Holy Baptism and the bread and wine in Holy Communion are called earthly *elements* because they are only a part of what is received in the sacraments.

Enlighten To give light to. The Holy Spirit enlightens people by bringing them out of the darkness of unbelief into the light of faith (see Question 190).

Enmity Hatred; hostility.

Entice To lure or attract to commit sin.

Epiphany 1. Christ's appearance to people as the Son of God and Savior of the world; 2. the festival of the church year (Jan. 6) when we celebrate Christ's showing himself as God's Son.

Epistle A letter.

Esteem To think highly of; to respect.

Eternal 1. Having no beginning or end (God is eternal); 2. everlasting, having no end (eternal life, eternal death).

Eternal Death Eternal separation from the blessings of God in the torment of hell.

Eternal Life Enjoyment of God's blessings eternally in heaven.

Eucharist Thanksgiving; same as *Holy Communion.*

Eunuch A man who is physically unable to father children.

Evangelist 1. Someone who shares the gospel with those who have not heard it; 2. writer of one of the four gospels.

Evil 1. Moral badness, wickedness; 2. any bad thing that is part of our lives on earth as a result of Adam's fall into sin.

Exaltation of Christ That part of Christ's ministry, beginning with his victorious descent into hell, when he made full and constant use of his heavenly power and glory.

Exasperate To make angry.

Excommunication The act of excluding from the congregation those who are plainly impenitent so that they may repent (see narrative following Question 334).

Exploit To take advantage of.

Extol To praise highly.

Faith Trust; saving faith is trust in the true God and in the salvation that Jesus won for us.

False Prophet Someone who claims to teach God's Word but whose teachings include doctrines that are not true.

False Visible Churches Groups that teach or permit false doctrine but are still to be recognized as churches because Jesus is taught as the Son of God and the Savior of the world (see Question 214).

Fasting The practice of voluntarily going without food for a certain period of time.

Fear of God 1. Being afraid of God's anger; 2. awe and respect for God and his commands as a result of faith in him.

Fellowship 1. Being united with others in the same faith; 2. an act of expressing this unity (e.g., by worshiping or praying together, doing mission work together, etc.) (see Question 213).

Firstfruits That part of a crop which is harvested first.

Flesh 1. The muscular tissue of a body; 2. human nature, that which makes up a human person; 3. same as *Sinful Nature* (see narrative following Question 6 and Question 128).

Folly Foolishness, especially the foolishness of disobeying God's law.

Forgiveness of Sins Forgiveness; the state of being pardoned for our sins. God does not overlook our sins as though they do not matter, but he punished Jesus for them instead of us and declares us innocent. We receive this forgiveness through faith in Jesus.

Formula A written statement of doctrine.

Fraud Crime that involves getting the possessions of others by dishonest dealing.

Fulfill To bring to completion. Jesus fulfilled the law by obeying it perfectly. God fulfills his promises and prophecies by carrying them out.

Futile Useless; without benefit or effect.

Gangrene Decay of tissues that starts in one part of the body and spreads if left untreated.

Garment An article of clothing.

Gentile A non-Jew.

Glory 1. Splendor of a very high degree: "The glory of the Lord shone around them" (Luke 2:9); 2. adoring praise: "[Abraham] gave glory to God" (Romans 4:20).

Godless Without faith in the true God.

Good Friday The Friday before Easter on which we observe the death and burial of Jesus.

Good Works Everything a believer does according to God's Word out of love and thanks for all of God's goodness (see Questions 195-202).

Gospel 1. The good news that God in love sent Jesus to take away the sins of all people; 2. one of the first four books of the New Testament.

Grace God's undeserved love that provides free forgiveness of sins, life, and salvation for all people.

Gracious Showing divine grace; merciful.

Guilt The state of someone who has done wrong and deserves to be punished.

Hallow To regard as holy.

Heaven 1. The sky; 2. the place of eternal life and perfect joy in the presence of God.

Hell The place of eternal death and punishment where the devil and his angels and all who die as unbelievers are tormented.

Heresy False doctrine.

Heritage Something that is passed on from one generation to the next.

High Priest The most important of the priests. According to the ceremonial law, only the high priest could enter the Most Holy Place on the Day of Atonement and atone for the sins of the nation. Jesus is our High Priest because he atoned for the sins of the world by offering himself as a sacrifice (see Questions 154-156).

Holy 1. Pure, sinless: "Be holy because I, the Lord your God, am holy" (Leviticus 19:2); 2. set apart for the holy God: "The seventh day shall be your holy day" (Exodus 35:2).

Holy Communion The Sacrament in which the body and blood of Jesus are given to us together with bread and wine for the forgiveness of sins.

Holy Spirit One of the three persons of the triune God; also called Holy Ghost, Comforter, Counselor, Paraclete.

Homosexuality The sin of having sexual relations with a person of one's own sex or of having a desire for such relations.

Hope A confident longing for the things God has promised.

Hover To remain in one place in the air.

Humiliation of Christ The part of Christ's ministry when he chose not to make full use of his heavenly power and glory so that he might live and die in a lowly way (see Questions 168-170).

Hypocrite One who pretends to be a believer but is not.

Idol A false god, especially one that is represented by a statue or image.

Idolatry The worship of a false god.

Image of God The holiness in which Adam and Eve were created, and the fact that their wills naturally conformed to the will of God. The image of God was lost through the fall into sin, but it is restored through the work of the Holy Spirit (see *New Self* and the narrative following Question 60).

Immanuel God with us; one of the names of Jesus (Matthew 1:23).

Immerse To put completely into water.

Immorality That which is contrary to the moral law.

Impenitent Not sorry for one's sins; not penitent.

Incarnation The taking on of a human nature by the Son of God. In this way God became a man. It refers to the conception and birth of Jesus.

Inclination A leaning or tendency; a liking or preference.

Indulge To give in to desire.

Iniquity Failing to measure up perfectly to God's law by breaking one of his commandments. Crooked or perverse behavior.

Inner Being Same as *New Self* (see Question 27).

Inspiration The miracle by which God "breathed into" the prophets and the apostles what he wanted them to write in the Bible. It is called *verbal inspiration* to show that God guided them to use the exact words he wanted them to write.

Institute To establish; to found.

Intercede To beg or plead on behalf of others.

Intercourse The bodily joining of a man and a woman in sexual relations.

Invisible Church The group consisting of all those everywhere who believe in Jesus as their Savior. This gathering of believers is visible only to God because he alone sees faith in the heart (see Question 207).

Justification God's declaration that people are not guilty because Jesus has paid for their sins.

Justify To declare not guilty. This word pictures a judge in a courtroom telling a criminal that there is no longer any charge against him (see Question 219).

Keys The power and right given by Christ to the church either to forgive sins or to refuse to forgive sins (see also *Binding Key; Loosing Key*).

Kingdom of God Christ's rule in the hearts of his believers through his Word.

Lavish To give or bestow generously.

Law 1. The commands that tell people what God wants them to do and not to do. 2. Sometimes in the Bible "law" refers to God's Word in general, even those parts that are not commands.

Lent The season of the church year between the Epiphany season and Easter during which we give special attention to Christ's suffering and death; also called the passion season.

Lewdness Indecency; lustfulness.

Loosing Key The power and right given by Christ to the church to forgive the sins of those who are penitent (see Question 324).

Lord When this word appears in all capital letters, it stands for

Yahweh, the name of God that emphasizes his grace and faithfulness to his promises.

Lord's Supper Same as *Holy Communion.*

Lord's Table Same as *Holy Communion.*

Lust Sinful desire.

Malice The desire to harm someone.

Marital Having to do with marriage.

Maundy Thursday "Thursday of the commandment" (John 13:34); the day on which we observe the institution of the Lord's Supper.

Means of Grace The gospel in Word and sacraments by which God offers and gives us the forgiveness of sins, life, and salvation (see the narrative following Question 298).

Mediator One who serves as a go-between or negotiator between two parties.

Meditate To think deeply.

Medium Person through whom one tries to communicate with the dead or with evil spirits.

Mercy God's kindness in not punishing sinners as they deserve but providing a Savior instead.

Minister Servant; especially someone called to serve people with the means of grace.

Ministry Service; the office or work of a minister.

Miracle A wonder or very unusual happening brought about by God beyond the natural order of things.

Mission Work The sharing of the gospel with those who have not heard it and believed.

Missionary A person who is sent to preach the gospel, especially to those who have not heard it.

Moral Law God's will for all people of all time; summarized in the Ten Commandments and the command to love God and other people, our neighbors (see Questions 12 and 13).

Most Holy Place Room in the tabernacle or temple where the ark of the covenant was kept and where the high priest sprinkled blood once a year to make payment for the sins of Israel.

Myth A story or teaching that may seem to be historically true but is actually made up by some person.

Name of God God's titles and everything else he has revealed about himself in his Word.

Natural Law The law of God as it is written on the hearts of all people.

New Man Same as *New Self.*

New Person Same as *New Self.*

New Self The new heart and mind that God creates in us by faith in Jesus. The new self delights in doing God's will and fights against the sinful nature. Also called *New Person; New Man; Inner Being; Spirit* (see narrative following Questions 27 and 232).

Oath A promise to do something, appealing to God as witness.

Observe 1. To celebrate (a festival); 2. to keep or obey, such as to observe the law.

Offense 1. A sin; 2. something that causes another believer to stumble in faith.

Offering A sacrifice or gift brought to God.

Office The work or service assigned to someone. In the church, the office of the public ministry is the work that the called ministers do. The office of Christ is the whole work Christ does as Prophet, High Priest, and King.

Old Adam The same as the *Sinful Nature.* It is called the old Adam because it is an inherited condition going back to Adam and Eve (see narrative following Question 6 and Question 128).

Old Man Same as *Sinful Nature.*

Old Self Same as *Sinful Nature.*

Omen A happening regarded as a special sign foretelling the future.

Omnipotent Almighty; all-powerful; able to do all things.

Omnipresent Present in all places.

Omniscient All-knowing; knowing everything past, present, and future.

Orgy A wild, immoral party.

Original sin The guilt and sinfulness inherited by all people as a result of Adam's fall into sin.

Pagan Unbeliever; heathen.

Palm Sunday The festival of the church year (the Sunday before Easter) on which we celebrate Jesus' triumphal entry into Jerusalem.

Parable A story told to teach a spiritual truth or lesson.

Paradise 1. The Garden of Eden; 2. a term that pictures heaven as a beautiful park.

Partake To receive a portion, especially of food.

Passion 1. Suffering (e.g., the passion of Christ); 2. very strong feeling (the passion of the sinful nature).

Passionate Having very strong feelings.

Passive Obedience of Christ Christ's suffering of the penalties that we deserve for breaking God's law (see Question 148).

Passover A yearly festival of the ceremonial law in which the Israelites sacrificed a lamb and remembered how God had rescued the nation from slavery in Egypt. The Passover lamb was a sign pointing to Christ, the Lamb of God.

Pastor Shepherd; someone called to serve a group of Christians with the Word of God.

Penitent Being sorry for sin and willing to stop sinning.

Pentecost The festival of the church year on which we celebrate the special outpouring of the Holy Spirit on Jesus' disciples 50 days after Easter.

Perjurer Someone who tells a lie when he or she has sworn to tell the truth.

Persecution Troubles that the unbelieving people of the world, because they are enemies of Christ, cause for a Christian.

Persevere To continue in spite of difficulties.

Perverse Having a twisted mind that is set upon wrongdoing.

Pervert 1. To corrupt (verb); 2. someone whose sexual desires are unnatural (noun).

Petition A request. Since there are seven requests in the Lord's Prayer, we call them the seven petitions.

Pharisee A member of a Jewish religious group who claimed to keep more laws than the ones God commanded and thought that this made him right with God.

Physical Bodily; not spiritual.

Praise 1. To speak joyfully and admiringly about God's goodness; 2. to commend someone for their actions.

Prayer An act of worship in which we speak to God from our hearts.

Prayer Fellowship A way of expressing unity in faith by praying with others.

Precept A command; a rule; a teaching.

Preservation God's work of providing all that we need to keep our bodies and lives (see Questions 130-136).

Priest 1. One who is permitted to deal with God directly in prayer and in the use of God's Word and sacraments (see *Priesthood of All Believers*); 2. one who is chosen to lead the people in worship and to offer sacrifices for them (Old Testament).

Priesthood of All Believers The priestly office held by all believers, which gives them the right to pray to God directly and to use his Word and sacraments.

Profane To treat something that is holy with disrespect; to dishonor (verb); unholy (adjective).

Prophecy Any message from God spoken or written by a prophet; often a message foretelling the future.

Prophet One who speaks a message from God.

Prostitute A person who commits sexual sins for pay.

Provision A supply.

Prudent Wise; having sound judgment.

Public Ministry The teaching of God's Word and the administering of the sacraments by workers (pastors, teachers, and others) who have a divine call. These workers act as representatives of the group of Christians who called them (see Questions 331-333 and the narrative following Question 330).

Quickening Making alive; raising from the dead. This is one way to picture the miracle of faith that the Holy Spirit works in us.

Radiant Bright; shining.

Ransom 1. Payment given to free people from captivity (noun); 2. to free people from captivity by paying a price (verb).

Real Presence The miraculous presence of Jesus' real body with the bread and of his real blood with the wine in Holy Communion.

Realm Kingdom.

Rebirth Being born again. This is one way to picture the miracle of faith that the Holy Spirit works in us (see Question 189).

Rebuke To scold someone for doing wrong.

Reconcile To restore someone to peace and harmony with another.

Reconciliation The restoration of peace between God and humans as a result of Christ's death.

Redeem To ransom; to buy back; to pay a price in order to free from slavery or captivity.

Redemption Christ's work of ransoming all people from the slavery of sin, death, and the devil by paying the price of his blood, suffering, and death.

Regeneration Same as *Rebirth*.

Render 1. To give; 2. to cause to become, to make.

Renewal The Holy Spirit's work of making us new by creating a new self inside of us through the gospel.

Renounce To give up; to intend to have nothing to do with.

Repentance A change of mind about one's sin. The Bible uses "repentance" in two senses: 1. sorrow over sin and desire to stop sinning; 2. sorrow over sin and faith in the forgiveness of sins.

Repentant Same as *Penitent.*

Resurrection Coming to life after death; refers especially to Christ's return to life on Easter and to the raising of all the dead on the Last Day.

Reveal To unveil; to make known something hidden.

Revenue A country's income from taxes, which is used to pay public expenses; incoming money.

Revile To use bad language about someone; to call someone bad names.

Righteous Sinless; morally perfect.

Righteousness Sinlessness; moral perfection. God has righteousness and demands righteousness from us. Through faith in Christ, his righteousness is given to us.

Robbery Taking the possessions of others by force.

Sabbath Hebrew word for "rest."

Sabbath Day The day of rest. According to the ceremonial law, the Israelites were commanded to rest from their work on the seventh day of the week (Saturday).

Sacrament A sacred act that Christ established for his church in which an earthly element is used together with God's Word as a means of offering, giving, and sealing to us the forgiveness of sins and thus also life and salvation.

Sacrament of the Altar Same as *Holy Communion.*

Sacrifice The killing of a living being (usually an animal) as an offering to God. The most important purpose of sacrifice was for atonement (see *Atone*).

Saint Holy one. Every believer in Christ is a saint because through faith in Christ each believer has the holiness of Christ.

Salvation Rescue or deliverance; especially the rescue from sin, death, and the devil accomplished by Jesus, the Savior.

Sanctification The work of the Holy Spirit through the means of grace. For the two different ways in which the Bible uses the word, see *Sanctify.*

Sanctify Set apart. The Holy Spirit sets us apart from the unbelieving world by calling us to faith in Jesus. The Holy Spirit sets us apart more and more from the sinful behavior of the world by strengthening our faith.

Sanctuary A holy place set apart for the worship of God. The tabernacle and the temple are each called a sanctuary.

Satan Adversary; a name of the devil.

Scripture Writing. Usually "Scripture(s)" refers to the Bible.

Second Birth Same as *Rebirth.*

Self-righteousness Same as *Work-righteousness.*

Sensuality Allowing oneself to pursue sinful bodily pleasures.

Sin Missing the mark of God's law by breaking one of his commandments.

Sin of Commission Doing something that God forbids (see question 41).

Sin of Omission Not doing something that God wants us to do (see question 41).

Sinful Nature A mind and heart inclined only toward evil. All people have a sinful nature because they are born of sinful parents. Also called *Flesh; Old Adam; Old Self; Old Man* (see narrative following Question 6 and Question 128).

Slander False statements that harm someone's reputation.

Sorcery Witchcraft; the magic of one who is aided by the devil.

Soul The immaterial part of a human being that continues to exist after separation from the body at death (it will be reunited with the resurrected body on the Last Day).

Sovereign 1. Having the highest ruling power (adjective); 2. highest ruler (noun).

Spell A formula of words believed to have magical power.

Spirit 1. A bodiless personal being (e.g., God, angels, the devil, demons); 2. "the Spirit" often means the Holy Spirit; 3. the new self that is given to believers by the Holy Spirit; 4. sometimes "spirit" means the same as soul.

Spiritist Someone who supposedly communicates with the spirits of the dead.

Spiritual Death Separation from the spiritual blessings of God. All people are born spiritually dead and remain that way until the Holy Spirit quickens them, that is, calls them to faith in Christ.

Sponsor Someone chosen in connection with the baptism of a baby who is to be concerned with the spiritual welfare of the child as he or she grows up. Sponsors are not mentioned in the Bible and are not necessary for a valid baptism (see the narrative following Question 307).

Statute A law.

Steadfast Firm; unmovable.

Subdue To take control of.

Substitute One who takes the place of another.

Suicide The sin of killing oneself.

Superstitious Trusting in powers that are not of God; belief in good luck charms, etc.

Sustain To hold up or support; to keep alive.

Swear To use God's name to assure someone that the truth is being told.

Synod A group of congregations that unite to help one another in the Lord's work.

Tabernacle The tent used by the Israelites as a place of worship from the time of the giving of the law on Mt. Sinai until the building of Solomon's temple.

Temple God's house; a building where he dwells and is worshiped. Believers are called the temple of God because he lives in them. The building in Jerusalem that God's Old Testament people used for their worship.

Tempt To try to lead someone into sin, false belief, or despair.

Temptation Any situation in which someone may be led into sin, false belief, or despair.

Testament A covenant. The Old Testament books of the Bible cover that portion of history when the old covenant (the law of Mt. Sinai) was in effect. The New Testament books describe the new covenant that Jesus established by fulfilling the law perfectly and by dying to earn the forgiveness of sins (see narrative following Question 351).

Testify To speak as a witness.

Testimony A statement of what one knows to be true. Frequently "testimony" refers to God's Word or a portion of it.

Theft Secretly taking the possessions of others.

Time of Grace The time of one's life on earth that God gives to an individual as his or her only opportunity to come to faith in Jesus and be saved (see Question 60).

Transform To change.

Transgression Crossing the forbidden line of God's law by breaking one of his commandments.

Trespass Same as *Transgression.*

Tribulation Suffering; affliction.

Trinity The triune God.

Triune Existing as both three (tri-) and one (-une). The triune God is three persons but only one God (see Question 118).

Unblemished Spotless; faultless.

Uncircumcision Not being circumcised; sometimes used as a picture of unbelief and disobedience.

Unrighteous Morally imperfect; sinful; contrary to God's will.

Unrighteousness Lack of righteousness; sinfulness.

Valid Legally binding; acceptable.

Verbal Inspiration See *Inspiration.*

Vicar A student training for the ministry who serves a congregation under the direction of a pastor.

Vicarious Performed by taking the place of another; substitutionary.

Vicarious Atonement The sacrifice of Jesus in our place, accepted by the Father as payment for our sins (see Questions 26 and 156).

Visible Churches Groups of people who gather to use the means of grace (see Questions 210-215).

Vision Something that is seen by other than normal sight, such as in sleep or in a trance.

Wickedness Great sinfulness.

Witch/Warlock One who seeks or uses supernatural power from the devil.

Witchcraft The attempt to do things by the power of the devil (see Question 40).

Witness 1. Someone who is an observer. The apostles were witnesses of Jesus' resurrection. Witnesses at a baptism observe the baptism to verify that it took place (noun). 2. The testimony that an observer gives. To bear witness means to give testimony (noun). 3. To testify; to speak as one who has seen (verb).

Word of God That which God has said either directly or through angels, prophets, or apostles. The Bible is the written Word of God.

Work-righteousness Trying to earn righteousness before God by one's own works.

Worship Any thoughts, words, or actions that we direct toward God as a way of praising him or praying to him.

Wrath Intense anger.

Written Law The law of God as it is written in the Bible.

Zion The hill on which Jerusalem stands. "Zion" is also used as a name for the church.

PRONOUNCING VOCABULARY

Aaron	AIR-un
Abednego	uh-BED-neh-go
Abel	AY-bul
Abiram	uh-BY-rum
Abraham	AY-bruh-ham
Absalom	ABB-suh-lum
Achan	AY-can
Adam	ADD-um
Ahab	AY-hab
Ananias	an-uh-NY-us
Antioch	AN-tea-uk
Arimathea	air-uh-muh-THEE-uh
Baal	BAY-ul
Balaam	BAY-lum
Balak	BAY-lack
Barabbas	bar-AB-bus
Barnabas	BAR-nu-bus
Bathsheba	bath-SHE-buh
Bereans	Burr-EE-uns
Caiaphas	KAY-uh-fuss
Cain	KANE
Canaanite	KANE-uh-night
Centurion	sen-TOUR-ee-uhn
Corinth	CORE-inth
Corinthians	cor-INTH-ee-uns
Cornelius	core-NEE-lee-us
Daniel	DAN-yell
Dathan	DAY-thun
David	DAY-vid
Egypt	EE-jipt
Eli	EE-lie
Elijah	ee-LIE-juh
Elisha	ee-LIE-shuh
Elymas	EL-ih-mus
Endor	EN-door
Esau	EE-saw
Ethiopian	EE-thee-OH-pea-uhn
Eunuch	YOU-nock
Eve	EEV
Gabriel	GAY-bree-el
Gaius	GAY-us
Galatians	gah-LAY-shunz
Golgotha	GUL-ga-tha
Goliath	go-LIE-uth
Gomorrah	guh-MORE-ruh
Hannah	HAN (*a* as in *bat*)-nuh
Herod	HAIR-ud
Hymenaeus	hi-men-EE-us
Isaac	EYE-zack
Isaiah	eye-ZAY-uh
Jacob	JAY-cub
Jairus	jah-EYE-rus
James	JAMZ
Jericho	JERR-ik-koh
Jerusalem	jerr-RUE-suh-lem
Jezebel	JEZ-uh-bell
Job	JOHB
Joel	JOE-el
John	JON
Jonathan	JON-uh-thun
Joseph	JOE-sef
Joshua	JOSH-ooh-uh
Judas	JEW-das
Lazarus	LAZ-zuh-rus
Lot	LOT (*o* as in *odd*)

Machpelah	mack-PEA-luh
Martha	MARR-thuh
Melanchthon	mel-LANK-thun
Meshach	ME-shack
Moses	MOE-zuz
Nabal	NAY-bul
Naboth	NAY-buth
Naomi	nay-OH-mee
Nathan	NAY-thun
Nazareth	NAZ-zur-reth
Nebuchadnezzar	NEB-uh-kud-NEZ-zur
Noah	KNOW-uh
Onesimus	oh-NES-ih-mus
Paradise	PEAR-uh-dies
Paul	PAUL
Pergamum	PURR-gah-mum
Peter	PEA-turr
Pharisees	FAIR-ih-sees
Philadelphia	fill-uh-DEL-fee-uh
Philetus	fie-LEE-tus
Philip	FILL-up
Philippi	fill-LIP-eye
Philippians	fill-LIP-eh-unz
Pontius Pilate	PON-chus PIE-let
Potiphar	POT-uh-fur
Rome	ROME
Ruth	ROOTH
Samaritan	suh-MARE-ih-tun
Samuel	SAM-you-ell
Sapphira	sah-FIE-rah
Sardis	SAR-dis
Saul	SAUL
Shadrach	SHA-drack
Shimei	SHIM-ih-eye
Silas	SIGH-lus
Sinai	SIGH-nigh
Sodom	SOD-um
Solomon	SOLL-uh-mun
Stephen	STEE-fun
Thomas	TOM-us
Uriah	you-RYE-uh
Zacchaeus	zak-KEY-us

SUBJECT INDEX

Locators refer to question numbers. An asterisk (*) indicates that the subject is found in the introductory paragraphs before the question or in the text box following the question's answer.

C

G

H

I

J

K

L

M

N

O

P

Q

R

S

T

U

V

SCRIPTURE INDEX

Locators refer to question numbers. An asterisk (*) indicates that the passage is found in the introductory paragraphs before the question or in the text box following the question's answer. A letter *c* indicates that the passage is found in the Connections section after the question.

Genesis

Exodus

Leviticus

Numbers

Deuteronomy

Joshua

1 Samuel

2 Samuel

1 Kings

2 Kings

1 Chronicles

2 Chronicles

Ezra

Nehemiah

Job

Psalms

Proverbs

Ecclesiastes

Song of Solomon

Isaiah

Jeremiah

Lamentations

Ezekiel

Daniel

Joel

Jonah

Micah

Haggai

Malachi

Matthew

Mark

Luke

John

Acts

Romans

1 Corinthians

2 Corinthians

Galatians

Ephesians

Philippians

Colossians

1 Thessalonians

2 Thessalonians

1 Timothy

2 Timothy

Titus

Hebrews

James

1 Peter

2 Peter

1 John

2 John

3 John

Jude

Revelation